THE GNOSTIC PROBLEM

THE GNOSTIC PROBLEM

A Study of the Relations between Hellenistic Judaism and the Gnostic Heresy

BY

R. McL. WILSON, B.D., Ph.D.

*Lecturer in New Testament Language and Literature,
St. Mary's College, University of St. Andrews*

LONDON
A. R. MOWBRAY & Co. LIMITED

© *A. R. Mowbray & Co. Limited, 1958*

First published in 1958

PRINTED IN GREAT BRITAIN BY
A. R. MOWBRAY & CO. LIMITED IN THE CITY OF OXFORD
7478

PATRIS MEMORIAE
FILIUS
D. D. D.

AUTHOR'S PREFACE

SOME fifty years ago Robert Law could write, 'The rise and spread of Gnosticism forms one of the dimmest chapters in Church history' (*The Tests of Life*, Edinburgh 1909, 26). It cannot be said that the researches of the past half-century have altogether removed the obscurity. The general nature of the heresy opposed by Irenaeus and Hippolytus is clear enough, and it may be summarily described as an assimilation of Christianity and contemporary thought which for a time threatened to deprive the Christian element of its identity and distinctive character; but once we go beyond such general statements, and more especially when we seek to place the movement as a whole in its context in the history of religion, then our difficulties begin.

This book does not profess to be a full-scale study of the Gnostic movement. The time for that has not yet come, nor can it come until all the documents of the Nag Hammadi library have been published and examined. What is presented here is rather an exploration of one small corner of the field, to which in the past too little attention has perhaps been given, although there have been in recent years indications of a growing recognition of the Jewish contribution to the development of Gnosticism. This study has been deliberately restricted to the Gnosticism of the second century, since it is here that the characteristics of the movement may first be clearly seen. Affinities with other systems of thought, both earlier and later, have been recognized, and some account has been taken of the earlier Coptic material, but the primary concern of this work is with the relation between the Gnosticism of the second century and the thought of Diaspora Judaism, especially in the works of Philo. In the past scholars have compassed the greater part of the Middle East in the search for 'sources,' but the alleged lines of connection have too often been highly conjectural and much has been claimed as 'Gnostic' which admits of another interpretation.

The book is based on a thesis accepted by the University of Cambridge for the Ph.D. degree. Since there is in English no recent book on the subject, an attempt has been made in it to provide as comprehensive a conspectus as possible of the literature now available. In the event, the footnotes have proved too extensive to be printed beneath the text, and have had to be relegated to the end of each chapter.

For the sake of brevity, the works most frequently quoted are generally cited by the author's name alone. Details will be found in the bibliography, but it may be noted that *Beginnings* refers to the five volumes edited by Jackson and Lake, *Jew and Greek* to the volume by G. H. C. Macgregor and A. C. Purdy. The latter is quite distinct from the book with the same title by Gregory Dix. Schürer GJV denotes the fourth German edition, other references being to the English translation.

Since the manuscript went to the press, information has been received of the publication of the first volume of a photographic edition of the Nag Hammadi texts: *Coptic Gnostic Papyri in the Coptic Museum at Old Cairo*, ed. P. Labib, Cairo 1956. An edition of the *Gospel of Thomas* is promised for 1958, and in the meantime some of the sayings in this document have been examined by G. Quispel in *Vigiliae Christianae* xi (1957), 189ff. The passages corresponding to the Oxyrhynchus Logia are presented in a Latin translation by G. Garitte (*Le Muséon* 70 (1957), 59ff.), who has also translated a number of Parables of the Kingdom examined by L. Cerfaux (*Le Muséon* 70, 307ff.). Cerfaux has noted a number of parallels between the *Gospel of Truth* and the *Gospel of Thomas*. On the *Gospel of Truth* reference may be made to the reviews by Barrett (*Exp. Times* lxix, 167ff.) and Leipoldt (TLZ 1957, 825ff.). Further references to the literature on Gnosticism will be found in the bibliographies appended to the various articles in the *Oxford Dictionary of the Christian Church*.

W. Schmithals' volume *Die Gnosis in Korinth* (Göttingen 1956) came to my notice only when the present work was complete. It must suffice to say that while there was clearly an incipient Gnosticism in Corinth, Schmithals seems to approach Paul's Corinthian correspondence too much from the developed Gnosticism of the second century. The book is notable for its full presentation of the theory of the redeemed Redeemer, but the inferences which must be made are so numerous and of such a character as to leave the whole theory still very much a matter of conjecture. On the Mandeans reference may be made to W. F. Albright, *From the Stone Age to Christianity* (2nd edition, Baltimore 1957), 364ff., which likewise came to hand too late to be fully utilized. It may be noted that Albright claims 'the central concept and myth of the Lesser Sophia is of Canaanite-Aramaean origin, going back at least to the seventh century B.C.' (ib. 369). Finally, reference should be made to the study of the allegorical method by R. M. Grant, *The Letter and the Spirit* (London, S.P.C.K., 1957). The Pythagorean background of the Simonian 'myth' of Helen has been examined by M. Detienne in *Rev. Hist. Rel.* clii (1957), 129ff.

The extent of my debt to the work of earlier scholars will be evident from the footnotes, in which I have endeavoured to make due acknowledgement in every case. At some points I have incorporated material already published in various articles. It remains for me to express my thanks to those who have helped by their advice and their encouragement. The suggestion of the theme came from the late Professor William Manson of Edinburgh, to whom I owe my first initiation into this department of learning and who was also good enough to read and comment on the original version of this book. My debt to my supervisor, the late Canon W. L. Knox, will be sufficiently evident from the references to his published works, but these references cannot reveal how much I learned from his criticism and suggestions. I am indebted also to Professor C. H. Dodd and Canon H. E. W. Turner for advice and encouragement, and to Professors van Unnik and Quispel of Utrecht for their interest in the book. I would thank the Rev. A. W. Matthews for assistance in the correction of the proofs, and Dr. D. A. Hubbard for some additional references in one of the notes. Finally, I must pay due tribute to my publisher and his staff for the skill and care which they have devoted to the production of the book.

R. McL. WILSON

ST. MARY'S COLLEGE
ST. ANDREWS
1958

CONTENTS

THE GNOSTIC PROBLEM

CHAPTER I

THE JUDAISM OF THE DISPERSION

THE fall of Jerusalem in 586 B.C., with the Captivity in Babylon which followed, marks the end of an era in the history of Israel. No longer an independent nation, the Jews were now to an ever-increasing extent dispersed abroad, living not only in their homeland but also in communities of varying size scattered over most of the known world.[1] This dispersion of the people inevitably exercised a very considerable influence on Jewish life and thought, since the members of these communities were brought into daily contact with men of other faiths and alien culture. The Jewish religion itself, as it developed after the downfall of the kingdom, is not identical with the religion of the pre-exilic period; as a living faith it had to adapt itself to meet the changing needs of the times. And within the Jewish faith as a whole the Judaism of the Diaspora is in some ways different from that of Palestine, and still more from the Rabbinic Judaism into which the Palestinian form was later to develop.[2]

The purpose of this study is first of all to examine the Judaism of the Diaspora in relation to its contemporary environment, in order to form some estimate of its character and of the features which distinguish it from the Judaism of Palestine, and also to determine the influences by which it was affected; in short, to discover how far the Judaism of the Diaspora was a legitimate development from its Old Testament beginnings, and how far it was modified by its contact with a wider world. A further question is that of the influence which the Diaspora itself was able to exert upon the ideas of contemporary culture, and the contribution which it had to make to the development of later thought. This is an aspect which is often neglected, as indeed is only natural, since it is easier to see alien forms in Judaism than to find Jewish features elsewhere; but, in Dodd's words, while the influence of Gentile thought upon the Dispersion was unquestionably enormous, 'it would not be safe to assume that where Hellenistic Judaism shows parallels with non-Jewish thought, the debt lies always and wholly upon one side.'[3] Moreover, in admitting the fact of Hellenistic influence on Jewish thought, it is necessary also to note its character, and the use which was made of the elements which were adopted.

The problem is complicated by a certain confusion of terms, which has been a fruitful source of misunderstanding in this field, particularly in regard to the word 'syncretism.' Etymologically it means the blending together of elements from diverse sources, and in this sense it is applicable both to Judaism and to Christianity, each of which has absorbed into itself elements from other systems of thought and belief; but, to anticipate, in these two cases the elements thus taken over have been thoroughly assimilated, and are employed to serve the ends of a faith which itself is not materially changed thereby. The same word, however, has to do duty also as a description of the very different process which is found in pagan circles. For the moment, it must suffice to draw attention to the distinction; it will become abundantly clear that 'syncretism,' used of Judaism or of Christianity, may mean something very different from the same word applied to the mystery religions or to paganism in general.

Traces of alien influence upon Israel have often been discovered, but it must not be forgotten that such influences did not operate only in the Greek period. The Jews did not begin their wanderings with the conquests of Alexander the Great, or even with the Captivity.[4] They were exposed to the influence of other cultures throughout their history, and some of the foreign elements were adopted at a very early stage. Even in the time of the kingdom, some Jews served as mercenaries under foreign colours,[5] others travelled abroad for purposes of trade, while political refugees sought asylum in Egypt or elsewhere during the ascendancy of their opponents.[6] Tablets have been found in Mesopotamia, which 'prove the existence in that region, in the seventh century B.C., of an important Israelite population participating in commercial and other affairs,'[7] and documents from Elephantine in Egypt seem to point to a community established before the Exile, and for some time out of touch with movements of thought and events in Palestine.[8] Nevertheless, the Captivity marked the beginning of a new era. The kingdom was no more; even the Hasmonean dynasty did not attain to the former glories of Israel, and save for a century under their rule the Jews were either a subject people or at most a dependent state, submissive to one or other of the great empires.[9]

When Cyrus gave them the opportunity to return to the land of their fathers, some of the exiles preferred to remain in Babylon, and formed a Jewish community there. Foreign settlers introduced by the conquerors had occupied part of the homeland, which could not contain the Jews as well, the more so since the Jews did not practise infanticide, and the population therefore increased more rapidly.[10] Palestine was a debated territory between Egypt and her rivals, Assyrian, Babylonian, and later Seleucid, on the north, and many no doubt sought a more settled abode. Finally Alexander, or at least his successors,[11] found the Jews to be admirable settlers for the new cities which were founded in the Hellenistic period, and for the most part these rulers were fully prepared to make use of Jewish industry and business capacity, while the Jews on their side were glad to take advantage of the opportunities offered. As a result, Jewish communities were to be found everywhere in the ancient world, from the Euphrates to Rome and even beyond,[12] in Asia Minor, Syria, Egypt, in Greek cities founded by Alexander and his successors, in towns, villages, and seaports, wherever the Jew could find scope for his talents and peace to live his own life—and sometimes where he lived in constant danger of hostile out-bursts from his Gentile neighbours. Philo and Josephus are at pains to stress the wide extent of the dispersion,[13] and even if they may be convicted of an apologetic bias we have ample evidence from the New Testament.[14] The mission of St. Paul and the spread of early Christianity owed not a little to the Diaspora,[15] which with Greek philosophy and the Pax Romana prepared the world to receive the Gospel.[16]

Before the Exile, the influences affecting Israel depended largely on the political situation; Egypt, Babylonia, Assyria, Phoenicia, all contributed in some degree, either through political ascendancy or by way of commercial relations.[17] After the Exile, Babylonian influence was probably stronger, until its eclipse by Persian,[18] and finally by Greek. Traces may be found of each, but it is dangerous to dogmatize.[19] Jewish exclusiveness may have maintained the purity of Judaism to some considerable extent, but, on the other hand, the conquests of Alexander, with the consequent diffusion of Greek language and culture, broke down many barriers.[20] This was particularly the case for religion. Cumont[21] has noted how the propagation of the Oriental mystery cults in the Roman Empire was facilitated by political and economic factors, the trading-journeys of merchants, the transference of slaves, soldiers or officials from one end of the Empire to the other, and the same is substantially true of the Greek period, though on a smaller scale. These cults spread beyond their homeland, winning new adherents and often causing modifications in the religions they met, but they themselves were also changed in the process.[22] A cult transplanted to alien soil took on new features, although it might remain nominally and on the surface the same as in the land of its origin. The mysteries influenced each other, and were themselves influenced in turn, and there seems to have grown up a sort of composite theology, compacted of popular belief and vague ideas about philosophy and astrology.[23] It was perhaps not very firmly settled, nor was it established with the authority of long tradition, but it was in the air, a spirit of the times. Many besides the Athenians were, in Paul's words, δεισιδαιμονέστεροι.[24] And this was the atmosphere in which the Jew of the Dispersion lived and moved.

Our problem is to determine how far Judaism was affected by this spirit of the age, a problem that is especially difficult in the case of the Diaspora. Our knowledge of Jewish exclusiveness leads us to expect a rigid determination to have no dealings with the Gentile, yet we have evidence which might suggest the other extreme. On the one hand we have the characteristic particularism that shunned all contact with other peoples and earned the Jew his reputation for μισοξενία among his contemporaries. On the other hand, cases of more or less complete apostasy are not unknown, and, short of that, we find considerable laxity in some quarters in regard to observance of the Law.[25] Here, however, an important distinction must be drawn. It is known that there were individual

Jews who, for whatever reason, lapsed into paganism,[26] but it is doubtful if such cases may legitimately be employed as evidence for Judaism as a whole.[27] We have to distinguish such aberrations from the general trend of thought. The vital question is not whether examples can be found of the kind of syncretism current in the pagan cults, but whether such syncretism was *characteristic* of the Diaspora, and to such an extent as to involve a radical departure from the ancestral faith. At the same time it has now become clear that Judaism as a whole was not so 'monolithic' as once was thought.[28] Thomas has pointed to the existence in Palestine itself of a fairly widespread 'baptist' movement,[29] while patristic references to Jewish sects have now been augmented by an allusion in one of the documents of the Jung Codex.[30] Moreover, there are in the Dead Sea Scrolls certain parallels to elements in the Fourth Gospel which once were considered Hellenistic but are now shown to have been at least naturalized in, if not indigenous to, the soil of Palestine.[31] The resultant picture is therefore one, not of a rigid and uniform orthodoxy, but rather of a great variety of different groups of a more or less orthodox character. Allowance must be made for these in forming any estimate, but our present concern is not with the sects but with the main stream of the Judaism of the Dispersion. Sects of a more or less heterodox character no doubt had their counterparts in the Diaspora, and there may have been some which appeared in the Diaspora alone, but was the main stream of Diaspora Judaism so deeply affected as to lose its specifically Jewish character? This is the essential question.

At this point it should be noted that Hellenistic influence was not confined to the Dispersion, since Hellenism made progress even in Palestine itself.[32] The foundation of Greek cities in their dominions by the Ptolemies not only provided for the military needs of Egypt, but also extended the range of Greek culture. The Greek language became the common speech almost everywhere, and these cities further afforded examples of Greek methods in municipal organization and administration which could be copied or adapted by the Jews for their own purposes. Again, Hellenistic influence was furthered by the considerate treatment accorded to the Jews by their Graeco-Egyptian rulers; it was the deliberate policy of these rulers to foster friendly relations between their Hellenic and Asiatic subjects.[33] For about 150 years there was opportunity for such peaceful penetration, and it was only the miscalculations of Antiochus Epiphanes that finally brought it to an end.[34] The opposition to his arbitrary legislation carried with it an opposition to alien elements which survived long after the Maccabean period.

The books of the Maccabees, written from a Pharisaic standpoint, depict a certain laxity among the Jews prior to the Maccabean Wars,[35] but their evidence should not be taken too much at its face value. According to Hecataeus of Abdera,[36] many of the ancestral customs of the Jews were altered as a result of their intercourse with the alien, but this again requires careful examination. Many of these customs may have been mere externals, matters of social or other legislation which did not affect religion, although, indeed, in some cases the outward change was no doubt only a symptom of a deeper transformation. In its fundamental beliefs Judaism remained firm, although it appropriated to itself such alien elements as were suitable and not incompatible with orthodox belief. As it has been put, 'Judaism was not only exposed to Hellenism, but maintained itself . . . in extraordinary ways, and also yielded . . . in ways equally unique.'[37] In its contact with the Graeco-Roman world, as Wendland says, Judaism was confronted by 'a culture not of a related character and to some extent highly superior. It was not exposed to forceful attempts at hellenization such as would provoke resistance, but rather to the slow and continually working contacts of the Greek spirit.'[38] But the same author says elsewhere: 'However much the development of Judaism and the moulding of its spiritual life was determined through its entanglement in world history and through foreign influences of many kinds, yet it cannot be proved at any point with certainty that the Greek spirit exercised any deep influence on the richly unfolding inner development of Palestinian Judaism.'[39] Elements absorbed in pre-Maccabean times remained, and Wendland admits a strong influence from the East, but so far as the fundamental tenets of the Jewish faith are concerned it cannot be said that there was any serious modification.

It must be remembered that the Judaism of the New Testament period is the result of a process extending over many generations. During the Exile and after, Jewish thought had undergone a great transformation, amounting to nothing less than a moral and spiritual regeneration of the nation. It was in the Persian period that Israel became the people of the Law; 'entrenched behind this rampart they were able ... to withstand the insidious encroachments of Hellenistic influence, and, as a nation, to remain faithful to the religion of their fathers.'[40] Again, it must be remembered that Judaism, at least under the Romans and to some extent earlier, was a privileged religion.[41] Antiochus stirred up a hornets' nest when he tried to hellenize Judaea by force, and in general the men in authority found that more was to be gained by leaving the Jew in peace than by endeavouring to compel him to conformity.

At the same time the fact of Hellenistic influence on Judaism cannot be denied. Antiochus in his misguided effort to hasten the hellenization of Israel was urged on by one of the two contending parties which claimed the High Priesthood, and this group is generally called the hellenizing, but the difference was probably rather one between an orthodox party, pro-Egyptian and agreeable to a gradual assimilation of the better elements of Gentile culture, and a more radical pro-Syrian party whose chief thought was for their own interests.[42] Certainly there is evidence that a desire to hellenize had been expressed by the Jewish leaders some years before Antiochus decreed the extirpation of the Jewish faith.[43] Moreover, even the Maccabean Wars did not put a final end to the process, since the festival of Hanukkah, which (if Rankin is correct) represents the transformation of a pre-Maccabean Dionysiac festival into a feast in honour of Yahweh, was instituted under Judas Maccabaeus.[44]

One result of the Maccabean Wars was an increased particularism and exclusiveness among Palestinian Jews, a particularism which was combined with nationalist hopes and expectations of a coming Messiah. This is one of the chief differences between the Diaspora and Palestine.[45] The Palestinian Jew tended to think of Yahweh as peculiarly related to Israel—Ruler of all the world certainly, but One who had chosen Israel as His people and who would vindicate them in His own good time before all men. The Gentile, except he became a Jew by adoption, was beyond the pale. This particularism had its roots in the Exile in Babylon, where it had been a condition of survival for Israel as a religious entity,[46] but its apocalyptic aspect belongs to Palestine. The keeping of the Law was the central feature; only those who obeyed could have a part in the promised glories.

The Diaspora, with some Jews of Palestine,[47] adopted the other view, that Yahweh, being the only true God, should alone be worshipped by all men. Universalist and Particularist alike looked upon it as a duty to win the Gentile, unless when particularism was united to a nationalism which barred the door to the alien, but missionary activity was greater in the Diaspora. Religious interest there was less concentrated on the more national and purely ceremonial part of the Law, and the Jew, from his inevitable daily contacts with the Gentile, had a wider and more sympathetic outlook.[48] It is perhaps significant that examples of the *kerygma* form narrating the mighty works of God are confined to Hellenistic as opposed to Palestinian documents. 'Judaism in Palestine was never concerned to be a missionary religion, except when it enforced a measure of conformity upon such parts of the population as it was able to conquer.'[49] The Diaspora Jew had learned to appreciate the value of Greek thought and philosophy, and was prepared to accept what he felt to be true in it. But again, he was convinced of the superiority of Judaism, and so sought to commend it to the Gentiles.[50] He did not as a rule share the Pharisaic passion for scrupulous attention to the ceremonial and ritual details of the Law, but concerned himself rather with the general religious principle; in other words, he kept the prophetic rather than the legalistic features of Judaism in the foreground.[51] Schürer and Bousset, however, maintain that the Diaspora differed from Palestine only in degree,[52] and stress the danger of making men like Philo and Josephus too much the mirror of their time.[53]

The attitude of the Jew towards the Gentile varied at different periods, and in the Diaspora no doubt in different regions.[54] The course of history had something to do with this, in the vicissitudes which attended the fortunes of the Jews under their Gentile overlords; where the past had left its mark we sometimes find various conflicting views held together. Generally the Jew kept to himself, but much of the Jewish literature of the period is in Greek, and it shows acquaintance in many cases with pagan thought. It would be convenient to divide Judaism into a particularist Palestinian and a more liberal Diaspora form, but this would be superficial. We know the general features of certain periods, and for some periods and some areas our evidence is fairly extensive, but we cannot always unravel the tangled skein and relate a particular trend to any one time or place. For our present purpose it is enough to say that most of the later tendencies, universalism and particularism, nationalism and missionary propaganda, zeal for the law, apocalyptic hopes, are foreshadowed, if not already present, before the Greek period.[55] They are therefore not necessarily to be ascribed to the impact of Hellenistic influence. In regard to the Messianic hope, it existed in the Diaspora, according to Weiss, but in a diluted form and less vividly. Certainly both Philo and Josephus minimize it in the interests of their propaganda for Judaism.[56]

Syncretism was always a strong tendency in the ancient world. To win the favour of the gods of a hostile state was one resource in time of war[57]; the gods of the country were often enrolled in the pantheon of the conquerors[58]; and as states extended their contacts men found gods bearing different names in different regions, but possessed of the same attributes. The course usually adopted was to assimilate the new god to the member of the existing pantheon who most closely resembled him.[59] It was taken for granted that the gods of other peoples were the same deities under different names.[60] One natural result of this was the growth of the idea of gods of many names, which ultimately blossoms forth in the view that all gods are simply the one god under various forms.[61] The Stoic philosophy[62] accommodated itself to current religious tendencies, and developed the literary form of apologetic, in which 'it interpreted the gods as ideas or natural forces and explained the myths allegorically.'[63] According to Reitzenstein, a similar process had begun in the mystery religions, and Stoicism provided the vocabulary for the restatement of these religions.[64] Certainly there was later a considerable syncretism in these cults, which could be linked with the Stoic system. The 'gods' are now manifestations of the one God or supreme principle, or natural forces controlled by him.[65] Syncretism and philosophy united to lead the Greek mind towards monotheism.[66]

For Israel, the process was rather different, although Judaism also could make use of the Stoic philosophy for its own purposes.[67] In the development of Hebrew religion we find first of all monolatry, the existence of other gods being admitted,[68] although any attempt at syncretism or worship of these other gods is fiercely denounced by the prophets. Then gradually there grows the conviction that there is only one God, who has chosen Israel as His special people. The other gods are degraded to the status of angels or similar subordinate powers, appointed as rulers of the Gentiles to lead them astray.[69] It was held that there were seventy nations in the world, and there were seventy lesser deities in ancient Semitic mythology, so that it was easy to associate these gods with the nations.[70] Again, the seven planets were gods in the Babylonian pantheon, and thus an astrological turn could be given to the system[71]; whether or not the number seventy had originally a planetary significance, 'it would tend to suggest an association between the planets and the nations, since for astral mathematics, no less than for Pythagorean, a nought at the end of a figure presents no difficulty.'[72] Astrological theories and a belief in fate, commonly associated with the influence of the planets, are prominent in pagan speculation at this period; thus, 'Gentile convention could regard the mysterious "powers" which upheld the cosmos as being in sympathy with, if not governed by, the planets which foretold or ruled the fate of man.'[73] By conflating all these doctrines, the Jews could conclude that the Gentiles were ruled by minor beings associated with the planets, or 'subject to a fate determined by the hostile powers which ruled the heavens.'[74] The Jew, of course, was free from the stars,[75] and just as Yahweh was the supreme God, so Israel, His chosen people, was held to be destined to rank above the nations.

Syncretism of this sort was mainly confined to Palestine, since the Alexandrians at any rate felt the danger of apostasy too strongly to make such concessions,[76] and in Palestine the hope that Israel would take precedence of the Gentile was linked to the Messianic expectation, with its vision of a king of Davidic race who would create a Jewish world-empire. This expectation contributed to Jewish exclusivism in Palestine, but the Jew of the Dispersion seems to have been less affected.[77] Yet though he abandoned or minimized the more material features of Palestinian eschatology, the Diaspora Jew almost always remained a Jew. He might adopt

Greek habits, and use Greek as his vernacular speech,[78] he might be lax in Pharisaic eyes in his observance of the Law, yet he remained essentially a Jew, and sometimes was more conservative than his kinsmen in the homeland. He might regard himself as a citizen of Rome or of Alexandria, but he still looked to Jerusalem as his mother-city.[79]

There are, however, two cases in which there does appear to have been some amalgamation of Judaism with other faiths, the cult of Zeus Hypsistos[80] and that of Sabazius.[81] It is perhaps significant that both are best attested for Phrygia, where the Jews seem to have been more lax than elsewhere, possibly because of the conditions under which their settlement was established.[82] Yet it is not clear that these cults represent more than an aberration by a number of Jews, who contributed some elements of their own to the formation of a composite cult. Oesterley says the cult of Sabazius 'offers perhaps the most astonishing example of religious syncretism on record,'[83] but his further statement that 'though it constituted a very un-Jewish cult, it was nevertheless a Jewish form of worship'[84] seems to go beyond the evidence. The inscriptions to which he refers prove no more than that certain Jews were lax in their observance, although, of course, those named were probably not the sole offenders. Laxity there was, to a considerable degree; wholesale syncretism is more doubtful.

The cult was certainly an 'astonishing example of religious syncretism,' but a great deal is purely pagan and some of the rest common ground for both Jew and Greek; the features which can definitely be assigned to Jewish influence are not many. Sabazius is identified with both Zeus and Dionysus,[85] and the symbols depicted on various monuments and votive offerings show that he was associated with other gods also.[86] This affords a clear example of the current monotheistic tendency, while the absorption by Sabazius of the functions and attributes of other gods leads quite naturally to the idea that he is the greatest and highest of them all. He is expressly designated as such in inscriptions, and Oesterley finds Jewish influence here.[87] This may have been a contributory factor, but ὕψιστος might mean to a Jew something very different from what it meant to a Greek.[88] Certainly there were points of contact which would make assimilation easy for those who chose: Yahweh in the Septuagint is ὕψιστος and κύριος Σαβαώθ, among other titles. Sabazius is also ὕψιστος, and is sometimes designated κύριος Σαβάζιος. If the original significance of Σαβαώθ were forgotten, as might well happen where Hebrew was no longer the common speech, and the word came to be regarded as a proper name, identification of the two deities was a simple matter.[89]

In point of fact, any one who was not closely acquainted with the two faiths might easily confuse them, and the Graeco-Roman world was distinctly vague in its conception of Judaism.[90] Again, both Greeks and Romans habitually identified strange gods with familiar deities of a similar name or character.[91] Thus the statement of Valerius Maximus,[92] that Hispalus *Iudaeos qui Sabazi Iovis cultu Romanos inficere mores conati erant repetere domos suas coegit*, need not mean that the Jews in Rome worshipped Sabazius, but simply that Yahweh Sabaoth and Sabazius were identified by the Graeco-Roman world.[93] Plutarch[94] identifies the God of the Jews with Dionysus, who is also identified with Sabazius,[95] and Tarn[96] suggests that Ptolemy IV may have driven the Jews into the arms of Antiochus by attempting to unite his subjects in a syncretistic cult of Sabazius-Dionysus-Sarapis.

The facts then are these: the Jews in Phrygia were known to be lax; there is evidence of Jewish influence on Phrygian belief,[97] apart from the cult of Sabazius, and the Jews presumably were not entirely free from influence from the other side; there was a syncretistic cult of a god Sabazius, who was sometimes identified with Yahweh Sabaoth; and there were a number of Jewish features in this worship. These facts do not justify the claim that the Jews of Phrygia amalgamated their ancestral faith with the local cult. Some may have done so, or some proselytes may have relapsed; but in ancient religion as in magic it was the normal procedure to invoke the god by every possible name and under every possible form, for fear of missing the correct formula of approach. Just as the magicians invoked Iao[98] and later Jesus,[99] so the Phrygians may have enrolled κύριος Σαβαώθ among the other aspects of Sabazius. We may in short be dealing not with Hellenistic influence upon the Dispersion, but with the influence of the Diaspora itself upon its environment.

The cult of Zeus Hypsistos is closely connected with that of

Sabazius; as we have seen, Zeus and Sabazius were assimilated, and Sabazius is sometimes designated Θεὸς ὕψιστος. The title is common, but not exclusively Jewish. Zeus bears it as the chief god of the pantheon,[100] and Sabazius and others derive it from their identification with him. According to Cumont,[101] it is one of the less frequent epithets for Zeus in classical Greek, but in the Semitic world it was used to translate *Elyon*.[102] This was the name of a pre-Israelite Canaanite deity, whose functions Yahweh absorbed; in later non-Israelite Semitic theology, influenced by astrology and Mazdaism, he became the supreme god, governing the stars and through them events on earth. In the Diaspora, ὕψιστος was a favourite epithet for Yahweh,[103] and was used by Gentiles of the God of the Jews. Thus, apart from Greek mythology,[104] there were two streams of thought using this title for a monotheistic God—Judaism and a Semitic variant of current astralism. These might easily be confused in popular belief, and this supreme God might also be identified with the chief god of any locality.

Here again, syncretism would be easy. Lake suggests that some Gentile sympathizers with Judaism may have developed an eclectic cult of ὁ Θεὸς ὁ ὕψιστος, minimizing the more objectionable Jewish features, while borrowing from Judaism.[105] This may be so, but on the other hand such a cult may have existed already, and derived certain elements from Judaism through the medium of apostate Jews or of Gentile sympathizers who relapsed into paganism. It may be remarked that Jewish features need not always imply Jewish co-operation; any element that seemed attractive or efficacious might be simply borrowed, perhaps by people who had no knowledge whatever of its real significance.

For present purposes the main point is that, while there is evidence of Jewish influence on Gentile thought and pagan influence on Jewish, there is nothing to prove syncretism in a major degree. The nearest approaches are to be found in these two Phrygian cults, both on the fringes of the Dispersion. Of the six inscriptions from the Bosporus referred to by Jackson and Lake,[106] only one is syncretistic, and even that may not be a true case. Moreover, if it were, it might once more be a matter of Gentile borrowing from the Jews, and not of pagan influence on a Jewish group. Canon Knox sees only one clear case of syncretism, in which a certain

Julia Severa is a High Priestess of the imperial cult and her husband a ruler of the synagogue for life[107]; for the rest, he is 'entirely unconvinced that we have anything more than a certain laxity in the remoter synagogues of the Dispersion.'[108] We may fairly accept Wendland's judgement, that 'Judaism was already in itself too firmly established to be lost in the mingling of the peoples,' and that it had itself an influence upon alien religions.[109]

It is, however, clear that the Diaspora was faced with a need to defend itself against the attractions of other faiths. If the majority of Diaspora Jews remained loyal to their faith, some did apostatize. Since toleration was normal in the ancient world,[110] and Judaism in any case was a privileged religion, such apostasy would be due in the main not to persecution but to the belief that the faith adopted was superior, or to a desire for the material advantages which might accompany adherence to the local cult.[111] And this was the point at which Judaism had its strongest defence—the synagogue. The character of this institution, its origin, and the extent to which it spread in the Dispersion, have been adequately treated by others.[112] Here we need only note that it formed a rallying-point, a centre which united the Jews in any region, binding them together and linking them to other synagogues and to Jerusalem. It was 'both prayer-house and school, the religious and therefore the civic centre of the community in any place.'[113] Regular instruction in the fundamental principles of the faith,[114] regular corporate worship, conducted in a language that all could understand, the sense of membership in an elect community, of fellowship one with another and with God,[115] these gave to the Jew a conviction of the superiority of his own faith. Moreover, the festivals of the Jewish calendar were so designed, as the Old Testament itself reveals, that the worshipper was constantly reminded of the great events of Israel's history. Further, amid the welter of competing creeds and cults of the ancient world, Judaism was able to offer something to the Gentile also, and it was to the synagogue that he came.

Schürer[116] remarks that the success of Jewish propaganda is at first sight strange, in view of the general disfavour with which Jews were regarded, even while they enjoyed a certain freedom of worship. He stresses three points: (i) the Jew knew how to commend his faith by keeping in the background whatever might not be acceptable to his hearers[117]; (ii) Judaism held out the prospect of the practical realization of a happy and moral life; (iii) it was the fashion of the time to patronize oriental religions generally.[118] Professor Dodd remarks that there is a good deal of evidence of widespread curiosity about the Jewish faith. 'The Jewish insistence on one supreme God, completely other than man and worshipped without images, appealed to the best pagan thought of the time, which was moving along different lines to monotheism.'[119] The existence of the Jewish Scriptures in Greek and the presence in the Diaspora of men ready and willing to commend their faith also played a part. Professor Nock[120] quotes Gressmann as noting the economic strength of the Jews, their freedom from crude mythology, their Book, their ethical standards, and their social rest-day. Judaism was one faith among many, but it claimed to be above all others.[121] The pagan cults combined with each other and assimilated their deities one to another. There was no limit to the number of cults a man might adopt.[122] But Judaism, like Christianity later, was firm and uncompromising—'this one faith and no other!' The very conviction of the believers must have been a potent factor.[123]

Judaism had come from the remote and mysterious East, but its sacred writings were available to all in the language of everyday life. Palestine concentrated largely on the Messianic hope, but the Diaspora took a more universal view.[124] The Diaspora Jew was bound by many ties to the Gentile world, and the more educated at least had some acquaintance with the ancient Greek philosophers, if only through the medium of the doxographers.[125] The Septuagint, translated in the first place for the benefit of Greek-speaking Jews,[126] was available also for the Greeks. Even at its most accurate the version suggested different concepts to the Greek, concepts arising out of his own religious background.[127] The words used might be the closest equivalents to the original Hebrew, yet their connotation and associations were bound to be different. Again, there was, so to speak, a vast deposit of ideas derived from philosophy, and possibly also from the mystery cults. Some of these ideas chimed in with Jewish doctrines.

The age was essentially syncretistic, and the different faiths drew

from the common store as they chose. But for Judaism syncretism
seems to have taken the form of pressing Gentile thought into the
service of the Jewish faith.[128] It was thus not the ordinary conflation
that we find in the mysteries, as, for example, in the merging of
Sabazius and Dionysus,[129] but a much more subtle inner modification. Dibelius has noted the taking over by Hellenistic Judaism of
arguments for the existence of God which originated in Greek
philosophy.[130] Again, catalogues of the vices of the heathen were
'a commonplace of the Jewish literature of the period preceding
and contemporary with the New Testament,'[131] and the warnings
against such vices were by no means unnecessary. St. Paul adopts
the form in his letters, and Deissmann[132] has shown a similarity
between Pauline and Hellenistic lists. The ultimate source of such
lists appears to be popular Greek philosophy as preached by itinerant
Stoics and Cynics.[133] The Jews would have adopted the form for
their own purposes, for example, in synagogue preaching,[134] and
St. Paul would derive it thence.

Again, at some points Judaism bore a close resemblance to
features in paganism.[135] The reservation of the Decalogue till after
initiation,[136] the withdrawal of the name of God from common
use, the treatment of the Exodus-narrative as symbolic of salvation,[137] and above all, the Paschal meal, all these had parallels, more
or less close, in the mysteries.[138] Professor Goodenough goes so
far as to suppose that there actually existed an organized Jewish
mystery cult, on the lines of the pagan religions, but this is un-
tenable.[139] Philo and others used the language of the mysteries,[140]
and even compared Judaism to some sublime mystery,[141] but no
more.

Parallels to current astralism, and possibly some adaptation of
astral ideas,[142] can also be found. The seven-day week[143] and the
emphasis on the Sabbath might seem to have astral associations, at
least to an outsider, and, in fact, St. Paul on one occasion turns this
against his Judaizing opponents.[144] Current Hellenistic and Roman
opinion linked the God of the Jews with Saturn,[145] while the idea
of the powers of God could also be adapted to astral beliefs.[146] In
all this, we have to think of the impression produced on a pagan
coming into contact with the Jew, and of Jewish devices to win the
Gentile to adherence. The various points of similarity need not mean

that the Jews transformed their faith to suit Greek models, nor that they copied the alien. They simply chose the points which could be paralleled, and claimed that all the best of pagan belief was to be found in a higher degree in Judaism, and more than this too.[147] There were points of contact also between Judaism and the dominant philosophy of the time, which was a synthesis of Platonism, Stoicism, and Pythagoreanism, ascribed with some probability to the work of Posidonius,[148] and here again the same holds good.

What the Jew did was not so much to assimilate alien elements, but to present his own faith in the form which approached most closely to current ideas. By elaborate systems of chronology and the skilful manipulation of history he sought to prove that all the wisdom of the Greeks was enshrined in the inspired teaching of Moses—in fact, the Greek philosophers had borrowed from Moses, without acknowledgement.[149] The mysteries were but poor shadows of the real religion, the true faith which alone could save. As for astrology, the Graeco-Roman world came to be more and more dominated by religions of an astral type, and Judaism might conceivably have come forward as simply another among many, but the Jews, though making use of such concepts on occasion, held rather that Judaism is beyond the power of the stars, and the Jew thus free from fate.[150] Such freedom from fate was one of the aims desired by the initiate in the mysteries, but Judaism could claim to offer it much more convincingly. In all this, the Jews were greatly helped by the allegorical method of interpretation then current, especially it would seem in Alexandria.[151] The Stoics had made use of it in dealing with Greek mythology, but our best source for it is Philo, the Jew of Alexandria.

NOTES TO CHAPTER I

[1] See *Beginnings* I. 137ff., *Jew and Greek* 144, and on the Diaspora in general Schürer, Bousset-Gressmann, Pfeiffer.

[2] Cf. *Jew and Greek* 43. For the distinction within Judaism of the Palestinian aspect, culminating in the Rabbinic Judaism which survived the fall of Jerusalem in A.D. 70, and the Hellenistic, which was absorbed in Christianity or ran out into the numerous Gnostic sects of later years, cf. Dodd *BG* xi–xii; see also Montefiore, *Judaism and St Paul*; and *Jew and Greek* 157ff.

[3] Dodd *BG* 247.

[4] See Causse *Les Dispersés d'Israel*; and cf. *Jew and Greek* 144.

[5] Schürer (*HJP* 2. 2. 227) speaks of Jewish mercenaries under Psammet-ichus I (664–610 B.C.) [cf. Causse 77ff., Swete, *Introd. to O.T. in Greek* (Cambridge 1914) 4], but in his 3rd and 4th German editions (Leipzig 1898, 3. 19 note 29; 1909, 3. 32) claims that the king in question is Psammetichus II (594–589 B.C.). Cf. Schürer's article Diaspora in *HDB* extra vol., 95; Hoonacker *Schweich Lectures* 1914, 5; Oesterley and Robinson 2. 159. The important point for our purpose is, however, the fact that Jews did serve as mercenaries before the Exile, and not so much the date, or the king whom they served. For the text of Aristeas which comes under review in this connexion see Swete 553.

[6] Cf. Causse 17. One such group of refugees went down into Egypt after the Fall of Jerusalem, taking Jeremiah with them, despite his protests. We have no record of their fate, but apparently they lapsed into idolatry. It has been suggested that they were either absorbed into the Egyptian population or else penetrated far to the south, to become the ancestors of the colonists at Elephantine (Oesterley and Robinson 1. 444). The refer-ences in Jer. 44 to other Jewish communities may indicate still further pre-exilic Jewish settlements in Egypt. Cf. also G. A. Smith, *Jeremiah* (4th ed. reprinted, London 1941) 309ff.

[7] J. W. Jack in *Exp. T.* 1942, 82.

[8] Hoonacker's suggestion (op. cit.) of a Judeo-Aramean community may be correct, but it is also possible that we have here a group who migrated before the reforms of Josiah, and hence adhered to less strict standards. Cf. Causse 83. Oesterley and Robinson (2. 159ff.) suggest that they came from Assyria. Cf. also C. H. Gordon in *JNES* 1955, 56ff.

[9] There is evidence of deportations by later rulers, e.g. Ochus (Schürer 223; cf. Angus *Environment of Early Christianity* 143ff.) and Antiochus III (Cumont *CR Acad. Inscrr.* 1906, 63). Schürer (220) refers to the transporta-tion of Jewish captives to Rome by Pompey, but thinks voluntary emigra-tion more important. Cf. Schürer for details of distribution, political status, religious life, etc., in the Diaspora, and see also Reinach in Daremberg-Saglio 3. 1. 620ff., Schürer in *HDB* extra vol. 91ff.

[10] Cf. Tarn *Hellenistic Civilization* 183.

[11] For Alexander cf. Swete 4f. [note that he refers only to Josephus and to Hecataeus ap. Josephus; the latter reference seems to concern ps.-Hecataeus (infra p. 20 note 36)]. For the Ptolemies among the Diadochi, see ib. 5ff. See also Oesterley and Robinson 2. 177, 189.

[12] Oesterley and Robinson 2. 177; *Jew and Greek* 144–5; Stewart, *A Man in Christ* 48ff. For details see *Beginnings* 1. 142ff., and refs. to Schürer above.

[13] Philo *in Flacc.* 7. 46, *Leg. ad Caium* 281; Joseph. *Ant.* 14. 7. 2, *BJ* 7. 3. 3. Cf. *Or. Sib.* 3. 271, Cic. *pro Flacc.* xxviii, and refs. in Johnston, *Doctrine of the Church in the NT* 27 note 8. Reitzenstein *HMR* 19 note 2 mentions a

similar stress on the diffusion of the Isis-cult in a Greek hymn to Isis (*P Ox.* 1380). It may be a current propaganda form.

[14] Cf. Acts 2. 5ff., and the narratives of St. Paul's missionary journeys. Cf. Juster 1. 180ff. for a 'tableau détaillé' showing the extent of the Dispersion. Based on documents of all kinds, this table strikingly confirms Jewish claims.

[15] Wendland *HRK* 208ff. Cf. Bousset-Gressmann 80f., Cumont *Rel. Or.* 20.

[16] Schürer 2. 2. 281ff. Cf. Wendland *HRK* 91ff. for the part played by philosophical propaganda.

[17] For a study of alien influences on Hebrew literature see Peet *The Literatures of Egypt, Palestine, and Mesopotamia* (Schweich Lectures 1929). Cf. Causse 103ff., and for the *religionsgeschichtliche* problem and contacts with other religions Bousset-Gressmann 469ff.

[18] Cf. Bevan *Hellenism and Christianity* 188ff., for a suggestion of Persian influence in the development of apocalyptic from prophecy. See also S. A. Cook in *CAH* 3. 478ff. for the influence of post-exilic conditions on the OT documents (Knox *Jewish Liturgical Exorcism* 191), and, for the effects of the contact with Babylon and Persia, Causse 143ff. Kuhn and others find Iranian influence in the Dead Sea Manual of Discipline (*ZTh.K.* 1952, 297 note 2).

[19] See also Kennedy *PMR* 60ff.

[20] See Wendland *HRK*, esp. 1–40; Nock *Essays* 63. See also Nock *Conversion*, and Knox *PCG* 56.

[21] *Les Religions orientales dans le paganisme romain* 17ff.

[22] Cf. Reitzenstein *HMR* 23: Schon die Verpflanzungen grösserer Volksmassen, die innerhalb eines Weltreiches oder Kulturgebietes ein Herrschergebot oder der friedliche Zwang des Handels bewirkt, lösen bis zu gewissem Grade den nationalen Charakter der Volksreligionen und beeinflussen ihr Wesen.

[23] For the Hellenistic popular philosophy see Bevan in *The Hellenistic Age* 79ff., and his *Hellenism and Christianity* 75ff., 92ff. For astrology see Cumont *Astrology*; Wendland *HRK* 132ff.

[24] Acts 17. 22.

[25] Knox *PCJ* 23 note 50. In *PCG* x, Knox refers to the need of countering anti-Semitic propaganda and to the requirements of Judaism as a missionary religion, as motives for Philo's labours to make Judaism 'intellectually respectable.' Cf. also Tarn 194ff.

[26] Cf. the case of Tiberius Alexander, on whom see *JRS* 1954, 54ff., *Gnomon* 1955, 461. On the apostates condemned by Philo see Wolfson, *Philo* 1. 73ff.

[27] This seems to be the point at issue between Friedländer and Schürer (see Friedländer, *Der vorchristliche jüdische Gnosticismus*, Göttingen 1898, and Schürer's review in *TLZ* 1899, 167ff.).

[28] See, for example, Goodenough, *Jewish Symbols in the Greco-Roman*

period (New York, 1953–), although the thesis of Goodenough's earlier *By Light, Light* must be received with reserve (see infra, p. 27 note 139).

[29] *Le mouvement baptiste en Palestine et Syrie* (Gembloux 1935).

[30] See Quispel in *The Jung Codex* (ed. F. L. Cross, London 1955) 62, and in *Evang. Theologie* 1954.

[31] See F. M. Braun in *Rev. Biblique* 1955, 5ff., W. F. Albright in *The Background of the NT and its Eschatology* (Cambridge 1956) 153ff. References to the immense literature on the Scrolls will be found in Rowley *The Zadokite Fragments and the Dead Sea Scrolls* (Oxford 1952), and in Fritsch *The Qumran Community* (London and New York 1956). The latest full study is that of Millar Burrows, *The Dead Sea Scrolls* (New York 1955; London 1956).

[32] For the influence of Hellenism on Palestinian Judaism see Oesterley and Robinson 2. 174ff., Angus 216ff., Wendland *HRK* 187ff. For a summary of Hellenistic influence on the Jews, see Oesterley, *Jews and Judaism in the Greek Period* (London 1941) 19ff.

[33] Oesterley and Robinson 2. 179.

[34] For Antiochus, see Oesterley and Robinson 2. 217ff., *Jew and Greek* 30ff., 60. For another estimate, see Tarn *The Greeks in Bactria and India* (Cambridge 1938) 183ff.

[35] E.g. 1 Macc. 1. 11–15.

[36] Quoted by Oesterley from Reinach *Textes d'auteurs grecs et romains relatifs au Judaisme* (Paris 1895) 19ff. Among the works of Hecataeus (*c.* 300 B.C.) was a book on Egypt, from which Diodorus Siculus (xl. 3ff., adduced in Reinach *Textes* 14ff.) summarizes a passage concerning the Jews. According to Josephus (*c. Apion.* 1. 22. 183) Hecataeus devoted a separate book to the Jews, but Origen (*c. Cels.* 1. 15; cf. Chadwick's note ad loc.) reports the doubts of Herennius Philo regarding its authenticity. These doubts are generally upheld, although some (e.g. Willrich *Judaica* 86, Thackeray on Joseph. ad loc.) would maintain that the quotations in Josephus are genuine. The point is that we can prove fairly conclusively the forgery of a work attributed to Hecataeus, and partly derived from him, but designed to serve the needs of Jewish propaganda. See further Schürer 2. 3. 302ff., *PW* 7. 2. 2750ff., Geffcken *Apologeten* xff., Willrich *Urkundenfälschung in der hellenistisch-jüdischen Literatur* (Göttingen 1924). On the work of the real Hecataeus see Wendland *HRK* 116ff.

[37] *Jew and Greek* 144.

[38] *HRK* 193; written of the Diaspora, this is largely applicable also to Palestine, and especially to the north.

[39] *HRK* 191.

[40] Oesterley and Robinson 2. 166.

[41] See Reinach in Daremberg-Saglio 3. 1. 622ff. for Jewish privileges under Graeco-Roman government. For Roman policy towards the Jews see *Beginnings* 5. 277ff., 1. 156ff.

[42] Cf. Tarn 184ff.

[43] Oesterley and Robinson 2. 217f.

[44] Oesterley and Robinson 2. 307, quoting Rankin *The Origins of the Festival of Hanukkah* (1930). See also Rankin's essay in *The Labyrinth* (ed. Hooke) 161ff. But cf. Farmer *Maccabees, Zealots, and Josephus* (New York 1956) 132ff.

[45] Cf. Angus 154: there were in Judaism 'two opposite tendencies—an expansive and an exclusive. The latter is largely Palestinian, the former of the Diaspora. The influence of Deutero-Isaiah and the great prophets, together with the experiences of the Exile and of the Diaspora, gave the upper hand to universalism.'

[46] Cf. Oesterley *Jews and Judaism* 111ff., and quotation from Rowley, p. 116. See also *Jew and Greek* 56ff.

[47] For examples see Oesterley 113.

[48] The conversion of the heathen is sometimes regarded as a necessary preliminary to the Messianic restoration, at least in Palestine (Causse 125). Elsewhere we find that the Messianic Kingdom is dependent on the keeping of the Law (Knox *PCJ* 24 note 52). In Alexandria there was no direct interest in the development of Law and cultus (Bousset-Gressmann 159).

[49] Knox *Jewish Liturgical Exorcism* 191–2; cf. *PCJ* 9 and notes. One such part of the population was the Idumaeans, conquered by Hyrcanus (Graetz *History of Israel* 2. 8). But cf. Rowley *The Unity of the Bible* 115 and note 5: 'While Judaism was never a missionary faith in the sense in which Christianity became missionary almost from its inception, it had a solid missionary achievement to its credit.' According to Bousset-Gressmann (76ff.), the sense of mission did not entirely perish even in Palestine, and it was only with the growing irritation of the Jews against Roman domination that the decisive reaction came (84). See also Bousset-Gressmann 432ff. on the relation between the Diaspora and Palestine.

[50] Cf. Bultmann *Primitive Christianity* 95.

[51] Schürer *GJV* 3. 136. According to Dodd (*BG* 34), 'for the Jews of Egypt in the Hellenistic period the developed meaning of *torah* as a code of religious observance, a 'law' for a religious community, was the normal and regulative meaning, and they made this meaning cover the whole use of the word in the OT. Thus the prophetic type of religion was obscured, and the Biblical revelation was conceived in a hard legalistic way. . . . Where thinkers bred in Hellenistic Judaism sought to escape into a religion of greater spiritual freedom and spontaneity, it was not by any way of return to the prophetic idea of *torah*, but by taking up a fresh attitude to religion conceived as Law. Philo accepted the Law as such and allegorized it: Paul declared that Judaism, being a legal religion, was superseded by the religion of the Spirit.' At the same time, a whole series of legal precepts had fallen out of use (Bousset-Gressmann 433). Cf. also Bousset-Gressmann 128.

[52] Schürer *GJV* 3. 137; Bousset-Gressmann 128.

[53] Bousset-Gressmann 136, 436.

C

[54] For Jewish attitudes to the Gentile see Knox *PCJ* 26 note 57 and 24 note 51. Cf. Loewe in Oesterley *Judaism and Christianity* 1. 112ff.: 'Friendship in social and business relations is more important than theoretical maxims of exclusiveness' (p. 116). Further references in Cadoux *The Historic Mission of Jesus* 137 note 3.

[55] Cf. Causse 116ff.

[56] Weiss *Primitive Christianity* 1. 221ff. For the suppression of the Messianic hope by Philo and Josephus, cf. Knox *PCG* 27 note 3, and for Philo in particular Bréhier 3–10. The expectation does, however, appear in the Sibyllines, and it is possible that Virgil's Messianic Eclogue was inspired by Jewish, or certainly by oriental, ideas (Bousset-Gressmann 206). For the concept of the Redeemer in other faiths, see Knox *PCG* 8ff., 27ff., and for the existence in the contemporary environment of 'messianic' ideas akin to the Jewish, Bousset-Gressmann 224ff.

[57] Cf. Reinach *Textes* 49f. and note to p. 50 there.

[58] Cf. Nock *Conversion* 6. So Israel was tempted to worship the Canaanite Baalim. The cementing of an alliance by marriage also involved some acceptance of the ally's divinities (cf. the cases of Solomon and Ahab).

[59] Cf. Wendland *HRK* 116, 131. For syncretism of Greek and Egyptian deities cf. Plut *de Is. et Os.* 354F ff. Cf. also Apuleius 11. 5, and see Reitzenstein *HMR* 240ff.

[60] Cf. Origen *c. Cels.* 5. 45, 6. 39.

[61] Thus Isis is addressed as *una quae es omnia* (cf. Reitzenstein *HMR* 27 and the quotation from Apuleius, ib. 240). Cf. also *Corp. Herm.* 5. 10, *Asclep.* 20; *Jew and Greek* 213, 222, 276; Causse 137ff.; Hatch *Influence of Greek Ideas* 173ff.

[62] Wendland *HRK* 110ff.

[63] Cf. Bréhier 162; see also Geffcken's index, *Apologeten* 325, and in particular ib. 205ff. on Athenagoras xxii.

[64] *HMR* 4, cf. ib. 28. Syncretism also made toleration easy. Jewish scruples and exclusiveness here partly account for the hostility so often met by the Jews. Cf. Moore *Judaism* 1. 323.

[65] Cf. Conybeare *Philo on the Contemplative Life* 195. See also Rohde's account of Orphism *Psyche* 339ff.

[66] Cf. Nock *Essays* 59ff., Kennedy *PMR* 4ff. For Greek religion and philosophy see especially Wendland *HRK* 95ff.

[67] Cf. Bultmann 96: 'The Stoic theology offered a ready instrument for the expression of Israel's faith in God as Creator.'

[68] Cf. Exod. 20. 3, 1 Kings 9. 3–7, and see Oesterley *Jews and Judaism* 94ff.

[69] See Causse 137ff., Dodd *BG* 17ff., Knox *PCJ* 96 and notes, *PCG* 52, 100, *Pharisaism and Hellenism* 97ff. Philo uses the same methods in adjusting Stoicism and Platonism to Judaism. The Logos, like the cosmos, the immanent divine principle, and all that to the Greeks meant God in the world, becomes an intermediary between the transcendent God of Judaism

and this merely material universe (cf. Bréhier). So also the early Christians explained the pagan gods as demons.

[70] Knox *Pharisaism and Hellenism* 97. See further Moore *Judaism* 1. 226f., 3. 62 and cf. Deut. 32. 8–9 LXX. Gressmann (*Der Messias* 217f.) derives the idea of an allocation of the nations to the different gods from Egypt via Phoenicia, quoting Philo of Byblos ap. Eus. *PE* 1. 10. 32, 38. Cf. also Bousset-Gressmann 246f., 326, 504 on the seventy 'shepherds' of 1 Enoch.

[71] Ibid. Cf. Causse 138ff. In *Tim.* 41A the heavenly bodies are included among the θεοί (but see Dodd *BG* 5ff. on the meaning of θεός).

[72] ibid.

[73] Knox *PCG* 51.

[74] ibid. 52.

[75] ibid. 100; *Pharisaism and Hellenism* 100f. Cf. Sukenik *Ancient Synagogues in Palestine and Greece* (Schweich Lectures 1930) 66.

[76] ibid.

[77] Cf. above, p. 8.

[78] For Greek as the language of the Diaspora cf. Angus, who remarks that in its attitude to Greek culture the Diaspora stands apart from Palestine (214ff.).

[79] Philo *in Flacc.* 7. 46; cf. *Leg. ad Caium* 281.

[80] See Cumont in *PW* 9. 444ff., art. Hypsistos in *Suppt. rev. inst. pub. Belg.* 1897, and *Rel. Or.* 59ff.; Schürer *SAB* 1897, 209ff.; also Roberts, Skeat, Nock: The Guild of Zeus Hypsistos, in *HTR* 29 (Jan. 1936), 39ff.

[81] See *PW* (2 Reihe) 1. 1540ff., Cumont in *CR Acad. Inscrr.* 1906, 63ff., Oesterley in Hooke *The Labyrinth* 115ff. Cf. also Reitzenstein *HMR* 104ff., Guignebert 311ff., McMinn in *JNES* XV (1956) 201ff.

[82] Oesterley *Labyrinth* 124ff. Cf. Knox *PCG* 146ff., Cumont loc. cit.

[83] ibid. 118.

[84] ibid. 119.

[85] Cf. Rohde *Psyche* 253ff. and notes.

[86] Oesterley 130ff.

[87] ibid. 148. For worship of Hypsistos by Sabazius-groups, cf. Reitzenstein *HMR* 99, 105, and cf. 145, 151.

[88] Cf. Dodd *BG* 11ff., and see p. 32f. infra.

[89] Cf. Cumont *Rel. Or.* 60 and note; Dodd *BG* 11ff., 16f.; Nock *Conversion* 64; *HTR* 29. 63.

[90] Cf. Reinach *Textes*, passim.

[91] Cf. Pettazzoni *The All-knowing God* (London 1956) index s.v. *interpretatio Graeca, Romana*.

[92] I. 3. 3, quoted by Reitzenstein *HMR* 104. Cf. Reinach *Textes* 258f. and notes.

[93] Cumont (*CR Acad. Inscrr.* 1906, 67) remarks: 'Nous nous trouvons donc en présence, non d'une méprise occasionelle, mais d'une identification constante, dont l'origine remonte au moins au IIe siècle avant notre ère.' Another possibility is that *some* Jews in Rome worshipped Sabazius, and

their more orthodox brethren incited the authorities against them. Cf. Rankin in *The Labyrinth* 189ff.

[94] *Quaest. conviv.* iv. 6, quoted by Oesterley 148 note 5.

[95] Rohde 286 note 10, Cumont loc. cit.

[96] *Hellenistic Civilization* 183; cf. his remark about Antiochus IV, ibid. 196. Cf. also Reitzenstein *HMR* 106 note 1.

[97] Oesterley 124ff.

[98] Cf. Nock *Conversion* 62, Knox *PCG* 41ff., 208ff., and especially Goodenough *Symbols* 2. 153ff.

[99] Cf. Preisendanz *Pap. mag. gr.* iv. 3019 (I p. 170), Reitzenstein *Poimandres* 187 note 3.

[100] E.g. Pindar *Nem.* xi. 2. Cf. Dodd *BG* 11ff.

[101] Summarized in *Beginnings* 5. 93ff., on which this account is based. See also *PW* 9. 444ff., *HTR* 1936, 55ff.

[102] Cf. Dodd loc. cit., Schürer *SAB* 1897, 214ff., Hooke *The Labyrinth* (index s.v. Elyon).

[103] Cf. *HTR* 1936, 66f., *OGIS* 96.

[104] For the Greek background cf. *HTR* loc. cit., where it is suggested that Jewish influence, though sometimes contributory to the later developments, is not all-important, and that the popularity of the epithet may be explained by the tendency to concentrate powers in the hands of one deity.

[105] *Beginnings* 5. 96. Such people might remain apart from the synagogue in groups of their own, or they might have a synagogue connexion of some sort. In either case they would be a fruitful field for Christian propaganda, although such groups persisted into the fourth century A.D. (Nock *Conversion* 63f., Cumont Hypsistos 2f., *CR Acad. Inscrr.* 64f.)

[106] *Beginnings* 5. 90ff. Cf. Knox *PCG* 147 note 1, *Pharisaism and Hellenism* 89 note. See also Goodenough in *JQR* XLVII (1957) 221ff.

[107] *Pharisaism and Hellenism* 88 (cf. 72), quoting Ramsay *CBP*, inscrr. 550 and 559, p. 649ff. Cf. also Johnston *Doctrine of the Church* 16.

[108] ibid. 89.

[109] *HRK* 193f., where a number of examples are cited.

[110] Juster 213ff. notes that religious toleration was normal in the ancient world. The Jews by refusing the customary reciprocation of worship left the authorities with the choice between persecution and privilege. Unilateral toleration of Judaism meant privileges for the Jews which were denied to others. Refusal of toleration involved compulsion and the abandoning of the time-honoured principle of religious liberty. Some states took one path, others the other, but the roots of anti-Jewish feeling are easily seen. So too the Christian apologists later complain of the inconsistency of the normal Roman tolerance and the intolerance which the Church had to face (cf. Geffcken *Apologeten* 161 *et al.*).

[111] Thus in Egypt citizenship was offered to Jews who would abandon Judaism for the mystery cults (*PCG* 56 note 5, *HMR* 105ff., quoting 3 Macc. 2. 25ff.). Cf. the case of Tiberius Alexander (see Graetz 2. 185 and

above, note 26), and see also the section below on the Wisdom literature. On the question of Jewish citizenship in the cities of the Diaspora, see Bousset-Gressmann 64, and especially 90 note 1, where the claims of Josephus that the Jews possessed isopolity are rejected as fabulous. See also Box's introduction to his edition of Philo *in Flaccum*, quoting Tarn for the view that the Jews possessed *potential* citizenship but not actual, since the latter would have involved participation in heathen worship.

[112] E.g. Schürer 2. 2. 52ff., 282ff., Juster 456ff., Moore *Judaism* 1. 281ff., Bousset-Gressmann index s.v. See also Sukenik *Ancient Synagogues in Palestine and Greece* (Schweich Lectures 1930).

[113] Johnston *Doctrine of the Church* 19.

[114] Some at least of the mystery religions had no fixed doctrinal system (cf. Reitzenstein *HMR* 27, Cumont *Rel. Or.* 81)—an asset for syncretism, but a defect in face of authoritarian Judaism.

[115] Knox *PCG* 27 refers to Josephus *C. Ap.* 2. 19 for the ὁμόνοια of the Jews.

[116] op. cit. 291. Reinach, however, says that the view of Judaism which we derive from the references of ancient authors (i.e. Schürer's 'general disfavour') is modified by the success of Jewish propaganda (Daremberg-Saglio 3. 1. 629). He ascribes the antipathy shown in the literary references to the influence of Alexandrian polemic, but this is perhaps unnecessary. There were features in Judaism which met with approval, others which found disfavour. Popular opinion would not always be consistent, especially where the mob was concerned, and the references in Greek and Roman literature are not uniformly unfavourable. Reinach loc. cit. gives details of Jewish proselytizing methods and of the attraction which Judaism exercised on Gentiles, as well as some examples of prominent proselytes.

The references to the Jews and Judaism in Greek and Latin authors are collected in Reinach *Textes*. Cf. also Juster 45ff. For the Hellenistic Jewish literature, largely composed as propaganda in reply to pagan slanders, see Schürer 2. 2. 156ff., Pfeiffer 197ff., Wendland *HRK* 197ff. The remains of this literature are collected in W. N. Stearns *Fragments from Graeco-Jewish Writers* (Chicago 1908). Cf. also *Recueil Cerfaux* 1. 65ff. (= *Muséon* 37 (1924) 29ff.).

[117] Cf. Josephus *c. Apion.* 2. 145ff.

[118] Cf. Angus 155ff., and for the religious curiosity of the period Nock in *Beginnings* 5. 183ff.

[119] *BG* 243. See also Stewart 52f., *Jew and Greek* 151. On the other hand we have the willingness of the age to listen to new religious teaching, of whatever sort, provided it was authenticated by miracles. Cf. the case of Alexander of Abonoteichus (Knox *PCJ* 305 note 20, Nock *Conversion* 93ff.). See Kennedy *PCR* 226 for Philo's description of 'false prophets' (*de Spec. Leg.* 4. 50).

[120] *Essays* 55 note 1. Conrad Noel (*Life of Jesus* 33ff.) claims that the Jews had attained commercial supremacy in the Diaspora, and with it

political power. The richer Jews, comfortably at home in the commercial world, had much to fear from nationalistic outbursts, and hence spiritualized away the more nationalistic hopes of world dominion by the Jewish race. Cf. above note 56.

[121] For Jewish apologetic cf. Josephus *c. Apion* 2. 145-296, and the literature referred to in note 116 above.

[122] Cf. Apuleius, who apparently tried them all; cf. also Reitzenstein *HMR* 28.

[123] Cf. Stewart, *A Man in Christ* 66. What he says there of the Church is true also of the Jews (cf. the references in Greek and Roman writers: see Reinach *Textes* s. v. Impiété). Cf. also Juster 1. 213.

[124] Thus Philo turns from the hope of a glorious destiny for Israel to concentrate on the future of the Law. All else in Jewish eschatology becomes 'a symbol of inward moral progress.' The Messianic hope is almost entirely neglected (cf. Bréhier 3-10). Schürer says it is characteristic that Jewish particularist ideas are not necessary for his philosophy (2. 3. 368).

[125] Cf. Knox *PCG* 69.

[126] Cf. Wendland *HRK* 196.

[127] See Dodd *BG* xi and Part I, and cf. Reitzenstein *HMR* 420: 'Ganz andere Ideenverbindungen gestattet, ja erfordert ... das griechische Wort πνεῦμα als das hebräische rūaḥ.' See also Deissmann, *Die Hellenisierung des semitischen Monotheismus*. Cf. *Corp. Herm.* XVI (Reitzenstein *Poim.* 348f.): δόξει τοῖς ἐντυγχάνουσί μου τοῖς βιβλίοις ἁπλουστάτη εἶναι ἡ σύνταξις καὶ σαφής, ἐκ δὲ τῶν ἐναντίων * * * ἀσαφὴς οὖσα καὶ κεκρυμμένον τὸν νοῦν τῶν λόγων ἔχουσα, καὶ ἔτι ἀσαφεστάτη .τῶν Ἑλλήνων ὕστερον βουληθέντων τὴν ἡμετέραν διάλεκτον εἰς τὴν ἰδίαν μεθερμηνεῦσαι, ὅπερ ἔσται τῶν γεγραμμένων μεγίστη διαστροφή τε καὶ ἀσάφεια.

(* Es fehlt ein Dativ: anderen, oder den Ungläubigen, oder dergl., vgl. IX (X) 10: Ps. Apuleius 10.—Reitzenstein loc. cit.) Cf. also the Prologue to Sirach.

[128] See Knox *PCJ* 96f.

[129] For syncretism in the mystery cults see Cumont *Rel. Or.* passim.

[130] *Studies in the Acts of the Apostles* (ed. H. Greeven; ET London 1956). Norden (*Agnostos Theos* 129ff.) argues for the existence of a propaganda-tradition regarding the true worship of God, which he traces from early Greek philosophy through Judaism to Christianity. See also Geffcken *Apologeten*.

[131] Knox *PCJ* 23 note 49; cf. Kirk *The Vision of God* 119ff., and for the catalogue-style in Paul ibid. 127ff.

[132] *Light from the Ancient East* 315: 'These were no new creations, but based on Jewish and pagan series.' Cf. the attacks on the vices of the heathen in the *Wisdom of Solomon*.

[133] Stoic and Cynic preachers were the chief agents in spreading such

ethical commonplaces. Deissmann (loc. cit.) stresses the importance of popular lists from papyri, etc., as against the philosophical literature, for what was really current among the people. Cf. Wendland *HRK* 75ff. on the philosophical propaganda, and Kirk loc. cit. on the characteristics of the Stoic-Cynic preaching. Some features may, however, have been developed independently by the Jews (Kirk 121ff.). See further Knox *Schweich Lectures* 1942, 5f. and notes there.

Hatch *Influence of Greek Ideas* 139ff. warns against overstress on the picture of the state of morals presented by satirists and apologists.

[134] Cf. Thyen *Der Stil der jüdisch-hellenistischen Homilie* (Göttingen 1955).

[135] See Kennedy *PMR* 31ff.

[136] For similar reservations in Christianity cf. Bethune-Baker, *Introduction to the Early History of Christian Doctrine* 34ff., and note on p. 39.

[137] This feature appears already in the prophets (Dodd *Apostolic Preaching* 95).

[138] See Knox *PCG* 27ff. (Exodus in Jewish *kerygma*), 29 (reservation of the Decalogue), 40 (withdrawal of the name of God). See also *Pharisaism and Hellenism* 82ff., and for Exodus, the *Wisdom of Solomon*, chapters x to end.

[139] Goodenough *By Light, Light.* See Johnston's criticisms, *Doctrine of the Church* 16ff., and references there. A similar view had been advanced by Conybeare op. cit. 303. See also Loisy in Montefiore op. cit. 234. For further criticisms of Goodenough's theory see Nock's review in *Gnomon* 1937, 156ff.; W. D. Davies *Paul and Rabbinic Judaism* (London 1948) 94ff., Wolfson *Philo* 1. 44f. Goodenough has replied in *Quantulacumque: Studies Presented to Kirsopp Lake* (London 1937) 227ff. to the earlier among these criticisms. See also his *Jewish Symbols in the Greco-Roman Period* 6. 198ff. The influence of the mysteries on Alexandrian Judaism before Philo has been examined by Cerfaux (*Muséon* 37 (1924) 29ff. = *Recueil Cerfaux* 1. 65ff.).

[140] For Philo's knowledge of mystery terminology see Reitzenstein *HMR* 97, 100, 247ff., 257 etc., and Conybeare on *De Vita Contemplativa*, excursus p. 303ff. Cf. also Knox *Pharisaism and Hellenism* 82ff., and Kennedy *PCR* 212ff.

[141] Josephus *c. Apion.* 2. 188. Cf. also Lewy *Sobria Ebrietas* 13 note 1, 15 note 3 *ad fin.*

[142] Cf. Causse 138ff.

[143] Cf. Wendland *HRK* 157ff. The seven-day week is Hellenistic, and owes its origin to the belief that the planets relieved each other as rulers throughout a seven-day period. The Roman week of eight days was superseded by the third century. The Jewish week, which was taken over by the oldest Gentile Christian communities, had long lost any relation to the planets which it may originally have had. Cf. also Schürer in *ZNW* 1905, especially 13ff.

[144] Gal. 4. 3, 9f. Cf. Bréhier 163. But see also below, p. 93 note 111.

[145] Tacitus, *Histories* 5. 4. See Knox *PCG* 44–54.

[146] Philo, while endeavouring to combat the astrological speculations of other Jews, incorporates such speculations elsewhere as his own. Thus in *De Fug. et Inv.* 103ff., the cities of refuge are interpreted in terms of the powers, which allows him to produce 'a celestial hebdomad to correspond to the planets.' So too in *Qu. in Exod.* 2. 62ff. Philo reduces these speculations to comparatively harmless dimensions, but the accommodation is apparent, and others were not so careful to avoid unorthodox views. See Knox loc. cit., especially 47ff., *Pharisaism and Hellenism* 94ff.

[147] Artapanus ap. Euseb. *PE* 9. 18, 23, 27 endeavours to prove that the Egyptians owed everything to the Jews [e.g. Abraham instructed king Pharethothes in astrology (cf. Wendland *HRK* 199; Knox *PCG* 37, 101); Moses instructed the Egyptian priests in hieroglyphics (cf. Willrich *Judaica* 114; Reitzenstein *Poim.* 182)]. Aristobulus also claims that the Greek thinkers borrowed from Moses, and that the essence of the Pentateuch had been translated into Greek long before LXX (Euseb. *PE* 13. 12. 1 (= Clem. Strom. I. 22. 150 = *PE* 9. 6. 6–8), 12. 4, 12. 13). Cf. Numenius ap. Euseb. *PE* 9. 6 (Clem. Strom. I. 22. 150): τί γάρ ἐστι Πλάτων, ἢ Μωυσῆς ἀττικίζων; See Gifford's notes on Eusebius ad loc., Schürer 2. 3. 238ff., Swete *Introd. to OT in Greek* 12f. and 1–2.

On the relation between Aristobulus and ps. Aristeas on the subject of LXX, see Swete loc. cit., Schürer 2. 3. 309–310, *PW* 2. 918f., and especially Gifford on Euseb. *PE* 410d. 13. See also Tarn *The Greeks in Bactria and India* 414ff., for discussion of certain resemblances between ps. Aristeas and Part I of the *Milindapañha* or *Questions of Milinda* (= Menander). Tarn argues that ps. Aristeas was acquainted with the original Greek *Questions of Menander*, written in India after 150–145 B.C., which was the basis of the *Milindapañha*.

[148] Knox *PCG* 63; cf. Bevan, *Stoics and Sceptics* 85ff., Reitzenstein *HMR* 134, Wendland *HRK* 60f., 134, 206–7. Further references in Kirk *The Vision of God* 33 note 1. See also Norden *Agnostos Theos* 277 note 2 and index.

[149] Schürer 2. 3. 240; cf. Swete 1–2, quoting Aristobulus ap. Clem. Alex. Strom. I. 22. The same attempt had been made elsewhere, e.g. Herodotus (Book 2) tries 'to derive all manner of Greek customs, ritual, and theology from Egypt' (Babbit in Plutarch *Moralia*, vol. 5 (Loeb) p. 4). Herodotus here as often seems merely to reproduce the claims of his sources, in this case the Egyptian priests. Cf. Philo *LA* 1. 108 (Heraclitus), and for Aristobulus Euseb. *PE* 13. 12. 1 (parallel to Clement), 7. 14. 1, 8. 10. 1, 9. 6. For the Greek attitude to other cultures in this period cf. Wendland *HRK* 38ff., 116ff., and for Jewish literary propaganda notes 115 and 146 above. See also Bousset's examination of Clem. Alex. *Strom.* in *Schulbetrieb* 205ff. Some at least of Clement's material goes back to Jewish sources.

[150] Cf. Knox *PCG* 37 note 3, and 100; *Pharisaism and Hellenism* 100ff., and for the desire for freedom from fate in the mysteries Reitzenstein

HMR 347 (quoting Karppe, *Les Origines du Zohar* 76–7), 302; *Poimandres* 78; Kennedy *PMR* 24ff.; Bevan in *The Hellenistic Age* 79ff.; Clement, *Exc. ex Theodoto* (ed. Casey) 72, 76, 78. Human destiny was regarded as subject to a fate governed by or at least in some way associated with the planets. Here we have the roots of the Gnostic systems of the planetary spheres, ultimately due to the influence of Iranian-Chaldean religion. For the Zohar, which is in some respects akin to certain Gnostic systems, though much later, see Gillet, *Communion in the Messiah*, 67ff. For Greek ideas about fate, good and evil, see Greene, *Moira* (Cambridge Mass. 1944).

[151] This is another example of adaptation of pagan methods in the service of Judaism. For a pagan example of the method, see Plutarch *de Is. et Osir.*, and for its use by the Therapeutae Philo *de Vita Contemplativa* 28, 78. Cf. Conybeare 249, Drummond *Philo Judaeus* 1. 121ff., Bréhier 35ff., Wendland *HRK* 112ff., Hatch *Influence of Greek Ideas* 50ff., Wolfson *Philo* 1. 115ff.

CHAPTER II

ALEXANDRIAN JUDAISM AND PHILO

ONE of the largest communities of the Dispersion was that of Alexandria,[1] where the Jews occupied two of the five regions of the city.[2] The political history of this community is one partly of official favour and partly of popular antagonism,[3] but for our purpose the feuds of Jew and Greek are far less important than the interaction of Greek and Jewish thought. The origins of Alexandrian Christianity remain obscure,[4] but we are fairly well informed about Alexandrian Judaism and its Hellenistic background. The danger is, indeed, that we should make Alexandria normative for the Diaspora as a whole and assume that every Jew of the Dispersion was another Philo. Alexandria was in some respects unique, yet in many ways it was representative of Diaspora Judaism; our difficulty lies in the fact that we have not always the material which would enable us to form a definite judgement. Some things are, however, clear.

In the first place, Alexandria had long supplanted Athens as the centre of learning for the Greek world.[5] Alexandrian products in the literary field may be mechanical and artificial, but we find here some of the first ventures in the scholarly editing of the Greek classics.[6] The library was one of the wonders of the world, and the Ptolemies did much to foster learning. According to tradition, it was the interest of one of these rulers that led to the translation of the Hebrew Scriptures into Greek.[7] The legend may be discredited, but it does convey some indication of the reputation of Alexandria. Here Jews, Greeks, and native Egyptians mingled with the motley rout of all nations that is to be found in any seaport. The language and culture were Greek in the main, but the city was open to influences from all quarters.

Secondly, Egypt to the Greeks no less than to men of later days was a land of mystery, of age-old monuments and ancient cities, where the mystic lore of centuries was zealously studied in the temples. Hellenized Egyptian cults took their place among the faiths which spread across the ancient world. Astrology, magic, and philosophy of various kinds mingled with and influenced religious beliefs and customs. In such an environment syncretism is only to be expected.

According to Wendland a Jewish 'Diaspora' in Egypt is attested by documents about the middle of the third century B.C.,[8] but this would seem to be too conservative, since we have seen that its origins may go back still further[9]; it is probable, however, that a Jewish community existed in Alexandria at that period. Wendland is inclined to accept the Jewish tradition which puts the origin of this community in early Hellenistic times, soon after the foundation of the city itself. At any rate, by the beginning of our era Alexandria was the chief seat of Hellenistic Judaism and consequently of Graeco-Jewish literature. It was eminently suited for the growth of such a literature, although we may not assume that there was no such activity elsewhere. Our knowledge of Egyptian Judaism apart from Alexandria is meagre, but Jewish elements are found in the magical papyri. On the other hand, Jewish features are absent from the earliest at least of Egyptian astrological writings, and Cumont uses this as proof that these documents were compiled outside the city, since within it Jewish influence would have been inevitable.[10]

The fundamental document is, of course, the Septuagint, which is linked with Alexandria in all forms of the tradition. This had a double purpose: first, to meet the needs of Alexandrian Jews who had become completely Greek in language and perhaps also to some extent in thought and customs; and secondly, to present the Jewish faith to the Gentiles in their own tongue. The translated Scriptures were no longer the private concern of a small group versed in a tongue which had passed from common use; they now belonged to all who chose to read. This same double purpose is also the motive for Philo's attempt to make Judaism intellectually respectable by linking it with Greek philosophy, and in a word it lies behind all the propaganda of the Jewish Hellenistic literature.[11]

Juvenal[12] speaks of some who, *sortiti metuentem sabbata patrem*, have gone yet further and given themselves over to Judaism. The danger was present also for the Jews, namely, that the younger

generation might completely lose the contact which their parents
had but half maintained, and pass as it were from palaestra and
gymnasium to the Greek temple.[13] The synagogue, the Septuagint,
and the writings represented above all by the works of Philo, are
all designed to meet this danger. Their success can be seen from
the comparative absence of syncretistic tendencies in Judaism, and
also from the spread of Christianity in the Hellenistic world.

It must be confessed, however, that the Septuagint itself gives
opportunity for syncretism of a sort. The namelessness of God in
the version, the result of Jewish scruples against the use of the
Tetragrammaton, 'chimed in with certain speculative tendencies of
Hellenistic thought.'[14] The use of ὁ ὤν in one passage,[15] and more
freely by Philo, suggests the identity of the personal God of the
Jews with the impersonal Absolute of the Greeks. The use of θεός
for Elohim had a similar effect, and this philosophic character which
Judaism might assume combined with its superior ethic and its
freedom from anthropomorphism to win the adherence of the
more thoughtful among the Gentiles. 'The tendency towards
monotheism (among the Greeks) was accompanied by a view of
the divine as immanent and impersonal,'[16] so that this translation
of the Hebrew names and titles of God might result either in 'a
far-reaching depersonalizing of the God of the Old Testament' or
in the revitalizing of the abstract monotheism of Hellenistic philosophy. As it happened, Hellenistic Judaism, together with its
adherents, was largely absorbed in the Christian Church.[17] New
elements entered into the conception of God, but the inherent
opposition between the Greek and Hebrew ideas was to cause
difficulties for the theologians who sought to fuse them into one.[18]
These difficulties are foreshadowed in Philo, who in the effort to
preserve both the immanence and the transcendence of God is
forced to postulate intermediaries, the Logos or the powers,
between God the Wholly Other and the κόσμος.[19]

Professor Dodd has examined several fundamental ideas of
Judaism from the point of view of the Greek world, as it approached
by way of the Septuagint.[20] In their Greek dress these ideas are not
exactly what they were in the original Hebrew. Judaism was
modified, though not in the same way as other faiths. Thus, in
addition to the two examples already noted, we find the title *Elyon*

rendered by ὕψιστος.[21] 'Jew and pagan could unite in the worship of θεὸς ὕψιστος, though the former might mean by it "God Most High,"[22] and the latter "the supreme Deity." ' Again, the title *Jahweh sebaoth* is rendered in three ways, all of which transform the primitive war-god Yahweh into something of a Hellenistic deity:[23] (a) The first simply transliterates *sebaoth*, with κύριος for *Yahweh*. This rendering κύριος Σαβαώθ, according to Dodd, 'is no doubt responsible for the treatment of Σαβαώθ as a proper name, which we find in Gnostic writings and in magical papyri.'[24] It is also not unlike the Phrygian κύριος Σαβάζιος, and may have led to some confusion between the two cults, if not to an attempt at syncretism by the Phrygian worshippers.[25] (b) The second rendering translates *sebaoth* by δυναμέων.[26] This admirably fits the tendency of the Greek world to represent the gods of polytheism as manifestations of the one supreme god, or as natural forces controlled by him, while at the same time it agrees with the tendency of Hellenistic Judaism to rationalize the angels of popular mythology, or for that matter the degraded gods of the Gentiles, as agencies or powers of God.[27] In Philo the doctrine of δυνάμεις is highly developed. 'On the one side they are attributes or qualities of God, on the other side they are emanations of the divine. . . . He identifies them alike with the Platonic ἰδέαι and with the angels of Scripture.'[28] (c) The third rendering παντοκράτωρ seems to be coined on the model of κοσμοκράτωρ, which has astrological associations.[29] The second rendering also might be astrologically interpreted, the δυνάμεις being conceived as cosmic powers such as the planets.[30]

These examples are simply illustrations of the new content which Jewish ideas received in their Greek form. In other respects the Greek version was deliberately modified to conform with more advanced ways of thought. Various devices are employed to remove the anthropomorphisms of the Hebrew original, as the Targums use the Memra and Philo the Logos or some other intermediary.[31] The Greek ἄγγελος seems to have had a Hellenistic usage which fitted it to represent an intermediary between God and the world, while it could be used to avoid either polytheism or anthropomorphism at need.[32] These are but a few examples, but they may suffice to indicate the nature of the syncretism which we may expect among the Jews of the Dispersion. It is not the combination of Yahweh with other gods, nor the application to Him of their attributes, but the much more subtle modification which arises from the translation of Semitic ideas into Greek forms of expression.

The position is well assessed by Schürer[33] when he says that Judaism and Hellenism 'now entered upon a process of mutual internal amalgamation. Judaism, which in its unyielding Pharisaic phase appears so rigidly exclusive, proved itself uncommonly pliable and accommodating upon the soil of Hellenism, and allowed a far-reaching influence to the ascendant Greek spirit.' But Judaism was at the same time very different from the other contemporary religions. 'Its internal power of resistance was incomparably greater than theirs. While the other Oriental religions were merged in the general religious medley of the times, Judaism maintained itself essentially inviolate.'[34] It thus proved its pre-eminent religious strength, and the consciousness of this pre-eminence left its mark on the Graeco-Jewish literature.

With the Septuagint and the other Hellenistic Jewish writings Judaism enters upon the field of history in Greek dress and no longer as an obscure semi-barbarian cult. The chief representative of this Jewish Hellenism is Philo of Alexandria, a contemporary of Jesus and the Apostles, whose works have been preserved, where others perished, largely because of the interest he aroused in the early Fathers of the Church.[35] 'A faithful adherent of the synagogue, its dogmas and its rites, Philo allowed himself to be influenced to a very high degree by non-Jewish speculations in his religious views and experiences. The similarities and the peculiar characteristics of biblical and Hellenistic piety are therefore clearly to be seen in him. The biblical scholar recognizes that the Greeks also, admittedly under oriental influence, had developed a piety corresponding to their own general frame of mind, which was able to draw the Jew under its spell, although he, of course, possessed from his fathers a book of revelation.'[36] This syncretism of Greek and Jewish thought, interesting in itself, has a special importance for the history of Christianity, but we are here concerned solely with its relation to that of Judaism.

We cannot say exactly how far Philo is typical of Alexandrian Judaism. Bréhier[37] says there was no one school, since Philo's predecessors do not all conform to the same type and style as he. Again, our evidence is scanty apart from his own works, and we have literally nothing by which to judge whether he really represents the Jews of Alexandria in his day in their attitude to Greek culture and their own religion. On the other hand, there are parallels and points of contact between Philo and his predecessors which seem to show that he was developing, modifying, and generally carrying to a conclusion the work of those who had gone before.[38] Moreover, there are indications that he was not working independently, that he did not simply concoct his theories and allegories for himself, but drew upon an existing tradition.[39] We know that Aristobulus worked in a similar fashion, and that the allegorical method had been practised earlier.[40] Finally, Philo's work is just what we might expect from a man of his type—versed in the Scriptures, acquainted to some extent with the Greek philosophers, and convinced that his own Scriptures contained the whole truth delivered to man by God. The man most like him among his contemporaries (of whom we have any knowledge), namely, the author of Hebrews, uses at times the same methods and for the same ends. Similar features may be found in other New Testament writers, notably in Paul and John.[41] All three move in the same circle of ideas as does Philo, although Paul is much less influenced than the other two.

Thus, although we cannot compare Philo's works with the ideas current among his fellow-Jews in Alexandria, we seem to have grounds for assuming him fairly typical of several schools of thought. In aim and methods he reminds us, though with differences, of Paul and Hebrews, while his contacts with his predecessors seem to show that he is but following in their footsteps, although in the end he goes far beyond the point they reached.[42]

It must not be forgotten, however, that not all Jews would have the same education, the same interest in Greek philosophy, the same temptation to abandon Judaism for one or other of the Greek systems of thought. The less educated would be drawn rather to the mystery cults,[43] and here the synagogue, with the awe inspired by doctrines inculcated from the cradle, would retain the allegiance of the majority. The greater danger was that the enlightened, priding themselves upon their intellectual powers, might be drawn

<u>away</u>.[44] Lucretius[45] had said that Reason drove away superstition, the *terrorem animi tenebrasque*, Plutarch[46] that philosophic reason 'does away with the wonder and awe due to unenlightenment and ignorance.' Philo seeks to show that Judaism, so far from being merely a vain superstition, is not incompatible with philosophy, but in fact embraces all that is best in philosophy—if it be approached in the proper way. Some of his arguments may seem to us fanciful and far-fetched, but of his sincerity and his loyalty to the faith of his fathers there can be no doubt.

The justification of Judaism in the eyes of the educated Jew was one side of the twofold purpose which Philo shares with the rest of the Alexandrian Jewish literature, but he has also the Greek world in mind. The decline of the old Olympian religion under the impact of philosophical criticism and the propaganda of the oriental cults left men at sea. All seemed at the mercy of blind Fate or Chance;[47] the gods who led a carefree existence in 'the lucid interspace of world and world'[48] either did not or could not come to the aid of their suppliants. Some turned to philosophy, but philosophy satisfied only the few; not all could attain to αὐτάρκεια,[49] the Stoic calm of a Cato or of Horace's *justum et tenacem propositi virum*.[50] Many turned to the new faiths which claimed divine authority and offered assurance of salvation to the initiate. Full initiation might be beyond the means of most, yet they could hope for something of the divine protection and trust to the god to deliver them from the sway of fate.

In Philo, Judaism appears as both a philosophy and a religion, embracing in itself the best that other faiths could offer and speaking with an authority which they could not claim. It is not simply another mystery but, above all others, the only complete and perfect faith.

Contemporary paganism was seeking to defend itself by a synthesis of Stoic, Platonic, and Pythagorean philosophy, apparently due largely to Posidonius.[51] This made the κόσμος a system in which one divine λόγος emanating from Zeus manifested itself in the gods, in men, and in nature. Judaism had developed a similar doctrine for Wisdom, and Philo uses the same principle: the God of the Torah creates through the λόγος, which manifests itself in λόγοι or angels or discarnate souls,[52] in man and in nature. Christianity adopted the scheme for its own purposes, regarding Christ as the Λόγος through whom all things were created, but in this system there was no interest in the subordinate λόγοι, which accordingly tend to disappear.[53] Regarding man as fallen, Philo has also a scheme of redemption[54] such as we find in Christianity, in the mysteries,[55] and in some philosophies,[56] although, of course, each scheme has its own characteristic features.

Early Greek philosophy had made several attempts to account for the origin of the universe, some thinkers assigning it either to some πρώτη ὕλη[57] or to the inter-action of atoms,[58] without any thought of a Creator in the biblical sense. Plato, on the other hand, argued that the κόσμος, being sensible, must have come into being and hence had a First Cause.[59] This First Cause he equates with a supreme God, who existed before the gods of the Olympian pantheon, his first creations.[60] Stoicism developed a suggestion of Heraclitus into a scheme in which one λόγος manifested itself in the universe in many σπερματικοὶ λόγοι, the Logos being the divine fire and the soul in man a spark from it enclosed in matter.[61] These schemes were conflated into a philosophic monotheism of a pantheistic type;[62] all the gods were emanations of the one God, or the one God under various aspects, an all-pervading Logos manifested in innumerable λόγοι. In this scheme it became possible to distinguish between 'the element of divine fire immanent in the cosmos and the concentrated element of fire in the firmament of heaven,'[63] and thus 'to vindicate the existence of God as a being whom man could know and worship in virtue of that affinity between God and man which was proclaimed by the very structure of his body, which enabled him alone of all the beasts to contemplate the stars without difficulty.'[64]

The Old Testament view was radically different, but in Egypt and Syria Judaism came into contact with the cults of Isis and Astarte.[65] Isis appears as an agent in creation, Astarte as a fertility-goddess, and Judaism, apparently to offset the lure of their cults, now developed the concept of Wisdom as an almost personified being,[66] the first of created beings, though as yet simply an assessor and not an agent in Creation.[67] Moreover, Yahweh had by this time been transformed by a natural process of development from the God of Israel to the God of heaven, ruler of the world which

D

He had created.[68] Here Judaism and philosophy could join hands; for the one, God dwelt in heaven, a holy spiritual being; for the other, the heaven itself was an intelligent being, sometimes designated νοῦς ἐν αἰθέρι.[69] So to Juvenal the God of the Jews is *caeli numen*.[70]

The immanent Logos presented more difficulty. Judaism could not admit a second deity,[71] but at the same time the Jewish conviction of the transcendence of God left a gulf between God and the world. Here the concept of Wisdom provided an intermediary, sufficiently vague to avoid offence to Jewish scruples, yet real enough to play the part. In this connection also Wisdom is a counterpart to Isis,[72] and, moreover, the concept proved a convenient way of obviating the anthropomorphisms of the Old Testament.

The first to identify Wisdom with the immanent cosmic principle seems to have been Aristobulus,[73] who was followed by the authors of the *Wisdom of Solomon*. The relevant passages are preserved in the *Praeparatio Evangelica* of Eusebius,[74] where Aristobulus is quoted to confirm a statement of Philo on the Logos. The fuller version begins with the claim that Plato had carefully studied the Mosaic law, and that he together with Pythagoras and Socrates had closely followed Moses. Orpheus and Aratus are quoted to show that all things are pervaded by the power of God. Then, according to Eusebius, Aristobulus adds after an interval that God in creating the cosmos 'has given us the seventh day as a day of rest, because for all men life is full of troubles; this day indeed might naturally be called the first birth of light, whereby all things are beheld.[75] The same title might be transferred to Wisdom, for all light comes from her.'[76] Hence some of the Peripatetic school have described her as a beacon, but Solomon much more clearly and beautifully said that she existed before heaven and earth.[77] This leads to an explanation of God's rest on the Sabbath, and to a selection of verses from Homer, Hesiod, and Linus—one verse being authentic!—in praise of the hebdomad.[78] The explanation of the Sabbath rest and the praise of the hebdomad, but not the verses, may be paralleled from Philo.[79]

Wisdom here appears in the character of pre-cosmic light, which also belonged to Isis, although the Jewish concept might have been derived directly from Genesis.[80] 'The attempt to place her at the beginning of all things and yet to identify her with the sabbath suggests that Aristobulus has in mind the equation of Wisdom with the Torah, as described in the interpolation in Ecclesiasticus and in rabbinical tradition.[81] His panegyric on Wisdom enables him to introduce the argument that the philosophers of Greece had really borrowed from Moses; unfortunately it also reveals the paucity of his acquaintance, and that of his successors, with the philosophy of the classical age.'[82]

The *Wisdom of Solomon* falls naturally into three parts, and the character of these sections is such as to suggest composite authorship.[83] The first five chapters deal with the righteous and the ungodly, and in these the word σοφία occurs twice.[84] Neither of these instances necessarily implies that Wisdom is a cosmic principle, although they could be so interpreted if read with the second section and similar works in mind. The concluding chapters of the book[85] represent Wisdom as active in history, but in these Wisdom eventually disappears,[86] to be replaced by the direct intervention of God. From the end of the tenth chapter to the close of the book there is but a single reference to Wisdom, and the general level of this section is lower than that of the earlier chapters.

With the second section the situation is altogether different. Some of the references here to σοφία apply to the 'understanding heart' for which Solomon prayed,[87] rather than to Wisdom as a cosmic principle, but the writer passes easily from the one sense to the other, and it is not always possible to make a clear distinction. Thus in vii. 7 we have his account of Solomon's prayer:

$$\delta\iota\grave{\alpha}\ \tau o\hat{v}\tau o\ \epsilon\vec{v}\xi\acute{\alpha}\mu\eta\nu,\ \kappa\alpha\grave{\iota}\ \phi\rho\acute{o}\nu\eta\sigma\iota\varsigma\ \vec{\epsilon}\delta\acute{o}\theta\eta\ \mu o\iota\cdot$$
$$\vec{\epsilon}\pi\epsilon\kappa\alpha\lambda\epsilon\sigma\acute{\alpha}\mu\eta\nu,\ \kappa\alpha\grave{\iota}\ \mathring{\eta}\lambda\theta\acute{\epsilon}\nu\ \mu o\iota\ \pi\nu\epsilon\hat{v}\mu\alpha\ \sigma o\phi\acute{\iota}\alpha\varsigma.$$

The following verses would naturally be understood in the former sense, but it is clear from verse 22 that the author has also the cosmic principle in mind throughout.[88] The ambiguity was an advantage, since the scrupulous Jew might understand it all of wisdom, which is the gift of God, while others thought of the cosmic principle Wisdom, almost as a second deity.

Wisdom is the gift of God,[89] and there is in her an intelligent spirit which pervades all things.[90] She is the exhalation of the power of God,[91] an emanation of the glory of the παντοκράτωρ,[92] an effulgence of the eternal light,[93] a perfect reflection of the action of God,[94] and the image of His goodness.[95] She is one and all-powerful,[96] fairer than the sun and above every rank of stars;[97] compared with light she proves superior.[98] She is the mother of all things,[99] initiated into the knowledge of God[100] and sharing in His works,[101] the partner of His throne[102] and His agent in Creation.[103]

Some of this goes back to the concept of Wisdom in Proverbs and Ecclesiasticus; other elements are derived from the various Greek systems of philosophy, as harmonized by Posidonius.[104] The details of the development do not concern us, since our aim is chiefly to demonstrate the growth of theories such as this before Philo.[105] In other parts of the book various Greek theories about the soul, life and death, and similar topics are adduced and refuted. Some of these we can definitely assign to a particular school.[106]

Philo, or some one not long before him, took a further step in reconciling Judaism and philosophy by substituting the term Logos for Wisdom.[107] The latter still appears, sometimes because Philo has not corrected his source or because of its greater aptitude for his purpose, but it has no real place.[108] The change had the advantage of removing the awkward female figure, while it also brought his scheme closer to the Stoic, and harmonized better with the narrative of Genesis.

Philo's interest, however, always remains the same—not to construct a more adequate philosophical system, whether based on those of contemporary schools or in opposition to them, but 'to justify Judaism in terms of contemporary thought,'[109] and to read into it as much as was possible of the conventional Hellenistic theology. 'When he gathered the beautiful blossoms of Grecian learning, it was to twine them into a garland for the better adornment of Judaism.'[110] He begins with the Jewish Bible, and reads Greek philosophy, as it were, between the lines. His work is determined throughout by the Scriptures. 'The fact that Philo in the closing sections of De Mund. Op. 61 (170ff.) summarizes the value of a cosmogony which is based on the Timaeus and Posidonius in terms of purely conventional Judaism which ignores alike the Logos and the divine pattern, seems a decisive proof that he did not really care about it; in the same way his "powers" are merely the Stoic manifestations of the one God in the figures of pagan religion.'[111] His teaching about the Logos and the powers may be something of a departure from strict monotheism, but he had precedents in rabbinic theology, and in any case his scheme could not be far removed from the popular concept of a hierarchy with God as supreme. For Judaism this hierarchy seems to be derived from Persian angelology;[112] for the Greek it was a question of the reduction of the Olympian gods to a lower grade.[113]

More important than the question of origins is the fact that there was such a hierarchy both in Jewish and in Gentile thought.[114] It was natural to identify the two, in spite of their differences, and here again we find results similar to those attendant on the Greek translation of the Jewish Scriptures. Background, origins and content were often different, but each party assumed that the other meant the same as he, to the great confusion of later generations.

Philo's treatise *De Opificio Mundi* has some very close resemblances to the *Timaeus*, although there are also points of difference. Philo builds his work round the narratives of Genesis, while Plato was endeavouring to construct a philosophical system with no such inspired book to guide him. Again, there are some things in the *Timaeus* which Philo would surely never have omitted had he known of them, so that it would seem that he did not have a very close acquaintance with it. This, coupled with the fact that Philo's scheme is more closely akin to the syncretistic system of Posidonius[115] (or what we know of it) than to Plato himself, suggests that he knew the *Timaeus* only at second hand, through Posidonius. It is only because this system could be read into the narrative of Moses that it is employed at all.

After praising Moses for the 'admirable and most impressive exordium' with which he introduced his code of laws,[116] Philo infers from the narrative of Genesis that there were two causes, an active and a passive.[117] The latter is incapable of life and motion until it is shaped and quickened by the active Cause, which is 'the perfectly pure and unsullied Mind of the universe, transcending virtue, transcending knowledge, transcending the good itself and the beautiful itself.'[118] Elsewhere he forsakes this for a fourfold Peripatetic scheme, in which God is the formal cause, the Logos the instrumental,[119] and goodness the final.[120] The material cause is the four elements, corresponding to the passive cause of *De Opificio Mundi*. In each case it is a question not of creation *ex nihilo* but of the shaping of material which already lay to hand.[121] He ascribes the origin of the world to a Creator who is Himself uncreated, and who cares for the work of His hands,[122] in contrast to some theorists who admire the world rather than its Creator.[123] The cosmos, being ὁρατός and αἰσθητός, must have had an origin.[124]

The first step is the formation of the intelligible cosmos, as the necessary pattern for the production of the material world.[125] This intelligible cosmos could have no other location than the divine Logos which devised this ordered frame.[126] In fact, the intelligible world is nothing else than the Logos of God when He was already engaged in the act of creating.[127] It is also the image of God: man was created 'after the image of God,' that is, as an image of that image; the cosmos, the whole of which man is a part, must be an image of the image also, and hence the pattern after which the cosmos was formed, the νοητὸς κόσμος which is the Logos, is the image of God.[128] In this passage the man created after the image of God is the natural man;[129] so too shortly afterwards the plural ποιήσωμεν of LXX is interpreted as indicating that lesser beings shared in this work, in order that God might not be held responsible for evil.[130] In the *Legum Allegoriae*,[131] however, a distinction is made, based on the double account of the creation of man in Genesis. One man is moulded from the dust of the earth, and is literally 'of the earth, earthy,' although God breathed into his nostrils the breath of life and he became a living soul.[132] The other, the heavenly man, was not moulded, but stamped with the image of God.[133] He is on the same level as the νοητὸς κόσμος and the Logos, and, indeed, is equated with them.[134]

In Plato's account, the κόσμος itself is ζῷον ὁρατόν, εἰκὼν τοῦ νοητοῦ, θεὸς αἰσθητός;[135] it is ζῷον ἔμψυχον ἔννουν τε,[136] and has a soul stretched throughout the whole.[137] For the Stoics, the whole universe is permeated by the divine Logos, which manifests itself in man as reason;[138] it is no different from the supreme principle, whatever be the name assigned to it.[139] Philo adopts these concepts where they suit him,[140] but generally distinguishes the Logos from God,[141] though sometimes very vaguely, and establishes a gulf between the transcendent God and the world.[142] In one case the world is the only-beloved perceptible son of God by Wisdom;[143] in another there are two sons, the κόσμος νοητός, closely associated with the Logos, and the κόσμος αἰσθητός.[144] He makes no attempt to devise a consistent system, but simply uses one theory or another as suits the biblical context with which he is dealing.

Of the other descriptions of the Logos, we find it to be ἑρμηνεὺς τοῦ θεοῦ καὶ προφήτης,[145] πρεσβύτερος τῶν γένεσιν εἰληφότων,[146] πρωτόγονος and πρεσβύτατος τῶν ἀγγέλων.[147] It is a work of God,[148] or again neither ἀγένητος like God nor γένητος like man, but a mean between the two extremes.[149] It is an emanation from God,[150] a first-born son whom God sets at the head of His flock (the elements);[151] in the cosmos, viewed as a temple of God, the Logos is High Priest.[152] The fountain of wisdom,[153] it is also the principle of unity[154] and stability in the world,[155] and the principle of virtue;[156] the intermediary between God and man, it plays a part in the ascent of the soul to God.[158] Sometimes it appears almost as a distinct personal being,[159] yet again it is less personal than the older Jewish concept of Wisdom.[160]

To sum up, the Stoics had found in Plato's *Timaeus* a cosmogony which could be adapted for their purposes. The older view of a divine reason immanent in the cosmos was transformed into one which retained the immanent reason but also conceived of a transcendent deity, equated with the firmament. As regards the relation of these two principles, the Stoics were not quite clear, and certainly they were not always consistent. But the *Timaeus* cosmogony became a standard for Hellenistic thought. Jewish speculation, in the face of the danger of apostasy owing to the attractions of other faiths, had to some extent diverged from the straight line of the Old Testament religion by developing the concept of Wisdom, employed by some writers as a counterpart to Isis, but soon to become the Jewish version of the immanent Logos. Alexandrian Judaism had by the time of Philo completed the assimilation by substituting the Logos for Wisdom. The course of the development shows that it was not merely a question of borrowing from Greek thought, for the germ was present long before. Rather should we say that when he came under the influence of philosophy, or encountered philosophical criticism of his beliefs, the Jew modified his ancestral faith to a form acceptable to the Gentile thinker. To avoid anthropomorphisms, some sort of intermediary became necessary; it was not God who spoke or visited the patriarchs or walked in the garden, but an angel. Subsequently, under the influence of philosophy, the figure of Wisdom or the Word was introduced. So Wisdom lay ready for use against Isis, and when Jews and Egyptians alike were confronted by the Hellenistic Greek cosmogony a further change took place in their schemes. The Jew had the advantage, since it mattered little to him whether he spoke of Wisdom or the Word; the prevailing fashion in Philo's day called for a Logos, so Logos it was. The variety of meaning which the Greek word possessed was also of use; the Stoic meant the immanent Reason, the Jew the Word or Reason or Mind of the transcendent God. Philo and his circle were not really syncretistic here; a philosophic interpretation on the lines of Posidonius' scheme was expected of any faith, and they sought to provide it by emphasizing features in Judaism which would otherwise have remained in the background.

With inconsistency among the Stoics and more of his own, besides the fact that the philosophy is only secondary, it is not surprising that Philo's work is not always coherent.[161] The Logos has no one special function; it can be 'the divine pattern of which the material world is a copy, the divine power immanent in the cosmos,[162] the divine agent in creation, or the divine purpose in creation, or the Platonic idea of the good. In fact, he can be anything that appears in Plato or the Stoics as the power of God acting upon the world, or as an intermediary between God and the world, or as the reason of God immanent in the world.'[163] There are two main reasons which account for the doctrine: one is Philo's desire to interpret Judaism in terms of current philosophy, the other the need for some link between God and this finite world. The latter, however, is bound up with the former, since it arises out of the conflicting views of God as transcendent and as immanent. When Philo thinks purely in terms of Judaism the Logos disappears.

God alone is good and perfect, nay rather, above the good and above the beautiful.[164] All existence cannot be traced back to Him, since evil cannot have its source in Him, even indirectly.[165] The world is created from a formless, passive matter, and it almost seems that Philo regards matter as evil.[166] Yet in his account of the Creation matter is said to be completely without properties.[167] It is only when we come to his view of man that this Platonic dualism fully appears.[168] Man, the natural man, is moulded from the dust of the earth, and God breathes His spirit into his nostrils;[169] or again, the whole atmosphere is filled with souls, of which those nearer to the earth are attracted by sense and descend into mortal bodies.[170] Drummond endeavours to save Philo's philosophical reputation by assuming that the distinction is between phenomenal and eternal, not between material and spiritual.[171] Matter is not an active principle of evil. 'The source of imperfection was not in the material as opposed to the spiritual, but in the phenomenal as opposed to the eternal. To have come into existence placed an infinite gulf between the Creator and the created. . . . Limitation belongs to the very notion of a cosmos composed of a variety of parts. . . . It is not to matter in its original essence, but to matter in its phenomenal and ever-changing aspects, that Philo attributes any power of limiting the agency of God.'[172] This seems to be true, although it might perhaps be doubted whether Philo could be so subtle. He is so often inconsistent, too, that it might easily be simply another case of inconsistency here.[173] He does not admit an evil Power or deity like the Persian Ahriman; matter must therefore be without quality, since there was nothing to sway it either way. But in dealing with man Philo has to account for the fact of evil, and here the widespread myth of the Fall was readily assimilable to Platonic ideas.[174]

The central thought is that man is akin to the divine, whether his divine part be a spark of the Stoic Logos or a portion of Dionysus devoured by the Titans.[175] All such ideas, Platonic,[176] Stoic,[177] Orphic, Philonic,[178] have as a basis a dualistic conception of the world as divided into regions of sense and of spirit, of noumenal and phenomenal, real and apparent. This world is evil, because matter is evil, whatever be the technical terms used to distinguish between the two spheres. Man really belongs to the higher sphere, but has fallen or been banished to the lower. The body is a prison from which the soul longs to escape.[179]

In some systems pessimism was carried even further. The Orphics and Pythagoreans, like the Buddhists,[180] conceived of an endless round of reincarnations, and some such idea was adopted in other views. Greek ideas about the soul, immortality, after-life, had undergone many changes, and each stage left its mark.[181] But the chief complication for the Hellenistic Age came from the influence of astrology.[182] The soul in its fall or descent passed through the spheres of the seven planets.[183] To reach its true abode it had to find its way back. Sometimes the soul is held to have taken on, as a garment, elements from each of the spheres;[184] these must be doffed on the journey home, until the pure spirit rises into the highest sphere. The gates are guarded, pass-words are required, and a knowledge of the way, if not a guide from above. This was the sort of view proclaimed by mysteries and philosophies alike in our period, and this was the need they sought to meet. This also is Philo's own background, and his view of man takes its colour from the contemporary world.[185] For Judaism too man was at variance with God, but in the details we find the Hellenistic idea dominant. Philo reads it into the Jewish Scriptures.[186]

The Logos is the agent of God in creation, but there are also other Logoi, of which it is the chief.[187] Philo speaks of logoi, of powers, of angels, but the exact relation of these to each other and to God is obscure.[188] He works on the lines of the Posidonian theory, yet there are differences due to his Jewish background. The Stoic logoi are emanations of the one Logos, but though Philo sometimes uses an emanationist manner of speaking, he does not develop the doctrine fully.[189] It is enough for him that he has a system of intermediate beings which could be read in Stoic terms. So in his doctrine of man he interprets the Jewish view of man as fallen in terms of Platonism.[190] Sometimes the soul is one of the lesser powers who has fallen into sense and matter; elsewhere the mortal clay is quickened by the inspiration of the breath of God. He seeks to combine Greek and Jewish thought, and the result is not always consistent. His background is that of the Hellenistic Age, and he uses the allegorical method to find hellenistic ideas in the sacred writings of his people.

Hellenistic popular philosophy sought release from the cares of this life by a reduction of interests.[191] The less a man had, the less he had to lose, the less he felt the pain of such loss. This ascetic strain appears in all schools of thought, but its chief exponents were the Stoics. The sole good is the good life, the life in accordance with nature; all else is secondary. The truly wise man is free from passions,[192] simple in his needs, aiming at morality;[193] though the world fall in ruins about him, he holds to that one purpose.[194] The mysteries offered freedom from fate and the prospect of future bliss by a union with the god, an apotheosis;[195] mystic secrets were imparted, sometimes by a redeemer from on high who would lead the soul to its true home.[196] Judaism proclaimed salvation through membership of the chosen race, using the Exodus as a type of the hellenistic journey of the soul.[197] Philo has something of all these, but the pagan elements have been fused together. The earlier Stoics looked for a cosmic cataclysm when the soul would be absorbed again into the divine fire; their successors admitted an ever-increasing possibility of survival, first for the great, then for all.[198] Their philosophy was popular because it met the desire of men for assurance about the future and could be combined with the religion of the mysteries; the Epicureans[199] bluntly denied survival, but their system did not appeal to men who cherished some hope of a future life.

The Jewish emphasis on the law harmonized with the Stoic insistence on morality, and so we find in Philo a view that man can ascend to God, by breaking from the bondage of passion and purifying himself in readiness to meet with God, who requires a pure soul as His dwelling.[200] But elsewhere he lapses into pessimism in an assertion of man's inability to free himself.[201] God plants and promotes virtue in him, and perfection is attained through surrender to Him. Man yearns to return to his rightful abode;[202] entangled in sense, he must struggle up to the vision of God, but it is God who sets him free.[203] The vision is possible on earth, in this life, when the truly wise and virtuous man is carried off in a prophetic rapture.[204] Death to such a man is but the separation of the soul from the body, the escape from the prison.[205]

For the mysteries, as interpreted by hellenistic philosophy, salvation was largely an escape from fate, from the power of the stars, effected by an almost magical process through initiation.[206] There is nowhere the same ethical emphasis as in Judaism, although ascetic tendencies are evident in all cults.[207] There are similarities between the mysteries and Judaism, due partly to Jewish use of mystery terminology, partly to the influence on both of their environment and of current ideas.[208] Some features again are natural developments such as may be found in any religion. Little or nothing can be adduced to prove that Judaism was influenced by or borrowed from the mysteries in any degree. It was modified, admittedly, because it was a living religion and reacted to its environment, but the modification was due rather to philosophy, and in particular to Stoicism. Philo and others used Greek terms and Greek ideas in presenting their faith to the world, but it was and remained Judaism. Throughout the history of the Diaspora the Jews accommodated their faith to current local views by emphasizing the similarities and neglecting the differences; some alien elements were assimilated, but they were transformed for the service of Judaism. This is what we find in Alexandria and in Philo; he is a Jew, fascinated by Greek culture, but still a Jew; he seeks to combine the two systems of thought that were dear to him, as men will, yet the fact remains true that his chief delight was in the faith of his fathers.[209]

Philo's disappearance from Judaism and his failure to exercise any appreciable influence upon rabbinic thought[210] may be attributed partly to reaction against his accommodating spirit, under the stress of the political and other troubles which the Jews of later days had to endure; partly to the use which was made of his works by the Christian Fathers;[211] and partly to the fact that the conditions for which he wrote no longer existed for Judaism. The interest of the Christian Fathers secured the preservation of his works, while his predecessors and contemporaries for the most part found at best a partial sanctuary in the pages of Eusebius. Within a century of his interview with Caligula, the Jews rose twice in revolt[212] and were ruthlessly suppressed; the Gentile inhabitants of Alexandria and similar cities doubtless took advantage of the unrest to put down their Jewish neighbours. Proselytism was forbidden by imperial edict,[213] and Judaism vanished from the ranks of the religions competing for supremacy. In Palestine, always less open to Greek influences, the Rabbis developed their faith along different lines, although some features show traces of the influence of the Diaspora.[214] Hellenistic Judaism was no longer active as in the centuries from Alexander to the Flavians, yet it left its mark upon the history of religion.

The traditions of Alexandria were continued by the Christian catechetical school, under men like Clement and Origen.[215] St. Paul used the methods and ideas of hellenistic Judaism in presenting the Gospel to a wider world, as also did other New Testament writers, notably the authors of Hebrews and of the Fourth Gospel. Some Jews and most proselytes became Christians;[216] they brought with them the type of speculation with which they had been familiar, and which later came to flower in Gnosticism. Others turned directly to sects of a Gnostic type outside the Church, or dabbled in magic.[217] The rest followed the Rabbis; the synagogue and its organization, despite oppression and persecution, united the Jews in every land. The proselytizing fervour of hellenistic Judaism was gone, and with it the propaganda it had inspired. Judaism developed into its Rabbinic form, and hellenistic Judaism was either absorbed in this or swallowed up by Christianity and the Gnostic sects. Jewish elements remain in magic and to some extent in astrology, elements assimilated long before, but the real heir of the Diaspora is the Church.

NOTES TO CHAPTER II

[1] Swete 5ff., Schürer 2. 2. 226ff.

[2] Philo, *In Flacc.* 55. On the question of Jewish citizenship in Alexandria cf. Wolfson *Philo* 2. 398ff., and references there. See also the Introduction to Box's edition of *In Flaccum* (London 1939) on the Jewish question, and on the events leading up to the outbreak of A.D. 38 in Alexandria; also Bell *Jews and Christians in Egypt* (London 1924), and *Cults and Creeds in Egypt* (Liverpool 1953).

[3] Cf. Schürer 2. 2. 275ff. and note 183; Oesterley and Robinson 2. 402ff. See also Philo *in Flacc.* and *Leg. ad Caium.*

[4] It has been suggested that Christianity entered Egypt in a heretical form. See Bauer *Rechtgläubigkeit u. Ketzerei im ältesten Christentum* (Tübingen 1934), 49ff., with Turner's criticisms, *The Pattern of Christian Truth* (London 1954), 39ff., especially 46ff.

[5] See Bowra, *Ancient Greek Literature* 217ff., Wendland *HRK* 21ff.

[6] *CAH* 7. 251ff., *Cambridge Companion to Greek Studies* 121ff., 744ff., Wendland *HRK* 55ff.

[7] Swete 9ff.; cf. Angus 158ff., Schürer 2. 3. 160. Philo's version seems to represent a tradition independent of Aristeas (Swete 12).

[8] Wendland *HRK* 192; cf. Sukenik 1. Deissmann (*Bible Studies* 222) refers to a synagogue inscription from Lower Egypt, belonging probably to the third century B.C.

[9] Supra p. 2f. See Causse 17ff., 77ff.

[10] *L'Egypte des Astrologues* 134: on devra constater que les premiers astrologues ne contiennent presque aucune trace d'une influence juive quelconque, alors que dans les papyrus magiques elles abondent. C'est un nouvel indice que les plus anciens traités grecs de divination sidérale n'ont point été composés à Alexandrie, où une action du judaisme eût été inévitable.

[11] See Knox *PCG* x; *Pharisaism and Hellenism* 72. Cf. Schürer 2. 3. 367.

[12] Sat. 14. 96.

[13] According to Clearchus (ap. Joseph. *c. Apion.* 1. 22), Aristotle spoke of a Jew who was Ἑλληνικὸς οὐ τῇ διαλέκτῳ μόνον, ἀλλὰ καὶ τῇ ψυχῇ (Reinach *Textes* 12). The extent of the danger may be gathered from the case of Philo's own nephew, Tiberius Alexander (see above, p. 19 note 26), who made a career for himself in the service of Rome. This would entail at least a considerable laxity, if not complete apostasy. Cf. Knox *Pharisaism and Hellenism* 72. Siegfried (in Kautzsch *Apoc. and Pseud.* 1. 478) thinks Soph. Sol. directed against influential Jews of this type.

[14] Dodd *BG* 3, quoting *Corp. Herm.* V. 10, *Asclep.* 20. Further references in Geffcken *Apologeten* 38, on Aristides i. 5. But Wolfson (*Philo* 2. 113ff.) claims that 'the conception of the ineffability or unnamability of God' is not found in Greek philosophy before Philo. See however Goodenough in *JBL* 67 (1948) 96f.

[15] Exod. 3. 14 (Dodd *BG* 4); cf. also Jer. 1. 6, 14. 13, 39 (32). 17. For Philo's use of ὁ ὤν, and also of τὸ ὄν, see Leisegang's index, 226f.

[16] Dodd *BG* 4–7, Wendland *HRK* 105. Cf. Plut. *de Is. et Osir.* ad init., where we find οἱ θεοί of the Greek pantheon, ὁ θεός and τὸ θεῖον of 'God' in a more abstract and impersonal sense. Nock (*Conversion* 222) remarks that δαίμων, θεός, θεοί, τὸ θεῖον 'are constantly used in Homer to denote the incalculable non-human element in phenomena.' His main point here is the development of the theory of *daimones*, but his argument is important as illustrating Greek views and ideas about deity.

[17] This seems the reason for the fact noted by Moore (1. 357), that Philo's work exercised no discoverable influence on Jewish thought. Such successors as he had were probably absorbed by Christianity and the Gnostic sects; the same may be true of the Essenes and the Therapeutae, although Schoeps (*Urgemeinde* etc.) would find the descendants of the Essenes in the Ebionites.

[18] For the clash of cultures see Dix *Jew and Greek* (Westminster 1953).

[19] Cf. Schürer 2. 3. 375, quoting Zeller. Thus Drummond (*Philo Judaeus* 1. 214) describes the philosophy of *Soph. Sol.* as 'an eclectic attempt to reconcile the dogma of a transcendent God with the pantheistic conception of His immanence in nature and in man.' Cf. ibid. 224, and 2. 107ff. See also the section on the Theology of Wisdom in Charles *Apoc. and Pseud.* 1. 527ff. Wolfson, however, declares that Philo had no reason to look for intermediaries (1. 282ff.).

[20] See *BG* part I.

[21] ibid. 11ff. See above, p. 13.

[22] e.g. *Soph. Sol.* 5. 15, 6. 3. Cf. Philo *LA* 3. 82 etc.

[23] Dodd *BG* 16ff.

[24] ibid. 17. For κύριος see ibid. 9–11. The absolute use has no parallel in Greek prior to LXX. For a later example see Plut. *de Is. et Osir.* 352A, 353B.

[25] Cf. Tarn 183. Valerius Maximus (1. 3. 3) may have made the same mistake (see above, p. 12).

[26] Dodd, loc. cit. Cf. Justin *c. Tryph.* 85. 1, on which see Cullmann, *Earliest Christian Confessions* (London 1949) 24, 61.

[27] See above, p. 9f. On the 'powers,' see Knox *PCG* 50ff., Dodd *BG* 17–19, 109–11.

[28] Dodd *BG* 18.

[29] ibid. 19. Cf. Cumont *L'Egypte des Astrologues* 27f. According to Moulton and Geden (*Concordance* 749), this word appears nine times in Revelation, once elsewhere in the NT, and is not found in classical Greek writers. Cf. also Schürer *SAB* 1897, 205.

[30] See Knox *PCG* 51; supra p. 10.

[31] Dodd *BG* 20ff.; cf. Knox *PCG* 52, Swete 327. On the Memra, see Moore 1. 417ff., who claims that it is in no sense an intermediary corresponding to the Philonic Logos, but simply provides a reverent periphrasis for 'God.' In Philo the Logos is no mere circumlocution, but has other functions besides. Cf. Knox *PCG* 82 note 3. Knox *HE* 43 suggests that the Memra may have at one time played a much greater part in Jewish speculation than appears from our extant evidence, in which it may have been suppressed through reaction against Christianity. Contrast Wolfson *Philo* 1. 282ff.

[32] Dodd *BG* 21ff.

[33] 2. 3. 157ff.

[34] ibid.

[35] Bréhier p. I. A general Bibliography of Philo by H. L. Goodhart and E. R. Goodenough will be found in Goodenough *The Politics of Philo Judaeus* (New Haven 1938).

[36] Windisch *Die Frömmigkeit Philos* 3f. For Philo's sources, see Windisch 86ff.

[37] op. cit. p. II. Cf. Kennedy *PCR* 8ff., Bousset *Schulbetrieb* ad. init.

[38] Cf. Wisdom in *Soph. Sol.* and the Logos in Philo; also Aristobulus' use of the allegorical method; and compare Philo's interpretation of the Sabbath rest (*LA* i. 5ff., *de Cher.* 87ff.) with that of Aristobulus (ap. Eus. *PE* 13. 12). See also *Recueil Cerfaux* 1. 65ff. Knox says Philo is not a philosopher but a compiler, and suggests that he has incorporated 'a whole body of traditional teaching of the schools and synagogues of Alexandria' (*Pharisaism and Hellenism* 62; cf. ibid. 69). Bréhier remarks that the Logos doctrine is introduced generally as well known, and hence is not Philo's own (op. cit. 86). Wolfson (*Philo* 1. 98ff.) takes a much more favourable

view of Philo; he is 'a philosopher in the grand manner, not a mere dabbler in philosophy' (114), and his teachings became 'the most dominant influence in European philosophy for well-nigh seventeen centuries' (115). But cf. Goodenough's criticisms, *JBL* 67 (1948) 87ff.

[39] Cf. Bousset *Schulbetrieb*, e.g. 43: Auch da, wo er direkt umfangreiches profanes Gut hellenischer Philosophie überliefert, sehen wir fast überall, dass zwischen ihm und seiner griechischen Autoritäten das Medium älterer Quellen jüdischer Uberlieferung steht. The conclusions to which Bousset comes are summarized ibid. 152ff. See further Knox *HE* 47ff.

[40] Note Philo's references to other philosophers, and his condemnation of those who spiritualize the law at the expense of literal observance (*Mig. Ab.* 89–90). See Bréhier 35ff., Wolfson *Philo* 1. 115ff., for full discussion of the allegorical method. Wolfson (1. 55ff.) sees three tendencies in Alexandrian Judaism, a traditional, an allegorical, and an extreme allegorical. See also his *Philosophy of the Church Fathers*, vol. 1.

[41] See Kennedy *PCR* passim, Windisch 104ff. Windisch (113ff.) stresses the links between the Philonic and Johannine literature, calling John 'the Philo of the New Testament.' In this, however, he seems to go too far. See further Kennedy *PCR* 47–50, 176f., Knox *HE* 42ff., and more recently Dodd *The Interpretation of the Fourth Gospel* (Cambridge 1953) 54ff.; also *Exp. Times* lxv. 47ff. The evidence of the Dead Sea Scrolls seems to make Philonic influence on the Fourth Gospel still less probable (above, p. 5) although Philo's writings remain of value for the understanding of the Gospel.

[42] In the following pages Philo's work is examined mainly from the point of view of his place in the chain linking Greek and Jewish speculation with Christian and Gnostic thought. For other aspects see Kennedy *PCR* and Bréhier.

[43] Cf. Knox *PCG* 56ff. for the danger of apostasy to the cult of Isis, and for Jewish counter-propaganda.

[44] Cf. Wolfson *Philo* 1. 78ff.

[45] Quoted in the Loeb Philo, vol. 1, p. 184 note b.

[46] ibid. Cf. Murray *Stoic, Christian and Humanist* 23ff., and especially 26: 'Classical philosophy (with some exceptions) represents the view of society and of duty which is natural to men of position, with a sense of responsibility. Christianity, and the various passionate religions which competed with it in the great industrial towns, represented the aspirations of the poor and outcast.' Cf. 1 Cor. 1. 18ff., Origen *c. Cels.* 3. 50.

[47] On the development of Greek religion, see Wendland *HRK* 96ff., and for $\tau\acute{\upsilon}\chi\eta$ etc. ibid. 104ff. See also Bevan in *The Hellenistic Age* 79ff., and cf. Cumont *Rel. Or.* 24ff.

[48] Tennyson, *Lucretius.* Cf. Lucretius v. 82, 145ff.

[49] On $\alpha\mathring{\upsilon}\tau\acute{\alpha}\rho\kappa\epsilon\iota\alpha$ as the aim of the Greek philosophical schools see Bevan loc. cit.

[50] *Od.* III. 3.

[51] See Knox *PCG* 62ff., *Phar. and Hellen.* 63ff., and references above, p. 28 note 148. For the Stoic theology, see Wendland *HRK* 110ff.

[52] Cf. Leisegang's index, 499ff., and especially section IV, p. 502; cf. also *de Fug.* 94ff.

[53] Cf. John 1, Col. 1. 15ff., *Const. Ap.* 7. 33ff., 8. 12, etc. See Sanders, *The Fourth Gospel in the Early Church.* The obvious reference is to the Fourth Gospel, but Sanders shows that the earliest writers make little use of it, even in discussing the Logos. This type of thought must therefore have been more widespread in Christian circles than we tend to think, and was not entirely due to the influence of the Fourth Gospel. See further Knox *HE* 43ff. and notes.

[54] See Windisch, *Die Frömmigkeit Philos.*

[55] Cumont *Rel. Or.* 39 etc., Kennedy *PMR.*

[56] Cf. Nock *Conversion* 164ff.

[57] See Burnet, *Early Greek Philosophy* (London 1920) 40ff. (Thales), 72ff. (Anaximenes); cf. 50ff. (Anaximander).

[58] ibid. 330ff. (Leucippus and Democritus). For Greek philosophy in relation to Philo see Drummond, vol. 1.

[59] *Timaeus* 28B.

[60] ibid. 38Dff., 40E. To be strictly accurate, the Olympians are the descendants of Ge and Ouranos. In 41A the θεοί include the deities of popular belief and the heavenly bodies.

[61] See Drummond 1. 102ff.

[62] Knox *PCG* 65.

[63] ibid. 66.

[64] ibid. Cf. *Pharisaism and Hellenism* 65.

[65] ibid. 56ff. For Egyptian influence on Jewish Wisdom-literature see Peet *The Literatures of Egypt, Palestine, and Mesopotamia* (Schweich Lectures 1929), 99ff. See also Causse 110ff.

[66] Prov. 8. 1–31, Ecclus. 24. See Knox loc. cit. and *JTS* 38. 230ff. Ringgren (*Word and Wisdom*, Lund 1947, 143ff.) criticizes Knox, but thinks it probable that Sirach meant the glorification of Wisdom in chap. 24 as a counterblast to the aretalogy of Isis. Cf. also Davies *PRJ* 163ff.

[67] Cf. *Soph. Sol.* 9. 4, 9 and contrast 7. 12, 22, 8. 1, 5, 6, 9. 1.

[68] Knox *PCG* 66ff.

[69] Cf. Hecataeus ap. Reinach *Textes* 16, and Reinach's note; Bidez-Cumont *Les Mages Hellénisés* 1. 66 and note, 241; Knox *PCG* 44, 67, quoting *Placita* 1. 7. 33 for νοῦς ἐν αἰθερι as God. Cf. also Windisch 20, Philo *Mig. Ab.* 181. Philo is not always consistent.

[70] Sat. 6. 545, 14. 97. For Caelus, see Cumont *Astrology*, index s.v., and references in *PW* 9. 446. 31f. Cf. Origen *c. Cels.* 6. 19.

[71] See, however, Drummond 2. 195ff. for the Logos as a second God in Philo. For Christianity, cf. Hatch 265ff.

[72] Knox *PCG* 68.

[73] ibid. See also Schubert in *TLZ* 1953, 495f., although his attempt to

E

show that in part of the Dead Sea Manual of Discipline we have the earliest Gnostic document extant ignores certain vital distinctions. On Aristobulus see Schürer 2. 3. 237ff., *PW* 2. 918ff., Drummond 1. 242ff. Wendland, however, seems to date him in the Christian era (*HRK* 204). Eusebius (*PE* 7. 13) introduces him to support a statement of Philo on the Logos, and later (8. 9) identifies him with the Aristobulus of 2 Macc. 1. 10, who was tutor to Ptolemy Philometor. Cf. Gifford's edition of Euseb. *PE*, vol. iv, 238, 270f., 290, 444f. Knox says 'it is unlikely that he is later than . . . the Wisdom of Solomon' (*PCG* 69). The earlier dating seems more probable. The discussion in Schürer *GJV* 4. 3. 512ff. is fuller, and examines some more recent theories.

[74] Euseb. *PE* 13. 12 and (abbreviated) 7. 14. The work of Aristobulus was known also to Clement of Alexandria and to Origen (Schürer loc. cit.).

[75] For the Hermetic view, see Dodd *BG* index s.v. φῶς.

[76] Cf. Gifford on Euseb. *PE*, vol. iv, 447f., for Clement's use of this passage.

[77] Cf. Prov. 8. 22, 27.

[78] Knox (loc. cit.) remarks 'it is clear that we have here a Jewish writer, not a Christian, since the sabbath has to play the part both of the first day on which light was created and also of the seventh.' Clement reconstructs the passage into a Christian ogdoad.

[79] e.g. *Op. M.* 89ff. (hebdomad), *LA* i. 5ff. (sabbath rest, followed 8ff. by hebdomad), *de Cher.* 87ff.

[80] Knox *PCG* 69 (cf. ibid. 45).

[81] ibid. 59ff. Cf. Davies *PRJ* 168ff.

[82] ibid. 69. 'He, like the rest of them, fails to notice the one passage in that philosophy in which a cosmic figure of Wisdom really appears,' viz. Plato *Philebus* 30C.

[83] See Knox loc. cit.; Charles *Apoc. and Pseud.* 1. 521ff., Kautzsch *Apoc. and Pseud.* 1. 476ff.

[84] 1. 4, 6. For the latter cf. 7. 23, 12. 19. It simply means (as 12. 19 suggests) that the wise (or righteous) man should be φιλάνθρωπος. Causse 129 calls φιλανθρωπία 'the characteristic virtue of cosmopolitan Hellenism.'

[85] 10–end. This division rests purely on subject-matter, and does not pretend to any critical authority. It may be that 11. 4ff. has been substituted for an original conclusion continuing the theme of Wisdom. Cf. Knox *PCG* 81.

[86] σοφία occurs once after chapter 10 (14. 2, cf. 7. 22). Much of this section is devoted to attacks on idolatry (cf. Isaiah), animal worship, and human sacrifice, as practised by the heathen, and to comparison of them with Israel, all set in a frame of the deliverance from Egypt.

[87] 1 Kings 3. 9. On the concept of Wisdom generally see Drummond 1. 214ff., and on Wisdom and Logos in Apocalyptic Dix in *JTS* xxvi (1925) 1ff.

[88] In other words Wisdom is a divine 'substance' in which individual wise men participate. Cf. Drummond 1. 214. The whole theory is based on the hypostatization and personification of the wisdom of God; hence the oscillation between abstract principle and particular manifestation. Cf. also Prov. 3. 13ff. The whole subject has been studied in detail by Ringgren (*Word and Wisdom*).

[89] 7. 7, 9. 6.

[90] 7. 22. Cf. Knox *PCG* 71ff.

[91] 7. 25.

[92] ibid. Cf. p. 33 above.

[93] 7. 26. Cf. Heb. 1. 3 and Philo.

[94] ibid.

[95] ibid. Cf. Philo (see Leisegang's index s.v. Λόγος); Col. 1. 15.

[96] 7. 27.

[97] 7. 29.

[98] ibid. Literally 'prior,' but it might be either in quality or in time.

[99] 7. 12 γένετιν A, γένεσιν al.

[100] 8. 4, 9. 9.

[101] 7. 22, 9. 1, 9.

[102] 9. 4.

[103] 9. 1. Cf. 7. 22, 14. 2.

[104] See Knox loc. cit. for the Greek elements, and for the development of the concept in its Greek and Jewish features. Causse 154 thinks Greek influence unnecessary, pointing to oriental parallels. The whole point is that the Jewish-oriental scheme, independently developed, could be harmonized with that of Greek philosophy. Cf. Knox *Pharisaism and Hellenism* 66ff.

[105] The germ of the Philonic Logos concept may be present in 16. 12, but it is here not a technical term, as v. 26 shows. Cf. also 18. 15.

[106] A detailed study of *Soph. Sol.* in the light of Cumont's *After-life in Roman Paganism* might prove profitable. For the author's acquaintance with Greek philosophy see Charles op. cit. 531ff.

[107] Knox *PCG* 70, 81. On the Logos see Bréhier 83ff., Drummond 2. 156ff.

[108] ibid. 85. Cf. *LA* i. 43, *QDPI* 114ff., *LA* i. 86, de Fug. 137, 166. On the relation of Logos and Wisdom, see Drummond 2. 201ff., Ringgren op. cit., Wolfson *Philo* 1. 253ff. Wolfson (loc. cit.) thinks the use of the term logos by the Stoics has been too much exaggerated.

[109] *PCG* x.

[110] Graetz 2. 186. Plutarch made a similar attempt for the cult of Isis in his *de Iside et Osiride* (cf. Knox *PCG* 86).

[111] Knox *PCG* x; cf. ibid. 82.

[112] Cf. Oesterley *Jews and Judaism* 266ff., Causse 141ff.

[113] Cf. above, p. 9f. The Jews also depreciated the gods of the Gentiles

into angels or similar subordinate powers. The two modes of thought intertwine here.

[114] For mediation in Philo and in contemporary thought cf. Kennedy *PCR* 157ff., Hatch 245ff. Contrast Wolfson *Philo* 1. 282ff. ('The Fiction of Intermediaries').

[115] Knox *PCG* 82: 'He has followed Posidonius in equating the Stoic reason with the divine pattern and the Platonic idea, adding the image of God from Hebrew cosmogony.'

[116] *Op. M.* 2.

[117] ibid. 8ff. Cf. *Timaeus* 28C.

[118] ibid. The Platonic Demiurge likewise is similar to the Anaxagorean νοῦς (cf. Bury in *Timaeus*, Loeb edition, p. 7).

[119] Cf. *Mig. Ab.* 6. This ὄργανον is also the παράδειγμα (*LA* iii. 96).

[120] *De Cher.* 127.

[121] Cf. *Timaeus* 30A, 31Cff., and Bury loc. cit.: 'The Demiurge is not a Creator *ex nihilo*, but imposes order on pre-existing chaos.' Kennedy, however, claims that the pre-existence of matter is not distinctly presupposed (*PCR* 67ff.). It might be argued from *de Cher.* 127 and *de Som.* i. 76 that matter was first created, and then shaped from its formless state into the cosmos. See also Drummond 1. 299ff., Bréhier 80ff., Moore *Judaism* 3. 119f., note 120, Wolfson 1. 300ff.

[122] *Op. M.* 10.

[123] ibid. 7ff. On the view that the κόσμος is ἀγένητον καὶ ἀίδιον cf. *Timaeus* 37D.

[124] *Op. M.* 12; cf. *Timaeus* 28B.

[125] ibid. 15ff.; cf. *Timaeus* 29A. On the divine pattern in Rabbinic and other Jewish literature, see Knox *Pharisaism and Hellenism* 75f., and for Babylonian religion Burrows in Hooke *The Labyrinth* 59ff.

[126] ibid. 20.

[127] ibid. 24.

[128] ibid. 25. Cf. *LA* iii. 96, *de Som.* ii. 45, *de Plant.* 20.

[129] ibid. 69. But contrast ibid. 134, *LA* i. 31. It is as if Philo gave the obvious Platonic interpretation for the first account in Genesis, and then produced the other version when he came to the second account, referring back in *Op. M.* 134 etc. to his earlier version. The ideal man has no part in corruption (*LA* i. 31). From *Op. M.* 72ff. Drummond argues that the man in question is the ideal man (2. 139ff.), while he infers that the powers who co-operate in the creation of man are not the divine powers but a lesser class such as the angels (ibid. 141ff., especially 144ff.). But in *Op. M.* 62ff. the animals are most naturally the actual beasts of this world, while in *LA* ii. 11ff. they are the ideas of the passions, the genera of which the species are now created. It seems therefore that the man of *Op. M.* 69ff. is the natural man and not the ideal. The key may perhaps be found in *de Fug.* 68ff., where Philo distinguishes the ideal from the natural man, the former being mentioned with the article, the latter without. In this case he takes

Gen. 1. 26 as marking the proposal, Gen. 1. 27 as the creation of the ideal man, and Gen. 2. 7 as the creation of natural man. He then interprets Gen. 1. 26 in Platonic terms as indicating that other beings shared in the creation of man (so also *de Conf. Ling.* 169ff.). The only exception seems to be *de Plant.* 19ff., where the men of Gen. 1. 27 and 2. 7 are identified, but the distinction appears again ibid. 44. Philo has not fully harmonized his sources here.

See further Drummond loc. cit., Kennedy *PCR* 76–7, Bréhier 121ff., Knox *PCG* 82f., Bousset *Schulbetrieb* 152 note 2, *Hauptprobleme* 194f. The suggestion made above has also been advanced by Dodd (*BG* 155). For Adam as an androgynous being in Jewish thought see Moore 1. 452f.— 'Probably a bit of foreign lore adapted to the first pair in Genesis.'

[130] ibid. 72ff.; cf. *Timaeus* 41Cff. On the early patristic exegesis of Gen. 1. 26 cf. *Studia Patristica* 1. 420ff.

[131] i. 31; cf. *Op. M.* 134.

[132] ibid. 32. Cf. the view of Saturninus, infra p. 103.

[133] ibid. The distinction, once made, is carried on into the account of Eden (*LA* i. 53, 88).

[134] Cf. *de Conf. Ling.* 146.

[135] *Timaeus* 92C. See Dodd *BG* 5ff. for the meaning of θεός. Cf. Reitzenstein *Poim.* 25 note 1, quoting *Corp. Herm.* xii (xiii): ὁ δὲ σύμπας κόσμος οὗτος, ὁ μέγας θεὸς καὶ τοῦ μείζονος εἰκὼν κτλ.

[136] ibid. 30B.

[137] ibid. 34B. Cf. *de Plant.* 8–9 and the Stoic theory.

[138] See Bréhier 84, quoting Plut. *de Stoic. repug.* xxxiv (v. Arnim *SVF* 2. 269). Cf. Knox *Pharisaism and Hellenism* 64. For the Logos as the bond of all things, see *de Cher.* 27, *de Plant.* 8–9, *de Fug.* 112.

[139] ibid. They called it common nature, destiny, providence, Zeus.

[140] e.g. *de Plant.* 8 (immanent reason); *de Ebr.* 30 (cosmos as son of God). For the former Knox refers to *Soph. Sol.* 8. 1 (*PCG* 81 note 9). Cf. also *LA* i. 91 (God as soul of the universe—see Colson's note ad loc.).

[141] See Bréhier 98ff.

[142] *De Spec. Leg.* i. 329. But cf. Leisegang's index p. 365, section 2b: ubique est praesens (of God). See also Drummond 2. 105ff., and generally in this volume, for other views.

[143] *De Ebr.* 30. Cf. Leisegang's index s.vv. υἱός, κόσμος, μονογενής.

[144] *QDSI* 31.

[145] *QDSI* 138; cf. *Soph. Sol.* 7. 27 etc.

[146] *Mig. Ab.* 6.

[147] *De Conf. Ling.* 146.

[148] *De Sac. Abel.* 65.

[149] *QRDH* 206. Cf. Drummond 2. 192.

[150] *De Post. Caini* 69.

[151] *De Agric.* 51.

[152] *De Som.* 1. 215.

[153] *De Fug.* 97; *QRDH* 191. But cf. *de Som.* ii. 242: κάτεισι δὲ ὥσπερ ἀπὸ πηγῆς τῆς σοφίας ... ὁ λόγος, and see Knox *PCG* 86ff., Drummond 2. 201ff., especially 211, Wolfson *Philo* 1. 253ff., especially 258-9, Dix in *JTS* xxvi (1925).

[154] See Bréhier 90.

[155] ibid. 84ff. (Logos as Stoic ἕξις).

[156] ibid. 93.

[157] *QDSI* 138. See Bréhier 98ff.

[158] Cf. *de Spec. Leg.* iv. 14, *Op. M.* 146, *de Post. Caini* 122, *QDSI* 138, *QDPI* 146, *Mig. Ab.* 174. See Kennedy *PCR* 165ff.

[159] Knox *Pharisaism and Hellenism* 68; Schürer 2. 3. 374f., Kennedy *PCR* 168ff., Drummond 2. 222ff.

[160] Knox *PCG* 82; cf. Bréhier 107ff.

[161] Cf. Knox *Pharisaism and Hellenism* 65. On the Logos generally, see Bréhier 83ff., Drummond 2. 156ff.

[162] In *QDSI* 173ff. Philo introduces the Logos as a rational principle directing the fate of nations, thus setting aside the current belief in Chance (Τύχη).

[163] Knox op. cit. 68.

[164] *Op. M.* 8. On Philo's conception of God see Bréhier 69ff.

[165] Schürer 2. 3. 376.

[166] But the world, modelled on the truly good, must itself be good. Philo does not follow the Platonic view to the full except in his anthropology. The need for intermediaries implies that the world is evil, yet it was created by God after the best pattern. Philo is simply not consistent.

[167] See references in Schürer loc. cit.

[168] ibid. 377. Cf. Windisch 4ff.

[169] *Op. M.* 134ff. Cf. Plato's version in *Timaeus* 41Eff., 44B, 86E, and see Kennedy *PCR* 75ff.

[170] *De Gig.* 6ff. This is Gen. 6. 2 interpreted in Hellenistic terms. Cf. Kennedy *PCR* 80.

[171] 1. 310ff. See also Kennedy *PCR* 71ff. 'We find no perfectly clear conception of Matter in Philo. . . . But there is nothing to show that Philo regarded Matter per se as evil' (ibid. 74). Contrast Bigg *Christian Platonists* 11. Similarly, in *LA* iii. 67, we find: ἡ αἴσθησις οὔτε τῶν φαύλων οὔτε τῶν σπουδαίων ἐστίν, ἀλλὰ μέσον τι αὕτη καὶ κοινὸν σοφοῦ τε καὶ ἄφρονος ... οὐ καταδικάζεται πρὶν ὁμολογῆσαι, ὅτι ἠκολούθησε τῷ χείρονι. But ibid. 69 τὸ σῶμα is πονηρόν τε καὶ ἐπιβουλον τῆς ψυχῆς. On the question of the eternity and pre-existence of matter in Philo, see Kennedy 68ff.

[172] ibid. 311f. This is one point at which we are in danger of attributing to Philo views which he may not consciously have held, although they were current in his time and seem to us to be implied in his doctrine, or which are really the result of later speculation.

[173] Within the simple dualism of body and soul Philo sometimes dis-

tinguishes two aspects of the soul, a rational and an irrational, and it is not so much the body as the irrational part of the soul which is evil. This distinction goes back, through Posidonius, to Pythagoras (Rohde *Psyche* 400 note 55). Elsewhere we find the Platonic myth of the charioteer and horses (e.g. *LA* i. 70, where see Colson's note, Loeb ed., vol. i. 478)—a triple division (for Posidonius see Bevan, *Stoics and Sceptics* 101ff.). See generally Drummond 1. 314ff., and for Philo and Paul, Kennedy *PCR* 75ff.

[174] Cf. Knox *PCG* 83f. The inconsistency seems to go back to Plato, whom Philo follows. The Cosmos created by the supreme Being must be good; the bodies created by the lesser gods are mortal and imperfect. But for Plato evil comes from matter, which is not quite consistent with the view advanced in the *Timaeus*. The inconsistency may arise from a combination of the Orphic σῶμα-σῆμα concept with a philosophical theory of the origin of the world. So too Philo sometimes wavers between a world-denying (ascetic) and a world-affirming view (cf. for example Windisch 62ff.). See also Bréhier 121ff. A similar difficulty also confronted the Stoics (see Drummond 1. 116ff.).

[175] For the Orphic myth see Kennedy *PMR* 11ff., Rohde *Psyche* 340ff., James in Oesterley, *Judaism and Christianity* 1. 43ff., and for the Thracian cult of Dionysus in relation to Greek philosophy and religion Rohde op. cit., chap. VIII *et seq.* Orphism was, however, no longer a vital force in the period (Cumont-Bidez op. cit. 1. 97). Cf. also Kennedy *PMR* 137 note 1.

[176] For the Platonic doctrine see Rohde 463ff., and cf. generally Nygren, *Agape and Eros* 1. 120ff.

[177] For the Stoics, this dualistic doctrine should perhaps be confined to the later school, influenced by Posidonius, the earlier thinkers being more consistently monistic. See Drummond loc. cit. and 96ff. for their attempts to deal with the problem of evil. See also Knox *PCG* 73ff., Wendland *HRK* 135, for the Stoic view of the soul.

According to Rohde (403 note 75), the Stoics and Epicureans (e.g. Luc. 3. 978ff.) took up the idea advanced by Empedocles that this earth is the real Hades. In this 'the Orphic idea of the σῶμα-σῆμα was thoroughly and energetically carried out.' See also ibid. 497ff., and 518 note 60. The emphasis of Stoicism is rather upon ethics, conduct in this life, and not on an approach to the divine by ascetic effort or by initiation. The philosophy of Posidonius, however, culminates in mysticism (Wendland *HRK* 134).

[178] For Philo cf. Bousset *Schulbetrieb* 11ff., who notes that Philo repeatedly rejects the Stoic view of the soul as ἀπόσπασμα τοῦ αἰθέρος in favour of a purely spiritual conception. The variations in his manner of expression are explained thus: where as in Stoicism the αἰθήρ is material, Philo rejects the association of the soul with it; where he speaks of the soul as ἀπόσπασμα τοῦ αἰθέρος the αἰθήρ is a 'spiritual' element, a πέμπτη οὐσία. This last conception is according to Bousset 'spezifisch unstoisch.' The soul is, however, still a higher element imprisoned in a lower.

[179] *LA* i. 108, iii. 42; cf. *Spec. Leg.* iv. 188 (σῶμα-σῆμα explicitly), *Soph. Sol.* 9. 15. Cf. Kirk *The Vision of God* 41 note 4.

[180] There are several close parallels between Buddhist and Hellenistic doctrines. Thus, the gods and goddesses are the creations of man (cf. Xenophanes, Euhemerus). Man is doomed to a round of reincarnations until by self-sacrifice, meditation, and the subjugation of the passions he attains to perfect conduct. Then he reaches Nirvana, which is the absorption of the Ego into the divine source from which it came (cf. the fate of the souls in *Timaeus* 42B, and the myth of Er, *Rep.* 10, 614ff. Cf. also Origen *ap.* Hatch 235). The relative dates suggest Indian influence upon Western thought via Persia and Asia Minor, but an independent development of primitive Indo-Germanic ideas might also be possible, under similar conditions of environment, etc. [For suggestions of Indian influence on the NT, see Clemen *RGE*, who considers such influence doubtful except in a few cases (46ff.).] The Persian Empire may have linked India and Ionia, while Alexander reached the Indus, and a further link may have been provided by trade-routes. One of the Greek kingdoms in India was possibly the last Hellenistic kingdom to survive in independence (Tarn *The Greeks in Bactria and India* 351). See also Rohde *Psyche* 346f. and notes.

For the Orphic doctrine see Rohde 342ff. They had also a way of salvation through the Orphic mysteries, which involved first redemption by the god and then an ascetic life. For the Pythagoreans, see ibid. 374ff.

[181] See Rohde *Psyche*; Cumont *After-life*. Rohde (569 note 117) observes the influence of Greek ideas on Jewish thought in this connection. For Philo cf. Drummond 1. 335–9, 2. 322–4.

[182] For this influence see Cumont *Astrology*, especially Lectures IV, V, and VI.

[183] Knox *PCG* 224. See Burrows in Hooke *The Labyrinth* 66ff., Wendland *HRK* 170ff., and cf. *Timaeus* 41E, where each soul is assigned to one star. Nygren overlooks the Hellenistic descent of the soul in his discussion of Plotinus (op. cit. 154).

[184] Servius ad Virg. *Aen.* 6. 714 (ap. Reitzenstein *Poim.* 53). See also Cumont *After-life* 41. Cf. Hooke in Oesterley *Judaism and Christianity* 1. 226, Bevan *Hellenism and Christianity* 100ff., Bousset *Hauptprobleme* 361ff.

[185] Cf. Charles *Apoc. and Pseud.* 1. 533 (of *Soph. Sol.*): 'Most writers are children of their time, and their work cannot but show traces of the intellectual atmosphere which they breathed.'

[186] Cf. Schürer 2. 3. 367: 'Philo deduces formally from the Old Testament all those philosophical doctrines which he had in fact appropriated from the Greek philosophers.'

[187] Cf. *de Fug.* 94ff. and see Bréhier 112ff., 126ff., 136ff., and Kennedy *PCR* 157ff. Cf. also Col. 1. 16, 2. 10.

[188] See Schürer 2. 3. 372. He claims that 'Philo conceived of them both as independent hypostases and as immanent determinations of the Divine existence.' Cf. Kautzsch *Apoc. and Pseud.* 1. 477 of *Soph. Sol.*: 'Like Prov. 8.

22 he conceives of Wisdom as God immanent, as something belonging to the divine essence, but on the other hand again as something independent, existing beside God, for which reason he often personifies Wisdom.' On the whole question of the hypostatization of Wisdom see now Ringgren *Word and Wisdom.* On the powers, see also Drummond 2. 65ff., 217ff., who regards the logoi or powers as manifestations of God under one aspect or another, while the angels are minor and created powers. The former share in the creation of the intelligible cosmos, the latter in that of the visible world and of man. The angels are 'powers,' but the powers are not necessarily angels (ibid. 147).

189 Schürer 2. 3. 373.

190 Cf. Drummond 1. 336ff., and on the essence of the mind as non-material ibid. 325ff.

191 See Bevan in *The Hellenistic Age* 83ff., and for the use of this concept by Philo cf. Windisch 68.

192 Cf. *LA* ii. 99ff., and note especially 102 *ad fin.*: ἐὰν γὰρ ἀπάθεια κατάσχῃ τὴν ψυχήν, τελέως εὐδαιμονήσει.

193 Cf. Schürer 2. 3. 378. See also Kennedy *PCR*, index s.v. Stoics.

194 Cf. Horace *Od.* iii. 3.

195 Cf. Reitzenstein *HMR* 49, 257; Kennedy *PMR* 199ff., Hooke in Oesterley *Judaism and Christianity* 1. 222ff. See also Hort-Mayor *Clement of Alexandria: The Seventh Book of the Stromateis* (London 1902), 203ff.

196 Cf. Reitzenstein *HMR* 54ff., Knox *PCG* 220ff., Bevan *Hellenism and Christianity* 102ff.

197 For this heavenly journey in Jewish apocalyptic and elsewhere see Kirk *The Vision of God* 16 and references there (note 1).

198 See Knox *PCG* 73ff., Cumont *After-life* 110ff., *Astrology* 167ff. Orthodox Stoicism, however, offered really no more than a limited immortality, and some of the later Stoics still denied any possibility of survival. See Rohde *Psyche* 497ff.

199 Cf. Rohde 504ff.

200 Cf. Windisch 11ff., Wolfson *Philo* 1. 424ff., especially 432ff. (Free Will and the Choice of Good and Evil). See also on the whole subject Völker *Fortschritt und Vollendung bei Philo von Alexandrien* (*TU* 49. 1, Leipzig 1938).

201 ibid. 15ff., Schürer 2. 3. 379. Thus sometimes the Logos itself guides the soul, but elsewhere a distinction is made: the Logos is the transcendent goal of man's endeavour, and there is also an inferior logos or νοῦς, the Stoic moral faculty, in man himself. Here we have the series: God—Logos —man κατ᾽ εἰκόνα θεοῦ—man. The Logos can only enter the soul of man if νοῦς gives place (see Bréhier 92ff.). On the metaphor of the μέθη νηφάλιος in Philo, see Lewy *Sobria Ebrietas*.

202 Cf. Heb. 13. 14, Phil. 3. 20. See Kennedy *PCR* 96ff.

203 For God's approach to man in Philo, see Kennedy 142ff., and for the

vision of God ibid. 192ff. Cf. Reitzenstein *HMR* 73 for a similar view in the mystery cults.

[204] *QRDH* 69–70; Schürer 2. 3. 380. Cf. Windisch 60ff., Conybeare *Philo on the Contemplative Life* 200; also Cumont's account of astral mysticism, *Astrology*, Lecture V, and for similar ideas in Plato Rohde 470ff. and notes. Yet the vision is not certainly to be attained even by the pure in heart, at all events in this life (Kirk *The Vision of God* 43f.). See Kirk generally on the whole subject of the vision of God in Christian and earlier thought.

[205] For the rest, according to Schürer (ibid. note 185), there remains but transition to another body and further torment. Cf. *Timaeus* 42B. This, however, is simply an inference by Schürer, based upon the views expressed in similar systems, and is doubtful for Philo. See also Legge, *Fore-runners and Rivals* 1. 175 note 1. For this view in Posidonius see Bevan *Stoics and Sceptics* 109, Cumont *After-life* 27ff. According to Wolfson (*Philo* 1. 409), Philo says that 'awaiting those who live in the way of the impious will be eternal death.' Again (ibid. 412f.) he sometimes speaks of the true Hades as 'the life of the bad, a life of damnation and blood-guiltiness, the victim of every curse,' by which he means that the punishment of sin consists in the torture of a bad conscience in this world. In Wolfson's view, this does not mean to deny punishment after death, but is only supplementary to it.

[206] Cf. Kennedy *PMR* 183 on Paul's thought in comparison with the mystery-idea of transformation by the vision of God. On immortality in the mysteries cf. Kirk *The Vision of God* 30 note 1.

[207] The high ethical standards of Mithraism, perhaps inherited from Zoroastrianism and based on the dualism of Good and Evil, mark it off from other cults. See Hooke op. cit. 227 and cf. Kirk 29ff., Nock *Essays* 70ff.

[208] Hooke op. cit. 239 claims that 'the same ancient ritual pattern which was the source of the most important elements in the mystery cults had already given to Jewish Apocalyptic many of the same elements in another form.' See his essay in *The Labyrinth* 213ff.

[209] Cf. Schürer 2. 3. 363ff. Some cautions against deriving Philo's doctrines purely from Hellenism will be found in Kennedy *PCR* 218ff. (with special reference to his mysticism). See also Windisch 86ff., and his conclusions ibid. 95, Wendland *HRK* 204ff.

[210] Cf. Moore 1. 107ff., 357; Wendland *HRK* 208. But Goodenough has collected material which seems to show the persistence of a hellenized Judaism well into the Christian era. See his *Jewish Symbols in the Greco-Roman Period.*

[211] So the Christian use of LXX led to fresh Jewish translations of the OT such as that of Aquila.

[212] See Oesterley and Robinson 2. 440ff., 459ff. Note also the minor

revolt of 115 A.D. (ibid. 458) in which the Alexandrian Jews suffered great losses.

[213] Cary *History of Rome* 614; cf. Oesterley and Robinson 2. 454–5. According to *Beginnings* 5. 292, Claudius had prohibited proselytism while allowing the Jews themselves freedom of worship. Juster, however, claims (1. 254ff.) that proselytism was not forbidden as such until the time of the Christian emperors, although the proselyte was liable to a charge of atheism. The *Historia Augusta* (see Reinach *Textes* 346) says that Severus prohibited conversion to Judaism under severe penalties. Hadrian's prohibition of circumcision was one of the causes which led to the Bar-Cochba revolt. See also Moore 1. 348ff., who claims that despite attempts to prevent the spread of Judaism the Jews persisted in their missionary efforts.

[214] Cf. Knox *Pharisaism and Hellenism* 74ff., 104ff. See also Loewe in Oesterley *Judaism and Christianity* 1. 120ff.

[215] Conybeare (op. cit. 198) claims, for example, that the Jewish writers of Alexandria, and Philo in particular, served as models for the Christian apologists in their attacks on polytheism and idolatry. Cf. Wendland *HRK* 56, Hatch 69ff.

[216] So too, no doubt, the majority of the groups who observed a syncretistic Judeo-pagan worship, such as that of Sabazius or Hypsistos. Thus the name of Sabazius does not appear in fourth-century epigraphy (Cumont *CR Acad. Inscrr.* 1906, 79), although Hypsistarii are known then (Cumont *Hypsistos* 2f.).

[217] This is, of course, but a continuation of earlier tendencies. See Knox *PCG* 41ff., and note II (ibid. 208ff.). Gnosticism and magic are not always clearly distinct. Cf. also Dieterich *Abraxas* 2, and especially the material collected by Goodenough *Symbols* 2. 153ff.

CHAPTER III

GNOSTICISM AND CHRISTIANITY IN NEW TESTAMENT TIMES

SPIRITUAL unrest was general in the Hellenistic world, and in the world of the Roman Empire which forms the background to the New Testament.[1] The decline of the old Roman religion under the impact of philosophical criticism and its attempted restoration by Augustus have often been described; so also have the political unrest of the period, with its concomitant yearning for peace and security, and the rise of the mysteries, with the syncretism characteristic of the time.[2] The Pax Augusta seemed the dawn of a new age, and was hailed as such by the poets.[3] Augustus was greeted as σωτήρ,[4] in his case no empty honour as it so often became,[5] but an expression of relief and of hope in a Golden Age that was now about to begin after the years of strife. Various factors led to the growth of a cult of the emperor,[6] but this tended to be a matter of court ceremonial, of rites which it was customary to perform on certain occasions, a test of loyalty rather than a faith. Moreover, there was among the people a consciousness of the limitations of the deified ruler. 'Caesar can give peace from war,' said Epictetus in effect,[7] 'but he cannot give peace from sorrow.' The need was felt for a deeper, more individual and personal religion, and this need philosophy and the mystery religions attempted to meet.[8] ὁ δὲ λόγος ὁ τῶν φιλοσόφων ὑπισχνεῖται καὶ ἀπὸ τούτων εἰρήνην παρέχειν.[9]

The early Christian Church adopted contemporary methods and ideas to present its own message; the itinerant philosopher was to some extent a model for the Christian preacher,[10] the allegorist for the Christian exegete,[11] but the Church had its own contribution to make. The real trouble was not external stress, but inward, and consisted in sin. The Golden Age was thought to have dawned with Augustus, but human sin remained. All have sinned, all come short of the glory of God; the wrath of God is revealed from

64

heaven against all ungodliness and unrighteousness of men.[12] The
bright hopes of Augustus' reign perished in misrule and decadence
under later emperors.

Undoubtedly the picture of contemporary life presented by
satirists and philosophers, by reformers and by Christian advocates,
is exaggerated in its gloom,[13] but Christianity could point to the
obvious fact that all was not well with the world, and it offered
new hope and new life in Jesus Christ.[14] Philosophy and the
mysteries made their own claims, and in some points they resembled
or even anticipated Christian thought, but with the Christian
Gospel a new element entered into religion, clothing itself in the
old forms, and filling them with a new content.

When it broke free from the limits of Judaism and turned to the
Gentile world, Christianity was faced with the need for a fresh
formulation of its message, and in the course of its mission it was
itself modified and transformed through the influence of its environment. This transformation is not simply to be deplored as a
declension from an original purity.[15] The new faith arose out of
Judaism, but it came with a mission and a message to all men; it
had therefore to speak in a language understood by all. Like the
Judaism of the Diaspora before it, it had to be reinterpreted in
terms of contemporary thought, its message expressed in the
language of its environment. Without such a reinterpretation
Paul's Gentile mission would have been a complete failure, but the
reinterpretation in itself was fraught with grave danger for the
Church. There were those without who were only too ready to
learn and appropriate any new religion, to merge it with those
which they had already accepted;[16] there were those within who
yielded too easily to the attractions of their environment, and who
in their reinterpretation lost their grasp of the essentials of the
faith. In each case we have a blending and merging of Christian
elements in what is ultimately a non-Christian scheme.

At this point we touch upon a question which is still to some
considerable extent a matter of controversy: the nature and origins
of the Gnostic movement; and once again the question is complicated by problems of terminology.[17] The title 'Gnostic' was
originally claimed for themselves by certain particular groups, but
in modern use it has been extended to the whole movement against

which Irenaeus and others directed their Refutations. In this sense, 'Gnosticism' is a general description of a series of related heretical schools which menaced the Church, particularly in the second century A.D. Irenaeus, and more especially Hippolytus, traced back the ancestry of these sects to the various schools of Greek philosophy, and this remained the traditional view until quite recent times.[17a] Thus Harnack in a famous phrase described Gnosticism as 'the acute hellenization of Christianity.' With the rise of the *religionsgeschichtliche* school, however, the range of the term was extended even further. Reitzenstein and Bousset pointed to similar features in other systems of thought, and in particular to parallels in ancient pre-Christian mythologies. They and their followers therefore argued that Gnosticism is not the product of the impact of Christianity on the Graeco-Roman world, but is in fact pre-Christian, and, moreover, that it was an important factor in the origins of Christianity itself. So for Jonas not only heretical, but also orthodox Christianity, and even certain strata in the New Testament, are included in the 'Gnostic' sphere.[18] The fact that the same term is employed by some writers to describe the Christian heresy and by others in this wider sense has inevitably led to confusion; it has, indeed, been said that no two writers use the word in the same way.[19] It is therefore of fundamental importance that some effort should be made at clarity and precision in the use of the term.

The school of Reitzenstein and Bousset is by now somewhat out of favour, but although some of their theories have had to be abandoned, they did a great service by showing the need to study primitive Christianity in the context of its contemporary environment; their main contention has come to be a permanent element in this field of research.[20] The weakness of their theory lies in the inferences which they drew from the material they collected, and in their disregard of chronology. For example, there can be no doubt that Gnosticism is in some way related to Manicheism and Mandeism[21] but, in the first place, Mani lived in the third century A.D., while our evidence does not seem to permit of our placing the Mandeans before 400 A.D.; and in the second place, the Mandeans seem to have been indebted to Mani for some of the ideas which they hold in common.[22] It is possible that the Mandeans are the ultimate descendants of the Palestinian baptist sects of New Testament times and the period immediately preceding,[23] but our evidence is not sufficient to justify the assertion that these sects were already 'Gnostic' in the second-century sense of the term. Even if we assume such a chain of connexion, we should still have to consider the possibility of a later influence from the 'Christian Gnostic' sects of the second century, or similar systems, upon the developing ideas of the baptist groups. The Hermetica again, in which Reitzenstein saw 'the end phase of a long development which had begun and reached its maturity before the beginning of the Christian era,' are in their present form scarcely earlier than the third century.[24] It is beyond question that certain particular ideas which are found in the Gnostic systems were already current long before the Christian era, and it is also true that we can trace back these ideas to Egypt or Persia or Babylonia, to Greek philosophy or ancient Semitic mythology; but we have not thereby accounted for the origins of Gnosticism. As Quispel has observed,[25] practically the entire Near East has made its contribution to the development of Gnostic theory. The important point is that we have as yet no conclusive evidence for the combination of these ideas into a coherent system before the rise of Christianity.[26] According to Bultmann,[27] 'the essence of Gnosticism does not lie in its syncretistic mythology but rather in a new understanding—new in the ancient world—of man and the world.' The question is: at what point does this new understanding first appear?

As Dodd has put it, 'there is a sense in which orthodox Christian theologians like Clement of Alexandria and Origen, on the one hand, and Hellenistic Jews like Philo, and pagan writers like the Hermetists, on the other, should be called Gnostics.'[28] Bultmann and Jonas would add Neo-Platonism, despite the attacks on the Gnostics in the pages of Plotinus.[29] But it is significant that both Bultmann and Jonas find it necessary to make certain distinctions: Gnosticism is not simply syncretism, nor is it Greek philosophy;[30] and 'in so far as Christian preaching remained true to the tradition of the Old Testament and Judaism and of the earliest Church, *definitive contrasts between it and Gnosticism are straightway apparent*.'[31] This in itself suggests that their use of the term is much too wide. It must be admitted that there was a good deal of 'gnosticizing' thought in the early years of the Christian era, for example in Philo, but this is not yet definitely 'Gnostic' in the full sense. It would therefore seem advisable to adopt the narrower definition, recognizing the affinities with Gnosticism of such as Philo on the one hand, and Mandeism and Manicheism on the other, but reserving the term 'Gnostic' with Dodd as 'a label for a large and somewhat amorphous group of religious systems described by Irenaeus and Hippolytus in their works against Heresy, and similar systems known from other sources.'[32] As will appear, our earliest definite documentary evidence goes back to the middle of the first century, to the New Testament period. It may be that 'Gnosticism' in the full sense is even older, but so far as can be seen at present it is more or less contemporary with Christianity.

As Bigg says, Gnosticism may on the whole be regarded as a phase of heathenism.[33] The way was prepared for it by the syncretism current in the Graeco-Roman world, and much in Gnostic theology goes back into Hellenistic thought. Gnosticism appears first as a heresy within the Church, but it is not simply a depraved form of Christianity.[34] It arises out of the attempt to express Christianity in Hellenistic terms, without the safeguards which Paul and his fellow-labourers imposed upon their work. Speculations of a Gnostic type, as has been said, were already current before Christianity appeared on the scene, and there were in later days pagan systems closely akin to the Christian Gnosis. On the other hand, Burkitt claims that Valentinus and others were Christians who sought 'to set forth the living essence of their Religion in a form uncontaminated by the Jewish envelope in which they had received it, and expressed in terms more suited (as they might say) to the cosmogony and philosophy of their enlightened age.'[35] The common origin of the different systems lies for him in 'certain widely-spread notions or ideas'—the Ptolemaic astronomy, the $\sigma\hat{\omega}\mu\alpha$-$\sigma\hat{\eta}\mu\alpha$ concept, and magic, with the use of magical or barbarous names—and the error of Gnosticism consists in the fact that it conceded more to the Hellenistic world than could be admitted by what was later to become orthodox Christianity. Burkitt is certainly right as against those who would derive everything in Gnosticism, nay, even Christianity itself, purely from Graeco-Oriental religion and philosophy, but he himself seems to err in not making sufficient allowance for the Hellenistic elements, and in passing over the similar phenomena in paganism.[36] Burkitt's view of the essential Christianity of Valentinus has been accepted by Dodd,[37] and appears to be confirmed by the *Gospel of Truth*,[38] but for the movement as a whole the problem is much more complex. 'If Valentinus is a Christian theologian of an adventurous type, Justin and the Naassene writer are nothing of the kind; still less "Simon." '[39] On the other hand, if it is reported that in some of the Nag Hammadi documents the Christian element is very slight,[40] there can be no question that the compiler of the *Gospel according to Mary* considered himself, and desired to be considered, as a Christian.[41] In fact, we have to envisage a wide range, from the nearly Christian to the almost completely pagan.

The characteristic of Gnosticism in all its forms is syncretism, blending together elements of every sort, and finding room for every type of thought, from the highest philosophical mysticism to the lowest forms of magic. There is in consequence no one uniform set of ideas that may be singled out as Gnostic; rather is it a matter of a type of thought which manifests itself in different ways in different groups.[42] Yet there are certain characteristic features which reappear in different forms and combinations in the different systems, ideas assimilated from various sources and not always co-ordinated into a consistent scheme.

The Hellenistic world considered the universe to be a system of concentric spheres, rising above and around the earth. Each was ruled by a minor divine being associated with one of the planets, and human destiny was believed to depend in some way upon these powers. The Platonic distinction between the ideal world and that perceptible to the senses was widely current; the ideal world to which man really belongs—or at least to which some men really belong—was set above the spheres, where also the transcendent God had his abode.[43] The Stoic doctrine that the soul was a spark of the divine fire enclosed in matter was also prevalent, and the combination of all these doctrines led to the conclusion that the soul was, essentially a fragment of the divine imprisoned in an alien medium, from which it sought to gain release. Return to its true abode in the higher regions was secured either by purification from fleshly lusts, by ascetic practices, by regulation of the whole life in accor-

F

dance with the dictates of the higher element within, or by a magic knowledge of the names of the ruling powers and of the passwords which were the keys to unlock the gates which barred the way, or by a mystic vision and enlightenment which raised the fortunate recipient above the limits of human nature and made him a god himself.[43a] Sometimes there is some idea of a redeemer sent from above to lead the soul upon its journey; elsewhere man is left to himself to struggle upwards towards the light by holy living. Sometimes the soul is condemned to endure a round of reincarnations in atonement for past errors, or again there is as in Stoicism a re-absorption of the several sparks into the one divine fire from which they came.

There is a wide cleavage between the heavenly and the earthly regions; in the former dwells the transcendent God, remote from the material world with its corruption, and this is also the true abode of the soul, which has been banished or has fallen into this world of sense and matter. Different views are expressed as to the origin of the world, and the manner in which the soul came to inhabit this prison of the body, but a fundamental conviction is that the world, the body, flesh, matter, all are evil; true being belongs to God alone, and to those whom He deigns to endow with the knowledge which alone can save.[44] Only to some is it given to realize their true state, and to appropriate the saving γνῶσις, upon which great stress is laid. In some cases it is no more than a crude magical knowledge of spells and passwords, for to know the name of a god gives power over the owner of the name.[45] In other cases γνῶσις meant an elevated mystical experience, a vision of the divine, a knowledge received by revelation from God Himself. Great stress is laid on the possession of this γνῶσις, and special gifts and privileges are attributed to—or claimed by—the classes who possess it. This leads to a considerable degree of spiritual pride and complacency among the more favoured members of the community, and to widely differing conclusions regarding the practical conduct of life. To some the possession of γνῶσις made ethics irrelevant, whereas others held that it was necessary to mortify the flesh by ascetic practices in order to free the soul from its prison.[46] The Gnostics adopted these features from their Hellenistic environment, and combined them in various ways, with the addition of elements from other sources. There is here little or nothing derived from the Judaism out of which Christianity arose. The importance of Judaism in this connexion, and of the Diaspora in particular, is that it had absorbed some of these concepts, and provided a link between the Hellenistic world and the infant Church.[47]

There are traces of the 'Gnostic' type of thought in Philo,[48] and more in Paul, who has with some justification been called the first and greatest Gnostic;[49] but Paul always maintains the essential Christian point of view, in contrast to the strictly Gnostic systems to be examined.[50] Philo is our chief representative of the type of Jewish speculation which sought to blend Judaism with Hellenism in order to give it a philosophic colouring in the eyes of the Gentile world, while Paul had to adapt the Christian Gospel to the minds of his hearers; naturally both at times come near to those who on the other side were trying to blend whatever seemed useful in Judaism or in Christianity with their own syncretistic scheme. But both remain loyal to their own faith, although of course there are differences between them due to their different aims and to the different message which they sought to convey.[51]

Here it may be appropriate to add a warning: if we approach Paul or Philo with the Gnostic theories in mind, it is easy to detect the similarities; but were the Gnostic theories present to the mind of these writers when they composed their works? Bultmann, for example, claims that Paul interpreted the death of Christ in terms of the Gnostic myth, but does not seem to consider whether this 'Gnostic myth' in fact existed in the time of Paul.[52] Again, when he says that Christianity 'may employ Gnostic ideas and terminology' to describe the situation of natural man in the world,[53] the adjective is accurate in the sense that the ideas and terminology were later to be adopted by the Gnostics; but were they already 'Gnostic' when they were used by Paul? The vital question is not whether a particular word or idea can be paralleled in the later Gnostic theories, or even whether its 'Gnostic' meaning can be read into its use in Paul or Philo, but whether this Gnostic meaning was in the mind of the author when he wrote. In point of fact, it would seem more accurate to suggest that the Gnostics derived their language and ideas from Paul, although they gave to both a new interpretation which in many cases made of them something Paul would never have countenanced.

The 'Gnostic' traits in Philo are chiefly borrowed from the Hellenistic world. His dualism is not so sharp as the Gnostic, and in this and other respects he presents a less developed form of the scheme. We find a similar condemnation of the world of sense as a prison, the same assumption of a kinship between the human soul and the heavenly world—though with elements derived more truly from Jewish thought in the view which he holds of the relations of God and man—the same demand for escape from the bondage of sense. His idea of God is Jewish in origin, but it is developed after the fashion of Aristotle. The growing sense of the transcendence of God and the evil of matter necessitated for Gnosticism a doctrine of intermediaries; Philo at times uses the same ideas, but such a doctrine is not essential for him except as a philosophic colouring for the benefit of his Gentile readers.[54] His account of the creation of man, in particular, bears a strong resemblance to that of Saturninus.[55] Again, the yearning of the soul for release and for union with God is a Greek concept which persisted into Neo-Platonism with Plotinus. It is closely connected with the idea that the human soul is essentially akin to the divine, that it is cut off from a higher world to which it seeks to return. The upward striving, with all the purifications and ascetic practices which it involves, is in one sense the Platonic Eros, although the Greek mind was really too conscious of the essential goodness of the world to accept readily an ascetic view.

There is no trace of a personal redeemer in Philo, and the idea that God has revealed Himself as $\theta\epsilon\grave{o}s$ $\grave{\epsilon}\pi\iota\phi\alpha\nu\acute{\eta}s$, or that a man like Augustus should be fêted as $\kappa o\iota\nu\grave{o}s$ $\tau o\hat{v}$ $\grave{\alpha}\nu\theta\rho\omega\pi\acute{\iota}\nu o\nu$ $\beta\acute{\iota}o\nu$ $\sigma\omega\tau\acute{\eta}\rho$, is foreign to Philo's thought, as also to most Jewish thought, though common enough in the Gentile world.[56] But as Windisch remarks,[57] if he has no redeemer he does have the thought of a redemptive mission, and knows the experience of redemption; he thinks of God sending His powers to the aid of man, and he is aware himself of a deliverance.[58] Indeed, the whole aim of his work is to present Judaism as the true $\gamma\nu\hat{\omega}\sigma\iota s$, revealed by God to Moses and handed down by him to posterity. Again, the Gnostic division of mankind according to capacity for $\gamma\nu\hat{\omega}\sigma\iota s$, which goes back to the Republic of Plato[59] and to the allegorizations of the philosophers,[60] has also its parallels in Philo,[61] as too the idea that γνῶσις conveys ἀφθαρσία.[62] We cannot, however, call him a Gnostic; his importance lies in the fact that he shows the type of thought current in his time, and provides a link in the chain which unites the later movements with earlier thought.[63] He has certain Gnostic tendencies, but is still far removed from the elaborate and detailed schemes of the later thinkers. The Hermetic documents are in some ways similar,[64] but may be independent of Philo, though certainly they contain features which point to Jewish influence; both show how such concepts developed either on purely pagan soil or in centres where Judaism and paganism combined. In one passage,[65] Philo seems concerned to combat the opinions of some Jews who carried their use of the allegorical method to the extent of denying the relevance of the Torah for them; this may indicate the presence in the Diaspora of groups who yielded even more than he did to current thought, a point of some importance in view of the tendency among some scholars to seek the origins of Gnosticism in a Judaism of a more or less heterodox kind.[66]

The present study is concerned primarily with the Judaism of the Dispersion, but it is inevitable in any modern investigation into the New Testament period that some consideration should be given to the Dead Sea Scrolls.[67] With Quispel,[68] 'we must inquire: Does there exist any connexion between Jewish heterodoxy as it finds expression e.g. in the "Essene" documents from the Dead Sea, heretical Gnosis which flows in the ancient world as a broad river at the side of Greek philosophy and orthodox Christianity, and the "true," that is the orthodox, Gnosis of the Alexandrians?' Legge long ago claimed the Essenes, with the Orphics, as pre-Christian Gnostics.[69] In the light of the new evidence now available, how does the situation appear to-day?

As is only to be expected, opinions have varied, and some scholars have not hesitated to retract their earlier views. Thus H. J. Schoeps, who had formerly denied the existence of a pre-Christian Jewish Gnosticism, was constrained by the publication of the Scrolls to change his mind.[70] Subsequently, however, he came to the conclusion that Gnosis is always *pagan* Gnosis; the Jewish 'pre-Gnosis' which seems to anticipate Gnosticism has in reality

nothing to do with it.[71]   K. G. Kuhn, again, is quoted by Fritsch
as speaking of 'a Palestinian-Jewish pietistic sect of gnostic structure,'[72] but in later articles draws some important distinctions
between Gnosticism and the doctrines of the Dead Sea sect.[73]   In
the present state of our knowledge any conclusion must be provisional; only when all the material has been published and subjected
to the closest scrutiny will it be possible to give a final verdict.

On the definition of Gnosticism adopted for the present study,
however, it would appear that while the Scrolls may fairly be
called pre-gnostic, they are not yet Gnostic in the proper sense.[74]
Perhaps the simplest statement is that of Fritsch: 'That there are
Gnostic elements in the sectarian documents of Qumran cannot be
denied; but one would hardly call this a Gnostic sect.'[75]   Once more
it is a question of ideas and terminology which were later to be
adopted by the Gnostic sects, and once more we must inquire not
whether these terms and ideas occur in the truly Gnostic documents,
nor whether they can be understood in a Gnostic sense in their
present context, but what was the meaning which they had for the
author when he wrote.

It is, for example, certain that the sect laid great stress upon
knowledge, but according to Millar Burrows the stress on knowledge is no greater in the Scrolls than in the wisdom literature of
the Old Testament.[76]   So also W. D. Davies rejects 'the temptation
of connecting the references to knowledge in these documents with
a second-century milieu when gnostic movements were a menace
to Judaism, as to the Church.'[77]   This knowledge again is associated
with the revelation of a divine mystery, entrusted to a limited
group, which is once more characteristic of Gnosticism; but the
difference becomes apparent as soon as we ask the content of this
knowledge. 'What is meant by knowledge in the scrolls has to do
with the wonders of God's creation, the fulfilment of prophecy,
and the meaning of the divine laws man must obey';[78] and this is
by no means characteristic of Gnosticism in the second-century
sense of the term.   Finally there is in the Scrolls a dualism of light
and darkness which strikingly recalls the Gnostic dualism, but here
once more there are important distinctions to be observed.[79]   The
dualism of the Scrolls appears in fact to belong to the Iranian ideas

which had been assimilated into Judaism, rather than to Gnostic thought.[80]

One of the factors which convinced Schoeps of the existence of a pre-Christian Jewish Gnosticism was the use in the Scrolls of the myth of the *descensus angelorum* in Genesis 6.[81] This myth admittedly appears in the Gnostic systems, but it is also employed in Jewish apocalyptic writings and an allegorical interpretation of it is to be found in Philo.[82] That the Gnostics derived it from Judaism would appear to be certain, but that it was already Gnostic in Jewish apocalyptic and in Philo is by no means so clear. Once again we are faced with the old fallacy of assuming that because a term or a concept was later used by the Gnostics it is therefore to be considered Gnostic from the beginning.[83]

To conclude this brief summary two points may be added: as Burrows notes, the conception of the soul as a spark of the divine light imprisoned in the dark world of matter does not appear either in the Scrolls or in the fragments so far published, and again, it would be difficult to find in the Scrolls any connexion with the Gnostic myth of the divine Redeemer.[84] In fact, if Quispel is correct, 'there would appear to be good grounds for supposing that it was from Christianity that the conception of redemption and the figure of the Redeemer were taken over into Gnosticism.'[85] It may therefore be said with some confidence that in the present state of our knowledge the sect of the Dead Sea Scrolls, although it certainly belongs to the general milieu out of which Gnosticism arose, is not to be considered Gnostic. As Burrows puts it, 'on the whole, it seems unnecessary and only confusing to apply the term Gnosticism to the form in which such ideas appear in the Dead Sea Scrolls.'[86] One question, however, which may be raised is that of the possibility that the ideas of this sect were known to one of the early Gnostics, who combined them with other theories in the formation of his Gnostic system.[87] With the Scrolls we are certainly near to Gnosticism, but we have not yet passed the point of transition between pre-gnosis and Gnosticism proper.

With Paul we proceed a stage further, but here, as in the New Testament generally, we have to deal not merely with Gnostic tendencies in the author himself, but also with the more extreme forms of Gnosticism and 'Gnostic' speculation which he seeks to

combat in his opponents.[88] A large part of Paul's contribution to
Christianity consists in a sifting of the wheat from the chaff, in the
sense that he used Hellenistic ideas for his proclamation of the
Gospel, while resolutely opposing any attempt to make Christianity
simply another and refined form of Judaism, or to merge it in the
general syncretism of the age. One thing which marks him off at
once from any and every system of a Gnostic character is his view
of the person and work of Christ, for whereas to the Gnostic the
Redeemer came primarily to convey to a favoured few the secrets
of salvation, Paul's thought is dominated throughout by the Cross.
Redemption is not a matter of knowledge, but of faith and love—
men are saved not by their works, not by an enlightened vision, but
by faith in the Christ who gave Himself for them. The true
believer, who has indeed surrendered himself to God in faith, is
known by his works, by the life he leads, for he has died to his old
life and lives now in and for Christ, and Christ in him.[89]

Even here there is a close similarity between Paul's language and
that of the Gnostics, but there is a fundamental difference in the
idea expressed; in neither case is it a matter of intellectual acceptance
of a formula, but of a change in the believer through the working
of the divine power in him; but whereas γνῶσις delivers its possessor
from this evil world of matter, to Paul the evil consists in sin, from
which Christ by His death has set men free. The difference is
significant. The Graeco-Oriental world had in mind the transience
of this life, the vanity of human wishes, the vicissitudes due to the
sway of Fate over human existence; hence redemption is freedom
from the power of Fate, from the limitations of earthly existence,
union with the divine. To Paul, the alienation of man from God
is not due to his creatureliness, but to his disobedience, his failure
to comply with the demands of a righteous God. Thus the forgiveness of sins marks off Christianity from all its competitors.[90] The
Gnostics transformed forgiveness of sins into release from Fate,
from the bondage of the flesh, from matter; in a word, they changed
the distinctively Christian view into the current Hellenistic conception. The whole distinction between Paul and the Gnostics is
that he accepts the contemporary *Weltanschauung* but rejects the
Gnosticizing interpretation.

Again, the Gospel of Christ had for Paul implications which

were unheard of to the Gnostic. Paul himself sums up the difference when he sets Agape above all mysteries and all knowledge, as one of the three things that abide,[91] or when in contrast to the proud and self-reliant Gnostic, sure in his gift of γνῶσις, he urges consideration for those less strong in the faith, on the ground that they too are brethren for whom Christ died.[92] There are points of contact and of agreement, but there are also points of difference, and Paul is at pains to make himself clearly understood.

At the same time, there is much in his thought which could appeal to the Gnostics, and which could be incorporated by them in their systems. The contrast between flesh and spirit,[93] the conception of Christ as victorious over the 'world rulers of this darkness,'[94] or as the Man from Heaven,[95] his use of the terms γνῶσις[96] and πνεῦμα,[97] the language which he borrowed from his environment to express to the Gentile the 'mystery'[98] of the Gospel, all could be interpreted in Gnostic terms by the men who came after, men who too often neglected the other elements in his thought, his stress on brotherly love,[99] on Christian conduct,[100] his opposition to any magical interpretation of the new relation of the believer to God. There are times when he seems to take an ascetic, world-renouncing view, holding the things of this life as worthless in comparison with the things of the higher world,[101] but in contrast to the Gnostics he always emphasizes the practical implications of the Gospel for this life; we may here be in exile, strangers and sojourners, looking for an abiding city,[102] but for Paul, as for the other New Testament writers—and, indeed, for some Gnostics, though not for all—this lays upon us an obligation to live worthily of our true nature, no longer unto ourselves, but unto Christ.[103] For the Gnostic, the gift of enlightenment was too often conceived as a magic power which in freeing him from the sway of Fate left him at liberty to please himself;[104] in this he made what must have seemed to many a natural inference, allowing for his background of thought. The ideas of magic, of the mysteries, of the later schools of Greek philosophy, prepared the way for Christianity; Judaism had also played its part, but both Judaism and Christianity contained elements which were alien to the environment in which they found themselves. The subtle modifications of meaning which Dodd has noted in the translation of the Jewish Scriptures into

Greek are symptomatic.[105] When the attempt was made to express Jewish or Christian ideas to the Gentile mind there was ever present the danger of misunderstanding; forms of thought as well as language differ among different peoples, and new teachings tend to be merged in and assimilated to the ideas already present.[106] It is to the mutual interpenetration of several strands of thought in the 'maelstrom of the syncretistic process'[107] that we must look for the origins of Gnosticism.[108]

Most of Paul's letters are called forth by some problem or difficulty which has arisen among his converts. In *Galatians* he seeks to meet attacks on his apostolic authority, and to combat the view that obedience to the Jewish law was necessary to the Christian, that the redemption in Christ was insufficient apart from such obedience. Here Paul contrasts law and grace, obedience and faith, but is careful to stress the fact that the liberty to which the Christian is called is not to be used as an occasion for licence, but for mutual love and service.[109] In *Colossians* we find a similar idea that the redemption in Christ is not enough, this time from certain 'philosophers' who seem to have sought to introduce pagan elements, especially from astrology, into Christianity. According to them, it was necessary to know also the hidden 'mysteries' revealed by 'philosophy,' and to observe certain rites and practices of an ascetic nature.[110] In the two letters to the Corinthians Paul has in view the grave disorders which had arisen in the Church there: some set undue stress on the possession of gifts such as prophecy and 'speaking with tongues,' while there were also divisions and factions in the Church, and some set themselves apart as specially endowed with the gift of the Spirit.

In *Galatians*, the question is that which inevitably arose when the Gospel was preached to the Gentiles: their position in regard to the law which the earliest Christians had continued to observe; but in the other letters Paul is dealing not with Judaisers but with Gnostics of a primitive type.[111] He is prepared to accept the current cosmogony, but he rejects the conclusions which were drawn by some from that cosmogony in its relation to Christianity. Thus in *Romans* he apparently accepts the Jewish interpretation of the fall of Adam as the fall of a spiritual being into matter;[112] this involved the subjection of man to the dominion of the planets, but the Christian is restored in Christ to the sphere of the Spirit. The Jews had ascribed this deliverance to the Torah, but to Paul the Torah, though divine in its origin, was 'merely a check on the sins of mankind, not a means of delivering them from the power of the "elements," the material world, which in virtue of its material character was subject to the power of the stars under which it lay.'[113] Paul here simply transfers the tradition of Judaism concerning the Torah to Jesus, employing the ideas of contemporary religion; for him, however, the deliverance is not from Fate, but from sin—the rulers of the world could still exert their power over the Christian in respect of the trials of this life, tribulation, distress, persecution, famine, nakedness, peril or sword, but they were powerless to do more; 'neither death, nor life, nor angels, nor principalities, nor powers . . . shall be able to separate us from the love of God, which is in Jesus Christ our Lord.'[114] As Canon Knox puts it, 'the form might be Hellenistic; the faith was the Jewish faith in the Torah transferred to Jesus as the Lord who had conquered death on the stage of history.'[115] There are traces which seem to point to astrological influence,[116] but Paul here passes over the current view that deliverance was to be gained by knowledge; Jesus is superior both to the Torah and to the hostile planets, and in him the Christian is delivered from the power of Fate. The Hellenistic cosmogony is only the framework in which the Gospel is presented.

The adoption of the Hellenistic cosmogony, however, involved a further development in Paul's thought. The dominant interest in his earlier letters had been to proclaim Christ as the Messiah, but if Christ were thus able to redeem men from the power of Fate and of the planets it was to be assumed that he was their superior in the order of things.[117] This meant a re-statement of the Gospel in terms of current cosmogony, which should explain the position of Jesus in relation to the powers that ruled the earth. Here Alexandrian Judaism had prepared the way with its accommodation of Genesis to contemporary philosophy. The Alexandrians were not concerned with the Messiah, or with speculation concerning the last things, but rather with the assimilation of Judaism to the current views of popular philosophy, and hence substituted for the Messiah the divine Reason immanent in the world, which they identified with Wisdom and with the Spirit of God.[118] So in 1 *Corinthians*

Christ appears as the wisdom of God and the power of God,[119] while in *Colossians* He is 'the image of the invisible God, the first-born of every creature; for by Him were all things created, that are in heaven, and that are in earth . . . and He is before all things and by Him all things consist.'[120] In these verses we have language which recalls that used by Philo of the Logos, or of Wisdom in Proverbs or the Wisdom of Solomon. It seems clear that Paul is adapting the teaching of the synagogues of the Diaspora in order to present his message to the Hellenistic world, although it is noteworthy that the Philonic concept of the Logos does not yet seem to be widely current.[121]

Other features of Paul's epistles concern the true nature of the gifts of the Spirit, and of the life of the world to come; there is much in his language that recalls the ideas of the contemporary world, but throughout he maintains the essential Christian position. In Christ dwelleth all the fullness of the Godhead bodily,[122] and He was therefore able to effect a complete reconciliation of man to God; Christians are complete in Him, no longer subject to the powers or to the 'rudiments of the world,' no longer subject to ordinances which belong to the wisdom of this world and not to the wisdom of God.[123] The redemption in Christ is full and final, and there is no need for any special gift of knowledge or wisdom to complete it.

Paul's teaching in these letters arises from the problems which arose in the Gentile churches, problems due to the attempt to relate the Gospel to contemporary thought. Other problems confronted the other New Testament writers, who used similar methods for their solution. All employed the current forms of thought and ideas, but employed them in the service of the Gospel. As Dodd has noted, the whole tradition of the New Testament is thoroughly Biblical, in contrast with the varied and uncontrolled speculations of the Gnostics.[124]

Here, indeed, we seem to have an important criterion by which to distinguish the 'Christian Gnostics' alike from orthodox Christianity and from other heretics. As Casey put it, 'a broad practical distinction must be drawn between those systems which as a whole and in their main structure were inconsistent with Christian theology and those which represent variations from Christian orthodoxy

only in points of detail.'[125]   It may be, indeed, that 'orthodoxy' in
the later sense does not exist in the earliest period, and that the
whole situation was extremely fluid, but we do have on the one
hand a firmly Biblical tradition, the tradition of the apostolic
preaching which is enshrined in the New Testament, and on the
other hand a tradition which is not controlled by the Biblical norm.
Casey continues: 'The admission of Sabellianism, Donatism or
Arianism would have altered the texture but not the structure of
Christian thought; the admission of Marcionite, Valentinian or
Manichean claims would have meant a complete change in the
edifice.' It is to the credit of Irenaeus that he saw this, and accused
the Gnostics of changing the very substance of the faith.[126] His own
reply is a thoroughly Biblical theology.[127] This would seem to
justify the position already adopted, in that we have here clear
grounds for distinguishing the tradition which runs from the New
Testament through Irenaeus from that which culminates in the
Gnosticism of the second century and its later developments. Some
at least of the Gnostics were Christians who sought to present their
faith to a wider world in terms which that world could accept, but
they failed to grasp the redemptive history related in the Scriptures,[128] and in the result it is the pagan element, not the Christian,
which is the dominant factor. Whatever the affinities which may be
detected, this distinction is and remains fundamental.

There are trends of thought and language in the Fourth Gospel
which are closely akin to the thought and language of Philo or of
the Hermetic literature, although as has been noted the evidence of
the Dead Sea Scrolls would seem to show that some at least of these
were already rooted in the soil of Palestine.[129] It is again a striking
fact that the earliest use of this Gospel appears to have been among
the Gnostics,[130] but Quispel would appear to be justified in claiming
that the Fourth Gospel is not Gnostic, and that Valentinus has in
fact transposed the Johannine data into a Gnostic key.[131] Certainly
the First Epistle of John is quite clearly *directed against* ideas of a
Gnostic type.[132] The Epistle to the Hebrews offers further evidence
of the same methods, although here it must be said that not all the
commentators are agreed on the subject of its 'Hellenistic' background.[133] But in each of these cases it remains true that the
writers abide by the fundamentals of the faith, although they

translate them into the language of the surrounding world. There was an obvious need for Christianity to adapt itself to its new environment, to become supranational instead of a mere sect of Judaism, yet the adaptation might destroy the essence of the faith, making it but another of the competing Oriental cults of the day. Some refused to make any concession, and faded away as small 'Puritan' sects in the course of time.[134] Others conceded too much, and these represent in one form or another the Gnostics with whom we have to deal. The genuine tradition which was to become that of the Catholic Church of later ages sought to admit such alien elements as were compatible, and strove to baptize the Graeco-Oriental philosophy, where it was possible, into the service of the Gospel. Some features there may be to deplore in this process, but the chief result of this contact of the Church with Hellenistic culture was to give Christianity a clearer and surer understanding of its message. There were many problems still to be solved, many false views still to be rejected, but a beginning had been made in the clarification of the doctrines of the Church.

The Greek world demanded a reasonable faith, compatible with the best truths of philosophy as it was then known, and this demand was met by the assimilation of Christianity to Hellenism, and of Hellenism to Christianity. Each had something to contribute, but the Church remained essentially true to its charge, while reformulating its teaching to meet new conditions. It is not simply a matter of syncretism; like the Jews before them, the Christians modified and adapted their faith, yet without losing their central message.[135] The beginnings of the process may be seen in the Pauline and Johannine writings, but in them may be seen also a firm and steadfast resistance to any weakening or modification of the fundamental Christian doctrines. There was much in Hellenistic thought that was incompatible with Christianity, but there was much also that might be usefully adopted, and this was taken up by the Church in the course of the early centuries of its life.

In the New Testament we are faced only with an incipient Gnosticism. The false doctrines which are refuted in Colossians and in 1 John are still far removed from the later elaborations, although they show already the main characteristics of the movement. Gnosticism is not entirely foreign to Christianity, and this fact added to the danger, since the Gnostic teachers could give a Christian colouring to their doctrines while yet employing to the full the pagan ideas which they drew from their environment.[136] Had Gnosticism been purely pagan it would have been more easily dealt with. The movement as a whole is the product of the contact of Christianity and 'Hellenism' in its wider sense, where the Hellenistic element is given free play and the ethical and practical emphasis of Christianity as preached by a Paul is neglected. It is 'the fullest accomplishment of that amalgamation of Hellenic and Oriental philosophical speculation with primitive Christian beliefs which was in greater or less degree in process in all Christian thinking,'[137] but in Gnosticism the Graeco-Oriental element tended to overshadow and even to obscure the Christian. There had grown up in the Hellenistic world a composite theology of a popular type which coloured the opinions of men on many subjects; the ideas of the mysteries and of philosophical mysticism were blended, and the system of Posidonius plays a prominent part. Greek philosophy, Oriental and Semitic religion, magic, and at least a flavour of astrology, all had their place. Paul and his fellows adopted some of the contemporary concepts for their own purposes, but there was always the danger of misunderstanding, while some went too far in their acceptance of current thought.

Given the Hellenistic cosmogony, the central problem was the relation of Jesus the Messiah to the powers that ruled the world, and the means whereby man could escape from their domination.[137a] In presenting a solution the Christian writers had also to combat the practical conclusions which were drawn by some from the new interpretation of the Gospel, conclusions both about the efficacy of the redemption in Christ and about the conduct of life in this world. The Gnostic, in common with the majority of his contemporaries, tended to think that the gift of the Spirit which was the earnest of the life to come set him free from all responsibility, although some took an ascetic view; Paul stresses the other side, responsibility to God if not to man.[138] Over against a purely subjective view of ethics he sets loyalty to Christ: the Christian is no longer his own master—nay rather, never was—but belongs to Christ, is one with Him, and loyalty to Christ involves also love to the brethren.[139] In the Johannine writings this love to the brethren becomes the touchstone of faith;[140] all alike now stand under the same judgement, all have the same obligation of love and service, since all alike are brethren for whom Christ died.

Again, some set undue stress on abnormal, ecstatic, experiences. The type of thought which lies behind this can be traced at many points in Greek religion, as in the inspiration of the prophet or the Sibyl;[141] in Hellenistic times this 'inspiration' was claimed by many, some in all sincerity, no doubt, though quacks and impostors were numerous. The trouble was that subjective experiences such as ecstasy came to be regarded as the whole end of human endeavour,[142] and the possessor of such gifts as prophecy tended to consider himself, and to be considered, as in a class apart from ordinary mortals. Prophecy and miracles, wonder-working of various kinds, were part of the stock-in-trade of the itinerant holy man. Some made a name for themselves, and were credited with super-human powers, or even worshipped as gods by their credulous followers. Now and then we read of the exposure of such claims, but many a quack seems to have practised with impunity.[143] For Paul, such gifts are not the highest ends of human life, and they are bestowed not for the elevation of the possessor but in order that he may use them for the good of the whole community;[144] but his references show how strong was the other view among his Gentile converts, while the frequent warnings against false prophets, both in the New Testament and in the early patristic writings, show the prevalence of charlatanry and imposture, even among those who claimed to be Christians.

To sum up, Gnosticism arises largely from an imperfect grasp of Christian principles by people brought up in the environment of the Hellenistic world, with its cosmopolitanism and its throng of competing cults; the Christian heresy is indeed only a part of a wider movement of which the origins are still obscure, although it would appear to be roughly contemporaneous with the rise of Christianity.[145] Even in its earliest stages Gnosticism in its Christian form was a danger to the Church, a danger which Paul and his fellows were not slow to observe and to resist.[146] In the New Testament we have as yet only the first murmurs of the storm, which reached its height in the second century, but they are enough to show that the danger had begun to make itself felt. The errors of the Corinthians or of the Colossians show how people with their background and outlook might react to the presentation of the new faith by a Paul. The same ideas were widely current, and the very number of the later theories shows the grasp which they had upon the popular mind. Not the least of the services done by Paul and his fellow-labourers was their exposition of the basic Christian doctrines in the light of contemporary thought, and their resolute rejection of any other Gospel.

NOTES TO CHAPTER III

[1] See generally Wendland *HRK*.

[2] For the contribution of Posidonius see Wendland *HRK* index, and references above, pp. 17, 36.

[3] Wendland *HRK* 142ff.

[4] *OGIS* 657. 1, cf. Wendland *HRK* 30f. and note, 143ff., Knox *PCG* 23. For the idea of σωτῆρες see Wendland index s.v. and *ZNTW* 1904, 335ff.

[5] Dittenberger (*OGIS* index s.v.) significantly remarks 'passim.'

[6] Cf. Wendland *HRK* s.v. Herrscherkult, Clemen *RGE* 29ff.

[7] 3. 13. 9.

[8] Wendland *HRK* 151ff.

[9] Epict. 3. 13. 11.

[10] Cf. Wendland *HRK* 75ff., 91ff. Compare the passages quoted by Hatch *Influence of Greek Ideas* 102, 111, from Epictetus and Dio Chrysostom. The Christian κήρυγμα was not, however, simply an imitation of the Stoic-Cynic ethical sermon (cf. Dodd *The Apostolic Preaching and its Development*), and while there are similarities in the *style* there is no evidence that Christians in the early period preached in the streets or in the market-place, like the itinerant philosophers. They began in the synagogue and later carried over its system into the Church, but a case like that of Paul in the school of Tyrannus is closely parallel to the practice of some at least of the pagan philosophers (Acts 19. 9; it was comparatively common by the time of Dio). See also Norden *Agnostos Theos* 129ff.

[11] Cf. Wendland *HRK* 112ff., Hatch 50ff.

[12] Rom. 3. 23, 1. 18.

[13] Cf. Hatch 139ff.

[14] Cf. for example Rom. 3. 23ff.

[15] The whole thesis of Hatch's book is the transformation of Christianity from the ethical emphasis of the Sermon on the Mount to the metaphysical doctrine of the Nicene Creed. Windisch 119 attributes the beginnings of the process to the work of John, but although we certainly have in the Fourth Gospel a presentation of the Christian message in terms of current thought (cf. Sanders *The Fourth Gospel in the Early Church*) the process had

G

already begun with Paul. See also Bethune-Baker *Introd. to the Early History of Christian Doctrine* 38, and Kirk *The Vision of God* 118 *et al.*, together with Hort and Mayor *Clement of Alexandria, The Seventh Book of the Stromateis* xxii ff. Some Hellenistic elements in primitive Christianity are examined by Canon Knox in his Schweich Lectures for 1942 under that title.

[16] Cf. the case of Simon Magus (Acts 8. 9ff. and see below, p. 99ff).

[17] See on the whole question Dodd, *The Interpretation of the Fourth Gospel* 97ff., Casey in *The Background of the NT and its Eschatology* 52ff.; also *Vigiliae Christianae* ix. 193ff., and Casey in *JTS* xxxvi (1935) 45ff.

[17a] On this 'classical' view of heresy cf. Turner, *The Pattern of Christian Truth* (London 1954) 217ff. *et al.*; also *Recueil Cerfaux* I. 263ff.

[18] *Gnosis und spätantiker Geist* I. 80.

[19] Cf. Schoeps, *Urgemeinde, Judenchristentum, Gnosis* 30.

[20] Cf. Kirk, *The Vision of God*, index, for references to Reitzenstein and Bousset, and see his criticisms of the *religionsgeschichtliche* method. See also Bethune-Baker's appendix, op. cit. 430.

[21] Cf. Jonas I. 6–8; Quispel *Gnosis als Weltreligion* 12: 'Der Gnostizismus ist ein grosser Strom, der von der vulgären Urgnosis zum Manichäismus führt.'

[22] Cf. Puech, *Le Manichéisme, son fondateur, sa doctrine* (Paris 1949) 40f. and notes 147 and 153.

[23] Cf. Thomas *Le mouvement baptiste en Palestine et Syrie* (Gembloux 1935).

[24] Casey in *The Background of the NT* 53. Nock (*Corpus Hermeticum*, ed. Nock-Festugière I, p. vii) observes that the Hermetica offer striking resemblances to Christian Gnostic writings, but thinks this due to a common background. The presence of Hermetica in the Nag Hammadi library indicates their use by the Gnostics (Quispel op. cit. 9f.), but not all these tractates are truly Gnostic (ibid. 28). Van Moorsel (*The Mysteries of Hermes Trismegistus*, Utrecht 1955, 20ff.) suggests that a term like *semignosticism* would be more satisfactory.

[25] op. cit. 9.

[26] Cf. Quispel in *Nederlands Theol. Tijdschrift* 11. 174. See also *Vig. Chr.* xi (1957) 96.

[27] *Theology of the New Testament* I. 165.

[28] *Interpretation of the Fourth Gospel* 97.

[29] Bultmann *Primitive Christianity* 163; Jonas I. 6: Plotinus is a Gnostic source 'not only through his writings against the Gnostics but also and above all, as we shall show, in essential parts of his own thought.' The section of Jonas' book relating to Plotinus has still to be published (cf. Jonas 2. ix). But cf. Quispel *Gnosis* 22ff.

[30] Jonas I. 77ff. See also his criticisms of Bousset (34ff.) and Harnack (50ff.).

³¹ Bultmann *Theology* I. 168 (his italics). For some further criticisms of Bultmann's approach see *Vig. Chr.* xi (1957) 93ff.

³² *Interpretation of the Fourth Gospel* 97. Casey (*JTS* xxxvi (1935) 55) points out that γνῶσις was used of the right apprehension of revealed truth by orthodox and heretics alike. So also Bouyer (*JTS NS* iv (1953) 200) observes that Irenaeus never uses *gnosis* and *gnostic* in a bad sense. It is *the gnosis falsely so called* (1 Tim. 6. 20) that he attacks. In this sense the *religionsgeschichtliche* view is correct—but we need a convenient term to designate the heretical *gnosis*, and 'Gnostic,' properly understood, is the most convenient and need not be confusing. See also Sagnard *La gnose valentinienne et le témoignage de saint Irénée* 81 note 1.

³³ *The Church's Task* 60; cf. Wendland *HRK* 165.

³⁴ Cf. Bevan *Hellenism and Christianity* 90: 'Christian Gnosticism, it is now recognized on all hands, was not a wanton perversion, a wanton sophistication, of a clearly articulated orthodox theology, but an attempt made by men who had received the Church's teaching when its intellectual expression was still more or less wavering and tentative, to combine that teaching with conceptions and aspirations prevalent in the Gentile world whence they had come.'

³⁵ *Church and Gnosis* 27ff. Cf. also Bethune-Baker 76, with, however, a slightly different emphasis.

³⁶ Cf. Harvey's edition of Irenaeus *adv. Haer.* cxliv, supporting Baur against Mosheim's view 'that we must look to the Oriental systems of philosophy for an explanation of the Valentinian theory.' It seems true to say that all the various systems, pagan and Christian, represent the type of thought then current, under the influence of Oriental religion and Greek philosophy, and that Christian Gnosticism is the attempt to bring Christianity into line with the rest. The pagan systems are important as showing the background of such ideas, the types of thought then in favour, and the variety of the different systems, from the primitive to the more developed forms. Gnosticism cannot be understood apart from this background, but the theories of a Valentinus need not have been borrowed purely from paganism, Greek or Oriental, while the similarities indicate a certain amount of common ground.

³⁷ *Interpretation of the Fourth Gospel* 100 note 4; cf. *BG* 207 note 1.

³⁸ On the attribution of this document to Valentinus see van Unnik in *The Jung Codex* 94ff., who would date the *Gospel of Truth* shortly before or shortly after Valentinus' breach with the Church (ibid. 103). See also below, p. 155ff.

³⁹ Dodd, *Interpretation* 101.

⁴⁰ Quispel, *Gnosis als Weltreligion* 5 (on the *Apocryphon Johannis*, for which see below, p. 149ff); Doresse in *Vig. Chr.* 2. 159. But against Doresse's view of the relation between the *Epistle of Eugnostos* and the *Sophia Jesu Christi* see Till *Die gnostischen Schriften des koptischen Papyrus Berolinensis* 8502 (*TU* 60), 54.

[41] See *New Testament Studies* iii (1957) 236ff., and for the text of this document Till op. cit. 62ff. So also Quispel notes that the people to whom the Nag Hammadi library belonged considered themselves more or less as Christians (op. cit. 5f.).

[42] The best description is that of H. R. Mackintosh: 'An atmosphere rather than a system' (*The Person of Jesus Christ* 134). See further *ERE* 6. 231ff., *PW* 7. 2. 1503ff.

[43] In some of the later systems there is a complete series of worlds in the ideal realm, corresponding to the spheres which surround this earth; of course the earth and the spheres were held to be copies of these higher worlds.

[43a] For this idea of deification cf. Hort and Mayor, *Clement of Alexandria: The Seventh Book of the Stromateis* 203ff.; Meecham, *The Epistle to Diognetus* 143f.

[44] On the nature of this Gnosis see Wendland *HRK* 166, Reitzenstein *HMR* 284ff., Kirk index s.v., Knox *PCG* 101ff., Harvey xl ff., lx ff., Bultmann in Kittel *TWB* 1. 688ff. There are three distinct types: (i) the mystic wisdom of the mysteries, the vision of the divine gained through revelation; (ii) a 'scientific' wisdom which leads the soul that is able to receive it out of the limits of the body and the world to the higher regions (cf. Knox *PCG* 120 and note 4 there); (iii) a cruder magical wisdom consisting in the knowledge of names and spells and passwords. The first two of these often blend with one another to produce a philosophical mysticism, and it is really only to these that Wendland's description applies: 'Gnosis ist nicht verstandesmässige Erkenntnis, sondern Schauen Gottes, Geheimwissen, das durch persönlichen Verkehr mit der Gottheit und durch Offenbarung gewonnen wird.' See also below, p. 107.

[45] Thus it was customary to invoke a god by every possible title, and even to guard against any omission by the use of some such formula as 'or whatever thou dost choose to be called.' The same thought lies behind the contemporary dedications 'to the unknown gods.' Cf. Knox *PCG* 40ff., Moore 1. 378, 426, 3. 119; Wendland *HRK* 128 and note 3 there, Norden *Agnostos Theos*, and *Beginnings* 5. 240ff. The idea of the power of the name goes back to a very early stage in history. For examples see Norden 216ff. Attention has been drawn to another aspect by Quispel (e.g. in *The Jung Codex* 69ff.), who emphasizes the importance for the study of Gnosticism of *Jewish* speculations about the Name of God.

[46] Cf. Bevan, *Hellenism and Christianity* 80ff.: 'Asceticism and lubricity are often plants springing from the same soil' (ibid. 81). Cf. Kirk 75ff. on rigorism in Paul, and see the whole chapter for the New Testament generally. For the Gnostics see ibid. 207ff.

[47] Cf. Hatch 128ff.

[48] Jewish 'Gnosticism' is, of course, most clearly to be seen in Philo, but Windisch remarks(87): 'Unter fremden Einfluss hat auch das palästinensische Judentum eine hypostatische Gotteslehre ausgebildet.' This may indicate

Gnostic tendencies even in Palestine (on the Dead Sea Scrolls see below, p. 73ff). Note that Simon Magus came from Samaria, while several of the other Gnostic leaders were natives of the same regions. It is to be presumed that the Jews did not remain unaffected. On the other hand it should be noted that Goodenough repeatedly emphasizes that despite their hellenization the Jews who employed the symbols which he examines were in their own way as loyal as the most Rabbinic (see his *Jewish Symbols in the Greco-Roman Period*).

[49] Reitzenstein *HMR* 86. See, however, Kirk's criticisms of Reitzenstein and Bousset (*The Vision of God* 86 et al.).

[50] Cf. Bultmann in Kittel *TWB* I. 709: 'Paulus hält ihnen gegenüber am Charakter echter christlicher Erkenntnis fest, aber indem er sich gnostische Terminologie und Fragestellung bis zu einem gewissen Grade aneignet' (this article has been translated and edited by J. R. Coates, *Bible Key Words: V. Gnosis*, London 1952). Cf. Reitzenstein *HMR* 258ff., 333ff.

[51] On the similarities and differences see Kennedy *PCR*, and Windisch 104ff.

[52] *Theology* I. 298 et al. But Quispel (*The Jung Codex* 76ff.) claims that it was from Christianity that the conception of redemption and the figure of the Redeemer were taken over into Gnosticism.

[53] *Primitive Christianity* 189; cf. *Theology* I. 174. It would seem more accurate to say that themes are already germinant in late hellenistic philosophy and in Philo which reach their full expression in Gnosis (cf. Bultmann in *JTS NS* iii (1952) 22), but this does not mean that these ideas are already 'Gnostic.' Sagnard (*La gnose valentinienne* 118 note 2) doubts the existence of a Gnosticism properly so called in the time of Paul, but Gnosticism was certainly present in an incipient form. Cf. Bultmann *TWB* (= *Gnosis* ed. Coates 111ff.), who finds Gnostic illuminati in Christian circles in Corinth. As Law long ago observed, the Corinthian letters show 'into how congenial a soil the seeds of Gnosticism were about to fall' (*The Tests of Life* 28). See also van Unnik in *The Jung Codex* 84f., 125.

[54] Cf. Sanders *The Fourth Gospel in the Early Church* for similar features in the Christian Apologists. In Philo, however, matter is not certainly said to be evil, although he comes near at times to this view. See above, p. 45.

[55] See below, p. 103.

[56] Windisch 88ff. Wendland (*ZNTW* 1904, 342) refers to Julius Caesar an Ephesian mention of τὸν ἀπὸ "Αρεως καὶ 'Αφροδείτης θεὸν ἐπιφανῆ καὶ κοινὸν τοῦ ἀνθρωπίνου βίου σωτῆρα, which may be the text Windisch has in mind. Cf. Wendland's article for parallels. The late Canon Knox referred me to *Leg. ad Caium* 13, 18, 149, where, however, Philo is either using conventional language in his address to the emperor, or possibly adapting a pagan source for his own purposes. Cf. also *In Flacc.* 74, and see Knox *HE* 37f. and notes there.

[57] op. cit. 107.

[58] Cf. Windisch's references, op. cit. 31. Philo is simply using figurative language to express the grace of God which he has experienced. It is indeed difficult to see how else he could have expressed himself, and there is no need to read into his words something which in all probability was not in his mind, such as the Gnostic descent of the Redeemer. Cf. also Wendland *HRK* 207 and note 3 there.

[59] The triple division of the soul would naturally lend itself to such a distinction, as would Plato's division of the citizens of his ideal state. The threefold classification is, however, later, the original comprising simply spiritual and carnal, so that Platonic influence may not have operated in the first instance. For the division of the soul, cf. Colson's note to L.A. I. 70 (Loeb Philo 1. 478).

[60] The philosophers discerned in Homer or in the Scriptures (according to their persuasion, whether Jewish, Christian or pagan) truths which were not revealed to the many. There thus arose a distinction between the enlightened and those who could not understand the allegorical interpretation which resolved the difficulties of the text, which could easily develop into a permanent division of mankind into two or more classes. New Testament analogies spring readily to the mind, but what is there largely a figurative use of language is by the Gnostics elevated into a permanent principle distinguishing one man from another on the basis of their 'spiritual' standing. Cf. Wendland *HRK* 160, etc. Cf. also Kennedy *PCR* 34 on Philo's use of allegory.

[61] Cf. Windisch 52 *et al.*

[62] Cf. Windisch 4ff.

[63] On Philo and Gnosticism see also Lewy, *Sobria Ebrietas* 73ff., where it is noted (74 note 1) that Philo almost entirely avoids the word γνῶσις.

[64] Cf. Windisch 89. See also Reitzenstein *HMR* and *Poimandres*, and Dodd *BG*.

[65] Mig. Ab. 89ff. Cf. Knox *PCG* 48, Friedländer, *Der vorchristliche jüdische Gnosticismus*.

[66] Cf. *ZRGG* ix (1957) 21ff., Quispel in *The Jung Codex* 62ff., and *Eranos Jahrbuch* XXII (Zürich 1954) 195ff., Schubert *Die Religion des nachbiblischen Judentums* 80ff., Goppelt *Christentum und Judentum* 125ff. As Cullmann notes (*JBL* 1955, 213ff.), the fact that the earliest forms of Gnosticism underlying Colossians and the Pastorals appear to be of a Jewish character suggests that there was a Jewish Gnosticism before the Christian. But see also Schoeps *Urgemeinde* 33ff.

[67] For references on the Scrolls see above, p. 20 note 31. The non-biblical texts are translated by Gaster, *The Scriptures of the Dead Sea Sect* (London 1957).

[68] *The Jung Codex* 38.

[69] *Fore-runners and Rivals of Christianity*, vol. 1. So also Dieterich (*Abraxas* 148) claimed the Orphics as the true birthplace of the earliest Gnosis.

[70] *ZRGG* vi (1954) 276ff.

[71] *Urgemeinde* 39f.

[72] *ZTK* xlvii (1950) 210, quoted by Fritsch *The Qumran Community* 118 note 11.

[73] *ZTK* 1952, 200ff., 296ff.

[74] Cf. Bo Reicke in *NTS* 1. 137ff., who warns against the temptation to seek for an elaborate Gnosticism in these Scrolls.

[75] op. cit. 74 note 22. On the whole question see Millar Burrows *The Dead Sea Scrolls* (London 1956) 252ff., and Nötscher *Zur theologischen Terminologie der Qumran-Texte* (Bonn 1956).

[76] op. cit. 255.

[77] *HTR* 46 (1953) 113ff.

[78] Burrows 256.

[79] ibid. 257f.

[80] ibid. 259ff. Cf. Kuhn in *ZTK* 1952, 296ff., who notes that Brownlee (*BASOR* Suppt. Studies 10–12, New Haven 1951) and Dupont-Sommer (*RHR* 142 (1952) 5ff.) had independently reached the same conclusion. Schubert, however (*TLZ* 1953, 495ff.) has some scruples about accepting this opinion. In any case, even if the *ultimate* source was Iranian, this dualism had been naturalized into Judaism (cf. Johnson in *HTR* 48 (1955) 161, Winter in *Vetus Testamentum* v. 315ff.).

[81] *ZRGG* vi (1954) 278.

[82] Cf. Moore *Judaism* 1. 406, 483; 2. 315; and for Philo, Drummond *Philo Judaeus* 1. 338, 2. 240.

[83] Schubert (*Die Religion des nachbiblischen Judentums* 85ff. and more fully in *TLZ* 78 (1953) 495ff.) attempts to show that part of the Dead Sea *Manual of Discipline* (iii. 13–iv. 26) is the oldest extant Gnostic text, but see *Vig. Chr.* xi (1957) 99ff. Quispel, however (*Ned. Theol. Tijdschrift* 11. 176) quotes Scholem for *tholedoth = natura* (cf. Schubert *Religion* 230 note 8), and for this meaning in *MD* iii. 13.

The later developments in Jewish 'Gnosticism' such as the Cabbala are beyond the scope of the present study. See Scholem, *Major trends in Jewish Mysticism* (New York 1946), and Lehmann in *Studia Patristica* 1. 477ff.

[84] Burrows 258f.

[85] *The Jung Codex* 78. Cf. *Jew and Greek* 314ff.

[86] op. cit. 259. It may be added that for Burrows the terms 'Gnostic' and 'Gnosticism' 'should be reserved for forms of religion, whether Christian or non-Christian, that exhibit at least the most characteristic features of Gnosticism as represented by the second-century Christian heresy' (ibid. 252).

[87] For an attempt to trace a possible line of connexion between the Scrolls and Gnosticism proper, through Simon Magus and Dositheus, see *ZRGG* ix (1957) 21ff. (cf. Quispel *Gnosis als Weltreligion* 7f., 51f.).

[88] Cf. in addition to Paul the Pastoral and Catholic Epistles, and the Johannine writings. See also Reitzenstein *HMR* 333ff., 'Paulus als Pneuma-tiker,' and Bultmann in *TWB* 1. 708ff. Dupont (*Gnosis: La Connaissance religieuse dans les Épitres de Saint Paul*, Louvain 1949) criticizes the view

that Paul was influenced by Hellenistic mysticism, and claims that the Pauline conception of *gnosis* is wholly in line with the tradition of the Old Testament and Judaism. But cf. Bultmann's review, *JTS NS* iii (1952) 10ff. Even if Dupont's argument be sustained, it does not seem to follow that his principal contention (Bultmann loc. cit. 20) is correct, viz. that the 'weak' in Corinth were Jewish Christians. Evidence that Paul's own background is Jewish and Biblical does not necessarily prove the same for his readers.

[89] Rom. 14. 7ff., 2 Cor. 5. 14ff., Gal. 2. 19ff.; cf. Rom. 6. 1ff. and especially verse 11.

[90] Norden *Agnostos Theos* 11 note 1; Reitzenstein *Poimandres* 180 n. 1. On the difference of the Greek and Jewish/Christian views of law, sin, etc., see Hatch 158ff., Bethune-Baker 74 note 3, and Dodd *BG* Part I.

[91] 1 Cor. 13. 13; note the whole chapter, and cf. 8. 1. See also Kirk 127ff.

[92] Rom. 14; 1 Cor. 8ff.

[93] Cf. Stevens *Theol. of the New Testament* 338ff., and on the Pauline and Philonic views Kennedy *PCR* 75ff. See also Kennedy *PMR* 135ff., and Kirk 88ff. Note especially Rom. 15. 27, 2 Cor. 7. 1.

[94] Col. 2. 15, Eph. 6. 10ff. Cf. Eph. 4. 8ff., and see Wendland *HRK* 177.

[95] 1 Cor. 15. 47.

[96] See Bultmann *TWB* 708ff., Kennedy *PMR* 167ff., Reitzenstein *HMR* 284ff.

[97] See Reitzenstein *HMR* 308ff., Kennedy *PMR* 135ff., and for comparison with Philo id. *PCR* index s.v.

[98] See Kennedy *PMR* 115ff., and for the word $\mu\nu\sigma\tau\acute{\eta}\rho\iota\nu$ itself ibid. 123ff. See also Knox *PCG* 227f.

[99] Rom. 12. 9ff., 13. 8ff., 1 Cor. 1. 10ff., 8, 13 etc. Cf. Eph. 2. 11–22, 4. 1ff.

[100] Rom. 6. 12, 12. 1ff., Gal. 5, 6 etc.

[101] Cf. Kirk 75ff.

[102] These phrases (from 1 Pet. 2. 11, Heb. 13. 14) are not Pauline, but the attitude is one that he might have adopted, and the inference of an obligation to righteous living is entirely in accord with his thought. For Philonic parallels cf. infra, p. 245 note 203.

[103] Cf. Rom. 8. 12 and references above, note 89.

[104] Cf. Hippolytus *Phil.* 6. 19 (Wendland p. 146 line 14, and the parallel there quoted). For Paul's view cf. 1 Cor. 10. 23.

[105] Cf. above, p. 32f.

[106] Some of the 'Hellenistic' features in Paul's writings owe their existence rather to his Old Testament background (in this Dupont is certainly correct). Similar features in the pagan world made it easier for him to convey his message, *but at the same time facilitated misunderstanding*, owing to the difference between the Jewish and the pagan modes of thought. It is to such misunderstanding that some at least of the Gnostic aberrations are due.

[107] Bultmann's phrase (*Theology* I. 171): here 'the genuinely Christian element is wrestling with other elements; "orthodoxy" does not exist at this early period but is still to develop.' So also Turner (*Pattern* 81ff.) suggests the existence of a penumbra between orthodoxy and heresy in the second century.

[108] But cf. Bultmann, *Primitive Christianity* 162: 'Since it appropriated all sorts of mythological and philosophical traditions for its expression, we may call it a synthetic phenomenon. Yet *it would be wrong to regard it only as such*. All its forms, its mythology and theology, arise from "a definite attitude to life and an interpretation of human existence derived therefrom."' Bultmann here quotes Jonas, who interprets Gnosticism in terms of Heidegger's existentialism (cf. Grant's review in *JTS NS* vii (1956) 308ff.).

[109] Gal. 5. 13.

[110] Cf. Knox *PCG* 154; cf. also ibid. 101: 'the Christian Gnostics later were uncertain whether it was baptism that delivered man from fate and the power of the stars, or whether Gnosis was needed as well' (quoting Clem. Alex., *Exc. ex Theod.* 76. 1 *seq.*). In Iren. I. 14. I the 'baptism of Jesus' is distinguished from the 'redemption of Christ who descended in him,' as psychic from spiritual.

On the Colossian heresy see Lightfoot *Col.* 73ff., and Dibelius in *HzNT*. Dupont (17 note 2) quotes Jülicher (*Enc. Bib.* 2. 1738–1742) as saying that the false teachers of Colossae 'become intelligible only if we take them as judaisers on the one hand, and gnosticizers on the other. . . . A gnosticizing Judaism of this sort they must have imported with them from without; that is to say, gnosticism already existed in the apostolic age, and *it was introduced into the Christian Church by the Jews*' (cf. also Cullmann in *JBL* 1955, 213ff.). This takes us back definitely to the middle of the first century, and offers one of the strongest grounds for assuming a pre-Christian Jewish Gnosticism, but unfortunately we have no documentary evidence to give conclusive proof of the existence of such a Jewish Gnosticism. See also Goppelt 137ff., who thinks these teachers came not from Palestine but from the strongly syncretistic diaspora of Phrygia. As Goppelt notes (138) the distinction between the 'Judaism' of Galatia and the Colossian heresy is particularly clear.

[111] Ropes and Lütgert have claimed that in Galatia Paul had to contend not only with Judaizers but also with a 'gnosticizing' group, but this is rejected by Duncan (Moffatt Commentary xxxiiff.; see also Goppelt 93 note 1, against Schlier and others). In point of fact, the 'gnosticism' would seem to be read back into the text. The primary question in Galatians is that of the law, and, moreover, if the epistle be dated (with Duncan and Knox) before the Apostolic Council this would appear to be too early for such a development to have taken place. Bultmann (*Primitive Christianity* 154f.) quotes Gal. 4. 3f., 9 in a series of passages which suggests a relationship between the Christian Gospel and Gnosticism, but (*a*) one of these passages

is from Apuleius (middle of second century A.D.), a second from the *Corpus Hermeticum*, and a third from the *Excerpta ex Theodoto*; (*b*) the interpretation of the passage is not beyond question: Bultmann takes the στοιχεῖα τοῦ κόσμου to be 'the elements of the world,' but commentators vary; if Duncan (134ff.) favours this interpretation, Lagrange (99ff.), Burton (510ff.), Lightfoot (167), and Knox (*PCJ* 113 note 13) are against.

[112] See Knox *PCG* 98f., discussing Romans 8.

[113] ibid. 108; see generally ibid. 104ff. on this subject. For Jesus as the new Torah, see Davies, *Paul and Rabbinic Judaism* 147ff.

[114] Rom. 8. 38–39.

[115] *PCG* 110.

[116] ibid. 107 note 1.

[117] ibid. 110. For this development in Paul's thought see 111ff.

[118] ibid. 113ff.

[119] 1 Cor. 1. 24.

[120] Col. 1. 15ff. Davies *PRJ* 150ff. presents this passage as a rabbinic meditation on the opening words of Genesis.

[121] Knox *PCG* 114 note 4.

[122] Col. 2. 9; cf. 1. 19, 3. 11, and see Knox *PCG* 163ff.

[123] Col. 2. 10, 20ff.

[124] *According to the Scriptures* 136f. See also Turner, index s.v. Gnosticism, appeal to Scripture.

[125] *JTS* xxxvi (1935) 58.

[126] *Adv. Haer.* 1. 10. 3 Mass. Cf. R. A. Markus in *Vig. Chr.* viii. 219ff.

[127] Cf. Lawson, *The Biblical Theology of St. Irenaeus*, and Markus loc. cit.

[128] Markus loc. cit.

[129] See above, p. 5. Cf. *Exp. Times* lxv. 47ff., *Novum Testamentum* 1. 225ff., and references there.

[130] See Sanders, *The Fourth Gospel in the Early Church* 47ff., 86.

[131] *Ned. Theol. Tijdschrift* 11. 173ff.

[132] See for example Law, *The Tests of Life*, and the commentaries of Westcott, Brooke (*ICC*) and Dodd (*MNTC*).

[133] See W. Manson, *The Epistle to the Hebrews* 16ff., against the views of Moffatt and E. F. Scott; also ibid. 123ff. on the 'Alexandrianism' of the epistle. Spicq (*L'Épitre aux Hébreux* 1. 91) subscribes to the formula of Menegoz, that the author is 'un philonien converti au christianisme,' but considers it hardly necessary to mention Weinel's view that the letter was written against Jewish Gnosticism (6 note 2). He finds in Hebrews an angelology which ignores Gnosticism but has in view contemporary Jewish speculations (2. 52, 60). See also his chapter 'Le philonisme de l'épitre aux Hébreux,' 1. 39–91.

[134] Cf. Goppelt 164ff., Schoeps *Urgemeinde* (who traces a connexion between the Dead Sea Scrolls and the Ebionites, but considers the Ebionites not 'Gnostic' but anti-Gnostic).

[135] For the similarity of the position of the New Testament writers and

the early Christian Fathers to that of Philo, cf. Kennedy *PCR* Introduction: the early Fathers 'found in Philo . . . a thinker who had already attempted to reconcile the claims of reason and revelation,' and they found his arguments apt for their own task (pp. 1–2). 'The Letters of Paul, the Epistle to the Hebrews, and the Fourth Gospel are also the products of devout Jewish minds. They all spring from an Old Testament soil. But they all presuppose a Hellenistic environment. Their authors have been more or less in touch with the currents of contemporary thought. . . .' (pp. 20–21). Christianity and Diaspora Judaism both sought to present their faith in an intellectually respectable form, both to hellenized Jews and to Gentiles. The lessons learned by the Jews were not lost upon the Church, although there was also a trend of Christian thought which rejected philosophy as irrelevant (cf. Wolfson, *The Philosophy of the Church Fathers*, 1. 10ff., 102ff.). The discovery of the Dead Sea Scrolls has inevitably led to an increased emphasis upon the Jewish aspects at the expense of the Hellenistic, but it would seem necessary to stress the fact that there was a considerable amount of common ground. As Dodd puts it, 'the old question whether these heresies (in Colossians and the Pastorals) were of Jewish or pagan origin loses much of its point when we recall that Hellenistic Jewish thought and pagan thought of the *Poimandres* type were already drawing together' (*BG* 248 note 1). This comment would seem to be more widely applicable.

[136] Cf. Bevan, *Hellenism and Christianity* 75ff. on the problems raised for the Church by Gnosticism.

[137] Walker, *History of the Christian Church* 56.

[137a] For the Gnostic, however, the central problem is that of evil. 'Comme tous les gnosticismes, le Manichéisme est né de l'angoisse inhérente à la condition humaine' (Puech, *Le Manichéisme* 70; cf. ibid. 152 note 271 and Jonas 1. 94ff.).

[138] Thus in 1 Cor. 2. 15, for example, he uses Hellenistic terms, but turns them to the service of the Gospel; he that is spiritual judgeth all things, yet he himself is judged of no man, but *the Spirit is the Spirit of God in Christ*. So in other passages there have been found uses of Hellenistic terms in a polemic against current misapprehensions of the Gospel. Cf. Bultmann *TWB* 708ff.

[139] Cf. Rom. 14 and references above, p. 92 notes 89, 99.

[140] 1 John 4. 7–8. Cf. Bultmann *TWB* 711.

[141] Cf. Rohde, *Psyche*, index s. v. ἔκστασις, Inspiration, Prophecy,

[142] Cf. Kirk 104.

[143] For examples of such religious leaders, who may or may not have been genuine, cf. Alexander of Abonoteichus and Apollonius of Tyana, and see the writings of Lucian. For the exposure of a quack, see Hippolytus *Phil.* 6. 8 (Wendland p. 135).

[144] Rom. 12. 4ff., 1 Cor. 12, Eph. 4. 11ff.

[145] 'etwa gleichzeitig mit dem Christentum' (Schoeps, *Urgemeinde* 35).

[146] Legge (*Fore-runners and Rivals* 2. 21) notes another aspect: the Gnostics spread the knowledge of Christianity in its hellenized form among the Gentiles, and thus won converts, but many of these converts later abandoned their Gnosticism and adhered to Catholic doctrines. Thus, though in itself a deviation and a danger to the faith, Christian Gnosticism could be a stage on the way to membership of the Church. Cf. ibid. 132ff.

CHAPTER IV

THE EARLIER GNOSTIC SECTS

IT has been recognized in the previous chapter that there are certain affinities between Gnosticism on the one hand and Judaism and Christianity on the other; it has been admitted that there was at the beginning of the Christian era a considerable amount of speculation which was at least moving in the direction of Gnosticism as it appears in full flourish in the second century; but it has been suggested that there are also differences sufficient to necessitate a distinction between what may properly be called Gnostic and what is not yet fully Gnostic but at most pre-gnostic, semi-gnostic, or gnosticizing. The Gnostic movement did not come into being in a day, although, indeed, some of the theories appear to have developed very rapidly. Allowance must be made for a gradual process of growth and development, and somewhere in the course of this development there is a point of transition. In the nature of the case it is inevitable that this point of transition should be differently placed by different scholars, but it has been urged that there is a real need for a clearer definition of terms, and a greater attention to questions of chronology.

On the definition adopted in the preceding chapter, Philo and the Dead Sea Scrolls are not yet Gnostic. The earliest clear evidence for anything comparable to the Gnosticism of the second century appears in Colossians, the Pastorals, and the Johannine literature, where the false doctrine combated would seem to be Gnosticism in an embryonic form. Here it appears as a deviation from Christianity, although, indeed, it may go back further. There is much to suggest a Jewish origin, and certainly it would seem that greater attention must be paid to the Jewish contribution than has been done in the past. At the same time, this is not to say that we may simply identify Gnosticism with Jewish heterodoxy, since other factors have quite clearly played their part. The problem is too complex to admit of a clear-cut simple solution. We may, however, distinguish three main stages: a pre-gnostic, to which may be assigned the various trends of Hellenistic syncretism, including Philo and the Dead Sea Scrolls; a Gnostic proper, represented by the sects of the second century; and the later developments in Manicheism, Mandeism, and other similar movements. The lines of demarcation are admittedly difficult to draw, but such a general classification may serve the purpose of introducing some degree of order into what is otherwise near to chaos. From this point of view the earliest signs of Gnosticism proper appear, in an incipient form, in the heresies opposed in the New Testament itself. That such men as Paul and John were deeply influenced by Gnostic ideas and terminology would seem to be doubtful, although certainly they did use language which the Gnostics were later to adopt. The 'Gnostic Redeemer-myth' is, however, largely a scholar's reconstruction, and it has not been satisfactorily shown that such a myth existed in pre-Christian times.

Up to this point no direct attention has been paid to the material collected by Goodenough in his study of Jewish symbols,[1] partly because the work is not yet complete, and, moreover, time is necessary for the proper evaluation of this material and for the testing of the conclusions that may be drawn; and partly because of the question of chronology. Goodenough argues that the evidence which he has gathered from the funerary ornament of Jewish tombs and the architecture of Jewish synagogues, not to mention the other material, proves the existence of a hellenized Judaism alongside the rabbinic *after* A.D. 70, when according to the current view rabbinic Judaism had become finally dominant. In his opinion there was a period from A.D. 70 down to the fourth or fifth century when this type of Judaism was widespread, both in Palestine and in the Diaspora. His evidence shows considerable use of pagan motifs, but Goodenough himself emphasizes that in their own way these Jews were no less loyal to the Torah than were the rabbis. The importance of this material lies in the light it sheds upon a Judaism which has been almost completely erased from our documentary sources, but its value as evidence for the pre-Christian period is more doubtful. It may be that the influence of Hellenism upon the Jews in the pre-Christian period was even stronger than has hitherto been allowed, but the evidence adduced appears to belong almost entirely to the Christian era. On the other hand, and more important for present purposes, it raises the question of the possible contribution of a hellenized Judaism to the development of Gnostic theory even in the second century. Philo may, indeed, have had successors who were able to exert a more direct influence both upon the Gnostics and upon more orthodox Christian thought; but this is a question which awaits further investigation.

The earliest Gnostic, according to the Christian Fathers, was Simon Magus, *ex quo universae haereses substiterunt*[2]—the magician of the Acts of the Apostles.[3] Haenchen has tried to prove that Simon was already a Gnostic before he came into contact with Christianity,[4] and could this thesis be upheld it would finally settle the vexed question of a pre-Christian Gnosticism. Unfortunately the evidence is inadequate at the crucial point. If Cerfaux is correct,[5] the Simonian theory was a 'gnosis,' and pagan, before Simon's contact with the Christian message, but it was not specifically a Gnosticism—there is a point in the development of the system at which the 'gnostic' themes appear. So also Quispel is doubtful whether Simon himself was fully a Gnostic, although the Simonian system is certainly the earliest known form of the Gnostic heresy.[6]

The problem is complicated by the fact that there is some question as to the accuracy of the accounts of his system which have been handed down to us.[7] There was a tendency for the Gnostics to refer their doctrines back to the oldest possible source, while there was also a tendency for the Fathers to assign all the later doctrines to the founder of the sect. Cerfaux notes that the primary concern for Irenaeus is to combat the theories of the Valentinians, and that one line of attack was to demonstrate that these theories were simply the invention of the magician of Samaria.[8] It may be, therefore, that some elements of later systems have been wrongly ascribed to 'the father of all heresies.' Cerfaux in particular finds Valentinian and Basilidian elements in the 'Simonian' system,[9] but it might also be claimed that these were original to Simon's theory and taken over from him by the later groups. Again, in many points Simon's system seems to have been mainly pagan, although with a few Christian traits. A comparison of his theory with that of Cerinthus[10] suggests either that the Fathers have read back later developments into Simon's scheme, or that he represents a Jewish-pagan Gnosticism faintly tinged with Christianity, while Cerinthus is the first Christian Gnostic in the full sense. For present purposes it is not necessary to enter into detailed criticism of the sources. It must suffice to summarize the account of Irenaeus, the earliest extended account at our disposal. One thing is, however, certain: the *Megale Apophasis* quoted by Hippolytus has nothing to do with Simonianism proper.[11]

Simon's system is very much the sort of theory which might be expected from the description in Acts, a syncretistic scheme with a few Christian elements grafted on. This 'father of all heresies' was worshipped by many as God, and claimed to be Father, Son, and Holy Spirit, in terms which recall the description of Isis given by Apuleius.[12] His companion Helen, he declared, was the first conception of his mind, emanating from him as Athena from the head of Zeus;[13] through her in the beginning he began to create angels and archangels. Helen then, as Ennoia or Thought, descended to lower regions and generated angels and powers, by whom this world was made. To these powers he himself was unknown, so they detained Ennoia in the lower world, *quoniam nollent progenies alterius cuiusdam putari esse*. Under their control she was subjected to all manner of insult, even to being imprisoned in a human body and compelled to suffer a round of incarnations. Hence she is the Helen who was the cause of the Trojan War, and is referred to in the Gospel as the Lost Sheep.[14] In the end he himself descended to redeem her, and to re-order the world, on account of the misgovernment of the angels. In this descent he was transformed so as to appear as man among men; he was thought to have suffered in Judaea, but did not.[15] The prophets were inspired by the lesser angels, and were therefore no concern of those whose hope was set on him and on Ennoia. Men were saved by grace, not by works, for no man was evil by nature, but only by law, and law was a device of the angels who created the world to enslave those who should obey them.

It is clear from this brief survey that Simon's system is nothing more or less than an assimilation of imperfectly understood Christian doctrines to a fundamentally pagan scheme. Something is due to Stoicism,[16] something to the Orient, something to Christianity, but the Christian elements play a relatively small part. Several features of later Gnostic thought are already present (unless they have been read back into the theory), such as the conception of emanations, the idea that the world is the creation of inferior powers, and that there is in it an element of the divine imprisoned and awaiting deliverance.[17] These views are foreshadowed in earlier thought, and it seems that Simon is simply another charlatan after the manner of Alexander of Abonoteichus[18] and his kind. Such elements of Christianity as are present are largely superficial, and there is no sign of any true conception of the message of the Gospel. It is subordinated to flights of fancy, while the antinomian strain at once cuts Simon off from the essentially Christian line of thought as it is presented by Paul and the Church.

Although he appears in the Fathers as a heretic, Simon is rather a rival of Christianity,[19] and represents clearly an attempt to merge the message of the Church in a farrago of alien thought. Hippolytus in recording his death takes a malicious joy in relating the failure of his promised resurrection.[20] As Harvey puts it:[21] 'Through some mismanagement the juggler's race was run.' After his death the sect maintained itself, although it never reached the importance of some of the later sects.[22] The succession was carried on first by Menander, the pupil of Simon, and later by Saturninus.[23]

The Nicolaitans, according to our authorities, drew from the Gospel the extreme conclusions which Paul had striven to combat in his letters;[24] they taught, in Harvey's words,[25] 'the complete indifference of human affairs in a moral point of view,' and were prepared to allow conformity to mysteries and official rites in order to avoid persecution.[26] This attitude is, indeed, open to any Gnostic; the Christian is no longer under law, but grace, and hence the works of the law and the things of this life no longer matter to him.[27] His γνῶσις sets him free, and all religious rites can be transformed by him to the true worship—he knows that the pagan gods are nothing, and may attend their rites without incurring any danger to himself. That Paul was aware of the interpretation which might be put on some of his sayings is obvious from many of his letters,[28] but some of his successors evidently did not know, or chose to ignore, his stress on Christian conduct.

With Cerinthus[29] we come to teaching of a much more definitely Gnostic character. Certain Judaizing elements in his system are

H

akin to Ebionite views,[30] but we are concerned rather with the Gnostic traits, which are presented here in one of their simplest forms. A sharp cleavage is made between God and the world: 'the creation ... was not effected by God Himself, but by angels— powers distinct from God—one of whom was the God of the Jews and the giver of the law.'[31] This view reappears frequently in the Gnostic systems, and, indeed, is singled out by Irenaeus in his preface to his work *Adversus Haereses*:[32] καὶ πολλοὺς ἀνατρέπουσιν, ἀπάγοντες αὐτοὺς προφάσει γνώσεως ἀπὸ τοῦ τόδε τὸ πᾶν συστησαμένου καὶ κεκοσμηκότος, ὡς ὑψηλότερόν τι καὶ μεῖζον ἔχοντες ἐπιδεῖξαι τοῦ τὸν οὐρανὸν καὶ τὴν γῆν καὶ πάντα τὰ ἐν αὐτοῖς πεποιηκότος Θεοῦ.

Whatever the origin of this idea, it is certain that there was a growing tendency to remove the Supreme Being ever further from contact with matter, and to interpolate intermediaries between Him and the world.[33] So the later Stoics made room for an increasing transcendence of God, where their predecessors had thought only of the immanent Logos,[34] and Philo, following to a great extent in their footsteps, developed his scheme of the Logos and the divine powers.[35] Something may be due to Zoroastrian or other Oriental systems of thought, but just how much is extreme- ly doubtful; certainly whatever Oriental elements are present have been worked over in the light of Platonic and other doctrines.

A second feature of Cerinthus' system concerns his view of the person of Jesus, who is regarded as a purely natural man upon whom the Spirit of God descended at His baptism.[36] This fore- shadows the later Gnostic doctrine of the pre-existent Aeon[37] who was united to the human Jesus during His mission, but left Him before the Crucifixion, although there is, according to Bethune- Baker,[38] no evidence that Cerinthus used the term Aeon of the pre-existent Christ. The object of the mission was primarily the revelation of doctrine, as in the case of the descent of the 'Redeemer' in some of the Hellenistic and later systems such as those presented in the Hermetic documents.[39] A second object was the inauguration of the millennium, conceived in the most material terms, but at this stage such views were not regarded with any suspicion, since millennarianism was widely accepted in the Church.[40]

There is one further representative of the earlier forms of

Gnosticism who must be noticed, namely Saturninus or Saturnilus,[41] who lived about the reign of Hadrian.[42] In his system there is one God the Father, who created angels, archangels, virtues, and powers.[43] The world and all that therein is was created by seven angels, as was man, the latter being made in the likeness of a divine image which came down from above, but which was too spiritual for this lower system.[44] This created man was unable to stand upright until the higher power took pity on him, as being made in his likeness, and sent into him a spark of life; this spark at death returned to its own kin, while the other elements were dissolved. The Saviour was unbegotten,[45] incorporeal, and without form, but appeared to seeming as a man.[46]

The God of the Jews was one of the angels, and because the ruling powers desired to destroy the Father,[47] Christ came for their destruction and for the salvation of those who believed in Him, namely those who possessed the spark of life.[48] Two kinds of men had been created by the angels, and since the demons aided the wicked, Christ the Saviour came to destroy the wicked, men and demons, and to save the good.

Marriage and the begetting of children were of Satan, while most of Saturninus' followers abstained also from animal food.[49] Prophecy was in part due to the creator angels, in part to Satan, who though an angel stood in opposition to the creators, and especially to the God of the Jews.[50]

In this system there are clear links with the earlier thinkers, as, for example, in the conception of God as unknown and completely transcendent, in the creation of the world by the angels, and in the view of the God of the Old Testament.[51] There is also the Docetic Christology, and the view that prophecy was due to the inferior angels. Some points recall the writings of Philo, such as the account of the creation of earthly man, although this seems more closely connected in some respects with Stoic doctrine. The most striking novelty is the ascetic strain. Saturninus is the first of those whom we have considered to present an ascetic system, most of his predecessors apparently proclaiming an antinomian doctrine, although asceticism was always a possibility and appears even in the earliest stages.

These writers, or perhaps teachers would be more correct,

illustrate clearly the nature of Gnosticism in its earliest manifestations. There is one general line of thought to be discerned in all, namely, that the supreme God is far removed from this world, and had no contact with it, even in its creation. Some men at least have a closer relation to the divine than their fellows, but there is always the feeling that man is not at home in this world, although he is unable to escape unless with the aid of a redeemer or by power from above. Redemption comes through γνῶσις, which gives power over the hostile divinities, and, indeed, makes man himself divine.[52] In the case of Simon we have little more than a travesty of Christianity, but the others seem genuinely to have sought to present the Gospel in language suited to their age. The systems grow more and more complex with the passage of time, as new elements are assimilated, but except for Simon, whose thoughts were mainly of his own prestige and interests, the dominant problem for all, as for their successors, is soteriological.[53] All begin with the current Hellenistic cosmogony, more or less modified, and seek to explain the position of man in the world and to fit their belief in Jesus as Redeemer into their 'philosophical' theory.[54] In so doing they came near to losing the essential Christian message altogether, and some of them did lose all sight of the need for Christian life and conduct. This was due to their background, and to an insufficiently clear grasp of Christian principles.

Much of the Gnostic theology comes directly from systems of the Stoic type like that of Posidonius, but for the Logos which orders the material world, Gnosticism, with a stronger sense of the evil of the material, substitutes a fall of a spiritual being into matter, symbolized by the fall of Adam.[55] So far we have not actually encountered the Adam myth, but a similar thought lies behind the Simonian account of the detention of Ennoia by the angels. The idea of a divine element enclosed in matter was a commonplace of current theology. The Gnostics laid more stress than earlier thinkers on the evil of matter, which made it impossible for them to accept a real incarnation of Jesus.[56] Again, granted that Jesus was a divine being, the Passion was unthinkable—it was not the Cross of Christ but the secret knowledge which he came to impart that conveyed salvation.[57] The problem was generally solved by a denial either of the real humanity of Jesus or of his divinity: either he was a man like other men, inspired by God after testing by reason of his perfect righteousness, or he was only a phantom, a vehicle for the divine being in his sojourn upon earth. In either case the divine being could not possibly have suffered—the Christ left the human Jesus before the Passion, or some other man was said to have suffered in his stead.[58]

The creation of the world, again, was ascribed to angels or similar inferior beings, themselves either the creation of the supreme God, as in Plato and Philo and other writers, or emanations from him, growing less perfect the more they were removed from their ultimate source.[59] Man was himself a creation of these lower powers, but his soul was either a divine spark or breath implanted in the mortal flesh by the supreme God, or a fragment of the divine, a divine being, imprisoned out of envy by the hostile powers. Here the biblical conception of the whole man as the creation of God has given way to the Greek dichotomy of immortal soul and mortal flesh. If astrology played a part in the scheme, the powers were located in the seven planets, and ruled over the seven spheres which separated the soul from its heavenly home. We have so far met with no specifically astrological trends of thought—there is nothing of the planets or of fate in the systems which we have reviewed—but Hellenistic thought was strongly influenced by astrology, and we need not go far to find features which seem to point to the influence of astrology on the early Gnostics.[60] Thus in Simon's scheme we find six roots and an unlimited Power, and in that of Saturninus seven creator angels. Even if these were not originally associated with the seven planets, the doctrines could readily be interpreted in astrological terms. Such features appear in the later systems also, but the astrological influence is there more pronounced.

In his earthly existence man is subject to the lesser powers. The view was advanced as early as Plato that the laws of a state were expedients of those in power to secure their position,[61] and in Gnosticism this theory reappears, with a transference of the initiative from earthly rulers to the cosmic powers.[62] Obedience merely extends their sway, and he who is endowed with γνῶσις is above law, free from their power and from the need to obey their commands—in fact, disobedience helps to break their power.[63] In contrast to this antinomian view, which may arise in part from anti-Semitism, since the law was given by the God of the Jews, now one of the lesser powers, Saturninus taught that marriage and the begetting of children were a device of the angels to increase the number of their subjects. Celibacy defeated their ends by reducing the number of mankind, and, indeed, it seems that some regarded any kind of indulgence as tending to increase the authority of the rulers of this world.[64] Moreover, very diverse conclusions were reached from the premise that the Gnostic was free from Fate and mortality. Some held that this made ethics irrelevant for them, and freedom for them degenerated into licence, while others held that it was necessary to preserve the soul from contact with matter in any form, and consequently turned to ascetic practices.

From this survey it is clear that Gnosticism is not simply a depraved form of Christianity; its roots go back into the Hellenistic world, and it seeks seriously to introduce the pagan system of thought into the fabric of Christianity, perhaps already into that of Judaism,[65] and to unite the Christian Gospel of redemption with the pagan idea of salvation as peace and security in this world, and a blessed immortality hereafter free from the power of the stars. The concept of a redeemer sent from heaven, which appears later in most Gnostic systems, is held by Bevan and others to be a derivation from Christianity,[66] although some contribution may have been made by Jewish Messianic speculation—but not through Philo—or through some development of the ideas of the mystery cults. A further possibility is that the Hellenistic σωτήρ-concept involved some idea of redemption from the power of Fate, as well as from more material ills such as war and famine. The New Testament writers would then have used Hellenistic terms to express the meaning and significance of the life and ministry of Jesus, and this in its turn would influence later thought. It does, however, seem that Christianity transformed whatever idea of saviours it may have found; there is nothing in pre-Christian times to justify the view that Christianity here was simply borrowing from the Gentile world. The nature and the manner of the redemption are both different from anything in the mystery cults, while the very frequency with which the title σωτήρ was bestowed in the Hellenistic age seems to show that it had no real religious significance.[67] The language of the mysteries was almost the only medium available to express to the Gentile world the meaning of the historical figure of Jesus, but the Christians in using that language set their own stamp upon it. Once the doctrine had been formulated, however vaguely, there would be a natural tendency to assimilate it in other cults, and in any case the Gnostics seem simply to have tried to conflate the Christian doctrine with the current pagan cosmogony and theology.

The idea of $\gamma\nu\hat{\omega}\sigma\iota\varsigma$,[68] again, did not first arise with the Gnostics. The word had a long history in the Greek language, but in this period it had been transformed from its original meaning. 'The knowledge about which the Gnostic is concerned is, in contrast to Greek ideas, torn out of its relation to all other cognition; and this corresponds to the limitation of the use of $\dot{\alpha}\lambda\dot{\eta}\theta\epsilon\iota\alpha$ and $o\dot{\upsilon}\sigma\dot{\iota}\alpha$ to the divine reality and the divine essence.'[69] $\Gamma\nu\hat{\omega}\sigma\iota\varsigma$ is now distinct from rational thought, a $\chi\dot{\alpha}\rho\iota\sigma\mu\alpha$ which transforms the possessor from man to god, makes him divine.[70] In this transformation the mysteries and magic played their part. Instead of being applicable to knowledge in general, the word comes to mean a particular kind of knowledge, open only to a few, and consisting in some esoteric doctrine which was carefully kept from the eyes of the uninitiated. It might be a mystic vision which conveyed it, and here there was a possibility of a real religious experience; or again, $\gamma\nu\hat{\omega}\sigma\iota\varsigma$ might be a philosophical or scientific knowledge of the secrets of the universe, and of man's place in it; the soul that once truly understood the mystery was naturally led to seek its way to its true home, to strive to rise beyond the limits of this world to the realm beyond the spheres.[71] And finally, it might be nothing more than a crude magical affair of the names and spells which would open the doors to the soul in its ascent. In the papyri adduced by Moulton and Milligan,[72] $\gamma\nu\hat{\omega}\sigma\iota\varsigma$ is more often used in its non-technical sense, but the technical use also appears. Dibelius[73] finds it in Philippians 3. 8, and quotes the Hermetic prayer from the Mimaut Papyrus,[74] but Deissmann thinks the New Testament reference applies rather to 'personal and pneumatic acquaintance with Christ,' and illustrates this meaning from a Byzantine decree of the first century A.D.[75] Dieterich's conclusion,[76] based on the use of $\gamma\nu\hat{\omega}\sigma\iota\varsigma$ in magic papyri, that 'the Knowledge which also plays so large a part in Christian teaching is specially due to Greek influence' is rejected by Norden.[77] The most that can be said is that there was a technical use derived from the mystery cults and from magic, but there is no ground for assuming that every use of the word, Christian or otherwise, implies this technical sense. More recently Dupont has underlined the thoroughly Jewish and Old Testament background of this and similar words in Paul.[78]

The same conclusions may be reached from a study of other keywords in the thought of the New Testament writers, such as πνεῦμα, χρίσμα, σοφία, πνευματικός, and τέλειος.[79] There are uses of these words in the magic papyri and in the pagan cults, as well as in Gnosticism and the Hermetic documents, which are similar to the Christian use, but before we can claim that the Christian authors borrowed their ideas from their environment we must have surer grounds of proof. As it was with Philo, so it is with them: they used the language of their neighbours, and translated their message into its terms, but their message itself did not owe its origin to that environment.[80] The contact with paganism made it necessary for the Christian missionaries to work out their message in new terms, to develop in fact a true and Christian Gnosis over against the 'gnosis falsely so called.' Their work has stood the test of time, but there were others who attempted a reinterpretation, less successfully and without retaining their grasp of certain fundamental elements. These have now fallen into obscurity, but their example warns us of the dangers that beset the path.

NOTES TO CHAPTER IV

[1] *Jewish Symbols in the Greco-Roman Period* (New York 1953–).

[2] Iren. *adv. Haer.* 1. 16. 2 (Harvey); see also Harvey lxv, Bethune-Baker 79, Casey in *Beginnings* 5. 151ff., and for the title Nock ibid. 164ff., and Cumont-Bidez, *Les Mages Hellénisés*. Legge 1. 176ff. claims Simon as a pre-Christian Gnostic, but he *has* some Christian traits, although these may have been added after his contact with the Church. For a critical study of the sources see Cerfaux, La Gnose Simonienne, *RSR* 15 (1925) 489ff., 16 (1926) 5ff., 265ff., 481ff. (= *Recueil Cerfaux* 1. 191ff.). See also Quispel, *Gnosis als Weltreligion* 45ff., Jonas 1. 353ff., Wolfson, *Philosophy of the Church Fathers* 1. 512ff., Goppelt 132ff.

[3] Acts 8. 9ff.

[4] *ZTK* 1952, 316ff. Cf. *Vig. Chr.* xi (1957) 107f.

⁵ *Recueil Cerfaux* I. 256: 'Dans son fond, la religion de Simon n'avait pas été, à ses débuts, du "gnosticisme." C'était une gnose à base de mythes païens et de magie. Un jour arriva cependant où . . . la doctrine s'incorpora un nouvel élément. Les themes *gnostiques* apparurent.'

⁶ *Gnosis* 52; cf. Schoeps *Urgemeinde* 36.

⁷ See the works of Cerfaux and Haenchen referred to above. On the other hand Sagnard (*La gnose valentinienne et le témoignage de saint Irénée*) seems to have established the essential reliability of Irenaeus in regard to Valentinianism, and Schmidt in a study of the *Apocryphon Johannis* (*Philotesia. Paul Kleinert . . . dargebracht*, Berlin 1907, 315ff.) identified this document as the source of Irenaeus' description of the Barbelognostics (see Sagnard 439ff., and for the text Till, *Die gnostischen Schriften des Koptischen Papyrus Berolinensis* 8502, Berlin 1955, 78ff.). The Apocryphon and Irenaeus clearly present the same system, although there are certain differences (cf. also *JTS NS* vii (1956) 248ff.).

⁸ *Recueil Cerfaux* I. 257; cf. Jonas I. 351f.

⁹ ibid. 206 (Basilides), 209 n. 1 (Valentinus); cf. also ibid. 256.

¹⁰ For Cerinthus see below, p. 101f.

¹¹ Cerfaux I. 221ff., Haenchen loc. cit.

¹² Iren. I. 16. 1; cf. Apul. xi. 5 (Reitzenstein *HMR* 240). According to Cerfaux (199, 203, 255) this formula first appears in Irenaeus, and represents an addition to the earlier *Syntagma* of Justin.

¹³ For the following account see Iren. I. 16. 2. See also Casey loc. cit. for the accounts given by other patristic writers. Cerfaux (I. 191ff.) seeks to reconstruct the lost *Syntagma* of Justin by comparison of the later sources. In Harvey's edition of Irenaeus the gaps in the Greek text are supplied from Hippolytus, who gives a fuller account, although its accuracy is doubtful. Here Simon's scheme contains a succession of worlds, in the first of which Ennoia or Thought ('Επίνοια Hippol.) is one of three pairs of roots emanating from the Boundless Power. The lower worlds also contain three pairs of roots emanating from a single source, but Thought is now singled out as springing from the mind of the Father, and the other roots, as Heaven and Earth, Sun and Moon, Air and Water, become the patterns of the created world, and also, apparently, the creator angels (see Legge loc. cit.). Against this, however, is the fact that νοῦς and ἐπίνοια are said by Hippolytus to have been equated with οὐρανός and γῆ. Simon's attempt to combine heterogeneous systems has led him into inconsistency, unless the fault be that of Hippolytus or his source. The solution seems to be that the Ennoia of the second world descends into a lower world created by the powers of the third, who are inferior copies of their patterns in the worlds above. Even this, however, does not solve all the problems, since on this account Simon is trying to combine several different schemes with the cosmogony of Genesis. The account in Irenaeus is shorter, and clear enough. For Hippolytus' version see *Phil.* vi, and for suggestion as to Simon's sources Legge, loc. cit., esp. 197. Reitzenstein (*Poimandres* 233f.)

finds traces of Egyptian influence in Simon's system. So also Cerfaux I. 268f., but see Sagnard 613 n. 1 (*Recueil Cerfaux* I. 263ff. = *Irenikon* 17 (1940) 3ff.).

[14] This is partly an allegorization and rationalization of Greek mythology, partly an attempt to assimilate every possible form of thought which has any relation, however obscure, to his system. See also Hippol. *Phil.* vi. 19 (Wendland), and for Simon's allegorizations of Scripture ibid. vi. 14. Cf. the Valentinian use of the parable of the Lost Sheep, Iren. I. 1. 17. According to Cerfaux (I. 227) Simon's allegories rest entirely on pagan mythology, the figure of Helen is derived from a lunar myth (233 ff.) and the Lost Sheep is derived not from the Gospel but from paganism (240ff.). The emanation of Helen as Ennoia, again, is the result of Gnostic influence (254). Wolfson, however (*Philosophy of Ch. Fathers* I. 514), suggests that Simon's original teaching included a third supramundane being called 'the Son' or 'Second Thought,' with which may be compared *Apoc. Joh.* 28. 9 (Till 96; see also Till's note, 297ff., Baynes *A Coptic Gnostic Treatise* 8f.). As both Baynes and Wolfson note, such a triad appears in other systems, e.g. among the Naassenes and Ophites.

[15] Here we have the beginnings of Docetism, although for Simon it seems more a matter of explaining his own presence than due to any theological grounds. For the descent of the redeemer see Knox *PCG* 220ff.

[16] For the Stoic elements see Casey 160.

[17] Thus Hippolytus declares that Valentinus drew the elements of his theory from that of Simon, although he used a different terminology (*Phil.* vi. 20). Quispel (*Gnosis* 51) notes that according to Irenaeus Valentinus was dependent on the 'gnostics,' who in turn were dependent on Simon. Cerfaux, on the other hand (I. 270) claims that the Ophites and Sethians reflect Valentinian influences, but cf. Sagnard 446 n. 1 (against Casey in *JTS* xxxvi (1935) 50). As Quispel observes, the link is provided by the *Apocryphon Johannis*, which has been identified as belonging to the 'gnostics' (see above, p. 109 note 7; also p. 149ff. below).

[18] Cf. Knox *PCJ* 305 n. 20; Nock *Conversion* 93ff.; Cerfaux I. 230ff. Haenchen, however (loc. cit.) argues that Simon was not promoted by his sect from magician to redeemer, but degraded in Christian tradition from redeemer to mere magician.

[19] Casey 163. For fuller details concerning Simon see *ERE* xi. 514ff., where the various problems and theories are discussed. See also Meyer, *Ursprung und Anfänge* 3. 277ff. Quispel (*The Jung Codex* 66) thinks it probable that Simon and Menander were developing further an already existing Jewish heresy. The contribution of magic was certainly strong, as Cerfaux and Quispel have shown.

[20] *Phil.* vi. 20; see Harvey 195 note 1, Casey 163. The story of Simon's visit to Rome may be pure legend (see Casey 154ff.), although it appears already in Justin Martyr (1 Apol. 26).

[21] loc. cit.

[22] Casey 163. Origen (*c. Cels.* I. 57) says there were no more than thirty Simonians in the world; but cf. Cerfaux I. 234, where it is suggested that this was the number of members in each group.

[23] For Menander see Iren. I. 17, Harvey lxix. For Saturninus, Iren. I. 18, Harvey lxxxviii, Bethune-Baker 81, and infra, p. 103.

[24] Iren. I. 23, Harvey lxix, Bethune-Baker 79. The Nicolaitans constitute something of a problem, since the patristic accounts seem ultimately dependent on Rev. 2. 6ff., with some legendary accretions, and the passage in Revelation may be metaphorical—someone was leading the Church astray, after the manner of Balaam (Nicolaus may be an attempt to render Balaam into Greek). At any rate there were certain Gnosticizing tendencies evident in Asia Minor at this date, whether we have here a real sect or not. See *HDB* iii. 547, *ERE* ix. 363ff., and the commentaries on Revelation ad loc. Also Strachan in *EGT* on 2 Peter, p. 118f.

[25] op. cit. lxx.

[26] The view which would admit of participation in pagan worship is expressly excluded by Paul (I Cor. 10. 14ff.), and also contravenes the decree of the Apostolic Council (Acts 15); but it was natural to a Gnostic, and its occurrence in Corinth and in Asia Minor is significant in view of later developments. See further Frend in *JEH* v. (1954) 25ff.

[27] Cf. Simon Magus, etc. Such an attitude might be suggested by words like those of Rom. 8. 1, but Paul is careful to stress even there the implications of the Gospel. A Gentile with only a Gentile background would find it quite natural. But some Jews apparently rejected the Torah as irrelevant for them, on the ground that they were above the material world [Knox *PCG* 48 n. 1, on Philo *Mig. Ab.* 16 (89f.)].

[28] Cf. Rom. 3. 1ff., 6. 1ff., 15ff., 8. 1ff., 11. 20ff. Cf. also the Corinthian epistles, and Galatians 5 and 6 for the implications of the Gospel.

[29] Iren. I. 21, Harvey lxxi, Bethune-Baker 65, Hippol. *Phil.* vii. 33, *ERE* iii. 318ff. Cf. Lightfoot, *Colossians* 107ff., Wolfson *The Philosophy of the Church Fathers* I. 504ff.

[30] Bethune-Baker 65. For the Ebionites, see ibid. 63ff., Iren. I. 22, Harvey lxxiii. Schoeps (*Urgemeinde* 30ff.) considers the Ebionites *anti-*Gnostic. Cf. also Goppelt 164ff.

[31] Bethune-Baker 66. To be exact, Irenaeus and Hippolytus mention only *a* power as creator; neither has anything to say of the God of the Jews here.

[32] Harvey's edition, p. 2.

[33] With this is connected the Hellenistic view of the universe as a system of spheres (see above, pp. 46, 69 and add to the references there Bevan, *Hellenism and Christianity* 99ff.). Thus in Simon s system the Supreme Being or Boundless Power dwells in the highest world, and the angels might be considered as each ruling one of the planetary spheres, through which the soul had to pass on its descent to the lower world, and similarly in the other systems.

[34] See above, p. 36ff.

[35] See above, chapter II. The Jewish scruple against the use of the Tetragrammaton, combined with the Hellenistic view that the supreme God should remain unknown, would lead naturally to the Philonic and Gnostic teaching. See above, p. 32, and Lake in *Beginnings* 5. 240ff. There may be little evidence that the Gnostics used the phrase ἄγνωστος θεός, but it is clear enough from Irenaeus and others that they regarded the supreme God as unknown, whatever the words they used to express the view. Cf. the passages adduced by Norden 71ff. Quispel (*The Jung Codex* 68ff.) lays great stress on Jewish speculations about the Name of God, which were taken over into Gnosticism. See also Goodenough *Symbols* 2. 161ff., 241, 293ff. (and his index, 2. 318, s.v. Iao).

[36] Iren. 1. 21, Harvey lxii, Bethune-Baker 66. Cerinthus, however, departs from the usual Gnostic view in allowing that the human body of Jesus was raised again. This may be a relic of a more orthodox statement of his views, or perhaps simply an inconsistency (see Harvey 211 note 1).

[37] On the Aeon see Legge 2. 97ff., Bethune-Baker 79, 89ff. The latter holds that the term is not used in the Gnostic sense of 'emanation' before Valentinus. On the history of the word in religious usage see Reitzenstein *Poim.* 274ff.

[38] op. cit. 66 note 1.

[39] ibid. 66. For revelation by the redeemer cf. *Poimandres*, and for the descent of the redeemer Knox *PCG* 220ff.

[40] Cf. Bethune-Baker 66, and his note on Chiliasm, 68ff.; also Harvey lxxii.

[41] Iren. 1. 18, Harvey lxxxviii, Bethune-Baker 81. The name is variously spelt in our authorities. Harvey again supplies the lacunae in the text of Irenaeus from Hippol. *Phil.* vii. 28.

[42] Bethune-Baker loc. cit.

[43] The Latin version of Irenaeus gives *Virtutes*, *Potestates*, while Hippolytus reads δυνάμεις ἐξουσίας. The account of the creation is based on that of Simon, which in turn may go back directly or indirectly to Persian mythology. See Harvey lxxxviii, 196 note 4.

[44] Cf. the theory of Basilides (Harvey lxxxix, xcix, and below, p. 125). Cf. also the theory of Philo, *Op. M.* 69ff., for the use of Gen. 1. 26 (on the early history of the exegesis of this text cf. *Studia Patristica* 1. 420ff.), and see Harvey's notes, loc. cit. The divine spark seems more akin to Philo's description in *Op. M.* 134ff., or to the Stoic doctrine, the latter especially (see Knox *PCG* 1ff.). Saturninus avoids the inconsistency of Philo's account, where the Heavenly Man is apparently created by lesser beings, the earthly by God Himself (but cf. p. 56 note 129 above). Philo has to fall back on the analogies of sculpture and the magnet (*Op. M.* 141) to account for human depravity, just as the Gnostics explained evil by assuming a series of emanations each inferior to its predecessor. For the creation of man in Simon's system see Hippol. *Phil.* vi. 14.

45 The Latin version here reads *Salvatorem* (cf. Theodoret H. Fab. I. 3), while the text of Hippolytus gives Πάτερα. The former seems the correct reading, although the origin of the error is clear enough. There seems to be no valid reason for regarding ἀγέννητος as 'nicht vom Weibe geboren' (Neander, and with some hesitation Harvey), since the 'Gnostic' sense may be paralleled from Philo, although admittedly it refers there to God Himself. Cf. also Lightfoot *Ignatius* ii. 1. 90ff. The word is of frequent occurrence in the Coptic Gnostic literature (cf. the indexes of Baynes and Till s.v.).

46 Again the Docetic view, as in Simon. Cf. Philippians 2. 5ff., and note verse 8, which excludes any Docetic interpretation of the passage: καὶ σχήματι εὑρεθεὶς ὡς ἄνθρωπος ἐταπείνωσεν ἑαυτόν, γενόμενος ὑπήκοος μέχρι θανάτου, θανάτου δὲ σταυροῦ.

47 Et propter hoc quod dissolvere voluerint patrem eius omnes principes Iren. (Latin: Harvey 197); διὰ τὸ βούλεσθαι τὸν πάτερα καταλῦσαι πάντας τοὺς ἄρχοντας Hippol. vii. 28. 5; τὸν πάτερα φησὶ τοῦ χριστοῦ καταλῦσαι βουλόμενον μετὰ τῶν ἄλλων ἀγγέλων καὶ τὸν τῶν Ἰουδαίων θεόν Theod. (ap. Hippol. ed. Wendland 209). If the Latin be correct we are reminded of the revolt of Satan (cf. the Titans). Some such revolt would seem necessary to account for the otherwise arbitrary wish related in the Greek versions. On the other hand the Latin is one of two possible renderings of the Greek of Hippol. (Theodoret gives the other) which may therefore be original.

48 In the Stoic view all men possessed a spark of the divine fire, but only some were released from the general absorption into the universal fire at the ἐκπύρωσις. Here it is the possession of the spark which marks some men off from the rest, although above it seems that all men are so endowed. Saturninus has overlooked the inconsistency of his Stoic cosmogony with his Gnostic scheme of redemption—or perhaps he has been misunderstood by Irenaeus. Knox (*PCG* 224) suspects a similar inconsistency in Posidonius, who might then be Saturninus' source here. Cf. ibid. 75, 117.

49 Cf. Harvey xc. Irenaeus refers to Saturninus and Marcion the origin of the Encratite sect (1. 26).

50 See Harvey loc. cit. Cf. the Epistle of Ptolemy to Flora (ed. Quispel, Paris 1949).

51 Saturninus, in contrast to most other Gnostics, presents a comparatively favourable view of the God of the Old Testament. The account in Hippolytus (τον ... θεόν MS for τῷ ... θεῷ Iren. Epiph. Theod.) seems to equate him with Satan, which is nearer to the usual Gnostic judgement. In general, Saturninus represents the normal early Gnostic scheme, with a few variations of his own.

52 Bultmann in Kittel *TWB* I. 695; cf. Kennedy *PMR* 163.

53 Cf. Bultmann 694: 'Der Inhalt der Lehre ist Kosmologie und Anthropologie, aber ganz unter dem Gesichtspunkt der Soteriologie.'

54 Cf. Bethune-Baker 76; Mackintosh, *The Person of Jesus Christ* 134: 'At the root of all Gnostic systems ... lay the idea of redemption, and the conviction that it was to be won by a rare kind of knowledge. In a way, Christ was made the centre of all.' But there were also other features which made Gnosticism really unchristian.

[55] See above, p. 45, and cf. Bréhier 122ff. Whatever its form this view represents the Platonic doctrine of the evil of matter, assimilated to some myth of the Fall. The assimilation may go back to Posidonius, or earlier, but appears most strongly in Gnosticism. Origen (ap. Hatch 234ff.) speaks of a lapse, but not into matter. See generally Hatch 171ff. for Greek and Christian speculation concerning God, the world, matter; see also Knox PCG 83ff. for the myth of the Fall.

[56] The Gnostic view here is dominated by the Hellenistic dualism, which regarded the body as evil. For Paul, the body, the flesh, is not necessarily sinful or evil, hence it is possible for him to hold both that Christ possessed a real human body and that he was sinless. 'To him belonged the σάρξ; but not a σάρξ ἁμαρτίας (Rom. 8. 3).' See Stevens, *Theology of the New Testament* 340, and cf. Kirk 88ff.

[57] Cf. the system of Cerinthus, supra, p. 101f. Others held that the redemption in Christ was only a preliminary step, to be completed by Gnosis (Knox PCG 158).

[58] On the Gnostic Christology see Mackintosh 134ff. Cf. also Legge 2. 14ff.

[59] Cf. Hatch 200ff., 227ff. Of those whom we have examined, Simon and Saturninus postulate several inferior beings as creators, Cerinthus only one. The whole point is that the divine cannot have contact with matter; the creators are a stage or more below the divine properly so called. *Seven* angels seem to be mentioned first in the system of Saturninus, but Simon had six roots and a Boundless Power in his (according to Hippol. *Phil.* vi. 12).

[60] See above, esp. p. 46. Astrological traits in Simon's system figure more prominently in the account given by Hippolytus than in that of Irenaeus, but his alleged descent seems in any case to indicate an astrological view. The probability of astrological features is increased by the fact of the accommodation of Judaism to astrology (see above, p. 10, and Kirk 16 note 1). As already noted, Cerfaux finds a lunar cult among Simon's sources. Canon Knox has referred me to Bidez-Cumont, *Les Mages Hellénisés* ii. 283. See also Knox PCG 46ff.

[61] Cf. Rep. I, 338D ff.

[62] It is not implied that there is any connexion between the Gnostic and the Platonic views. Such a connexion is indeed possible, and might be of some importance, but there seems to be no evidence to prove its existence. Cf. Cicero *de Natura Deorum* i. 42. 118 (Geffcken *Apologeten* 161).

[63] To Paul on the other hand the law—the Jewish law, which is probably in the minds of some at least of the Gnostics—is holy and righteous and good, in fact πνευματικός (Rom. 7. 14), despite his depreciation of it over

against faith. See Dodd *BG* 25ff., Gillet *Communion in the Messiah* 60f., for the difference in the Greek and Jewish/Christian concepts of law.

[64] Cf. the Orphic view (Legge I. 128f.).

[65] Thus Friedländer (*Der vorchristliche jüdische Gnosticismus*, Göttingen 1898) argues for the existence in the Diaspora of two parties, a conservative and a radical, with several gradations between them of accommodation to the contemporary environment, and claims that these Jewish groups lie behind the later Christian Gnosticism. See, however, Schürer's review in *TLZ* 1899, 167f.

[66] *Hellenism and Christianity* 89ff., esp. 106; cf. Quispel in *The Jung Codex* 76ff. See below, p. 218ff.

[67] Cf. Knox *PCG* 11, Wendland *HRK* 123ff., 142ff., and his article in *ZNTW* 1904, 335ff., Knox *HE* 37ff. On the relation between Christianity and the Mysteries cf. Metzger in *HTR* 48 (1955) 1ff.

[68] Cf. above, p. 88 note 44. See also Wolfson, *Philosophy of the Church Fathers* 1. 498ff., and Davies in *HTR* 46 (1953) 113ff.

[69] Bultmann *TWB* i. 693 (the translation in the English version by Coates, *Bible Key Words: Gnosis* 8, is slightly different); see also Norden *Agnostos Theos* 87ff.

[70] Bultmann 695; cf. Kennedy *PMR* 163.

[71] The first of these is a wisdom gained through initiation into the mystery religions, the second that of the religious philosophy represented by the Hermetica, in which the only initiation recognized is 'a purely spiritual initiation into the truth about God, man, and the world, revealed to prophets and seers' (Dodd *BG* 245).

[72] *Vocabulary of the Greek New Testament* s.v., from which the following notes are derived. On the use of the word in Biblical literature cf. Norden 63f., and on Luke 11. 52 Kirk 153 note 1. In view of the frequency with which the idea of knowledge of God recurs in the Bible, Kirk's suggestion of 'a large concession to incipient Gnosticism' seems unjustified, although the Lucan version of the saying readily admits a Gnostic interpretation. See Norden 64 note 1, and the Matthean parallel, Matt. 23. 18.

[73] *HNT* ad loc.

[74] Cf. Reitzenstein *HMR* 285f.

[75] *Light from the Ancient East* 383 note 8 (new edition 378 note 6); cf. Kennedy *PMR* 170.

[76] *Abraxas* 134 note 1.

[77] *Agnostos Theos* 96 note 1.

[78] *Gnosis: La connaissance religieuse dans les épitres de Saint Paul*, Louvain 1949.

[79] See Moulton and Milligan, and references there s.vv., and for πνεῦμα and τέλειος Kennedy *PMR* ch. iv.

[80] Cf. Kennedy's criticisms of attempts to derive Philo's mysticism from Hellenistic thought, *PCR* 218ff., and see above, p. 16.

CHAPTER V

LATER GNOSTICISM AND THE CHRISTIAN PHILOSOPHERS

ENOUGH has been said in previous chapters to indicate that Gnosticism is not simply a second-century aberration from orthodox Christianity. It is rather a development of the syncretism characteristic of the Hellenistic world, and even in the first century various trends of thought were already moving in a Gnostic direction. Both Paul and Philo are influenced by their environment in their presentation of the message which each had to convey, and similar phenomena appear also in circles where no influence from either, or from the groups which they represent, can be postulated. The syncretistic religious thought of the period was full of such ideas and concepts, which Jews and Christians appropriated for the purposes of their own mission. Again, both Paul and Philo on occasion join issue with others who strayed from the true path, as each saw it, and both seek to safeguard the truth for which they stand. The contemporary systems of thought had affected both Judaism and Christianity to some degree, and were in their turn affected, but some thinkers tended to yield too easily to 'the wisdom of men,' and these are resolutely resisted.

There is, however, some truth in the statement of Hegesippus[1] that heresy did not venture to raise its head in the lifetime of the earliest disciples, in the sense that the Gnostic sects only come to full flower in the second century, and that in earlier years speculations of this type remain more or less obscure. The loss of most of the early Gnostic literature adds to the difficulty, since we are left without much evidence for pre-Christian phenomena of the same sort, and it seems almost as if the Patristic writers have entered into a conspiracy of silence on the subject.[2] For present purposes, however, it is sufficient to observe that in addition to the Christian elements Gnosticism contains both non-Christian and pre-Christian elements. The controversy is but a stage in the process of reinterpreting the Christian Gospel to meet the needs of the contemporary world, and in that process elements from various sources were blended, some of them dating back beyond Christianity itself.

Our immediate task in this chapter is to complete our survey of the main schools of Gnosticism, and to examine the form which Christianity has taken in the works of the Alexandrian Fathers who follow almost directly in the wake of the controversy. There is in Alexandria a tradition of scholarship which reaches back to Ptolemaic times, although we are concerned rather with the tradition which runs from the Jewish schools represented by the Wisdom of Solomon and by Philo to Clement of Alexandria and Origen.[3] Moreover, we are concerned with this tradition primarily in relation to the growth and development of Gnosticism, so that there is no need for a detailed study of the views of the writers mentioned.

The first body of doctrine to engage our attention is that of the Ophites. This name is used in two distinct senses, first for the Ophites proper, with whom the Naassenes may be connected,[4] and secondly, as a general term for a whole group of sects with certain common features.[5] In the latter case it serves to distinguish the numerous 'anonymous' sects from those such as Valentinianism which are named after their founder. The name is derived from the place which is given in these sects to the serpent,[6] but the role which the serpent plays varies in the different doctrines, and is sometimes purely incidental.

The general character of the Ophite system properly so called may be seen from the description in Irenaeus.[7] Their supreme Being is called Anthropos, and also Light, and has his abode in Bythos;[8] his Thought they call the Son of Man, and Second Man.[9] Along with these there exists the Holy Spirit, a female principle,[10] and below them four elements. Illuminated by the First and Second Man, the Spirit produces another male principle, Christ, who with her is caught up into the incorruptible Aeon, the true Church. The overflow of the light communicated to her falls down as dew, and penetrating into the waters assumes from them a body.[11] This dew, the hermaphrodite Sophia or Prunicus, being in danger of submersion, struggles to rise, and from her body forms the heaven. Finally, leaving the body behind, she returns to her mother, but

I

meanwhile she gives birth to a son, Ialdabaoth.[12] By virtue of his origin he also possesses a yearning for incorruptibility. He becomes the first of a group of seven angelic powers, each of whom creates a heaven over which he rules, the mother forming the Ogdoad.[13] The other six powers rebel against Ialdabaoth, who in despair begets another son, Nous, in serpent form. Exulting in his power, he believes himself to be the supreme Being, but his mother reveals to him the existence of the true God, and in order to distract the attention of the other powers in the prevailing confusion he unites with them in creating man.[14]

This man is at first inert and lifeless, but Ialdabaoth breathes into him the breath of life, thereby losing his own power and inspiring man with the redeeming powers of Nous and Enthymesis;[15] passing over his creators, man gives thanks to the First Man. Ialdabaoth seeks to deprive man of his power by creating woman,[16] but his mother induces Adam and Eve to disobey his commands,[17] and he expels them from Paradise. The course of Biblical history is presented as a struggle between Ialdabaoth and Sophia, in which the former's efforts to consolidate his power and hinder the redemption of man are continually thwarted by his mother, who through the prophets keeps alive in man the memory of the primal light.[18] Finally her mother, the First Woman, takes pity on her, and obtains from the First Man the sending of Christ. He descends through the seven heavens, assimilated to their sons, and gathers together all the dew of light. United with Sophia, he enters into Jesus, who had been prepared beforehand as a fitting vessel. The powers crucify Jesus, but Christ and Sophia ascend into the incorruptible Aeon, whence Christ sends to Jesus the power of resurrection.[19] Raised in a spiritual body, Jesus for eighteen months[20] teaches to such of his disciples as could receive them the mysteries of γνῶσις; then he is exalted to heaven, where Christ sits at the right hand of Ialdabaoth,[21] drawing to himself those who have known him as Jesus Christ, that is, those who possess the spiritual nature. He thereby deprives the unconscious Ialdabaoth of his power, in proportion as he himself is enriched, so that Ialdabaoth is no longer able to send souls into the world, save only the psychic.[22] The consummation is effected when all the dew of light is gathered together and restored to the incorruptible Aeon.

Such is the Ophite system described by Irenaeus. The other sects classed under this head seem to have held the same general theory, although with some variation in details. The chief characteristics of this group of sects may be summarized as follows:[23] (i) the highest being is generally designated by the name Anthropos, the First Man. (ii) Prominence is given to a female principle (Μήτηρ), who is conceived as presiding over the work of redemption. (iii) In almost all the systems a triad stands at the beginning of the cosmic process.[24] (iv) The systems are mythological rather than philosophical, and the mythology is based largely on astral conceptions. (v) A notable feature is the anti-Jewish bias, which leads to the identification of the God of the Old Testament with the chief of the angelic powers who hold man in bondage,[25] and to reverence for the serpent and for characters condemned in Biblical history. (vi) These systems are less impregnated with Christian ideas than the classical Gnostic schools. In some the Redeemer is absent, in others he is a purely mythological being, while in others again the Christian elements 'seem to be little more than an embroidery on a pagan groundwork.'[26] In one case (the *Naassenerpredigt*) a purely pagan document has been detached from the Christian commentary with which it is interwoven, but it is significant that Old Testament elements remain firmly embedded in the text.[27]

To endeavour to discover the relations of this group of sects to each other would involve an examination of critical questions and difficulties which are beyond the scope of the present study. Their relation to Valentinianism and other systems will be noted in due course,[28] but there are certain points which call for attention here. The first is that the Ophites would seem to have anticipated Valentinus in calling their supreme Being Bythos.[29] This Bythos is, however, remote and transcendent, unknowable and inaccessible, and to all intents and purposes the supreme Being is the First Man. Bythos is only mentioned in passing in the account of Irenaeus, and it is perhaps rash to assume that he has any place at all, especially since he does not seem to figure in the account of the Naassenes and other sects elsewhere.

Secondly, there is the variation in the view taken of the serpent. Irenaeus[30] says that some held Sophia to be the serpent, but in his survey of the system the serpent is the offspring of Ialdabaoth;[31] at first apparently friendly to man, he becomes hostile after the expulsion from Paradise, and begets six other malevolent demons who form with him an infernal hebdomad corresponding to that ruled by Ialdabaoth.[32] There is also apparently a 'heavenly' hebdomad headed by Bythos.[33] Again, the serpent is revered as the bringer of γνῶσις, though elsewhere hostile to man.[34] It seems that the narrative of Genesis has been conflated with some myth, derived perhaps from snake-worship, as, for example, in the cults of the chthonian deities,[35] but the assimilation is not complete. Given the conception of the God of the Old Testament as head of the hostile powers, we should expect the serpent, the bringer of the knowledge of good and evil, to be regarded uniformly as beneficent, but in fact traces of a different view persist in the idea of a lower hebdomad of demons, the chief of whom is Ialdabaoth's offspring, degraded for his share in bringing the redeeming γνῶσις to man.[36] A further inconsistency is that this γνῶσις appears to be due first to the breath inspired by Ialdabaoth, then to the fruit of the tree, and finally to the teaching of the redeemer.

Some modern authorities identify the Ophites and the Naassenes, but others reject this view. The names are similar, one derived from Hebrew, the other from Greek,[37] but the Naassenes lack the Mother, though traces appear, and the Seven. The three primary Aeons are here reduced to a single First Man, whose nature is threefold, and in whom the whole universe potentially exists. In Creation, this Being purifies himself of the material and psychical natures, thus attaining his true life as pure spirit. The three natures are again united in man, and the process whereby the spirit is released is revealed by the Saviour Jesus.[38] The Naassenes incidentally seem to have been the first to adopt the name Gnostic.[39]

Further evidence for the Ophite system comes from a diagram described by Origen.[40] Celsus had charged the Christians with certain errors which Origen refutes, among them being the possession of this diagram, which Origen ascribes to 'a very insignificant sect of Ophites.' The general features are similar to those of the system outlined above, but there is no indication of a descent of Christ into this world.

The diagram is divided into three parts, the lowest being the world of earth, the next the heavens, and the highest the realm of light. Earth consists of ten small circles within a large circle called Leviathan,[41] and this region apparently is governed by seven powers in animal form.[42] According to Celsus, the diagram is divided by a thick black line which, his informants told him, represented Gehenna or Tartarus;[43] another part of the diagram portrayed the Gates of Paradise and the flaming sword.[44] The heavens are ruled by Ialdabaoth and his six angels, the names corresponding to those given by Irenaeus;[45] of these, four are Scriptural names for God,[46] the rest drawn from magic.[47] These are the seven spirits who created the planets. The chief features of the higher regions are two pairs of concentric circles, separated by a double-headed axe;[48] of these, one represents Father and Son, but of the other Origen says only that the outer circle was coloured yellow and the inner blue.[49] There are also certain other figures, which are somewhat confusedly represented, and bear various names. The rest of the account contains the spells and passwords by which the Gnostic is able to make his way through the spheres to the highest realm.[50] The whole agrees fairly closely with the account given by Irenaeus, although there are certain differences of detail.[51]

There were several sects of this type, now generally classed under the name of Ophites, but there is no single form of thought or system of doctrine to which all adhered.[52] The general features are similar, and there is agreement on certain points of detail, but there are also differences which must not be overlooked. Again, some of them seem to have been more pagan than Christian, and Origen, indeed, emphatically distinguishes those of whom he speaks from the adherents of orthodox Christianity.[53] It is not only their fundamentally Gnostic cosmogony, nor their degradation of the God of the Old Testament into the chief of the archons; they also required of every candidate for initiation that he should curse Jesus. This recalls the words of the letter to the Corinthians,[54] although there may be no connexion whatever; but it does seem from the primitive form of some of the systems that Ophitism is a quite early stage of Gnosticism. The question is complicated by the possibility that later developments have been absorbed, or that elements from some later theory have been assimilated to an early scheme, but Ophitism certainly appears to show more possible links with pre-Christian thought than any of the systems so far examined. There are points of contact on the one hand with the Hermetica and the magical papyri,[55] both of which contain material which dates from an early period, although its present form may be late, and on the other hand with Valentinianism.[56] The links with Judaism[57] and with Christianity are also clear, although it is dangerous to theorize about the inter-relation of all these systems.

As Dodd puts it, the Book of Baruch attributed to the Gnostic Justin is 'in the main a mythical adaptation of Old Testament material,' although the writer also 'freely illustrates his points by reference to pagan myths.'[58] In this system there are three primal principles, two male and one female.[59] The supreme God, 'Ἀγαθός, dwells in light above, and plays but little part in the myth, which is chiefly concerned with the relations of the other two: the father of all, who is called Elohim, and the female principle, Eden,[59a] also called Israel, who is described as part woman and part viper. From their union spring twelve angels associated with Elohim and twelve associated with Eden, the third of the angels of Elohim, Baruch, being identified with the tree of life, the third of those of Eden with the tree of the knowledge of good and evil. Man was made by the angels of Elohim from the finest earth,[60] that is, from the better or human part of Eden, not from the animal, and Eden endowed him with soul, Elohim with spirit. Heaven and earth were created by Elohim in agreement with Eden, but he then aspired upwards, leaving Eden behind. On his arrival at the boundary of heaven he saw a light better than that which he had himself created, and sought entrance. A voice out of the light bade him enter,[61] the gates were opened, and he went in to Agathos, who made him sit at his right hand.

Eden then sought to avenge herself upon the spirit of Elohim which was in man, and for this purpose gave great power to Naas, the third of her angels.[62] Elohim sent Baruch to man's assistance, but Baruch's efforts were repeatedly frustrated by Naas until finally he found Jesus, the son of Joseph and Mary, who resisted the blandishments of Naas and was crucified; leaving the 'psychic and earthly' man to Eden on the Cross, he committed his spirit to the hands of the Father and ascended to the Good. Elohim is thus himself the cause both of good and evil: 'by ascending to the Good the Father showed a way for those who desire to ascend, but by departing from Eden he wrought a beginning of evils for the spirit of the Father that is in men.'

As Dodd notes, 'there is a short Christian episode in the scheme, which presents Jesus as the first initiate into true *gnosis*, and this could be removed without seriously affecting the system.'[63] More important for present purposes is the fact that the whole system is so clearly based on an allegorization of the Old Testament, which would seem materially to strengthen the case for a Jewish origin of the Gnostic movement.[64] There are obvious links with other forms of Gnostic thought, but once more the question of chronology arises: Is Justin earlier or later than such systems as those of the Ophites or of Basilides? It may be noted that there is a distinction between the supreme God and the Creator, but the latter is not represented as hostile to man. Again, it may perhaps be asked if the comparative simplicity and lucidity of Justin's scheme, in contrast to the bewildering labyrinths of other systems, may not perhaps be an indication of an early date.

It remains to consider the two great Gnostic leaders of the second century, Basilides and Valentinus, and once again we are faced with the difficulty which attends all study of the Gnostic schools, namely that the later members of the school often improved upon the teaching of the master, while yet ascribing all their doctrines to him.[65] Of the two, Valentinus is considerably the more important, but both present Gnosticism in its more advanced form. Their systems are more elaborate and complicated, with a larger number of emanations and divine beings than the earlier schemes. Both borrowed from their predecessors, Basilides following in the steps of Simon and Saturninus, Valentinus in those of the Ophites,[66] although, indeed, he also borrowed from Basilides.

According to Irenaeus,[67] whose account is thought to be closer to the original than that of Hippolytus,[68] Basilides set at the head of his system an unbegotten Father, of whom was born Nous; from Nous was born Logos, from Logos Phronesis, from Phronesis Sophia and Dynamis, and from these the virtues, powers and angels, by whom the first heaven was formed.[69] Other angels came into being by a series of emanations from these first angels, and each group created a heaven, to the number of three hundred and sixty-five in all.[70] The angels of the lowest heaven, which is that visible to us, were responsible for the creation of this world. Their chief was the God of the Jews, who wished to subject the other peoples to his own, but was opposed by the other powers. Seeing this, the Father sent his first-born Nous, who is Christ, to free those who believed in him from the power of the creators. Nous appeared on earth as a man, and performed wonders but did not suffer, Simon of Cyrene being transformed so that he was thought to be Jesus.[71] Nous had in the interval returned to the Father. For salvation it was thus necessary to confess not the crucified but the incarnate Jesus who was thought to have been crucified; those who confessed the crucified were still slaves to the creators of the body, but those who denied him were freed. Salvation was of the soul alone, since the body was corruptible by nature.

Prophecy was due to the creator powers, the law to their chief; sacrifice to idols was of no importance, and food thus offered might be used without fear, while the other operations of human life were likewise irrelevant. This school employed magic, images, incantations, invocations, and similar curious practices. They professed to give the names of the angels in the several heavens,[72] and claimed that only a few could know their secrets. Their mysteries were not to be disclosed, but preserved in silence. The three hundred and sixty-five heavens were distributed according to the views of the Mathematici,[73] whose doctrines they had adopted; the chief of the heavens is called Abraxas, who contains in himself the number 365.[74]

Hippolytus[75] is chiefly concerned to demonstrate the dependence of Basilides upon Aristotle. According to this account, Basilides and his son and disciple Isidore claimed to have received secret teachings from Matthias.[76] They held that there was a time when there was nothing;[77] the non-existent God willed to create a world, not the visible world but a σπέρμα κόσμου[78] containing in it the seed of all that was to be in the future world. This world was created not by emanation but by the spoken word of God, and all things derived their being from this cosmic seed.[79]

Inherent in this seed was a threefold Sonship,[80] which was consubstantial with the non-existent God, and begotten of that which was not. As soon as the seed was deposited, the first and most subtle Sonship returned to the non-existent; the second, being more dense, could not follow, but took to itself the Holy Spirit as a wing,[81] and both ascended to the first Sonship. The Spirit, not being consubstantial[82] with the Sonship, could not remain in the non-existent, but stayed in the intermediate confines, though not entirely deserted by the Sonship. This is the type of man's yearning for better things.[83] The third Sonship, being in need of purification, remained in the material world.[84]

A firmament was next established between the world and the realm above the world, and from the cosmic seed was begotten the Great Archon, whose influence filled the world up to the firmament, so that he thought himself supreme,[85] and set about creating the rest of the cosmos. First he created for himself a son, much better and wiser than himself; then with his son's assistance he set in order the ethereal region or Ogdoad.[86]

Another Archon now arose, inferior to the first and also to the third Sonship which was still imprisoned in matter, but superior to the underlying substance. This was the Demiurge,[87] whose realm was the Hebdomad. He also engendered a son from matter, and reduced the world to order, in accordance (although he did not know it) with the plan of the non-existent God.[88]

The third Sonship remained in the cosmic seed, and required to be revealed and restored above the intermediate Spirit to its place with the other Sonships and the non-existent. Combining two texts from Paul,[89] Basilides argued that the πνευματικοί were the sons of God, placed in the world to perfect the souls whose nature it was to abide in this region.[90] The Great Archon, the Ogdoad, ruled as far as the firmament, the Hebdomad the lower sphere, and the latter was the God of the Old Testament.[91] When the time came for the revelation of the sons of God, the Gospel entered into the world, passing through every principality and power; yet nothing descended from above, nor did the blessed Sonship depart from the non-existent God.[92] The power of the Holy Spirit imparted the light of the Gospel, flowing like a current, to the son of the Great Archon.[93]

The Archon now learned from his son Christ that he was not the supreme God, and was seized with the fear of the Lord that is the beginning of wisdom;[94] the entire creation of the Ogdoad was likewise enlightened. The light was then imparted to the Hebdomad, in the same way and with the same results, and finally the mystery was revealed to the hitherto abortive Sonship imprisoned in the formless matter. The light descended upon Jesus the son of Mary, fulfilling the prophecy of the descent of the Holy Spirit uttered to Mary by the angel.[95] The world was to continue until the whole of the third Sonship should be transformed by following Jesus, and enabled of itself to rise as had the first; it possessed the power when confirmed by the light which shone from above.[96] When the time comes, the souls which remain below, together with the Ogdoad and the Hebdomad, will be seized with ignorance, so that they do not desire the things above, for to them such desire is death. Thus shall all things be restored.[97]

To Basilides the Gospel was the knowledge of the things beyond the world,[98] a knowledge which the Great Archon did not at first possess. Everything concerning Jesus happened as it is written in the Gospels, but the purpose was that he should be the first-fruits of the distinction of that which had been compounded.[99] His corporeal part suffered, and returned to formlessness; so too the parts which belonged to the Hebdomad and the Ogdoad were restored to them, and that which was of the intermediate Spirit ascended thither and remained,[100] but the third Sonship was purified through him and ascended through them all to the blessed Sonship. The whole theory is summed up[101] as a compounding of the cosmic seed and the distinction and restoration of the several ingredients to their proper place. Such was the fruit of the wisdom Basilides learned in Egypt.[102]

The relation of these two accounts to each other, and to other reports concerning the views of Basilides, constitutes a problem which bristles with difficulties. Arguments may be advanced on either side, but it does seem more probable that the account of Hippolytus is the later; if it were truly the teaching of Basilides it is hard to see why Irenaeus shows no knowledge of it.[103] The closing remark of Hippolytus' account might possibly suggest that he is presenting an Alexandrian version of the system, the account of

Irenaeus in that case being Basilides' earlier views, before he went to Alexandria.[104] A similar suggestion has been made to account for the differences in the two accounts of Simon Magus.[105] The theory presented by Irenaeus is much more akin to the ordinary Gnostic views, as we have seen them in earlier systems; that given by Hippolytus is quite original, although the idea of the triple Sonship recalls the Naassene First Man, as does the concept of the distinction of the different elements and their restoration to their rightful abode.[106] Other sources contributing to the scheme as presented by Hippolytus are astrology, which is, however, a common element, Greek philosophy, although the influence here seems rather Stoic or Platonic than Aristotelian, and Zoroastrianism; some hold that Indian influence has also been operative, but this is by no means certain.[107]

The fundamental difference between the theory of Basilides, as presented by Hippolytus, and those of other Gnostic leaders lies in his rejection of emanation;[108] for him, once the creation has begun, the whole tale is one of effort to rise. The Sonships burst from the seed, the Archons rise as far as they can, the third Sonship ascends to join the others when it has been purified and quickened by the light of the Gospel. The goal of history is 'the establishment of all things in their proper rank.'[109] Basilides begins with the confusion of the world and seeks to explain the process of restoration; his cosmogony does not really explain the presence of the living spark in matter in a satisfactory way. Valentinus 'starts with the principle that evolution is degeneration';[110] the process of Creation is described as a series of emanations each inferior to its predecessor. In the one we have a decline from perfection followed by a return to the heights; in the other, a thinly-veiled dualism in which the creature from the beginning is always striving upward. Basilides teaches almost a doctrine of evolutionary progress. The same idea that all movement is upwards appears in his rejection of any descent of a supernatural being when the Gospel comes into the world.[111]

From Hippolytus' account we can understand the reputation which Basilides gained; from it too we are 'enabled to understand why the Basilidean influence ceased to play a part in the later history of Gnosticism. The cardinal Gnostic positions had been gradually abandoned by the disciples of Basilides, and his Gnosis merged itself at last in the ordinary philosophical speculations of the age. The Valentinian movement, on the other hand . . . never ceased to be faithful to the distinctive Gnostic ideas, and drew into itself practically the whole stream of later Gnosticism.'[112] Basilides was more philosopher than theologian, and his speculations were too exalted for the many.

Our evidence for the Valentinian theory is rather more extensive than that which we possess for the other systems, as, indeed, is to be expected since it was Valentinianism that Irenaeus was especially concerned to refute. Moreover, in this case we are able to some extent to check the patristic accounts from the fragments which have been preserved. Once again our main sources are Irenaeus and Hippolytus,[113] who agree on the whole, although it has been suggested that they present different versions of the scheme.[114] If this be correct, then each shows knowledge of the version used by the other. Some fragments of the work of Valentinus himself are extant,[115] while Origen has embodied considerable extracts from Heracleon's commentary in his own work on the Fourth Gospel,[116] in addition to various references, and Clement of Alexandria has preserved a number of excerpts from Theodotus amongst other notes.[117] The Valentinian school divided at an early date into an Eastern branch, which included Theodotus, and a Western which included Heracleon and Ptolemaeus, of whose writings also some fragments remain.[118] According to Brooke, Heracleon did not depart to any great extent from the teaching of his master,[119] and the same appears to be true also of the others.[120]

The Valentinians abandoned Basilides' view of the non-existent God and reverted to the usual Gnostic scheme, combining elements from various systems in such a way that all could recognize their own views to some extent in the developed Valentinian theory.[121] The supreme Being is the Perfect Aeon, also called $\Pi\rho o\alpha\rho\chi\dot\eta$, $\Pi\rho o\pi\dot\alpha\tau\omega\rho$, and Bythos, who is invisible, incomprehensible, eternal, and unbegotten. With him is associated Ennoia,[122] who is also $X\dot\alpha\rho\iota s$ or $\Sigma\iota\gamma\dot\eta$, and from these was born $No\hat\upsilon s$, who alone can comprehend the greatness of the Father,[123] and $'A\lambda\dot\eta\theta\epsilon\iota\alpha$. $No\hat\upsilon s$ is also called $Mo\nu o\gamma\epsilon\nu\dot\eta s$, $\Pi\dot\alpha\tau\eta\rho$, and $'A\rho\chi\dot\eta$ $\tau\hat\omega\nu$ $\pi\dot\alpha\nu\tau\omega\nu$, and from him emanated another pair, $\Lambda\dot o\gamma os$ and $Z\omega\dot\eta$, and from these in turn $"A\nu\theta\rho\omega\pi os$ and $'E\kappa\kappa\lambda\eta\sigma\dot\iota\alpha$. These form the archetypal

Ogdoad, composed of four 'syzygies.'[124] The four last Aeons then produced further emanations, ten from Logos and Zoe,[125] and twelve from Anthropos and Ecclesia,[126] to form a Pleroma of thirty Aeons in all.[127]

The supreme Being is known to Monogenes alone, who conceived the notion of imparting his knowledge to the others but was prevented at the behest of Bythos by Sige.[128] The other Aeons, however, longed to see the author of their being, the youngest of all, Sophia, being particularly eager. As a result of this 'passion,' this yearning to know the Father, she was in danger of being swallowed up and resolved into the Infinite, had she not encountered the guardian power, Horus,[129] by whom she was restrained and confirmed, and with difficulty restored to her senses, abandoning her intention and the passion which arose from it.

Others,[130] however, relate that she attempted the impossible, in trying to generate without the assistance of her partner, in imitation of Bythos; the result was a formless substance, such as her female nature enabled her to produce.[131] Stricken first with grief since the birth was incomplete, and then with terror lest it should be the end of her own existence,[132] she sought to conceal her offspring, but turned in her agony and threw herself on the mercy of the Father, the other Aeons joining in her prayers. Hence material substance took its origin, from ignorance, grief, fear, and amazement. The Father produced the above-mentioned Horus, through Monogenes, in his own image, a hermaphrodite being with no partner. Horus is also called Σταυρός, Λυτρωτής, Καρπιστής, Ὁροθέτης, and Μεταγώγευς; through him Sophia was purified and restored to her spouse,[133] and remained within the Pleroma separated from her desire and her passion, which were excluded from the Pleroma as a formless spiritual substance.

Monogenes now produced a further syzygy, according to the providence of the Father, namely Christ and the Holy Spirit,[134] by whom the Pleroma was completed. Christ taught the other Aeons that the Father was incomprehensible, and known only through Monogenes, and that they needed no higher knowledge. The knowledge that the Father was incomprehensible secured to the Aeons their continued existence; the knowledge of the Father which Monogenes alone possessed gave him his special status as Son.[135]

The Holy Spirit made all the Aeons equal, and led them into the
true rest; in their gratitude for this the whole Pleroma with one
accord brought each his best gifts, which were united in Jesus, the
perfect fruit and star of the Pleroma,[136] who is also called Saviour,
Christ, and Logos. Angels were, moreover, provided as a bodyguard for him.

All this takes place within the Pleroma, and the mystery is not
openly revealed, since only a few can receive it, but described in
parables, which simply means that an esoteric significance was read
into the Biblical narratives.[137] In the earlier examples which
Irenaeus adduces, the emphasis rests in each case on the use of the
word αἰών, or upon the occurrence of the numbers 10, 12, 18, 30,
which correspond to different groups of Aeons. In the later, various
texts are interpreted in terms of the Valentinian theory. 'Valentinus
is nowhere accused of having altered the text of Scripture, as
Marcion did, but of having perverted its meaning.'[138]

The Enthymesis of Sophia, also called Achamoth,[139] remained in
the darkness of the void outside the light of the Pleroma, until
Christ took pity on her and conferred on her form, but form κατ᾽
οὐσίαν μόνον, and not form κατὰ γνῶσιν. He then left her and
returned within the Pleroma, in order that she might strive after
better things, being now aware of her misfortune and possessing
still a savour of immortality left her by Christ and the Holy Spirit.[140]
Hence she is called Sophia, from her ancestor, and Holy Spirit,
from the Spirit that is with Christ. Striving after the light which
had left her, she was prevented by Horus, who pronounced the
name Ἰαώ,[141] from ascending higher, as being bound to her
passion.[142] From this passion, and from her 'conversion' to him
who had given her life, arose the material universe; from the
conversion the soul of the world and of the Demiurge, from her
tears the moist substance, from her laughter the light,[143] from her
grief and amazement the corporeal elements of the world.

After passing through this agony, to which she all but succumbed,
Achamoth appealed to Christ.[144] He hesitated to descend a second
time, but sent the Paraclete,[145] that is, the Saviour, to whom the
Father gave all power, setting all under his authority, while the
Aeons granted that 'in him might all things be created, both
visible and invisible, thrones, divinities, and dominions.'[146] With

him were sent also the angels, his bodyguard.[147] Achamoth at first veiled herself for shame, but then came to meet him, and received from him form κατὰ γνῶσιν, and the healing of her sufferings.[148] Her passions could not be done away, like those of the first Sophia, but were separated from her, and then blended and transformed into incorporeal matter.[149] They were thus adapted to enter into compounds and into bodies, so that there should be two substances, the base arising from the passions while the other arising from the conversion was capable of passion. Hence the Valentinians said that the Saviour virtually acted as Demiurge.[150] Achamoth then conceived spiritual offspring in the likeness of the angels who accompanied the Saviour.[151]

There were thus three substances, matter from the passions, the psychic from the conversion, and the spiritual which had been conceived. The spiritual she was unable to shape, since it was consubstantial with herself, but turning to the formation of the psychic she produced what she had learned from the Saviour. The first of these formations was the Demiurge, the father and king of all, both of those who were consubstantial with himself, that is, of the psychic, and also of the hylic. All the lower creatures now produced were images of the Aeons, produced ultimately by the Saviour working through Achamoth, as she worked through the Demiurge. Achamoth became the image of Bythos, the Demiurge of Monogenes, and the angels and archangels under them images of the other Aeons.[152]

The Demiurge is God and Father of all outside the Pleroma, the creator of all things psychic and hylic. He separated the two confused substances, and created things heavenly and earthly, heavy and light, higher and lower. He formed seven heavens, whence he is called the Hebdomad as their ruler, Achamoth being the Ogdoad, recalling the archetypal Ogdoad of the Pleroma.[153] These heavens and the Demiurge himself were angels, and Paradise was situated above the third heaven;[154] here Adam dwelt, and hence he derived certain qualities. In this creation the Demiurge thought he was acting of his own accord, although in truth Achamoth acted through him; he thought he himself was all in all, and spoke through the prophets, thinking himself the only God.[155] Achamoth, who is also the Mother, the Ogdoad, and Sophia,[156] dwelt in the intermediate region, above the Demiurge but below the Pleroma, until the fullness of time was come.

From the grief came the spiritual powers of evil,[157] among them the Devil, or Cosmocrator,[158] and the demons. This Cosmocrator was a creation of the Demiurge, and dwelt in this world of ours. The elements arose from the other parts of the passion.

Having created the world, the Demiurge formed earthly man,[159] and breathed into him the psychic substance; this was man κατ' εἰκόνα καὶ ὁμοίωσιν, who was finally clothed in a coat of skin, the perceptible body of flesh.[160] The spiritual seed conceived by Achamoth as a result of her vision of the angels was secretly infused into the Demiurge, and passed from him into man; this seed was the Church, the counterpart of the heavenly Ecclesia.[161] The Valentinians thus claimed to possess a soul from the Demiurge, a body from 'earth,' flesh from matter, and a spiritual principle from Achamoth.

The hylic were destined to perish, the psychic had freedom of will to be good or bad, to ascend or descend, being intermediate, while the spiritual were sent to undergo the discipline of life in conjunction with the psychic.[162] For this reason the world was created, and the Saviour came, to save the psychic. He received a spiritual element from Achamoth, and put on the psychic Christ, although he derived nothing from the hylic.[163] The fullness of time came when the spiritual were perfected in γνῶσις. The psychic, equated with non-Valentinian Christians,[164] were instructed in psychic things, and for them good works were necessary to salvation. The Valentinians were spiritual by nature, and hence destined to be saved. This, according to Irenaeus, led to licence and antinomianism.[165]

When all the seed is perfected, Achamoth ascends within the Pleroma to form a new syzygy with her bridegroom the Saviour, while the πνευματικοί, stripping off the psychic element, enter as intelligent spirits to become the brides of the angels.[166] The Demiurge, with the souls of the psychic righteous, ascends to the intermediate region, vacated by Achamoth, for the psychic cannot enter the Pleroma. The fire latent in the world will consume all matter, and itself be consumed, to exist no more.[167] Irenaeus concludes his survey with a note of some variations in Valentinian

Christology, and an exposition of some of the scriptural exegesis of the school, which he criticizes at length.[168] Truly, the Christian controversialist 'felt that he had nothing to do but set out at unsparing length their tedious pedigrees, in the well-grounded confidence that no one would care to peruse them a second time.'[169]

It has already been noted that the Valentinian school divided at an early stage into two branches. Further, some of the disciples differed from their master in various ways.[170] The variations in our evidence show that there was no real consistency or agreement in points of detail, although the basic scheme is the same. The Valentinian theory represents Gnosticism at its prime, with the ideas of the earlier thinkers blended into a system which could for a time compete seriously with orthodox Christianity. Allegorizations of Scripture, ideas from the religion and philosophy of the contemporary world, astrology, magic, all made some contribution. To us the recital of Aeons, of a triple world without the Pleroma, a triple Fall and a triple Redemption,[171] is tedious if not absurd, and the tedium is not relieved by the manner in which the patristic writers set out the opinions which they seek to refute. But farfetched though they be, these speculations made a contribution to Christian thought, if only by compelling the orthodox to think out the implications of their faith, and to present it to their contemporaries in the language of the time.[172]

There is, of course, much more to be said, and there are several other systems and several other leaders who would come under review in any complete survey of Gnosticism. Irenaeus devotes some space to the examination of the views of some of the disciples of Valentinus, and of the ways in which they diverged from the teaching of the master;[173] other sections deal with the Rule of Faith,[174] others again with various Gnostic schemes, some of which we have already considered. He is concerned to refute errors, not so much to set out his own views against them, and in consequence the first book of his work is largely polemical;[175] only in the later books does he go on to develop his own Biblical theology. The case is different a generation or so later, when the greatest danger was past.[176] The Alexandrian Fathers are still concerned for orthodoxy, as they saw it, but there is a difference in their attitude. They no longer devote their energies to the production of volum-

K

inous Refutations, but are even prepared on occasion to adopt the work of the Gnostics for their own purposes. The obvious instance is Origen's use of Heracleon's commentary on the Fourth Gospel, which he does not always cite with disapproval, but Clement before him had also made use of Gnostic ideas and concepts, and, indeed, goes so far as to appropriate Gnostic terms to the use of the Church. They are loyal to the Creed, but 'outside the circle of Apostolical dogma they held themselves free.'[177]

The fundamental difference between them and the Gnostics lies in their view of the God of the Old Testament,[178] and in their teaching on the Person and Work of Christ.[179] Where the Gnostic could see in the God of Israel only a hostile being who sought to bend men to submission to himself, a God who was just, admittedly, but no more, a stern ruler and the giver of the law, but not the God and Father of all mankind of whom the Gospel spoke, Clement asserts that the Justice of God is but the reverse side of His Love, and that the Jewish Law is a preparatory discipline to the full Christian life, a tutor unto Christ. Again, where the Gnostic could not admit that Jesus had a human body, or at any rate claimed that he could not have suffered, the Alexandrian Fathers return to the thought of Paul, and regard the death of Christ as the means of redemption. The Gnostic was governed by his view that the divine as such could have no contact with matter or the flesh, which were of themselves evil, and that a divine being could not suffer as Christ had suffered, while the Alexandrians, although Clement came near to Docetism,[180] were less convinced of the evil of matter, and found the source of sin in the freedom of the human will.[181]

On the other hand, both Clement and Origen employ the allegorical method in the interpretation of Scripture, in order to reconcile the truths of the Christian faith with the doctrines of philosophy.[182] In consequence there arises a dual standard, a higher life open only to a few and a lower open to the many who are unable to comprehend the deeper mysteries.[183] In this they are close to the Gnostics, although even here there are characteristic differences; thus to Clement the two lives are not essentially different, but rather different stages in one process of development. The less perfect Christian should in his view have it as his object to grow in the knowledge and love of God to a more perfect faith, in which the truths of reason and of revelation are blended; but although the spiritual life is one, a single process leading from simple faith and trust to a full knowledge of God, yet Clement's formulation of the distinction between the two lives brings him close to the Gnostics. 'The supreme end is not Love but Know-ledge, and this misplacement of the Ideal involves an egotism which he vainly struggles to escape.'[184] Faith is not enough by itself; it must be supplemented by knowledge—the position opposed by Paul in the Epistle to the Colossians,[185] although knowledge to Clement might mean something very different from the knowledge required by the 'philosophers' of Colossae.

There are differences of view between Clement and Origen, but both seek in their own way to unite Christianity and Hellenism, and especially to reconcile Christian beliefs with Platonic thought. In this they had been preceded by Philo in his efforts to attain the same end for Judaism, and their debt to their predecessor is shown by many features in their work.[186] At some points they do not go beyond the position he had reached, but at others there is a great advance; it was, indeed, in some ways easier to combine Christianity with the contemporary philosophy than it had been to blend that philosophy with Judaism, but the three writers may fairly be regarded as adherents of the same long tradition. There are in the works of Clement and Origen many parallels to Philo, and many indications of his influence; there are also many points of agreement between them and the Gnostics, although again there are decisive differences.[187] The Gnostics, in their attempt at the co-ordination of Christian doctrine and its expression in terms of current thought, had introduced elements from other sources which threatened to destroy the essential Christian message and submerge the Gospel in contemporary religious thought.[188] The reaction had tended to reject philosophy altogether, and to base everything upon Scripture alone. The Alexandrians sought to find a *via media*: 'their object is to show ... that neither Faith without Reason nor Reason without Faith can bring forth its noblest fruits.'[189] Later ages were to condemn some of their teachings, to brand the men themselves with heresy, but whatever their faults, whatever their failures, they did to a great extent succeed in their aim.

A full study of the doctrines of Clement and Origen lies beyond the scope of the present work,[190] but some indication of their views has seemed necessary in order to complete our survey of the principal Gnostic schools, and to demonstrate the way in which the more orthodox Christian thinkers attempted to solve the problem of presenting the Gospel to their time. The Gnostics had found in Paul much that they could employ; they had adopted the current Stoic-Platonic cosmogony with its theory of the universe and of man, and sought to fit the Christian doctrine of Christ into that scheme. The Alexandrians also followed Paul, but more closely, although here and there they departed from his guidance; they also adopted to a very large extent the contemporary philosophy, but for them the philosophy was only the framework, not as with too many Gnostics the greater part of the whole. They were first and foremost loyal to the Christian faith and this sets them apart. The philosophy was but a tool for the work of explaining and expounding the doctrines of the faith to which they adhered.

NOTES TO CHAPTER V

[1] Ap. Euseb. *HE* 3. 32. 7–8.

[2] Cf. Friedländer, *Der vorchristliche jüdische Gnosticismus* 12ff. Here, of course, the library of Nag Hammadi is of the first importance, as providing an extensive collection of Gnostic texts, many of them hitherto unknown. See *The Jung Codex*, and below, p. 149ff.

[3] Cf. Bousset, *Jüdisch-christlicher Schulbetrieb in Alexandria und Rom*; Bigg, *The Christian Platonists of Alexandria*. Unfortunately the origin and early history of the Christian Church in Alexandria remain obscure (see above, p. 30).

[4] See below, p. 120.

[5] On Ophitism in general see *ERE* 6. 237ff., 9. 499ff., *Dict. Théol. Cath.* 11. 1063ff., and on the Ophite sect proper, in addition to these, *PW* 18. 1. 654ff. See also Legge 2. 25ff. Further evidence is now provided by the *Apocryphon Johannis* (see below, p. 149ff.).

[6] Cf. *Dict. Theol. Cath.* 11. 1070f. on Hippolytus and Epiphanius.

[7] I. 28; the Greek text is supplied by Harvey from Theodoret, *H. Fab.* I. 14. Cf. Harvey lxxviii ff., although this analysis is inaccurate at several points; Scott in *ERE* 6. 237ff.

[8] Theoretically Bythos seems to be the supreme Being, but he is too remote to have any real place. Cf. infra, p. 119.

[9] For Ennoia (here, however, a male principle) cf. Simon Magus (supra, p. 100).

[10] The Hebrew *ruaḥ* is normally feminine; cf. here Gen. 1. 2 LXX. For the triad, cf. Norden 229ff.

[11] For the waters cf. Harvey 228 note 1, and note the place of Leviathan in the diagram preserved by Origen, infra, p. 120ff. For the idea of a creative dew or rain cf. Dieterich, *Abraxas* 24ff.

[12] On Ialdabaoth see Bousset *Hauptprobleme* 351ff., Dieterich 24, 26, 46, Legge 2. 46f. According to Legge (2. 45), Sophia in Ophitism = the Great Goddess of Asia Minor = Ishtar = Isis. Cf. p. 37ff. supra, and references there to Knox *PCG*.

[13] The eighth heaven being the body left by Sophia-Prunicus, and the others obviously the planetary spheres. On their names, see below, p. 139.

[14] Another use of Gen. 1. 26; cf. Philo (supra, p. 42) and Saturninus (supra, p. 103).

[15] Cf. Saturninus again (supra, p. 112 note 44). Rabbinical parallels are quoted by Harvey 232 note 3.

[16] On the generation of the angels from Eve by the lower powers, see Harvey 233 note 3. Cf. also the *Apocryphon Johannis* (below, p. 152).

[17] By the agency of the serpent (cf. Genesis), who is thus the bringer of γνῶσις. For Rabbinical parallels to the account of the Fall see Harvey's notes. But see also the *Apocryphon of John* (below, p. 152).

[18] In 1. 28. 5 ad fin., however, the OT writers are distributed among Ialdabaoth and his powers. Sophia apparently intervenes without their knowledge.

[19] 1. 28. 7. The Docetic view seems here developed in greater detail than in earlier systems.

[20] This appears also in the Valentinian theory; cf. Harvey 26 note 1, 240 note 1.

[21] According to Harvey and others, this means that Christ sits among the Aeons of the Pleroma, who are δεξιοί with reference to the lower or left hebdomad headed by Ialdabaoth (240 note 4). Others interpret more literally, viz. that Christ and Ialdabaoth sit together in judgement. Cf. Casey, *The Excerpta ex Theodoto of Clement of Alexandria* 20, and for the Valentinian use of the concept Exc. 38. 3, 62. 1. It may be simply a Gnostic adaptation of such a NT passage as Col. 3. 2f.

[22] i.e. the souls that he himself has breathed into men. There appears, however, to be some inconsistency here, as at some other points. Cf. Legge's notes (2. 58ff.).

[23] See E. F. Scott in *ERE* 9. 500, and cf. ibid. 6. 238f. Bousset (*Hauptprobleme* 319ff.) sketches primitive Gnosticism on the basis of the common features of these systems, which he considers to be offshoots from the original movement.

[24] Wolfson (*Philosophy of the Church Fathers* 1. 527) thinks the triad a survival of the pre-Christian syncretic stock, accommodated to the Christian doctrine of the Trinity.

[25] This identification is not, however, peculiar to the Ophites, being a

common feature of Gnosticism; but the other results of the anti-Jewish bias do seem to be peculiar.

[26] This lends support to Bevan's view (supra, p. 106) that the Gnostic Redeemer was derived from Christianity. Bousset (238ff.) thinks this Redeemer is due to an artificial combination of an earlier mythical figure with the historic Jesus.

[27] Cf. *Dict. Théol. Cath.* 11. 1071ff., and Reitzenstein *Poim.* 81ff. quoted there; but cf. also Burkitt in *JTS* xxvi. 117ff., Goppelt 134 ('erweisen sich die christlichen Züge als nachträgliche Einfügung; die atl. aber lassen sich nicht ausscheiden'). See also Dodd, *Interpretation* 98.

[28] De Faye argues that this group of sects is dependent on Marcion, and hence late. Scott rejects this view, and in fact there are indications that the sect may be pre-Christian. See *ERE* 9. 501, *Dict. Théol. Cath.* 11. 1065ff., Friedländer passim, Dieterich *Abraxas* 28, etc., Bidez-Cumont *Les Mages Hellénisés* (index s.v. Seth). According to Casey, 'Tertullian maintained that the gnostics were secondary to the Valentinians,' but this is refuted by Sagnard (*La gnose valentinienne* 446 note 1). Harvey (lxxviii) rejects the assertion of Philastrius that the Ophites formed a sect before the time of Christ, but does not allow for the possibility that Christian elements may have been assimilated by a pre-Christian group.

[29] Cf. Legge 2. 37ff., Harvey 236 note 3. This, however, may be an inference from insufficient evidence.

[30] 1. 28. 8.

[31] 1. 28. 3. Cf. Legge 2. 77ff., Dieterich *Abraxas* 111ff., 149ff.

[32] 1. 28. 4 ad fin.

[33] Harvey 263 note 3. There seems to be some confusion here, since immediately below the *sancta hebdomas* is associated with the stars (i.e. Ialdabaoth and the planetary powers). Cf. Legge 2. 64.

[34] The solution to this apparent inconsistency seems to be provided in the *Apocryphon Johannis* 57f., where the tree of the knowledge of good and evil is identified with the ἐπίνοια of light, and it is Christ himself who encourages man to eat of that tree. Cf. below, p. 152.

[35] Cf. *Dict. Théol. Cath.* 11. 1074f., Dieterich *Abraxas* 111ff., 149, Legge 2. 49. For Hermes or the Ἀγαθὸς Δαίμων as ὄφις cf. Reitzenstein *Poim.* 20 note 6; 27, 29, 31, and for the identification of Hermes with the Δαίμων ibid. 18. Cf. also ibid. 133f. A tradition in Philo of Byblus (ap. Euseb. *PE* 1. 10. 46ff.) 'lasst Tauthos oder Thot in "heiligen Schriften" die Verehrung der Schlange erklären und rechtfertigen' (ibid. 162).

[36] Cf. also Orig. *c. Cels.* 6. 29 (trans. Chadwick, 344).

[37] Hippol. *Phil.* 5. 6. 3, 9. 11f. Cf. Harvey lxxviii ff., *PW* 18. 1. 658, *Dict. Théol. Cath.* 11. 1073. Legge (2. 63ff.) combines the accounts of the Naassene and Ophite theories into one. Cf. also ibid. 53ff. Bousset indicates several points of contact (see his *Hauptprobleme*, index s.v. Gnostiker, Naassener, Ophiten). In Hippol. *Phil.* 8. 20. 3 the Ophites are cursorily mentioned; they may not be identical with the Naassenes of Book 5.

[38] *ERE* 6. 239. Here, too, man is inert and lifeless until he is endowed with a soul (cf. note 14 supra).

[39] *Phil.* 5. 6. But cf. Legge 2. 27.

[40] *Contra Celsum* 6. 24-39 (see Chadwick's translation and notes, Cambridge 1953). Cf. *Dict. Théol. Cath.* 11. 1067ff., *ERE* 9. 499f., Legge 2. 66ff., Wendland *HRK* 173. See also Friedländer 83ff., although his theory that such diagrams are meant by the Talmudic Giljonim seems quite unwarranted. Chadwick (338f.) reproduces Hopfner's reconstruction of the diagram.

[41] *c. Cels.* 6. 25; cf. ibid. 35, where Leviathan contains the circles of the seven 'archontics.' Lipsius and Hopfner therefore emend (Chadwick 340 note 1). Leviathan ($\delta\rho\acute{a}\kappa\omega\nu$ in Ps. 103 LXX etc.) is the serpent who embraces the earth in his coils. The type appears on seals and amulets. See further Chadwick 340 note 2.

[42] ibid. 30. One of these is Michael, on whom see Dieterich *Abraxas* 122ff. The Jewish archangels here appear as demons. Cf. Harvey 236 note 4.

[43] ibid. 25f.

[44] ibid. 33.

[45] ibid. 31; cf. Iren. 1. 28. 3, *Apoc. Joh.* 41-44 (see Till's summary, *JEH* 3 (1952) 18).

[46] Iao, Sabaoth, Eloaeus (Elohim), Adonaeus (Adonai). See Orig. *c. Cels.* 6. 32. In *Apoc. Joh.* 42, Adonaeus and Adoni are separate powers and Sabaoth is missing; but in 43. 20 Sabaoth replaces Adonaeus. Till notes 'nach 42, 3 sollte es Adonaios heissen,' but the error may be there and not in 43. 20 (for the text, see Till, *Die gnostischen Schriften des koptischen Papyrus Berolinensis* 8502 (*TU* 60), Berlin 1955, 126). Three of these names appear also in magic (see below, p. 241 note 160).

[47] Ialdabaoth, Horaeus, Astaphaeus. Magic need not, however, be the ultimate source. Of these, Ialdabaoth is the Demiurge in the *Apocryphon of John*, Astaphaeus one of the planetary powers, but Horaeus does not appear in this document. It should be added that in the *Apocryphon* (41. 18) Jaoth, the first of the planetary powers, is described as 'lion-faced.' In *c. Cels.* 6. 31 Ialdabaoth is 'the lion-like Archon' (see Chadwick, 347 note 2).

[48] On its possible significance see Legge 2. 67 note 3, Chadwick 353 note 2.

[49] *c. Cels.* 6. 38.

[50] On these see Legge 2. 71ff., and compare the text cited by Norden (218f.) from the Book of the Dead.

[51] Notably that the Ophites of Origen have no place for Jesus (6. 28).

[52] See refs. supra, p. 136 note 5 and p. 119; also Legge 2. 76ff.

[53] *c. Cels.* 6. 28. Chadwick (343 note 1) observes that Celsus is well informed and never makes the charges against 'the great church.'

[54] 1 Cor. 12. 3: $o\mathring{v}\delta\epsilon\grave{\iota}\varsigma$ $\mathring{\epsilon}\nu$ $\Pi\nu\epsilon\acute{v}\mu\alpha\tau\iota$ $\Theta\epsilon o\mathring{v}$ $\lambda\alpha\lambda\hat{\omega}\nu$ $\lambda\acute{\epsilon}\gamma\epsilon\iota$, $'A\nu\acute{a}\theta\epsilon\mu\alpha$ $'I\eta\sigma o\hat{v}\varsigma$. Cf. Origen ad loc., quoted by Chadwick 344 note 2.

[55] See Dieterich, *Abraxas*.

[56] See below.

[57] See Friedländer op. cit., although care is necessary here, and Bousset *Hauptprobleme* 324ff.

[58] *Interpretation* 99. See Hippolytus *Phil.* 5. 23ff., 10. 15f. (Wendland 125ff., 276–7; part of the first passage is included in Völker, *Quellen zur Geschichte der christlichen Gnosis*, Tübingen 1932, 27ff.). Hippolytus notes the similarity between Justin and Basilides.

[59] Cf. Dodd's summary, 104f.

[59a] There seems to be confusion here between Eden (LXX Ἐδεμ) and the Hebrew *'adamah* (see Scholem in *Eranos Jahrbuch* xxii (1954) 242, Rudolph in *ZRGG* ix (1957) 17 note 1).

[60] Cf. Philo (above, p. 42), Saturninus (above, p. 103) and Valentinianism (below, p. 132).

[61] Dodd compares *CH* 1. 4–5.

[62] In this account Eve is seduced by Naas. Cf. Ialdabaoth in the *Apocryphon of John* (62. 3–11, Till *TU* 60, 164); in this document Eloim and Jave are the two sons of this union. Naas is, of course, the serpent of the Naassenes and Ophites, but does not appear as such in Justin's system.

[63] *Interpretation* 99.

[64] It should be noted, however, that Justin's allegorization is in many respects distinct from that, for example, of the *Apocryphon Johannis*.

[65] Another complication arises from the tendency to interpenetration of doctrines, which makes it difficult to trace the origin and descent of any particular idea. Cf. Legge 2. 20.

[66] *ERE* 6. 239. On points of contact between Valentinus and Basilides, see Harvey cxi ff.

[67] 1. 19 (Harvey xc ff., 198ff.). Only the Latin is extant, and there are some textual problems. Mansel (*The Gnostic Heresy* 145) considers Clem. Alex. and Hippol. more reliable than Iren., who used less direct sources. He thinks the account in Iren. a later modification, influenced by the school of Valentinus (ibid. 161). For the texts and fragments see Völker, *Quellen* 38ff. See also Quispel, 'L'homme gnostique: doctrine de Basilide,' in *Eranos Jahrbuch* xvi (1948), 89ff.

[68] *Phil.* 7. See *ERE* 6. 239, and for full discussion ibid. 2. 426ff. E. F. Scott (*ERE* 6. 240) suggests that the account in Hippolytus 'may reflect a further development of that teaching (in Irenaeus) in its progress towards pure monism.' A. S. Peake, however (*ERE* 2. 430) considers the account of Hippolytus to be more original. See also Bousset *Hauptprobleme* 330f.

[69] In Hippolytus' account Basilides rejects the theory of emanations (*Phil.* 7. 22. 2).

[70] Thus corresponding to the days of the solar year (Harvey ci note 1). In Egyptian belief there was a god to govern each day of the calendric year (Herod. 2. 82), i.e. 360, with five more for the five intercalated days (cf. *ERE* 3. 91ff., esp. 99, Erman, *Handbook of Egyptian Religion* 180: the

reference to Brugsch *Matériaux* 47 in the former is incorrect). Cf. further Reitzenstein *Poim.* 256ff., esp. 272ff. In Hippolytus *Phil.* 7. 26. 6–7, Abraxas is the Great Archon of the heavens in the Hebdomad (cf. infra, n. 74). See the references in Wendland's edition of Hippolytus, 205.

[71] This, however, seems contrary to the view assigned to Basilides by Hippolytus and Clement (Harvey cvi; cf. *ERE* 2. 428).

[72] On the term Caulacau which occurs here see Harvey 201 note 4, *ERE* 2. 428f. Mansel (162f.) derives it from the Hebrew of Is. 28. 10. It appears also in Hippolytus' account of the Naassenes, *Phil.* 5. 8. 4 (cf. Legge 2. 94). See also Bousset *Hauptprobleme* 240 and note there, Creed in *JTS* xxvi 118.

[73] Vulgus autem quos gentilicio vocabulo Chaldaeos dicere oportet, Mathematicos dicit (Aul. Gell. *NA* 1. 9, quoted by Harvey 203 note 4, who refers to Hippolytus *Phil.* 4. 4–12 for the Chaldeans).

[74] See Harvey 203 note 6; Abraxas $= 1 + 2 + 100 + 1 + 60 + 1 + 200 = 365$. Cf. Hippolytus *Phil.* 7. 26. 6, Dieterich *Abraxas* 46. The occurrence of the name on amulets, etc., does not necessarily involve the influence of Basilides (cf. Goodenough *Symbols*, index s.v.). On the text here see Harvey cii note 3.

[75] *Phil.* 7. 14; 19. 9. Cf. Harvey xcff. Hippolytus describes this system more briefly in *Phil.* 10. 14.

[76] ibid. 20. 1. Matthias is the disciple elected to the apostolate in place of Judas (Acts 1. 23). According to Clem. Alex. *Strom.* 7. 106 the teaching came from Glaucias.

[77] On ἦν, ὅτε ἦν οὐδέν Wendland refers to Norden 370ff., *Clem. Hom.* 6. 3, Iren. 1. 1. 1–2 (Harvey 8ff.). Cf. *ERE* 2. 428ff.

[78] 21. 1–2. Cf. 10. 14. 1–2.

[79] 22. 2ff. The cosmic seed is also described as πανσπερμία, or again as a heap of seeds. Cf. Dieterich *Abraxas* 72ff.

[80] 22. 7ff. Cf. 10. 14. 2ff. Compare the account of the Naassenes, p. 120 above.

[81] For the idea of πνεῦμα $=$ ὄχημα cf. *Vig. Chr.* viii. 15ff. Hippolytus compares the *Phaedrus* of Plato (ibid.). Philo (*de Gig.* 3. 13) says the souls which are immortal soar back to the place whence they came (Wolfson *Philo* 1. 396), following Plato. Cf. also Wolfson 1. 367.

[82] ὁμοούσιος: 'possibly the earliest use of the orthodox watchword in repelling the Arian attack' (Harvey xcix). On the intermediate Spirit see Bousset *Hauptprobleme* 119ff., and for its occurrence here ibid. 127. Bousset has confused the Spirit with the second Sonship, but the correction only improves his argument. His rendering, however, finds some support in *Phil.* 7. 25. 7. On the Gnostic use of the Homoousion cf. Turner *Pattern* 161ff.

[83] Harvey c; Hippol. *Phil.* 10. 14. 3.

[84] 23. 1ff.

[85] He was indeed superior to the underlying cosmic seed, but not to the

third Sonship, nor, of course, to the Non-existent, of whom he was ignorant.

[86] Hippolytus here notes the similarity to the theory of Aristotle (24. 1–3).

[87] This figure corresponds to the Demiurge of other systems, but the Great Archon is also called δημιουργός (23. 7). The term is not yet restricted to a particular figure (infra, p. 233f).

[88] τὸ δὲ ἐν τῷ διαστήματι τούτῳ ὁ σωρὸς αὐτός ἐστι καὶ ἡ πανσπερμία, καὶ γίνεται κατὰ φύσιν τὰ γινόμενα ὡς φθάσαντα τεχθῆναι ὑπὸ τοῦ τὰ μέλλοντα λέγεσθαι .... λελογισμένου· καὶ τούτων ἐστὶν ἐπιστάτης ἢ φροντιστὴς ἢ δημιουργὸς οὐδείς. Cf. 10. 14. 8–9.

[89] Rom. 8. 19, 22.

[90] τὰς ψυχὰς κάτω φύσιν ἐχούσας μένειν ἐν τούτῳ τῷ διαστήματι, i.e. apparently the souls of the ψυχικοί—cf. Valentinus. See Bigg, Christian Platonists 205, for a similar view held by Origen.

[91] 25. 2ff.

[92] 25. 5ff. Harvey compares 'the vibration of light, the radiation of heat, or an electric current' (cii ff.).

[93] Who is Christ, as appears from 26. 2.

[94] Cf. Clem. Alex. Strom. 2. 35. 5–36. 1 (Wendland Hippol. 204).

[95] Luke 1. 35.

[96] 26. 10; cf. Harvey cviii.

[97] 27. 1–4. Harvey's inference (cv and note 2 there) seems unwarranted.

[98] 27. 7ff.

[99] ἀπαρχὴ τῆς φυλοκρινήσεως τῶν συγκεχυμένων. Cf. Quispel, Eranos Jahrbuch xvi (1948) 117ff.

[100] Basilides' version of the astrological ascent of the soul. Harvey wrongly identifies the Spirit with the Ogdoad (cvi).

[101] 27. 11: ὅλη γάρ αὐτῶν ἡ ὑπόθεσις σύγχυσις οἱονεὶ πανσπερμίας καὶ φυλοκρίνησις καὶ ἀποκατάστασις τῶν συγκεχυμένων εἰς τὰ οἰκεῖα.

[102] 27. 13.

[103] For details see ERE 2. 426ff. Scott in ERE 6. 240 remarks that the two accounts agree 'in not a few important details.' Bousset (Hauptprobleme 92ff.) finds the original views of Basilides in a third account, of a predominantly dualistic character, preserved in the Acta Archelai. Cf. ibid. 106. But see also Quispel in Eranos Jahrbuch xvi (1948) 92ff.

[104] Cf. the quotation from E. F. Scott in ERE, supra, p. 140 note 168.

[105] Cf. ZNTW 1904, 121ff.

[106] See above p. 120; cf. also Legge 2. 93f.

[107] See ERE 2. 432 on the formative influences, and Quispel loc. cit.

[108] ibid. 430. If we accept the account of Irenaeus, the following remarks require modification.

[109] ibid.

[110] ibid.

[111] ibid. 429, based on Hippol. Phil. 7. 25. 6.

[112] *ERE* 6. 240. Harvey (civ) notes analogies with Plotinus.

[113] Iren. *adv. Haer.* 1. 1. 1ff., Hippol. *Phil.* 6. 21ff.

[114] See Foerster, *Von Valentin zu Herakleon* (Beiheft 7 zur *ZNTW*, Giessen 1928); *Sagnard, La gnose valentinienne*; and for a reconstruction of the original doctrine of Valentinus, Quispel in *Vig. Chr.* 1. 48ff.

[115] See Hilgenfeld, *Ketzergeschichte des Urchristentums*, Leipzig 1884; Foerster 91ff., Sagnard 121ff. The fragments are collected in Völker *Quellen* 57ff. To these must now be added the *Gospel of Truth* (see below, p. 155ff.).

[116] Ed. Brooke, *The Fragments of Heracleon* (Texts and Studies i, Cambridge 1891); Völker 63ff. See also Foerster and Sagnard, opp. cit.

[117] Ed. Casey, *The Excerpta ex Theodoto of Clement of Alexandria* (Studies and Documents i, London 1934); Sagnard (Sources chrétiennes 23, Paris 1948). See also Bousset *Schulbetrieb* 157ff.

[118] *Epistle to Flora* ap. Epiph. *Haer.* 33. 3 (Legge 2. 131); ed. Quispel (Sources chrétiennes, Paris 1949); Völker 87ff. See also Foerster 81ff., Sagnard *La gnose valentinienne* 451ff., and Quispel in *Vig. Chr.* 2. 17ff.

[119] op. cit. 38, 104f.

[120] According to Harvey (8 note 1), Hippolytus and the *Didasc. Or.* of Clement of Alexandria (i.e. the *Excerpta ex Theodoto*) give the Oriental phase of this heresy, which Legge (2. 98 note 1) thinks more likely to represent the teaching of Valentinus himself. *ERE*, however, says (12. 572): 'A number of indications make it almost certain that Irenaeus is closer to the original sources, although he has presented his material with little discrimination, and has confused the teaching of Valentinus himself with that of his disciples.' For details, see the studies by Sagnard and Foerster noted above. For Ptolemy in this connexion see Legge 2. 119, *ERE* 12. 576.

[121] See Legge 2. 95ff., *ERE* 12. 572ff. The following account is derived from Iren. 1. 1. 1ff., which, however, purports to represent the views of Valentinus' disciples, his own views being given in 1. 5. See Foerster op. cit., Sagnard 140ff., and Quispel's reconstruction of the original theory, *Vig. Chr.* 1. 48ff.; also Quispel, *Gnosis als Weltreligion* 71ff.

Harvey reproduces the Greek text from Epiphanius. For comparison with Hippolytus see Foerster and Sagnard, and cf. Harvey's notes. Harvey links this account with the system of Ptolemaeus, holding Hippolytus to be nearer Valentinus' own views (11 note 4, cf. Legge 2. 108 note 1). Cf. also the exegesis of the Fourth Gospel ap. Iren. 1. 1. 18, and the references in the Excerpta and Heracleon.

[122] Cf. Simon Magus (above, p. 100). According to Hippolytus (6. 29) Bythos is alone. Hippolytus is concerned to show that Valentinus was indebted to Pythagoras, as Basilides to Aristotle (cf. Legge 2. 97ff.).

The *Gospel of Truth* (37. 10ff.) speaks of 'the mind which pronounces the unique word in silent grace,' with which may be compared the references in Ignatius to a word proceeding from silence (*Mag.* 8. 2, cf. *Eph.* 19. 1, 15. 1f.). See Stauffer, *New Testament Theology* (*ET* London 1955),

44, 57 and 267 notes 116 and 125, who quotes ps.-Philo 60 (*Texts and Studies* ii, 1893, 185), IV Ezra 6. 38f. Cf. also Baynes *A Coptic Gnostic Treatise* 48f.

[123] Cf. Exc. 7.

[124] This term is derived from the statement that Anthropos and Ecclesia were produced κατὰ συζυγίαν by Logos and Zoe. Man and the Church are born of the *union* of Reason (or the Word) and Life, themselves the offspring of Mind, which with Truth is the first product of Ultimate Being. According to Tertullian, some regarded all this as a figure of speech (Legge 2. 99). The Aeons are attributes of God, or names of God in different aspects.

[125] The Decad, according to Hippolytus assigned to Nous and Aletheia. On the names, see Legge 2. 101ff.

[126] The Dodecad, according to Hippolytus assigned to Logos and Zoe.

[127] The account in Hippolytus makes Sige a nonentity and leaves Bythos outside the Pleroma, which is completed by Christ and the Holy Spirit (6. 31). But he knows of this version.

[128] Cf. Exc. 29.

[129] According to Legge (2. 105 note 2), the name was probably suggested by that of the old Egyptian god, but this, although attractive, must be regarded as doubtful. In the one case we have Ὧρος, in the other Ὅρος (boundary or limit), although a Doric form ὧρος is given for the latter by Liddell-Scott-Jones. The Greek ὧρος (year) may also have contributed to the general syncretism. For Horus in Valentinianism cf. Knox *PCG* 155 note 2.

[130] Cf. Hippol. 6. 30.

[131] The male was considered to give form, the female substance; Bythos, being (on this account) hermaphrodite, gave both form and substance, but Sophia being female could only give substance without form. Cf. Hippol. 6. 30. See also Williams, *Ideas of the Fall* 235 note 6.

[132] Hippolytus (6. 31) refers this fear to the whole Pleroma. Cf. Exc. 31.

[133] Hippolytus (ibid.) refers this function to Christ and the Holy Spirit, who were produced for this purpose. Horus was then projected to shut off the passion outside from the Pleroma. Cf. Legge 2. 105f.

[134] Cf. Hippolytus ibid. The Spirit is again female here (cf. the Ophite system, above, p. 117). According to another version Christ is the offspring of Sophia (cf. Foerster op. cit. and Bousset *Hauptprobleme* 265ff.).

[135] Cf. Exc. 7 and 31, with Casey's notes. Norden (72) notes the similarity between Exc. 7 and the Hermetic κόρη κόσμου, for which see ibid. 65ff. Cf. also Philo *de Post. Caini* 15, where the realization that τὸ ὄν is incomprehensible is itself a boon.

[136] Cf. Col. 1. 19, 2. 9.

[137] See Iren. 1. 1. 5–6. On the significance of this first part of the Valentinian theory cf. Mansel 182f.: 'Stripped of its allegorical imagery, the general meaning ... seems to be the exposition of a doctrine in itself far

from heretical . . . that the representation of the divine nature by a plurality of attributes . . . is but an inadequate and imperfect manifestation of the Unlimited.'

[138] Harvey 30 note 2.

[139] Achamoth is the Greek transliteration of *Hochmah*, or according to Harvey (31 note 3) its Syriac equivalent. Cf. Legge index s.v., and the Ophite Sophia-Prunicus (above, p. 117). Mansel (169 note 2, 184 note 2) derives the name from Proverbs, esp. Prov. 9. 1. Cf. Exc. 47.

[140] So in the Hippolytan account of Basilides the Spirit retains a savour of the second Sonship (7. 22. 14, where Wendland compares 5. 19. 3ff.). According to another version Christ is the offspring of Sophia, but leaves her to enter the Pleroma (above, n. 134). It may be worth noting that in Tatian (Or. 7) man who was made in the likeness of God became mortal by reason of the fall, when 'the more powerful Spirit' departed from him. Cf. *Studia Patristica* 1. 427ff.

[141] Cf. Knox *PCG* 41ff., and for the use of the name in magic Goodenough *Symbols* 2. 318 (index s.v.).

[142] So too the Ophite Ialdabaoth and the Basilidean Archons are able to ascend only as far as the firmament, here in a sense represented by Horus.

[143] Cf. Dieterich *Abraxas* 30, etc., and note that Iao also appears in the text which he is discussing. Irenaeus here waxes eloquent in his scorn (1. 1. 8). See also Bousset *Hauptprobleme* 233f.

[144] In Exc. 23 the appeal is made by Christ to the higher Aeons.

[145] Cf. Exc. 23–24.

[146] An adaptation of Col. 1. 16; cf. Exc. 43, and see also *Vig. Chr.* viii. 48ff. on the *Epistle to Rheginus* in the Codex Jung.

[147] Cf. Exc. 21, 44.

[148] Cf. Exc. 44–45.

[149] Cf. Exc. 45f. On the meaning see Harvey 40 note 3. Cf. also Dieterich *Abraxas* 86ff.

[150] Iren. 1. 1. 8 (Harvey 41); cf. Exc. 47.

[151] Cf. Eve in the Ophite system (above, p. 137). These angels are the spiritual spouses of the souls of men (cf. Legge 2. 110 and notes there; Heracleon fr. 35. 17f. Brooke; Exc. 64).

[152] According to another version the Demiurge himself became the image of Bythos, and put forth first the psychic Christ and then the angels and archangels [Exc. 47, cf. Iren. 1. 1. 13 (Harvey 60)].

[153] Cf. above, pp. 118 (Ophites), 125 (Basilides).

[154] Cf. 2 Cor. 12. 2. In Exc. 51, man is created 'in Paradise in the fourth heaven.' Casey (144) refers to Ginzberg, *Die Haggada bei den Kirchenvätern, Monatschrift für Gesch. u. Wissenschaft des Judentums* 42, 1898, 547ff., for this location of Paradise in Jewish literature.

[155] Cf. Hippol. 6. 33–34, Exc. 49, and cf. the other Gnostic systems for this ignorance of the Demiurge.

[156] Also called Earth, Jerusalem, Holy Spirit, and κύριος.

[157] Cf. Exc. 48.

[158] On this see Harvey 47 note 3; the term itself is astrological (Knox *PCG* 202 note 5).

[159] Cf. Exc. 50, Philo Op. M. 136ff. This man was created not from the earth we know, but from 'an invisible substance' [Iren. 1. 1. 10 (Harvey 49)] Cf. the system of Justin (above, p. 122). On the early history of the exegesis of Gen. 1. 26, which is clearly in view in this context, see *Studia Patristica* 1. 420ff.

[160] Cf. Exc. 50, 55, and the references to Philo, etc., in Casey 143. The coat of skin is derived from Gen. 3. 21. Cf. Dodd *BG* 191ff. According to Origen (*c. Cels.* 4. 40) the statement 'has a certain secret and mysterious meaning' (see Chadwick 216 note 5).

[161] Cf. Harvey 50 note 2. In Iren. 1. 1. 13 the souls which receive the seed are said to be better than the rest, and to be especially loved by the Demiurge, who knows not why. He makes them therefore prophets, priests, and kings. Cf. Soph. Sol. 7. 27, where Wisdom 'passing into holy souls makes them friends of God and prophets.' If the equation of the Demiurge with the God of the OT be kept in mind, some connexion may be suspected.

[162] Cf. Exc. 56. The accounts vary between a view in which the three natures are combined in each individual and one in which there are three different classes of men, hylic or material, psychic and pneumatic. Cf. Iren. 1. 1. 14, Exc. 54. In contrast to the Ophites, for whom it was possible for men to pass from one class to another, Valentinus appears to have made the distinction one of essence. See Legge 2. 111ff., Foerster op. cit. Of course it was possible to combine both, the three natures being combined in each man, and the classification depending on the predominance of one over the others, but it is not clear that this was the view which was taken. One of the documents in the Jung Codex has been given the title *The Treatise on the Three Natures*, and has been ascribed to Heracleon. See Quispel in *The Jung Codex* 57ff., and Puech-Quispel in *Vig. Chr.* ix. 65ff.

[163] Cf. Harvey 52 note 5.

[164] On the 'psychic' see Kirk 217 and note 2 there, with the additional note ibid. 487ff.

[165] 1. 1. 11 *ad fin.*, 12. But cf. Foerster 78ff. Irenaeus and Heracleon generally agree, but here differ; for this and other reasons Foerster concludes that this section does not really refer to Valentinianism, but belongs to the account of some other system.

[166] Cf. Exc. 64, Heracleon fr. 18 Brooke. Sometimes it appears that such a union of the soul with its angelic complement ($\pi\lambda\acute{\eta}\rho\omega\mu\alpha$ Heracleon; see Foerster 16, 21, 85 and compare the *Gospel of Truth* 41. 12ff.) is a necessary preliminary to salvation; this in some respects recalls the myth of the *Symposium*. As each Aeon has its partner ($\sigma\acute{v}\zeta\upsilon\gamma o\varsigma$, $\pi\lambda\acute{\eta}\rho\omega\mu\alpha$) so has each soul, the things of the highest world being exactly paralleled in the lower. Cf. also Dieterich *Eine Mithrasliturgie* 129.

[167] Cf. Exc. 48, 81 and the Stoic ἐκπύρωσις. Also *Ev. Veritatis* 25. 15f.

[168] On the Christology of Valentinus see Legge 2. 115ff. The section of Irenaeus in question here is 1. 1. 13ff. See further Bousset *Hauptprobleme* 265ff., Mansel 192ff., and cf. Houssiau, *La Christologie de saint Irénée* (Louvain 1955).

[169] Bigg *Christian Platonists* 28. Applicable though it may be to such documents as *Pistis Sophia* and the anonymous work in the Codex Brucianus (cf. Schmidt, *Koptisch-gnostische Schriften* 1, 2nd ed. revised by Till, Berlin 1954; Baynes *A Coptic Gnostic Treatise*, Cambridge 1933; Till in *La Parola del Passato* 1949, 230ff.), this judgement would now appear to be not altogether justified. It may be too much to claim, with Harnack, that the Gnostics were the first Christian philosophers, but some at least of them were original and independent thinkers of considerable power. See below on the *Apocryphon Johannis* and the *Gospel of Truth*. According to Quispel (*The Jung Codex* 59), the author of the *Treatise on the Three Natures* 'stood consciously apart from Greek philosophy,' but this attitude can be paralleled among more orthodox Fathers (cf. Wolfson, *Philosophy of the Church Fathers* vol. 1).

[170] On the followers of Valentinus see Legge 2. 117ff., Foerster *Von Valentin zu Herakleon*, Sagnard *La gnose valentinienne*, Goppelt 275ff.

[171] Strictly speaking, only two falls are mentioned, that of Sophia and that of Achamoth, but a third seems to be implied in the infusion of the spiritual seed into man. Certainly there is a triple Redemption, although the sources are not very clear on the subject.

[172] On the results of Gnosticism cf. *ERE* 6. 240ff., and on Valentinianism and orthodox Christianity Legge 2. 121ff. For Gnostic influence on Origen see Daniélou *Origen* (*ET* London 1955) 191ff. and cf. below, p. 134ff.

[173] *Adv. Haer.* 1. 5ff.

[174] ibid. 1. 2ff. For Irenaeus' own theology see Lawson, *The Biblical Theology of St. Irenaeus* (London 1948), Houssiau *La Christologie de saint Irénée* (Louvain 1955), and cf. Markus in *Vig. Chr.* viii. 193ff.

[175] Irenaeus does, of course, demonstrate his own position, but his primary purpose is to refute the Gnostic theories. The emphasis of his work is therefore different from that of Clement and Origen, who seek to construct a Christian philosophy.

[176] Legge, however, notes (2. 95) that the orthodox who wrote long after Valentinus' death are most bitter against him.

[177] Bigg *Christian Platonists* 51. For an example of Clement's use of Gnostic terms see Legge 2. 100. See also Völker, *Der wahre Gnostiker nach Clemens Alexandrinus* (*TU* 57, Berlin 1952). Quispel (*The Jung Codex* 61) claims that the 'true Gnosis' of Clement and Origen 'is to be regarded as in a certain sense a progressive Christianization of the "Gnosis falsely so called" of the Valentinians.'

[178] Bigg 55ff.

[179] ibid. 71ff., 189ff.

[180] ibid. 71f. Compare ibid. 190f. and note 1 to 191 for Origen's view.

[181] ibid. 78ff., 198ff. Cf. Quispel *The Jung Codex* 61, *Gnosis als Welt-religion* 24ff.

[182] ibid. 56, 134, 145. For Origen see also Daniélou.

[183] ibid. 58, 86, 140. On the double standard generally see Kirk, index s.v.

[184] ibid. 88f.

[185] See above, p. 78ff.

[186] See, for example, Bigg 67 note 4. Quite apart from the numerous references given by Bigg, Philonic parallels frequently come to mind as we read his account of the teaching of the two Alexandrians. For one particular aspect, see *Studia Patristica* 1. 420ff. (the interpretation of Gen. 1. 26).

[187] Cf., for example, ibid. 77ff., 136ff., and for similarities 63ff., 155ff. (view of God), 113 (the seven heavens); compare also Origen *in Joh.* i. 20 (ibid. 171) with the view of Basilides as given by Irenaeus (supra, p. 124). Cf. also *Vig. Chr.* viii. 46.

[188] Bigg 49.

[189] ibid. 52. Cf. Bousset's description of Clement: Der Schöpfer der temperierten, ganz und gar vom Geist griechischer Philosophie durch-drungenen, entorientalisierten und damit für die Kirche erträglich gewor-denen Gnosis (*Schulbetrieb* iii).

[190] For fuller discussion see Bigg op. cit.; Turner *The Pattern of Christian Truth*; Wolfson *Philosophy of the Church Fathers* 1; and for Clement, Bousset *Schulbetrieb*, and Hort-Mayor, *Clement of Alexandria: The Seventh Book of the Stromateis*, Introd.

CHAPTER VI

TWO ORIGINAL GNOSTIC DOCUMENTS: APOCRYPHON JOHANNIS AND EVANGELIUM VERITATIS

U P to this point our study has inevitably been based on the Greek sources, in other words upon the evidence afforded by the Christian refutations. Apart from fragments, and the quotations embedded in the writings of the Christian Fathers, there has been until recent years no other evidence for Gnosticism in its earlier stages, or even in its prime. Certain original Gnostic documents in Coptic have long been known, but these date from a period a century after Valentinus, when any pretensions to philosophy had disappeared and Gnosticism had degenerated into the purest fantasy.[1] Our evidence is in consequence open to suspicion as the propaganda of the opposition, composed by the party which eventually emerged victorious and which was therefore in a position to control the record transmitted to posterity.

The situation is now completely transformed by the discovery of the Nag Hammadi library[2] and the publication of the Berlin Gnostic papyrus.[3] The latter has long been known, and one of the documents in it, the *Apocryphon Johannis*, was identified by Schmidt as the source employed by Irenaeus in his description of the Barbelognostics,[4] but only in 1955 did the full text become available. If there is now any hesitation about accepting Schmidt's conclusion, it is only because Nag Hammadi may yet provide an even closer parallel.[5] Of this library one document only has as yet been published,[6] but it may well prove to be the most important of them all: it has been identified as the *Gospel of Truth* mentioned by Irenaeus, and has been claimed as the work of Valentinus himself.[7] To these we may now turn our attention, although it must be emphasized that at this stage any conclusions are subject, for obvious reasons, to correction in the light of further research.

The importance of the *Apocryphon* is immediately clear from the fact that it occurs in three different recensions in the Nag Hammadi library, one of them closely similar to that of the Berlin Codex.[8] This shows, as Till has observed, that the document was very highly esteemed among the Egyptian Gnostics.[9] There are clear signs that it was originally composed in Greek, and if it was used by Irenaeus it must have been compiled before A.D. 180. According to Puech,[10] it almost certainly appears again in Babylonia, under the name of the *Revelation of John*, in the seventh or eighth century, so that it enjoyed a prolonged and widespread influence.

The treatise begins with a vision granted to John the son of Zebedee on 'the mountain,'[11] in the course of which, in answer to the questions which have perplexed him, he receives instruction in the doctrine, which is to be imparted only to those who are able to receive it. Towards the end[12] a solemn curse is pronounced upon any one who shall transmit this doctrine to another for the sake of merely material advantage.

In this system 'the true God, the Father of all, the Holy Spirit, the Invisible, who is above all, who exists in his incorruptibility, dwells in pure light which no eye may behold.' This supreme Being is described at length in purely negative statements,[13] as absolutely beyond human understanding or comprehension; not even perfection, blessedness or divinity may be predicated of him, for 'he is quite different from anything of which we can think, imagine, or speak.'[14] He perceived his own image in the pure water of light which surrounded him, and his "Εννοια[14a] came into existence, the image of light, the εἰκών of the Invisible, Barbelo. At her request the supreme God then created four further Aeons: a second Ennoia,[15] Prognosis, Aphtharsia and 'Eternal Life.' Barbelo then brought forth a divine spark, Monogenes, the first-born son. The invisible Spirit rejoiced over this new light, and anointed him with his goodness, so that he became perfect, without blemish, and Christ.[16] This son requested a single boon, Nous, which thereupon came into being, followed by Will and Logos. According to Irenaeus the eight Aeons created after Barbelo formed four syzygies.[17]

Christ was appointed god of all the universe, and given all power by the true God; from his union with Aphtharsia came the four great lights, whose names are Harmozel, Oroiael, Daveithe, and Eleleth. Each of these has three attendant Aeons.[18] Then from Prognosis and Nous arose the true and perfect man, Adam, who was established in the first great light.[19] The second light is the residence of Adam's son Seth, the third that of Seth's offspring, the souls of the blessed,[20] while the fourth is reserved for those who follow the Gnostic way only after some hesitation.

The last divine being to come into existence was Sophia, the third Aeon of the fourth light, who now without the consent of the Spirit or the approval of her partner[21] brought forth a son, Ialdabaoth. Ashamed of her offspring, who was of a different form from his mother, she hid him in a cloud that none of the other aeons might see him. Departing from the place in which he had been born, he created a world of his own, with twelve angels after the pattern of the immortal Aeons and subordinate angels for each of them, to the number of three hundred and sixty.[22] He also appointed seven kings of the heaven and five to rule over the chaos of the underworld (among the names here mentioned are Iao, Eloaios, Astaphaeus and Sabaoth[23]). To these his creatures he gave no part of the power which he had inherited from his mother, and so could rule over them. Ignorant of any higher being, he looked round upon his creation and declared: 'I am a jealous God; beside me there is no other'[24] (on which the author comments: 'Were there no other, of whom would he be jealous?').

Sophia now began ἐπιφέρεσθαι, having recognized her fault and realized that she had thereby lost her perfection. This ἐπιφέρεσθαι, however, does not have its Old Testament[25] meaning, but signifies that Sophia in her penitence went to and fro in the darkness. The other aeons[26] heard her prayer of repentance, and interceded for her; the invisible Spirit gave his approval. Sophia could not, however, return to her own place, but remained in the Nonad until her fault should be put right.

The Father now revealed to Ialdabaoth's seven archons his own image reflected in water, and they were so impressed that they resolved: 'Let us make a man after the image and likeness of God.'[27] Each contributed of his power, so that the man thus formed incorporated in himself the powers of all seven;[28] but for the moment he lay inert and lifeless, since neither they nor their three hundred and sixty angels could quicken him to life. The Mother, however,

now desired to recover the power which she had given to Ialdabaoth, and therefore approached the supreme God, who sent
Christ and the four great lights to Ialdabaoth in the form of his
(Ialdabaoth's) angels. They advised him to breathe into the face
of the new creature the power which he had inherited from his
mother.[29] He did so, and thereby transferred to Adam this power,
so that Adam became superior both to his creators and to Ialdabaoth
himself. Now begins the struggle for the soul of man between
the world of light and the world of darkness.

Ialdabaoth and his powers brought Adam down to the material
world and fashioned for him a body from the four elements;[30] this
is the grave of the light that is in him, and fetters him to the material.
The supreme God, however, in his mercy sent him a helper, the
Epinoia of light,[31] whom he called 'Zoe'; this was hidden in Adam,
that the archons might not become aware of it.

Ialdabaoth now set Adam in Paradise, to deceive him, for its
bliss was illusory, its fruits poison. The tree of life was, in fact,
intended to lead Adam astray and prevent him reaching perfection;
the tree of the knowledge of good and evil, on the other hand, was
no other than the Epinoia of light—hence the command (from
Ialdabaoth) not to eat of it. It was Christ, not the serpent,[32] who
encouraged man to eat of it. The serpent was in the service of
Ialdabaoth, and implanted in man sexual desire; procreation
increases the number of men in the world, and therefore the
number of divine sparks in the power of Ialdabaoth, and so serves
his purpose.

To prevent Adam from perceiving the truth, Ialdabaoth brought
forgetfulness[33] upon him, and then created another human being
in the form of a woman.[34] At the instigation of the Epinoia of
light they ate of the tree of knowledge, and so became aware of
their true being. Realizing that Paradise had failed in its purpose,
Ialdabaoth cursed man and expelled him. Filled with passion at the
sight of Adam's virgin wife, Ialdabaoth desired to have offspring
by her,[35] and begot two sons: the righteous Eloim and the un-
righteous Jave, whom men call Cain and Abel.[35a] These he set
over the four elements from which the material body of man had
been made. Ialdabaoth also implanted sexual passion in Adam,
whose son was Seth. There are now two spirits in man, one divine,

the other an ἀντίμιμον πνεῦμα.[36] The former seeks to arouse him
from forgetfulness and the 'wickedness' of the grave, the latter is
the sexual instinct which serves the ends of Ialdabaoth.

The narrative is here interrupted by questions from John, to
which the Saviour replies. Those upon whom the Spirit of Life
descends are redeemed and become perfect, worthy to ascend to
the Great Light. Purified from all wickedness and from every
temptation of evil, they set their minds on nothing but the incorruptible assembly, untouched by wrath, fear or desire, but only
bound for a season to the flesh. Not all, however, are capable of
this, since in some the ἀντίμιμον πνεῦμα is dominant. These
remain subject to Ialdabaoth and at death must be fettered in a
new body until they can attain to knowledge and be redeemed.
Those who have attained to knowledge and have turned away,
and thereby have sinned against the Holy Spirit,[37] are doomed to
eternal punishment.

A question from John about the origin of the ἀντίμιμον πνεῦμα
leads to a continuation of the reinterpretation of Genesis.[38] Ialdabaoth and his powers brought εἱμαρμένη into being, and by times
and seasons fettered the gods of heaven, angels, demons, and men,
but then he repented and resolved to destroy his creation by a flood.
The Epinoia of light warned Noah, who told the other men, but
they did not believe him. Noah and a few elect companions
covered themselves with a cloud of light,[39] and so were delivered
from the darkness which Ialdabaoth poured out over all things.
The powers then sent their angels to the daughters of men,[40] but at
first had no success and so resolved to create the ἀντίμιμον πνεῦμα,
which they implanted in the women. Their offspring were children
of darkness, in whom the ἀντίμιμον πνεῦμα was so strong as to
prevent them learning the truth. The treatise ends with a brief
reference to the descent of the redeemer to bring the saving knowledge, the curse against any who shall impart it merely for gain,
and the statement that John on the departure of the redeemer began
to tell his fellow-disciples what the redeemer had said to him.

As Till says, 'the Gnostic doctrine as we can gather it from the
Apocryphon of John is on a high intellectual and moral level.'[41] Here
we have a consistent and well-articulated system which in the later
Coptic Gnostic works has been shattered into fragments. For

present purposes, however, the chief interest of this system lies in the light it sheds upon the theories already considered, since here we seem to have the key to the enigmas of Ophite doctrine. Indeed, when the Ophite theories are examined in the light of the Apocryphon much that was obscure becomes perfectly clear and lucid, and it is evident that the disparaging comments sometimes directed against the Gnostics are not altogether justified. If it is perhaps too generous to describe the Gnostics as the first Christian theologians, it is now clear why Irenaeus and others devoted their energies to the refutation of this heresy. Some at least of the Gnostics were independent thinkers whose works, in an age when doctrine was still in its formative stages, must have exercised a real attraction for many minds as presenting a reasonable and consistent explanation of the nature and destiny of man and the universe.

One striking feature is the reinterpretation of the Genesis narrative which forms so large a part of the treatise. The strictly Christian elements in comparison are far less important, and in particular little place is given to the person and ministry of Jesus. This might seem once more to point to a pre-Christian Jewish Gnosticism which has been but slightly christianized; but, in the first place, we have no evidence for the date of this document save that it seems to have been known to Irenaeus,[42] and secondly, there is the fact that the God of the Old Testament has been degraded into the chief of the rulers of this world.[43] The latter feature does not seem to occur in the earliest forms of Gnosticism but appears to have been introduced somewhere about the time of Marcion. Again, comparison with such definitely Jewish writings as the Book of Jubilees or the recently published Genesis Apocryphon is instructive.[44] Here also we find expansion and interpretation of the narratives of Genesis, but the tone is completely different: in the eyes of the Gnostic writer this world is evil, its creator hostile to man and bent on retaining his control over the creatures who have come under his sway. In Gnosticism, in fact, as Jonas has observed,[45] a new and revolutionary element has entered in, an element neither Greek nor Hebrew, despairing of this world and all that it contains.

Again, the *Apocryphon of John* itself presents a number of questions for investigation: Is it, for example, an early and pure form of Ophitism, which Irenaeus has distorted in his efforts to present a concise statement, or is it a later, more coherent and more systematic version of a theory known to Irenaeus only in a cruder form? Do the evident links with the Valentinian theory indicate, as Quispel claims,[46] that Valentinus endeavoured to hellenize and christianize an earlier pagan Gnosis, or do they point rather to the influence of Valentinianism itself upon the sect from which this treatise[47] came? Here two points must be noted: in the first place, assuming that Irenaeus knew the Apocryphon substantially as we now have it, there is a period of about a generation from the time of Valentinus to that at which Irenaeus wrote, and secondly the *Gospel of Truth*, claimed by its editors as Valentinian, was found in the library of a group which appears to have been Sethian, i.e. of an Ophite type. Clearly much remains to be done before we can reach a final solution.

A 'Gospel of Truth' was known to Irenaeus,[48] who declares that the Valentinians had reached such a pitch of audacity as to entitle their own comparatively recent writing 'the Gospel of Truth,' although it agreed in no respect with the Gospels of the Apostles. Now the newly-published treatise from the Jung Codex begins with the words: 'The Gospel of Truth is joy for those who have received from the Father of Truth the grace of knowing him through the power of the Word which has come forth from the Pleroma, which is in the thought and mind of the Father, (the Word) which is he who is named 'Saviour' because that is the name of the work which he must accomplish for the redemption of those who knew not the Father.'[49] It is therefore natural to identify the two writings, the more especially since the new text is clearly Valentinian.[50] Moreover, as van Unnik observes, 'the one concrete point that Irenaeus tells us, viz. that it agrees at no point with the Gospels of the Apostles, fully accords with the character of the recently discovered writing.'[51] Here, it may be noted, there is a difference of opinion already among those who have had opportunity to study the text: Puech and Quispel have argued that the *Gospel of Truth* should be regarded as a fifth Gospel side by side with the canonical four, but van Unnik disagrees.[52] For him the word 'Gospel' must be understood 'in the light of early Christian linguistic usage, when it was not yet limited to a species of book.' The 'Gospel' is the message, the glad tidings of salvation, not yet the book in which the message is contained;[53] and, indeed, this view would seem to be justified by the facts. The document bears no resemblance to other Gospels, canonical, apocryphal or Gnostic; it contains no narrative, no account of the life or work or words of Jesus. It pre-supposes the Synoptics and the Fourth Gospel, but is itself rather a meditation or homily than a 'Gospel' in the familiar sense of the word as applied to a book.[54] On this point van Unnik would seem to be certainly correct, but his further hypothesis must await a critical examination: that the document was composed by Valentinus himself, at Rome, round about A.D. 140–145, before the development of the typically Gnostic dogmas.[55] The importance of the treatise is already clear.

To summarize this document would be quite impossible, which may, indeed, be part of the reason why Irenaeus has so little to say about it.[56] The writer does not present a system from which an outline may be extracted, as in the *Apocryphon of John*. Rather does the system seem to be pre-supposed, and, moreover, it is a system simpler than either the Valentinian or the common Gnostic type.[57] There is here no elaborate doctrine of aeons, nor is there any mention of a Demiurge in contradistinction from the supreme God; again, the primal sin is not associated with the fall of an aeon, but is ignorance of the Father, or more accurately a forgetting of the Father.[58] There is no reference, again, to an ascent of the soul, nor does the 'Gnostic myth' of the redeemed Redeemer find any place in this treatise. On the other hand, van Unnik has noted a number of traits which we know from other sources to have been characteristic of Valentinus, and much of the terminology is quite certainly Valentinian.[59] Moreover, as van Unnik observes, there are certain parallels between the *Gospel of Truth* and the works of Justin Martyr and Aristides which seem to indicate that the author was not so far removed from the 'orthodox' Christianity of this period as was the Valentinian theory in its developed form;[60] and further investigation may bring other parallels to light. All this would seem to lend weight to van Unnik's theory, already mentioned, that the document was composed by Valentinus himself shortly before or shortly after his breach with the Church.

This 'Gospel' is not a systematic treatise, and does not readily lend itself to analysis, but this is not to say that it is formless or

devoid of structure. As in the First Epistle of John, the writer seems
to return again and again to certain familiar themes, which he
weaves together in constantly changing patterns. His fundamental
concern, however, is with the knowledge which stands over
against the error which is the forgetting of the Father. 'The
Gospel is a revelation of hope, since it is a discovery for those who
seek him.'[61] The root of man's alienation from God, and hence
of all his perplexities and anxieties, lies in his forgetfulness of the
Father. To overcome this error God has revealed himself in his
Word. Thus expressed, the message of the treatise would appear
entirely orthodox,[62] yet the document as a whole is genuinely
Gnostic. As van Unnik puts it, the *Gospel of Truth* 'seeks to build
on the foundation of the New Testament, but with a plan of its
own which was not that outlined in the New Testament.'[63]

The supreme Being of this system is the Father of Truth (16. 33),
who is incomprehensible and inconceivable, and, indeed, above all
thought (17. 7ff.). He is 'the perfect Father who produced the All,
in whom the All is, and whom the All needs' (18. 33ff.).[64] Immanent
in his thought and mind is the Pleroma (16. 35f.); indeed, all
things are within the Father (17. 6). At the same time all things
are in search of him from whom they came forth, because he is
beyond comprehension. Ignorance of the Father produced anguish
and terror, and the anguish grew thick like a mist so that no
one could see. Thus Error became strong, and wrought at its
own matter in the void, without knowing the truth. 'It applied
itself to the modelling of a creature, trying to provide in beauty
the equivalent of Truth,'[65] but anguish, oblivion, and this
'creature of falsehood' are all as nothing over against the established
truth (17. 10ff.). The works of error are wrought to attract
and imprison 'those of the midst' (i.e. the $\psi\upsilon\chi\iota\kappa\omicron\acute{\iota}$?),[66] but
oblivion is destined to be abolished by knowledge (17. 30–18. 10).[67]
'Since Oblivion came into existence because they did not know
the Father, therefore if they attain to a knowledge of the Father,
Oblivion becomes, at that very instant, non-existent' (18. 7ff.).

This is the Gospel revealed to the perfect by Jesus Christ, through
whom the Father has enlightened those who were in darkness,[68]
and therefore Error oppressed him. 'He was nailed to a tree, and
became a fruit of the knowledge of the Father, but yet a fruit

which did not cause the destruction of those who ate it' (18. 10ff.).[69] On the contrary, to those who ate he gave joy because of this discovery. He came as the messenger of one unknown to many, who yet desired to be known and loved (19. 10ff.), and constituted himself a guide. Those who were wise in their own estimation[70] put him to the proof, but he confounded them, and they therefore hated him; but after them came the little ones[71] to whom belongs the knowledge of the Father, who both knew and were known,[72] were glorified and gave glory. In their hearts was manifested the Book of Life,[73] written in the thought and mind of the Father, which none could take since it was reserved for him who should be sacrificed. Jesus therefore endured suffering until he had taken the Book, knowing that his death was life for many.[74] As the fortune of the master of the house remains concealed until his testament is opened, so did the All remain hidden as long as the Father of all was invisible. 'This is why Jesus appeared and took that Book. He was nailed to a cross of wood, and he attached the deed of disposition of the Father to that Cross' (20. 22ff.).[75] He humbled himself even to death, although clothed with life eternal, and having stripped off these perishable rags, clothed himself with incorruptibility, which none can take from him.

Those who are to receive the teaching, the living inscribed in the Book of the Living, receive it from the Father and turn anew to him. He who is ignorant is deficient, 'and it is a great deficiency, since it is precisely that which ought to perfect him which he lacks.' He who remains ignorant to the end is a creature of oblivion and will be destroyed with it, whereas those who possess knowledge are known in advance, their names are registered and are pronounced by the Father (21. 23ff.). He who has knowledge is a being from on high. 'If he is called, he hears, replies, and turns towards Him who calls him, in order to reascend to Him. . . . Possessing knowledge, he performs the will of Him who called him. He desires to do that which pleases Him, receives repose. . . . He who thus possesses knowledge knows whence he is and whither he goes.' (22. 4–15.)[76]

The writer goes on to speak of letters which are not merely vowels or consonants but 'letters of truth which one does not pronounce unless one knows them.'[77] These are written by the

Father that the aeons by means of them might attain to a knowledge of himself. 'His wisdom meditates on the Word; his intelligence projects it;[78] his knowledge has been revealed' (23. 3ff.). He reveals that of himself which was hidden (which was the Son[79]), that through the compassion of the Father the aeons might know him and cease their striving in search of him.[80] 'Having filled deficiency, he abolished form' (here identified as the κόσμος); 'for the place in which there is desire and dissension is deficiency, but the place which is unity is plenitude' (24. 21ff.). Deficiency came into being through ignorance of the Father, and disappears with knowledge, as darkness at the appearance of the light. Matter is swallowed up as in a flame, darkness by light, and death by life. Those for whom such things have happened should take care 'that the house be holy and silent for Unity' (25. 19ff.).

The 'form' above mentioned is that 'of this world,' but there is another, for which a different word is used (μορφή as distinct from σχῆμα).[81] The aeons have recognized that they have come forth from the Father, but they have not yet received 'form' or a name. This they receive through knowledge. All is of the Father. If he will, he can make manifest any one whom he wishes, by giving him a form and a name. Before anything has become manifest, he knows what he is going to produce, but the fruit which is not yet manifest knows nothing, and does nothing (28. 5ff.).

The state of ignorance with its terrors is vividly described: 'What then is that which he desires man to think? This: "I am as the shadows and phantoms of the night." When the light of dawn appears, then this man understands that the terror which had seized upon him was nothing. Thus, they were ignorant concerning the Father whom they did not see. As long as ignorance inspired them with terror and confusion, there were many illusions by which they were haunted, and empty fictions, as if they were sunk in troubled dreams. . . .' When they awake, those who have been experiencing all these confusions see nothing, for they *are* nothing. 'It is thus that each one has acted, as if he were asleep, during the time when he was ignorant, and thus he rises again as if he were awakening. Joy to the man who has rediscovered himself and has awakened! And blessed is he who has opened the eyes of the blind!' (30. 6ff.).[82]

Here follows a curious passage: 'And the Spirit came to him in haste when it resuscitated him. Having helped him who was stretched out upon the ground, it placed him upon his feet, for truly he had not yet reappeared' (30. 16–23). In this context it evidently refers to the Resurrection of Jesus (the editors compare *Exc. ex Theod.* 61. 6–8), but it offers also a striking parallel to the account of the creation of man in Saturninus.[83] The passage continues: 'When they had seen and heard him, he allowed them to taste and feel and touch the beloved Son.[84] He appeared, instructing them concerning the Father . . . and breathed into them that which is in his mind, accomplishing his will.' Many received light and turned towards him, but material man (the ὑλικοί) did not recognize him, for he came in the likeness of flesh.[85] He became 'a way for those who erred, knowledge for those who were ignorant; a discovery for those who sought, assurance for those who wavered, immaculate innocence for those who were defiled' (31. 29ff.). Then follows an elaboration of the parable of the Lost Sheep which by its use of the Roman method of reckoning suggests a Roman, or at any rate a Western, origin for the treatise.[86] At this point occurs a lacuna of four pages in the text.[86a]

The document resumes in the middle of a sentence which refers to 'accomplishment by the Mind of the Father' (or 'perfection in the thought of the Father'?), and proceeds to a discussion of 'the words of his meditation.' Each of these is the work of his unique will, in the revelation of his Word. 'While they were still in the depth of his thought the Word, which was the first to come forth, caused them to appear, united to the mind which pronounces the unique Word in silent grace, and which was called "thought" because they were in it before they became manifest' (37. 7ff.).[87] Nothing takes place without the will of the Father, but this will is incomprehensible and cannot be sought out. The Father knows the origin of them all, as well as their end . . . but the end is the receiving of knowledge of him who is hidden, the Father from whom came forth the beginning and to whom are to return all those who came forth from him.

The next section is a meditation upon the mystery of the name of God.[88] One does not pronounce the name of God, but he reveals himself through a Son. The name of the Father indeed *is* the Son, to whom alone is given the name. The Father is absolute goodness, and sent the Son 'in order that he might speak about the Place,[89] and about his place of repose from which he had come forth, and that he might glorify the Pleroma, the greatness of his name and the gentleness of the Father' (40. 30ff.). He will speak of the place from which each has come, and strive to make him return to the region from which he has derived his essential being. 'His own place of repose is his pleroma. For this reason, all the beings which have emanated (?) from the Father are pleromas,[90] and all the beings which have emanated from him have their roots in him who caused them all to grow in himself.' Those who have something from on high strive towards that unique one who is perfect. They do not go down to Hades, nor do they experience desire or lamentation; no more is there death in them, but they repose in him who is in repose. The Father is in them and they are in the Father, perfect and inseparable from the truly Good. On this note of the blessed destiny of the children of God, 'children such as he, the Father, loves,' the treatise ends.

Much inevitably remains to be done before we can finally place the *Gospel of Truth* in its true perspective in the history of the development of Gnosticism. Despite the labours of the editors and translators, there is still much that remains obscure.[90a] In part this is due to the very nature of the work, in part to the fact that we have to deal with a Coptic translation of a Greek original, and, moreover, we have to reckon with the possibility of textual error both in the Coptic and in the underlying Greek tradition. On the other hand, if the manuscript is rightly dated in the middle of the fourth century (not earlier than the second quarter nor later than the end of that century), it provides us with the text of an original Gnostic document not much more removed in point of time from the autograph than the earliest extant manuscripts of the New Testament itself.

Even so inadequate a summary as that supplied above may serve to reveal the exceptional interest of the document. It is certainly Valentinian in character, and if it is correctly identified as the document mentioned by Irenaeus it must go back before A.D. 180. But no less certainly it is not the developed Valentinianism presented by Irenaeus; on the contrary, it is much more definitely

Christian. The prominence given to the person and work of Jesus is in fact a striking feature, although that work is transposed into Gnostic terms as one of revelation rather than of redemption.[91] There would seem to be two possibilities: either this document represents an attempt to christianize the Valentinian theory, and must be ascribed to some disciple of Valentinus who stood much nearer to orthodoxy than either the master himself or his more prominent successors, or with van Unnik we must assume that it belongs to an earlier stage in the development of the heresy. The time is not yet ripe for a final decision, and the editors themselves suggest no more than that the composition of the work may go back to about 150, and that it may be attributed either to Valentinus himself or to one of his immediate disciples; but van Unnik's hypothesis at the moment seems to have much in its favour.[92]

If this theory is correct, however, it would follow that Valentinus originally stood much nearer to orthodox Christianity than did the 'vulgar Gnosticism' of the *Apocryphon Johannis*, and the trend of the development within the school would have been away from orthodoxy and in the direction of a syncretizing system. Burkitt's contention[93] would be justified, at least for Valentinus, but it must be emphasized that this conclusion would be valid only for the Valentinian school. Indeed, it would seem necessary to think in terms of the individual sects, and not of the Gnostic movement as a whole.[94] Only when we have isolated the several sects and traced their development and their mutual relationships will it be possible to examine with some confidence the development of the movement, and here the publication of the Nag Hammadi library may provide important evidence.

It remains to be seen whether the *Gospel of Truth* will provide the proof that Valentinus when he wrote it already knew such a system as that of the *Apocryphon Johannis*. A first impression suggests that he did not.[95] It is, however, clear that he did both know and use the greater part of our New Testament, and one notable feature of the treatise is the way in which New Testament ideas and terminology are transposed into a Gnostic key. This must provoke a reconsideration of Bultmann's claim that Paul and John employed Gnostic terms for the presentation of the Gospel, since in the *Gospel of Truth* we seem to have rather an adaptation of

Christian terms to Gnostic use.[96] On the other hand, as van Unnik notes,[97] the Old Testament background 'is essentially weak, and makes itself felt in only a few places'; which would seem to indicate that in this case the Jewish influence was not so strong as in the cases of such as Justin and the Ophites. Quispel has urged that the long passage about the Name of God is to be linked with Jewish theories,[98] and certainly the references to a name which none may pronounce suggest the 'hidden name' of Jewish speculation; but although it may be that such 'more or less heterodox Jewish conceptions' were the *ultimate* source, the comparative absence of Old Testament material would seem to make caution advisable. Moreover, there would seem to be a closer parallel: the passage reads in some respects like a meditation on the christological hymn of Philippians 2. 5ff., 'being found in fashion as a man, he humbled himself, and became obedient unto death, even the death of the Cross. Wherefore God also hath highly exalted him, and *given him a name which is above every name.*'[99] This New Testament passage, indeed, recalls another striking feature of the *Gospel*, the emphasis upon the death of Jesus. Van Unnik speaks of 'a certain reserve in its attitude to Docetism,'[100] but this would seem to be an understatement. In view of the constant tendency in the Gnostic systems to minimize or even eliminate all references to the Passion, the statement, twice repeated, that 'he was nailed to a cross of wood,' and again that Jesus 'knew that his death meant life for many,' must be considered quite remarkable. Such statements are possible only to one who was consciously trying to accommodate his views to Christianity, or as van Unnik suggests, to one who, although he had Gnostic leanings, had not yet moved fully over to the Gnostic position.[101]

If van Unnik is correct, the *Gospel of Truth* belongs to an early stage in the development of the Valentinian theory. Alongside it we must place the older 'vulgar Gnosticism' of the Ophites, perhaps already in the form in which it appears in the *Apocryphon of John*. And it was under the influence of this 'vulgar Gnosticism' that Valentinus and his followers developed the final form of their system. So far as can be seen at present, such a reconstruction would certainly appear to meet the facts, but even should further investigation prove it without foundation, this much at least is clear: the two newly-published Coptic documents are of the first importance.

NOTES TO CHAPTER VI

[1] Cf. Till in *La Parola del Passato* 1949, 230ff.

[2] See *The Jung Codex* (London 1955), and literature cited there, esp. Puech in *Coptic Studies in Honor of W. E. Crum* (Boston 1950) 91ff. To this list may now be added Puech-Quispel, 'Le quatrième Écrit du Codex Jung,' in *Vig. Chr.* ix. 65ff.

[3] See Till *Die gnostischen Schriften des koptischen Papyrus Berolinensis* 8502 (*TU* 60, Berlin 1955); cited as Till *BG*.

[4] *Philotesia, Paul Kleinert . . . dargebracht* (Berlin 1907) 315ff. Cf. Sagnard *La gnose valentinienne* 439ff. for a summary in parallel columns of Iren. 1. 29 (1. 27 Harvey) and the Apocryphon (based on Schmidt).

[5] Cf. *JTS NS* vii. 248ff.

[6] *Evangelium Veritatis*, ed. Malinine, Puech and Quispel, Zürich 1956.

[7] Cf. Quispel in *The Jung Codex* 47ff., Puech-Quispel in *Vig. Chr.* viii. 22ff., and especially van Unnik in *The Jung Codex* 81ff.

[8] See Till *BG* 33ff., and his summary in *JEH* 3 (1952) 14ff., to which the following account is much indebted.

[9] *JEH* 3. 14f.

[10] Puech *Coptic Studies in Honor of W. E. Crum* 113.

[11] Page 19 of the Coptic MS (Till *BG* 78). The 'mountain' is identified by Till (*BG* 81) as the Mount of Olives, frequently in Gnostic and apocryphal literature the scene of such revelations (cf. James *Apoc. NT.* index s.v.).

[12] 76. 10ff.

[13] 22. 19–26. 13. German translation in Till *BG* 85ff., French (after Schmidt) in Sagnard 588f. Portions in English in the notes to Baynes *A Coptic Gnostic Treatise* (Cambridge 1933).

[14] Till *JEH* 3. 16.

[14a] Quispel (*Gnosis als Weltreligion* 62) compares Helen in the Simonian theory (above, p. 100).

[15] See Till's note, *BG* 297ff.

[16] 'This passage seems to me to try to explain the name χριστός in a double way: by "anointing" and by χρηστός' (Till *JEH* 3. 17). But if 'Iudaeos impulsore *Chresto* assidue tumultuantes' (Suet. *Claud.* 25) refers to Christians we may have here a similar confusion.

[17] Cf. Till *BG* 299f. There is no mention of syzygies in the Coptic text, but it does present two of the pairs referred to by Irenaeus (Thelema and Zoe Aionios, Nous and Prognosis, 31. 19), and in the sequel we read that the four Great Lights came forth from Christ and Aphtharsia (32. 19ff.), and that the perfect man Adam was produced by Nous and Prognosis (34. 19ff.). Schmidt's suggestion to emend on the basis of Irenaeus, which Till calls 'verführerisch,' is therefore fully justified. The parallel text from

Nag Hammadi (*CG* I) here agrees exactly with *BG*, so that the passage must have stood thus in their common source (Till *BG* 299).

[18] Here again there are differences between Irenaeus and the Coptic (cf. *JTS NS* vii. 250). For comparison with other Coptic texts see Till *BG* 41.

[19] Irenaeus, apparently through a misunderstanding, has here :qui et remotus est cum primo lumine ab Armoge (Harvey 224).

[20] Till remarks: 'This seems to show that the Gnostics to which the *Apocryphon of John* belonged were Sethians' (*JEH* 3. 17). The prominence of Seth in the Nag Hammadi documents appears to indicate that the community to which this library belonged was also Sethian, which gives an added significance to the discovery there of documents which are Valentinian in origin. Cf. *The Jung Codex* 20ff.

[21] Cf. the Valentinian theory ap. Hippol. 6. 30 (above, p. 129).

[22] 39. 6ff. Till compares 44. 5–9, 49. 2–5. For the twelve angels (corresponding to the Zodiac) cf. Justin (above, p. 122) and for the 360 Basilides (above, p. 124).

[23] Cf. the Ophites (above, p. 139), and see Till's summary, *JEH* 3. 18.

[24] 44. 14ff. Here the extract in Irenaeus ends (for a possible reason see Schmidt, *Philotesia* 334). The *Gospel of Truth* (18. 38ff.) denies that the Father (i.e. the supreme God, not the Demiurge, who does not appear) is jealous: 'what jealousy could exist between Him and His members?' The quotation of Deut. 5. 9 and Exod. 20. 3 in *Apoc. Joh.* proves the identity of Ialdabaoth with the God of the OT. Cf. Till (*JEH* 3. 18): the author's comment is 'characteristic for the standpoint of our Gnostics towards the Old Testament. The statements of the Old Testament are true but they are given in the sense of Ialdabaoth and are to be corrected or interpreted in the Gnostic way.'

[25] 45. 1–19; cf. Gen. 1. 2.

[26] 46. 15 reads *afsōtm* (sing.), but is probably to be emended to *ausōtm*, the reading of *CG* I (Till *BG* 132).

[27] Gen. 1. 26; cf. Philo, Saturninus, etc., and see *Studia Patristica* 1. 420ff., also Rudolph, Ein Grundtyp gnostischer Urmensch-Adam-Spekulation, *ZRGG* ix (1957) 1–20, Quispel in *Eranos Jahrbuch* xxii (Zürich 1954) 195ff., Scholem ibid. 235ff.

[28] In the Apocryphon literally so, each being associated with the 'soul' of some part of the body (see Till *JEH* 3. 18, *BG* 44f.). The actual material body is formed only later. On the Jewish background see references in previous note, and Quispel *Gnosis als Weltreligion* 31f.

[29] 51. 12ff. This is the Gnostic re-interpretation of Gen. 2. 7, the text in which Philo found the creation of earthly (as distinct from ideal) man; cf. *Studia Patristica* 1. 429. 'Adam' is the name given by the archons to their creation (49. 6f.).

[30] Cf. Exc. 50: 'On Adam, over the three immaterial elements, a fourth, "the earthly," is put on as the leathern garments' (tr. Casey 77).

M

[31] Till (*BG* 147) comments: 'Zoe = Eva. Die *BG* 38. 12 erwähnte Zoe ist wohl auch die Epinoia des Lichts.' In *JEH* 3. 19 he notes that the name 'Eve' never occurs. Scholem (241f.) quotes the (admittedly late) tradition of the creation of a woman (Lilith) before Eve, and notes 'Offenbar war aber schon viel früher den jüdischen Quellen der ophitischen Baruch-Gnosis die Vorstellung gelaufig, dass Eva "auf ähnliche Weise" wie Adam, aber unabhängig von ihm entstanden sei.'

[32] Cf. some forms of the Ophite theory (above, p. 119f.).

[33] Cf. Exc. 2. 2: 'Adam's sleep was the soul's forgetting' (the text of the *Excerpta* at this point appears to be corrupt). It may be worth noting that the Coptic word here used (*ibše*: 'it is explained by the Greek ἀναισθησία "lack of sense-perception,"' Till *JEH* 3. 19) is employed also in *Ev. Ver.* for the ignorance which is the forgetting of the Father (see below).

[34] 59. 12ff. The creation of this woman is part of Ialdabaoth's plan for the recovery of the power breathed into Adam. For the use of Gen. 2. 23 here, cf. Exc. 51.

[35] For legends of Satan's intercourse with Eve cf. Ginzberg *Legends of the Jews* 1. 105, 5. 333; *Targ. Jon.* Gen. 4. 1, *Yebamot* 103b, *Pirke R. Eliezer* 21; Epiph. *Haer.* xl. Cf. also the *Protevangelium of James* xiii (James Apoc. NT 44). Some such tradition (or one based on Gen. 6) appears to underlie the doubts of Lamech in the *Genesis Apocryphon* col. ii (Ed. Avigad and Yadin, Jerusalem 1956).

[35a] Quispel in *Eranos Jahrbuch* xxii (1953), 202 note 8, 205f.

[36] For the origin of the ἀντίμιμον πνεῦμα see below. There may be some connexion with the rabbinic doctrine of the *yetser hara'*. Quispel (*The Jung Codex* 64) draws attention to the Qumran *Manual of Discipline* (iii. 18), where it is said that God has appointed two spirits, a spirit of truth and a spirit of perversity, that man may walk with them until the day of his visitation, but rightly observes that all the heretical groups in Palestine 'cannot be described simply as "Gnostic" without more ado' (ibid. 63). Cf. above, p. 73ff.

[37] 70. 15ff. Cf. Mark 3. 29. Here, however, the Holy Spirit is the supreme Being (cf. above, p. 150).

[38] 71. 2ff.

[39] 'The Gnostic explanation of the Biblical ark' (Till *JEH* 3. 20).

[40] Cf. Gen. 6. 1–4 and see below, p. 200.

[41] *JEH* 3. 21; but cf. Puech in *The Jung Codex* 26: 'We may even suppose that the *Apocryphon of John* ... may have contained a more or less mythical system of Gnosis, which Valentinus would have partly taken over.' Puech wrote, however, before the publication of the Berlin Codex.

[42] According to Quispel (*Eranos Jahrbuch* xxii. 197), the Apocryphon 'kann schon um 120 verfasst worden sein.' Certainly if it was known to Valentinus it must be placed in the first half of the second century; but how early did Valentinus use it?

[43] The figure of the Demiurge seems to appear first in Cerinthus. The

distinction between the supreme God and the Demiurge is not yet complete in the Syrian Gnosis of the beginning of the second century (Quispel, *Eranos Jahrbuch* xxii. 199), although Jonas (1. 356f.) quotes ps.-Clem. *Recog.* ii. 49, where it is ascribed to Simon Magus.

⁴⁴ For Jubilees see Charles, *Apoc. and Pseud.* 2. 1–82; for the *Genesis Apocryphon* Avigad and Yadin (see note 35 above).

⁴⁵ Jonas 1. 214ff., cf. Quispel *Gnosis als Weltreligion* 30f.

⁴⁶ *Gnosis als Weltreligion* 12; cf. Puech in *The Jung Codex* 26.

⁴⁷ Cf. Cerfaux 1. 269: 'C'est le système de Valentin, mais abaissé et grossièrement demarqué, que reflètent encore les systèmes des Barbélognostiques. . . .' See also Baynes, index (228) for correspondences between Valentinian doctrines and those of the anonymous treatise in the Bruce Codex. 'Valentinus undoubtedly based much of his doctrinal system on that of his predecessors. Also many of the early doctrines may have come down to us only in their Valentinian dress, for the reason that in this latter form they were more accessible for purposes of criticism by the Church Fathers of the second and third centuries. As the influence of the developed Gnosis of Valentinus became widespread, the more primitive forms of doctrine would be superseded' (ibid. 14).

⁴⁸ Iren. *Adv. Haer.* 3. 11. 12 (Harvey ii. 52): Hi vero qui sunt a Valentino iterum existentes extra omnem timorem suas conscriptiones proferentes plura habere gloriantur quam sint ipsa evangelia. Siquidem in tantum processerunt audaciae uti quod ab his non olim conscriptum est Veritatis Evangelium titulent, in nihilo conveniens apostolorum evangeliis, ut nec evangelium quidem sit apud eos sine blasphemia. Si enim quod ab eis profertur veritatis est evangelium, dissimile est autem hoc illis quae ab apostolis nobis tradita sunt; qui volunt possunt discere (quemadmodum ex ipsis scripturis ostenditur) iam non esse id quod ab apostolis traditum est Veritatis Evangelium.

⁴⁹ Cod. Jung 16. 31ff. (ed. Malinine, Puech, Quispel, Zürich 1956, p. 2, *ET* p. 88) (cited as EV). The English translation is not altogether satisfactory (e.g. in the use of 'Verb' for 'Word'), and does not always tally either with the French or with the Coptic. At some points, however, the deficiencies are due to the effort to make the translation correspond with the lines of the Coptic text. The following account is based partly on the English, partly on the French and German translations, and partly on independent rendering of the original, but an attempt has been made at all points to control it from the Coptic text. Some passages are translated in *The Jung Codex* (see references below). Cf. also *Vig. Chr.* viii. 22ff.

⁵⁰ *EV* xi; cf. Quispel in *The Jung Codex* 47ff., van Unnik ibid. 81ff. It may here be noted that van Unnik has argued that one document in the Codex Jung (*The Epistle of James*) is not, like the rest, of Valentinian origin (see *Vig. Chr.* x).

⁵¹ *The Jung Codex* 94f.

⁵² Puech-Quispel in *Vig. Chr.* viii. 23f., Quispel in *The Jung Codex* 48,

van Unnik ibid. 106 note 1. Cf. *EV* xv: 'De toute façon, il paraît être, bien plutôt qu'un "évangile" à proprement parler, une méditation, une "éléva-tion" sur l'Evangile, une sorte de commentaire enthousiaste, d'effusion spirituelle, exaltant ce qu'est, en son essence, dans son effet le plus pur et le plus profond, le Message évangélique.'

[53] Van Unnik 104ff.

[54] *EV* xv; van Unnik 94f.

[55] Van Unnik 104; cf. *EV* xiv f., where the editors comment: 'Il nous semble, quant à nous, plus sûr, plus prudent, de nous en tenir pour le moment à l'opinion—elle-meme insuffisamment étayée—que nous avons avancée ailleurs (*Vig. Chr.* viii. 31 and 39): la composition de l'écrit pourrait remonter à 150 environ et la paternité en être rendue soit à Valentin soit à un de ses disciples immédiats.'

[56] Van Unnik 101ff. raises the question, and suggests that Irenaeus had indeed seen the document, but had little to say about it because although its content is Gnostic its Gnosticism is not emphasized.

[57] ibid. 98ff.

[58] ibid. 98, 106. Cf. *EV* 18. 8ff.: 'Since Oblivion came into existence because they did not know the Father, therefore if they attain to a know-ledge of the Father Oblivion becomes, at that very instant, non-existent.' As already noted (above, note 33) the Coptic word is used in *Apoc. Joh.* for the sleep of Adam.

[59] *EV* xii f.; cf. van Unnik 94ff.

[60] Van Unnik 101ff. 'In this connexion it is important to observe that various words which to our ears sound typically Gnostic had not yet become such by themselves' (ibid. 103); cf. above (p. 74) on the Dead Sea Scrolls.

[61] 17. 2ff. Van Unnik (105) renders 'This name of the Gospel is the revelation . . .,' linking with the previous line, but the photograph now makes it clear that some letters are missing.

[62] Cf. *Ep. ad Diog.* vii–viii. Van Unnik observes that for purposes of comparison the material supplied by such contemporary 'orthodox' writers as Hermas and Justin may be of the greatest value. 'I do not think that enough attention has been paid to this point, nor to the fact that the Old Testament also makes mention of "knowledge" ' (104 note 1). Cf. Dupont *Gnosis* (Louvain 1949). The theme of ignorance of God in particular goes back through Rom. 1. 20 to Soph. Sol. 13. 1–9 (cf. also Eltester in *NTS* 3. 93ff.).

[63] Van Unnik 126; see ibid. 107ff. for comparison of the *Gospel of Truth* and the NT. References to NT and patristic literature are provided in *EV* 51ff., but the editors have deferred detailed commentary to a later date. R. M. Grant (*Vig. Chr.* xi (1957) 149ff.) finds some parallels in the Odes of Solomon.

[64] Van Unnik (92. 99) notes from Tertullian that there was a difference here between Valentinus and Ptolemy, namely that for the former Nous,

Ennoia, etc., 'are extant *within* the Godhead and not outside it.' The editors cite Col. 1. 17, Rom. 11. 26 (a misprint for 11. 36), 1 Cor. 8. 6. Eph. 4. 6. Cf. also Acts 17. 27f. [Van Unnik has already remarked, 'We might describe the theme of this book as an elaboration of the thoughts contained in Acts 17. 25–30' (106).]

65 The editors here quote Philo *Op.M.* 48. 139 and Valentinus ap. Clem. Alex. *Strom.* 4. 90. 2 (II. 287. 29 Stählin). In *Apoc. Joh.* (48. 17) the word here rendered 'creature' ($\pi\lambda\acute{a}\sigma\mu a$) is applied to Adam; in 55. 10 this psychic Adam is distinguished from the material body ($\pi\lambda\acute{a}\sigma\iota\varsigma$ 55. 3) which is 'the grave of the $\pi\lambda\acute{a}\sigma\mu a$.' Cf. *BG* 119. 12, 18 (Till *BG* 279).

66 For 'the Midst' cf. Baynes, index (215).

67 On 18. 2–4 the editors compare John 1. 1–4; cf. Baynes, index (213).

68 18. 17–18. The editors quote John 1. 5 (cf. Iren. 1. 8. 5–6 = 1. 1. 18 Harvey; on this see Sagnard *La gnose valentinienne* 306ff.).

69 'Behind this lies the conception of the Cross as the tree of life' (van Unnik 116). See also Chadwick 350 note 3, van Unnik 110–111. In Iren. 1. 1. 4 (Harvey 23) Jesus is the $\tau\acute{\epsilon}\lambda\epsilon\iota o\varsigma\ \kappa a\rho\pi\acute{o}\varsigma$ (cf. above, p. 130).

70 See van Unnik, 117. The editors refer to Rom. 12. 26 (another error—Rom. 1. 21ff.?). Cf. also Eph. 4. 17: 'darkened in their understanding, alienated from the life of God because of the ignorance that is in them.'

71 In Exc. 23. 4 the little ones are identified with the elect; the face of God is 'perhaps now the Son (cf. Exc. 10. 6, 12. 1), now as much of that comprehension of the Father as they perceive who have been instructed by the Son.' But these sections are not, properly speaking, Valentinian (cf. Casey's notes and introduction, and *EV* 52). Cf. also Baynes 38, 42.

72 Cf. Dupont 51ff.

73 Lit. 'of the living.' The passage is translated and examined by van Unnik 108ff., who notes the use of the Passion Narrative in the Gospels and of Rev. 5.

74 Cf. van Unnik 111f. It should be noted that there is no indication of a Docetic view of the Passion [van Unnik 99 notes 'a certain reserve in (the attitude of *EV*) to Docetism,' and compares fr. 3 of Valentinus (Völker *Quellen* 58 = Clem. Alex. *Strom.* 3. 59. 3)]. But cf. Exc. 62. 3.

75 Van Unnik 111, 117 quotes Col. 2. 14f.

76 The passage 22. 2–19 is translated by Puech (*The Jung Codex* 30), who remarks (ibid. 29): 'What above all else we shall discover in the writings of the Jung Codex . . . is the significance of Gnosis for a Gnostic.' At 22. 13–15 occurs the well-known Gnostic formula: 'He who thus possesses knowledge knows whence he is come and where he is going' (cf. Exc. 78). Cf. Tert. *de Praescriptione* vii (ap. Burkitt *Church and Gnosis* 48): Unde malum et quare? Unde homo et quomodo? And Unde deus? Some connexion may perhaps be suspected between 22. 16f. ('He knows even as a person who, having been intoxicated, becomes sober') and the metaphors employed by Philo [cf. Lewy *Sobria Ebrietas*, and Corp. Herm. 1. 27, 7. 1,

quoted there (Lewy 74)]. Van Unnik notes an allusion to Luke 15. 17 in 22. 18 ('having come to himself').

[77] 23. 8–10. Is this a cryptic reference to the Tetragrammaton? Cf. the passage later on the Name of God (below, p. 160f).

[78] Perhaps better: 'his intelligence *pronounces* it.' Cf. 37. 7ff. All things are in the mind of the Father until the Word is first pronounced [cf. the Genesis cosmogony as interpreted by Philo (above, p. 41ff.) and in *Poimandres* (cf. Dodd *Interpretation* 40f.). Dodd (12 note 2) dates *Poimandres* before Valentinus.] It may be conjectured that the Greek original of 23. 21f. was ἡ γνῶσις αὐτοῦ ἐφανερώθη, and that the Coptic translator has rendered an objective genitive by a possessive. The whole passage may then be linked with the Prologue to the Fourth Gospel, which presents the first verse of Mark in terms of the Jewish Wisdom-Logos interpretation of Genesis (cf. Knox *HE* 55ff.). In 23. 35–24. 3 the Word is 'the fruit of his heart and the expression of his will.' The former phrase recalls the reference to Jesus as the perfect fruit (cf. above, note 69); on the latter the editors refer to Iren. 1. 14. 1, 15. 5. (1. 8. 1, 16, Harvey 129 and 154), where the Word is the μορφή of the Ineffable. If this be correct, reference may be made to Phil. 2. 6 and possibly also to Heb. 1. 3.

[79] Cf. Exc. 10. 6 ('the Son, through whom the Father is known'), 7. 2. Cf. John 1. 18, 14. 9, etc. The editors comment: 'Affirmation en désaccord avec Irénée 1. 2. 5 (1. 1. 4. Harvey), où c'est, au contraire, le Fils qui est le καταληπτόν, le *comprehensible* du Père.'

[80] Cf. Iren. 1. 1. 2 (Harvey 13), Exc. 31. 3 ('The aeon which wished to grasp that which is beyond knowledge fell into ignorance and formlessness').

[81] Van Unnik (119) quotes 1 Cor. 7. 31 (τὸ σχῆμα τοῦ κόσμου τούτου); the μορφή in this context recalls the μόρφωσιν τὴν κατὰ γνῶσιν of the Valentinian theory (Iren. 1. 1. 8 (Harvey 39)). Some connexion with Phil. 2. 6 (ἐν μορφῇ θεοῦ ὑπάρχων) may perhaps be suspected. Cf. Sagnard *La gnose* 647 (index s.v.).

[82] Translated in *The Jung Codex* by Puech (31f.) and Quispel (51f.), who compare Homer *Iliad* xxii. 199–201.

[83] The explanation would seem to lie in the Adam-Christ typology, the Resurrection being interpreted as a new creation. Cf. Acts 13. 33 (? and Rom. 1. 4); also Brownlee in NTS 3. 29 note 2.

[84] For NT references see van Unnik 120.

[85] 31. 5: lit. 'a flesh of similitude.' Cf. Phil. 2. 7.

[86] Cf. van Unnik 96f., where the passage is translated. For the Valentinian use of the parable see Iren. 1. 1. 17, 1. 9. 1–2, 2. 36. 4 (Harvey 73, 157ff., 341f.), and cf. Sagnard *La gnose* 364 note 2.

[86a] These pages have, however, been identified among the texts now in the Coptic Museum in Cairo (see Puech in *Rev. Hist. Rel.*, 1957, 269).

[87] Cf. above, p. 143 note 122.

⁸⁸ See Quispel, *The Jung Codex* 68ff., where the passage is translated (73ff.). According to Casey (*Excerpta* 18), 'Theodotus' view is derived from Philo, who identified the Logos with the name of God.' See also Sagnard *La gnose* 650 (index s. v. ὄνομα), and cf. Quispel *Gnosis als Weltreligion* 55ff.

⁸⁹ Cf. Quispel *The Jung Codex* 75 note 1, Sagnard 656f. (index s.v. τόπος). Casey (*Excerpta* 131 on Exc. 34. 2) quotes Philo *Op. M.* 20: οὐδ' ὁ ἐκ τῶν ἰδεῶν κόσμος ἄλλον ἂν ἔχοι τόπον ἢ τὸν θεῖον λόγον τὸν ταῦτα διακοσμήσαντα.

⁹⁰ Cf. Exc. 63–65, Heracleon fr. 18 Brooke (above, p. 132). In the Excerpta the 'repose' is in the Ogdoad. Here the 'repose' appears to be with the Father.

⁹⁰ᵃ The study of this document has only begun, and the above notes are not intended to be exhaustive. It is, however, hoped that they may make some contribution towards the eventual preparation of a definitive edition. For more detailed references see *EV* 51ff.

⁹¹ But note the references to the Crucifixion (18. 24, 20. 25), and the statement that Jesus knew his death meant life for many (20. 13f.).

⁹² See van Unnik 94ff., *EV* xiv f.

⁹³ See above, p. 68.

⁹⁴ Cf. van Unnik 85 and the quotation there from Kretschmar.

⁹⁵ Quispel's claim that Valentinus and Basilides hellenized and christian-ized the earlier 'vulgar' Egyptian Gnosis (*Gnosis als Weltreligion* 12) must then be referred to the later developed system. It should be noted in favour of van Unnik's theory that it so admirably fits the facts at present known. Valentinus began within the Church, but passed over to 'the opponents of truth' (Tertullian, quoted by van Unnik 92, 'possibly points in a veiled way to the Ophites'). The clear connexion between the *Apocryphon Johannis* and the later Valentinian theory indicates some kind of 'Ophite' influence, but the absence of this influence from the *Gospel of Truth* would seem to place it in the period of transition.

⁹⁶ Cf. van Unnik 125, who says: 'As far as the *Gospel of Truth* is con-cerned it is in my opinion not certain that we should here accept pre-New Testament influences.'

⁹⁷ ibid. 95.

⁹⁸ *The Jung Codex* 68ff.

⁹⁹ But in view of Casey's reference of Theodotus' doctrine of the Name to the influence of Philo it may perhaps be better to suggest 'a meditation on the hymn of Phil. 2. 5ff. under the influence of Hellenistic Jewish speculations.'

¹⁰⁰ Van Unnik 99.

¹⁰¹ But such passages as Exc. 61, 63 show how the Gnostics could re-interpret the Passion to suit their own theories.

CHAPTER VII

JUDAISM AND GNOSTICISM

CERTAIN conclusions may at once be drawn from the survey presented in the preceding chapters. At various points in this survey we have observed similarities between Jewish and Gnostic ideas, some consisting only in a common use of a particular Old Testament narrative in a particular way, others more far-reaching in their importance.[1] Both Judaism and Gnosticism maintain the transcendence of God, and both interpose one or more intermediaries between Him and the world. The Gnostic aeons and emanations are parallel to the Jewish angels and the Philonic Logos and powers, although, of course, there are differences which fall to be noted in a more detailed comparison. Both Judaism and Gnosticism accept the Hellenistic cosmogony, with its astrological associations, although astrology is less prominent in the more orthodox Jewish circles. The Gnostics do not, however, seem to have elaborated such a Platonizing account of the creation of the world as Philo's *De Opificio Mundi*, although they apparently move at times in the same fields of thought. The absence of such a creation story may be due to a defect in our sources of information, but it may, on the other hand, be the result of the typical Gnostic depreciation of the world and its creator. At least in the later and more developed forms the primary concern of the Gnostic cosmogonies is not to explain the creation of the world but to account for the origin of man and of evil.

In several cases there is a close parallel in Gnosticism to Philo's account of the creation of man, while other Gnostic accounts recall the other view which has been regarded in some quarters as Pauline, the interpretation of the Fall of Adam as a fall of a spiritual being into matter.[2] Further points of contact are provided by the σῶμα-σῆμα conception, with the idea that the soul of man is essentially akin to the divine, and that salvation consists in an ascent of man to his true home with God, however this is thought to be effected.[3]

172

The rebellion of the powers against Ialdabaoth in the Ophite system recalls the Jewish theory of a conflict among the angels on behalf of the nations over which they preside, while the names of these powers are either Old Testament names for God or names of a Hebraic type. Again, the union of the angels or lower powers with Eve or Achamoth is based on an Old Testament narrative, and has parallels in Jewish thought,[4] while the association of the angels with the seven heavens, and in particular the location of Paradise above the third heaven, with the idea that Adam had his abode there, also points to Judaism. The Valentinian concept of the final union of the elect soul with its divine counterpart has its parallels in Philo, and finally, perhaps most important of all, the conception of the Spirit as a female power seems only possible under Semitic influence, since the Hebrew *ruah* is feminine while the Greek πνεῦμα is neuter. The idea may have some other source, but Semitic influence here seems indisputable. It must, however, be admitted that such influence might not be Jewish, but any decision regarding the ultimate origin of the idea would involve an examination of cognate terms in other languages which is beyond the scope of our present study.[5]

These points lead to the general conclusion that Judaism was a contributory source to the origin and development of Gnosticism.[6] This, however, is only a provisional judgement, which must be checked and where necessary modified by further and more detailed examination of certain special aspects. The purpose of the following chapter is, so far as is possible in the existing state of our knowledge, to carry out this further examination. But first there are certain points which call for attention.

In the first place, there is a natural tendency for the individual worker in this field to lay special stress upon the particular aspect with which he is dealing. As Reitzenstein puts it: 'It is hardly to be avoided that according to inclination and the direction of his studies one scholar should claim too much as Egyptian, another too much as Babylonian, and a third all as Persian, and that the individual worker should be afflicted with a certain colour-blindness which renders him insensible to important distinctions. Only the common work of many can bring us nearer to the goal of understanding Hellenistic mysticism.'[7] The same is equally true of

Gnosticism, which is intimately related to this Hellenistic mysticism of which Reitzenstein speaks. The general tendency of research has been to seek the ultimate source of Gnosticism in one or other of the religions of the East, and there is no doubt that elements from each can be discovered in Gnostic thought; but no one of these religions is in itself sufficient to account for the development which we know as Gnosticism. The ultimate source of this or that element of a particular Gnostic system may be traced back into some religious belief of remote antiquity, but Gnosticism itself is essentially syncretistic, and the various elements are blended with and assimilated to elements of widely differing origin. What we require to discover in order to account for the origins of the Gnostic movement is therefore not the ultimate source but the point at which these diverse elements were first combined into a more or less coherent system.

The purpose of the present study is not to seek for ultimate origins, but to isolate one of the contributory factors. When we ascribe a particular feature to Jewish influence it need not mean that Judaism was the ultimate source, but rather that Judaism was the intermediary through which it entered into Gnostic thought.[8] We are dealing not with single elements, but with groups from different sources combined in various ways. One idea from Egypt may be combined with another which we can trace to Persia, but the combination of the two may have taken place in Palestine. If we can prove this combination Jewish we have discovered a proximate source, one of the junctions on the road, in Judaism.

It has already been remarked that Judaism underwent an influence from each of the great powers that controlled the Holy Land for a period, Assyria, Babylon, Persia, Egypt. Other influences came from Phoenicia and Greece, and all these have left their mark on the religion and literature of Israel. But these influences were absorbed into the Jewish faith and later, many of them, into Christianity. This explains some, although not all, of the contacts found between Christianity and the faiths of its environment. It remains to be seen whether it also explains some of the phenomena of Gnosticism. In the Hellenistic world ideas from all the ancient religions of the East were blended into a composite theology which is preserved for us in Gnosticism and the Hermetic literature and other similar documents. By its situation and its history the Jewish people was ideally placed to contribute to the process of syncretism, at least in so far as Christian Gnosticism is concerned.[9] Our purpose now is to seek for signs of such a contribution, and to form some estimate of its nature and extent.

A second point concerns the method of approach. Some of the common features may be due to Christianity, part of the stock which the early Church carried with it from the Judaism out of which it arose. These obviously prove nothing for Jewish influence on Gnosticism as such, and may be left out of consideration. Again, other features are common to Judaism and to Gnosticism and also to some of the systems of the contemporary world. Here the influence of that world upon Gnosticism may have been mediated by Judaism, but this does not prove anything for the influence of Judaism itself upon Gnosticism, since such influences might quite as easily have operated directly on the Gnostic thinkers. To prove beyond doubt that Judaism, and in particular the Judaism of the Diaspora, exercised an influence upon the origins of Gnosticism, it would be necessary to show not only that certain elements in Gnostic thought can be paralleled from the Diaspora, but also that some at least of these cannot be accounted for by any other source. This, in view of the influences exercised upon Judaism itself by other cultures at earlier stages in its history, might be wellnigh impossible, but there is the alternative of showing that the combinations in which these elements appear are due to Judaism and to Judaism alone. There is, of course, the possibility that some of the features shared by Judaism with Gnosticism and with paganism may be Jewish in origin, and their presence in pagan thought due to Jewish influence there. Finally, attention must be paid to a fact too often neglected: that similarity of language does not always imply identity of meaning. We must consider not the words only, but their content, and ask what it was that the writers intended to convey.[10]

Taking everything into account, it is probable that where a feature of Gnosticism can be paralleled from the Diaspora then Judaism is to be considered as a source, even if it be only as an intermediary between paganism and Gnosticism, but this remains only a probability until a number of elements or combinations of elements are shown to be of purely Jewish origin. When this is done, the fact that certain elements are purely Jewish, or that certain groups of elements derive their peculiar grouping from Judaism, renders it still more probable that the other common elements were derived from Judaism, even although that be not the ultimate source. If the Jewish-Christian elements be excluded, then Diaspora Judaism is established as a contributory source not only for the development of Christianity but also for that of Gnosticism. Pagan elements with no Jewish connexion are of interest here only as pointing to further sources, which operated together with Judaism to form the complex systems of thought which are known to us as Gnostic.

In all this the possibility of a pre-Christian Jewish Gnosticism is not excluded. In view of the general tendency of contemporary thought in this period such a Jewish Gnosticism must be considered highly probable, although conclusive proof may be lacking for its existence.[11] It should also be borne in mind that the various possibilities outlined here—Jewish influence, direct or through Christian mediation, pagan influence, direct or through Judaism or Christianity or both—are not altogether mutually exclusive. More than one may have been operative at one time, and the very fact that a particular idea was current in a more or less similar form in different groups, with whatever differences of meaning or significance, would contribute largely to its more general acceptance.

Before we turn to the more detailed examination of the parallels between Gnosticism and the Judaism of the Diaspora it may be remarked that the geographical distribution of the Gnostic sects is not without interest for our purpose. It is not possible to locate certain forms of Gnosticism with any certainty, and our patristic authorities must often be handled with great care, but still a general geographical classification may be made.[12] Simon Magus, according to our authorities, was of Samaritan origin; he is said to have journeyed to Rome, but this may be pure legend, or due to a mistaken inference by an early writer.[13] It has been suggested, moreover, that his system underwent a process of modification at Alexandria, represented by the account preserved by Hippolytus.[14] Saturninus and Basilides were Syrians, the former remaining in his native region while the latter according to Hippolytus came to

Alexandria. Cerinthus is located in Ephesus by the tradition of his encounter with John,[15] and Valentinus lived at first in Alexandria before going to Rome. The Ophites are placed by Legge[16] in Asia Minor, on the strength of the part played in their systems by the Mother, in which he sees the influence of the Phrygian cults. If this be correct, we may recall the notorious laxity of the Phrygian Jews. The tendencies manifested in the syncretistic cults of Sabazius and Hypsistos may have operated here also, and certainly there are numerous Jewish features in Ophitism. On the other hand, as Legge himself notes,[17] in the contemporary religious syncretism the Great Mother is equated with Isis and Astarte; Egypt has its triad of gods as well as Asia Minor, and the birthplace of Ophitism might well have been either. The case for Egypt is perhaps strengthened by the links between Ophitism and Valentinianism, but this point is not conclusive.[18] The interpenetration of the different theories is a notable feature of Gnosticism, each school borrowing from its predecessors and in turn furnishing elements which were adopted by its successors. Again, conditions in the period of the early Roman Empire were such as to favour communication between one part of the Mediterranean world and another. The points adduced by Cumont[19] for the spread of the mystery religions are applicable also to Gnosticism, while the journeys of Paul and the spread of early Christianity are in themselves sufficient evidence of the ease of communication and the opportunities for the dissemination of new doctrines.

In regard to Ophitism it must also be remembered that we are here dealing not with a single system but with a number of systems more or less closely related and holding certain common views.[20] Since the prevailing syncretism blended together elements derived from Egypt, Syria, and Asia Minor, it seems most probable that the Ophites simply adapted it, with local variations according to the region in which they found themselves. Thus the Naassenes may have given more place to Phrygian elements, while the Ophites of Irenaeus seem nearer to Egypt than to Phrygia.

Whatever our doubts as to the trustworthiness of our sources, and however obscure the relation between one sect and another, it is clear that the main source of Gnosticism was the eastern part of the Mediterranean world.[21] For Asia Minor we have Cerinthus, the Naassenes, and possibly the Ophites; for Syria, Simon, Saturninus, and Basilides; for Egypt, Basilides again and Valentinus, with possibly a modified form of the Simonian theory, and also perhaps the Ophites, or at least some branch of the 'Ophite' movement.[22] This does not exclude the possibility that some of the leaders sojourned for a time in different regions, where their views may have undergone some modification, but there is one factor common to all these areas which must not be overlooked: all are regions in which a native population had been more or less hellenized, and in which native religious beliefs had been combined with Greek philosophical speculations and alien religious doctrines; all had at one time been under the sway of Persia, when the teachings of the Magi[23] and of Chaldaea might have penetrated and been absorbed into their beliefs, and all are on the border of the empire nearest to those lands of the East from which came so many influences of different kinds. Finally, all were centres of the Jewish Dispersion, and this is especially true of Alexandria in Egypt. The fact that Gnosticism originated in the very lands where syncretism is most strongly marked, and where the Jewish Diaspora is most prominent, suggests in itself that there may be some deeper connexion.[24]

Judaism had itself been modified by influences emanating from these same lands of the East, influences which contributed to the development and expansion of Jewish thought, but such new ideas were absorbed to become part of Judaism, subordinated to its essential and fundamental message. On the other hand, certain individual Jews, and possibly certain groups of Jews, seem to have gone further in accommodating their faith to their environment than was allowed by the general consent of the people, even in the more liberal Diaspora. Jews of this laxer sort, and apostates or relapsed proselytes, might contribute Jewish elements towards the development of the cult which they favoured, and there was in any case a sufficiently close resemblance between the developing thought of Judaism, especially in the Dispersion, and the beliefs of the surrounding world for some confusion to arise, or some synthesis to be made, in the mind of the more casual observer. The Jewish Scriptures, moreover, read in their Greek translation by a man with a pagan tradition of centuries behind him, might convey to him an impression of the Jewish religion very different from the truth.

Consequently, although the Diaspora as a whole held apart from such aberrations, and although our evidence shows little sign of any real syncretism among the Jews, yet there was always the possibility of a Gnosticizing interpretation of Judaism; and there was also the possibility of Jewish influence upon the contemporary pagan cults.

Christianity was born, so to speak, in Palestine, but grew up in the Dispersion. Judaism had helped to prepare the way for it, and Jewish methods were adopted to further its growth. This again suggests that Judaism may have played a part, and possibly a considerable part, in the rise of such movements as Gnosticism. Attempts to prove the existence of a pre-Christian Jewish Gnosticism have not produced any very conclusive results, largely owing to lack of adequate evidence, but it is clear that there were varying degrees of observance of the law, and varying degrees of approximation in belief between the Jews and their contemporaries. Those who adopted Christianity, whether they had been Jews or pagans, naturally brought with them a certain deposit of religious thought, with which their Christian beliefs were combined and which coloured these beliefs to a greater or less extent. Others again outside the Church sought to appropriate something of Christianity for themselves,[25] and to blend it into schemes of their own. The result would be a number of stages of interpretation, from Gnostic to orthodox, according to the extent to which the 'convert' allowed his old ideas to colour his new beliefs. In Judaism, the interpretation would vary according to the extent to which the Jew or proselyte allowed the ideas of the surrounding world to colour his Jewish faith.

The attempt to assess the relation of Diaspora Judaism to Gnosticism is rendered more difficult by the absence of evidence for the beliefs of the Dispersion, apart from Philo, who represents at most only Alexandria, and probably only one aspect of Alexandria at that.[26] Judaism in Antioch or in Ephesus might have been very different from Alexandrian Judaism, and not every Jew even in Alexandria had the acquaintance with or interest in Greek culture which inspired Philo's efforts. On the other hand, there can be no doubt that in many respects the Diaspora adhered to the same beliefs as Palestine, although with less strictness and a more accommodating spirit.

The lack of direct evidence for the Diaspora itself is to some extent offset by our knowledge of the later Rabbinic Judaism, although this source of information must obviously be used with great care, and of the views held by Paul and the other New Testament writers, themselves for the most part Jews. Rabbinic Judaism is very different from Hellenistic Judaism, but where they are in agreement we may safely assume that the belief in question had a wide currency; and even when one directly contradicts the other it may be only an indication that a particular view was current in Judaism which one group or the other rejected. Paul was himself a Jew of the Dispersion, from Tarsus, though educated partly at least in Jerusalem; the Fourth Evangelist is traditionally associated with Ephesus, and has a distinctively Hellenistic or Jewish-Hellenistic background.[27] Where they agree with Philo, or where they seem to be moving in the same fields of thought, even though they may differ in points of detail, we may with some justification claim to find a fairly widespread belief of the Dispersion.[28] Could the Ophites be placed definitely in Asia Minor we might derive important information from their teachings, but otherwise there is danger of arguing in a circle. Where Philo stands alone, or in agreement only with Alexandrian doctrines such as those of Valentinus or the Christian Philosophers, we cannot argue for the Diaspora as a whole, but only for Alexandria, and, indeed, for Philo's own immediate circle, although with more extensive evidence the view might be shown to be much more widely spread. The *Corpus Hermeticum* provides further evidence, since the documents which it contains represent a syncretism of Hellenistic-Jewish and pagan elements, parts of which at least may be much older than the Corpus itself as it has come down to us.[29]

Our chief concern is naturally with those features of Gnosticism which betray the influence of Judaism, but there are other features which also have a bearing on our main problem. Among these are certain anti-Semitic tendencies, such as the depreciation of the God of the Old Testament into the head of the angelic powers who hold mankind in subjection,[30] and the rejection of the Jewish law. These may be due to hostility engendered by the opposition

which the Church had to face from the Jewish side after the breach
with Judaism, and also to a survival of the dislike which the Jew
has encountered in every age. In one aspect, indeed, Gnosticism
might be regarded as an attempt to eliminate Jewish elements from
Christianity, in favour of a closer understanding with the contemporary philosophy, but such a definition is inadequate. The
attempt, if such it was, did not succeed, and in fact only Marcion[31]
could really be said to have ventured upon it. Moreover, Gnosticism itself is too closely linked with Judaism for this definition to be
valid. On the other hand, it is no less clear that there can be no
question of trying to find in Judaism the one and only source of the
Gnostic movement.

The antinomian position may be a development of Paul's
teaching on law and grace, although Friedländer has attempted to
prove the existence of pre-Christian sects of an antinomian Gnostic
character.[32] These sects he considers, significantly enough, to be of
an Ophite type, revering such Old Testament personages as Cain,
Seth, and Melchizedek, but although there is a certain amount of
truth in his theory he seems to read too much into his sources.
The Ophite sects are among the oldest of all Gnostic sects, the
nearest to Judaism, although with marked anti-Jewish features, and
probably the most likely to be pre-Christian, but Friedländer's
arguments, though ingenious, seem inadequate to prove his case.
In reviewing his book, Schürer[33] admits the evidence of Philo to
the effect that some Jews on the ground of their allegorical interpretation paid little heed to the literal sense of the law, but claims
that there was no advance from such depreciation to non-observ-
ance of the law within the Jewish community. More recent
authorities seem to tend rather towards Friedländer's position,
although not necessarily admitting all his claims. It may be that
the significant words for Schürer's view are 'within the Jewish
community,' in which case he has perhaps misunderstood Friedländer's thesis. The latter's view, while hardly applicable to the
Diaspora as a whole, may well hold good for Jews on the fringe
of Judaism or for apostates. Schürer maintains that all Jews,
however lax, adhered to certain basic essentials of observance, but
it has already been noted that instances of apostasy are not unknown.
It may be that the two views are really much closer than appears

N

at first sight: for Friedländer, apostates are relevant evidence because they are or have been Jews; for Schürer, however, they are no longer within the Jewish community.

Whatever may be the true nature of the case, the fact remains that Judaism had preceded Christianity in adapting itself to its environment. This makes it probable that the speculations of the less orthodox in Judaism led to a result similar to that produced by those of the less orthodox in Christianity later. Many Jewish features were absorbed into Christian thought, and persisted even after the breach with the synagogue; others appear, as it would seem, in Gnostic thought, although they were rejected by the Church itself. Other features again were of pagan origin, but Judaism seems to have been the medium through which they passed into Christian speculation. Some of the features which can be traced to Jewish influence may derive ultimately from another source, but have been as it were naturalized in Judaism for so long as to be almost completely Jewish for our purposes. We may conclude, then, subject to further examination, that Judaism, and in particular the Judaism of the Diaspora, preceding Christianity as it did in its relations with Hellenism, provided a bridge across the gulf which separates the Graeco-Oriental and the Jewish-Christian worlds of thought. Its contribution to the development of Gnosticism was not only direct, through the absorption of Jewish ideas into Gnostic thought, but also in part indirect, since it was through the medium of Jewish speculation that certain pagan elements came into Gnosticism. At the same time, it must not be forgotten that in several respects Gnosticism stands apart not only from Christianity but also from Judaism. There are traces of both, but the dominant feature is a syncretism which is quite un-Christian and un-Jewish in character. The nature of the syncretism which we find among the Jews of the period has already been indicated, and further light will be shed upon it in the course of the examination which follows. Whatever may have been the case with individual Jews or groups of Jews, the syncretism most commonly manifested in the Diaspora as a whole is of a very different character from that current in the pagan world, and also from that represented by Gnosticism.

For the purposes of this study it seems advisable to divide the examination into a number of sections, grouping the various subjects together so far as possible. The most natural division seems to be as follows: (1) the idea of God, with the intermediaries and other subordinate powers; (2) the nature of the world, and the various accounts of its creation; (3) the nature of man, his origin, and his place in the universe; (4) closely connected with this, the idea of salvation, including the views held concerning man's present state and the means of escape therefrom; (5) the Gnostic doctrines of the Redeemer, in relation to Jewish and Christian doctrines of a similar type.

1. *The Idea of God*

It might seem at first sight that the only point of similarity between Judaism and Gnosticism in regard to the idea of God is the fact that both in Philo and in Gnostic thought the supreme Being is completely transcendent, and that in both a series of intermediaries is interposed between God and the world as we know it. Moreover, since Moore[34] claims this idea of a remote and extra-mundane God to be a misrepresentation of Judaism, due to an exaggeration of the importance of the apocalyptic writings as evidence, and since even Philo not infrequently presents the more normal Jewish view of God as the Father of His people, infinitely near to them and manifesting towards them a loving and tender care—an idea which has little if any place in Gnosticism[35]—the possibility of Jewish influence on Gnostic thought in this connexion might seem to be almost completely ruled out.[36] But in fact this is not the case. Jewish thought during and after the Exile underwent a considerable development, and in particular as regards the idea of God. Yahweh becomes the God of Heaven, throned high above the world,[37] while the later prophets developed an uncompromising monotheism which succeeding generations of Judaism never entirely lost. These and similar developments in Judaism afforded points of contact with the current Hellenistic philosophy.

Again, although apocalyptic may not accurately represent Judaism as a whole, it may be that it does represent the more popular ideas of the period,[38] over against the more strictly Jewish views of the schools upon whose work Rabbinic Judaism is based.

The ideas of Diaspora Judaism as presented by Philo may then represent a popular Judaism translated into Greek idioms and to some extent accommodated to contemporary philosophical theories, although as a rule adhering to the fundamentals of Judaism throughout. The concurrence of apocalyptic and Hellenistic Judaism is not lightly to be set aside in favour of Rabbinic evidence where popular thought as distinct from scholastic theological speculation is concerned. On the other hand, the Philonic theories tend to be more philosophical and less popular, so that this concurrence represents a convergence of educated and popular views, and may therefore be quite characteristic for our period.

A further point to be observed is that in Gnosticism there is a hierarchy, at the head of which stands the supreme God; below him is the Demiurge, and below him again the remaining subordinate powers. In the more elaborate systems other powers are associated with the supreme God, as emanations from him or as his attributes, and others again with the Demiurge as his collaborators in the work of creation; these powers, interpolated between one rank of the classification and the next, serve also to enhance the remoteness of God from the world. In Judaism, God stands alone on the one hand, the intermediaries on the other, although there is sometimes a tendency to admit of subordinate creators,[39] or at least of assessors,[40] especially with a view to accommodation of the Jewish conception to that of contemporary thought.

Leaving the other powers out of consideration for the moment, we have thus as the Gnostic counterpart to the God of the Old Testament not only the supreme God but also the Demiurge. For the Jew, the Creator and the supreme God are one and the same, the God of the Old Testament; the more objectionable features of the Biblical description are explained away by allegorization. The Gnostic, convinced of the evil of matter and regarding this world as under the sway of powers hostile to man,[41] considered the Creator as one of these powers, and so introduced a distinction between him and the supreme God. Such a distinction was almost inevitable in view of the fundamental Gnostic dualism, but anti-Semitism may also have contributed to the depreciation of the God of the Jews. In examining Gnostic thought about God for Jewish influence we have therefore to consider the Gnostic Creator as well as the supreme God in relation to the one Jewish God. This greatly extends the possibility of Jewish influence.

Attention has already been drawn to the convergence of the Jewish and Hellenistic ideas of God.[42] The avoidance by devout Jews of the use of the divine name, the conviction of the transcendence of God, the prohibition of images, all impressed the pagan, and all combined to exalt the mysterious supreme Being still more.[43] Jew and Greek alike could unite in the conception of a supreme God, nameless and invisible, but whereas the Hellenistic view tends to be impersonal and philosophical, and the supreme Being is there a metaphysical Absolute, the Jewish view retains—even in Philo— the sense of the personality and, indeed, of the Fatherhood of God.[44] Windisch[45] considers that the idea of the transcendent God in Philo shows Greek influence in addition to the Jewish elements, and this provides a link with Gnosticism, where the idea is developed more on Hellenistic than on Jewish lines. Philo's interpretation is a stage on the way from Judaism in the stricter sense to the Gnostic view.

Norden[46] claims that the phrase ἄγνωστος θεός cannot be found in purely Greek documents, which is all the more notable in view of the frequency of related terms such as ἀόρατος and ἀκατάληπτος. It may also be remarked that it does not occur in the Septuagint, and only once in the New Testament.[47] Plato had held that God is invisible, but comprehensible to the mind (νοητός), and that this world is a perceptible god, the image of the intelligible;[48] the Stoics had held that God is invisible, but may be known from his works,[49] and the concept was taken over from them into Hellenistic Judaism,[50] whence it passed into Christian thought with Paul. But where Paul could speak of the revelation of God in nature[51] the Gnostics removed Him beyond the knowledge of all save the enlightened few. Natural theology could attain only to the Demiurge, who as Creator of the world is known by his works.

This theory that God is invisible, which is maintained by a long tradition of thought from Plato onward, is not the same as the view that He is unknowable or unknown;[52] it is this latter view that marks the difference between the normal Greek idea and that which came into favour with the Gnostics, and this difference appears to begin with the penetration into the Graeco-Roman world of the Oriental religions.[53] With it is associated a change in the idea of man's knowledge of God. 'The Greek sought his *Weltanschauung* on a speculative path. With the clarity of abstract thought which is characteristic of him, he allowed his *νοῦς* to knock at the gates of knowledge. His aim was intellectual comprehension along rational lines, and the mystic-ecstatic element is at least in principle eliminated. The Oriental did not gain his knowledge of God by the path of speculation, but an emotion (*Gefühlsleben*) dormant in the depths of the soul and aroused by a religious need allowed him to attain to a union with God. . . . Thus faith and enlightened intuition take the place of knowledge and comprehension, a deeply inward experience that of reflection.'[54]

A similar result is obtained from an examination of the use of the phrase *γνῶσις θεοῦ* and the related verbal forms.[55] These also are rare in earlier Greek thought, but become more common later, again with the appearance of the Oriental cults upon the stage of the Graeco-Roman world. At the same time there is a change in the connotation of the word: the possibility of a rational knowledge of God is now denied; *γνῶσις* is imparted by revelation or by a mystic vision, and not by speculation or by inference from the natural world.[56]

The importance of this for our purpose is that from the Greek point of view Judaism was one of the competing Oriental cults. Moreover, the terms *γνῶσις θεοῦ*, *γινῶσκειν θεόν* and so on are frequent in the Septuagint,[57] which was one of the chief means by which Jewish thought became known to the Greeks. The evidence thus points to a development in Hellenistic thought concerning God which took place with the rise to prominence of the Oriental religions and which culminated in the Gnostic doctrines.[58] Jewish influence played a part in this development, but Judaism on the whole was not itself greatly affected. Philo stands nearer to the Gnostic view than do the Greek philosophers proper,[59] but he still makes room for an effort on the part of man to attain to the knowledge of God, in addition to employing the concept that such knowledge is the gift of divine grace. Again, he does not seem to use the term *ἄγνωστος* of God.[60] The type of thought which he represents is a combination of Judaism with Greek philosophy, together with elements from other cults which shared in the contemporary syncretism; his position is intermediate, since although the process of syncretism had already been begun, it was either not yet complete, or more probably he was not so strongly influenced by it as were the Gnostics later.

In the nature of the case there is not much that can be said about the unknown God, since such knowledge as was claimed by the Gnostics was a secret confined to an inner circle, but we can point to a concurrence between one aspect of Jewish theology and certain tendencies of current thought, both Greek and Oriental. The common elements are elaborated by the Gnostics in a way that leads them far from Judaism, and there is little that can confidently be attributed to Jewish influence. The dominant factor in the process of development is the current religio-philosophical syncretism,[61] but Judaism itself contributed to this syncretism, and hence to the growth of the Gnostic view. The new connotation which was given to the word γνῶσις would in itself transform the Old Testament for the Hellenistic reader, although there is not much evidence that it affected the Jews themselves. The Gnostic doctrine of the unknown God is therefore neither Greek nor Jewish, but the product of a blending of Jewish and Graeco-Oriental thought which dates perhaps from shortly before the Christian era,[62] and with which is connected the new connotation given to the concept of γνῶσις. It is not so much a question of religious dogma as of the reinterpretation of religious ideas in the light of current philosophical speculation.

If there is not much evidence of connexion between Judaism and Gnosticism in the case of the supreme God, there is more when we turn to the Demiurge.[62a] This is only to be expected, since in most Gnostic systems the Demiurge, or at least one of the creator angels, is explicitly identified with the God of the Jews. Whatever be the ultimate origin of this figure, it is interesting to note that the Gnostic theory here runs counter to all earlier tradition. Plato regarded God as creator of the world, but presents as His first creatures the lesser gods who co-operate in the creation of man.[63] This removes from Him the responsibility for human evil. To the Stoics, God is the λόγος immanent in the cosmos, or later the transcendent λόγος who manifests himself in the cosmos in innumerable λόγοι.[64] Here again God Himself is the creator, although this raised problems concerning the evil that is in the world which the Stoics strove in vain to solve.[65] To Philo, as an orthodox Jew, God is again the creator;[66] the Hellenistic scheme of the mediating λόγος is adopted to suit his purpose, but abandoned where it is not required.[67] The same is true of Christianity, save that the cosmic activity of Christ as the creative λόγος is here more integral to the scheme.[68] On the pagan side, certain Hermetic prayers invoke Hermes or the Ἀγαθὸς Δαίμων as creator, and similar features appear in the papyri.[69] Thus in general, despite differences of cosmological detail, the tradition is the same throughout. Lesser powers may be assigned a part to avoid the ascription of evil to God; a hostile power may appear in opposition to Him, thwarting His purpose, but the Creator is always the supreme God.[70] The emphasis of Athenagoras in his apology for the Christians might almost suggest that he is opposing any other view.[71]

In Gnosticism we find the creator as a being hostile to man over against the supreme God, and here the fact that the Demiurge is so frequently equated with the God of the Old Testament suggests the influence of anti-Semitism. This is probably true, but anti-Semitism is only a contributory factor. The real source of this peculiar phenomenon is the predominant Gnostic sense of the evil of human existence, which forces them into a dualism far more radical than any previously known, at least in the Greek world.[72] Persian dualism admitted two creators, in the words of Plutarch, τὸν μὲν ἀγαθῶν, τὸν δὲ φαύλων δημιουργόν,[73] which lends support to the view that we have here ultimately to do with Persian influence; but the relations of Ormuzd and Ahriman, and of these two to Zervan, where he appears, are somewhat obscure, while it must be noted that the parallel is not exact. Ahriman contends with Ormuzd for the mastery of the world, and is the creator of the evil in the world; he is not the creator of the world, nor is he subordinate to Ormuzd, while the latter is not removed from contact with the world like the Gnostic ἄγνωστος θεός.[74] A closer parallel to the unknown God would be Zervan, who, however, seems to belong to less orthodox speculations.[75] If Persian dualism did play a part, therefore, it was in a much modified form. Again, the fact that the Demiurge does not appear at all in certain systems, or as in *Poimandres* is distinct from the supreme God but not yet hostile to man, seems to indicate a development within the Gnostic movement.[76]

Bousset argues that Ialdabaoth is not originally Jewish, but represents an ancient Babylonian deity, degraded as a result of the victory of Persia, with whom Yahweh was later identified.[77] The process would be facilitated by the fact that Yahweh, the creator-god of the Old Testament, was already associated with Saturn in Hellenistic thought, while Saturn in turn is associated with the Babylonian god in question.[78] However this may be, we are not at present concerned with ultimate origins, but rather with the more immediate links in the chain. Various factors combined to exalt the supreme God and to remove Him from the world, and it is probable that suitable ideas from ancient mythological tradition were taken up and adapted by the thinkers of our period to express the views which they sought to advance. Thus the similarity of some Gnostic concept to some strand of ancient mythology need not involve a more direct dependence of Gnosticism on the mythology in question. Magian theories of Zervan may have contributed to the growth of the idea of the unknown God, and some such Babylonian deity as that proposed by Bousset may have served as the model for the Demiurge, but the particular application of these various theories which we find in Gnosticism was the work in the main of men of a much later day, who blended into a comprehensive system elements old and new, mythological and metaphysical, from religion and from philosophy. Given the strong sense of the evil of this life, and the view that this world was the creation of hostile powers, any creator-god becomes automatically hostile. The fact that this degraded the God of the Jews was only an additional source of satisfaction to anti-Semites, or to those who sought a closer rapprochement with the Gentile world of thought over against the Judaism from which Christianity had sprung.

We have, then, two theories of Creation. In the Gnostic the Demiurge is a hostile being who holds mankind in subjection, and seeks to prevent their return to God. Here God and the πνευματικοί, if not the rest of men, are ranged against the Demiurge and his powers. In the other theory we have a series descending from God through His powers or the Logos or the Demiurge to man. Here the source of evil is usually held to be matter rather than any specific hostile being. In both theories room is made for demons at a still lower level. It is interesting now to observe that in Valentinianism an attempt is made to merge these theories together: the statement that the Saviour virtually acted as Demiurge seems an attempt to harmonize the Christian doctrine of Christ as the Logos in Creation with the Gnostic theory.[79] A similar feature occurs in the *Poimandres*, where the λόγος ascends to unite with the Demiurge.[80] Here Dodd sees a fusion of two theories, a Hellenistic-Jewish and a Platonist, concerning the power intermediate between God and the world. This fusion is less awkward than the Valentinian, since the Demiurge is not regarded as hostile to man,[81] while it has a 'subtle appropriateness' in this connexion. 'The λόγος ... remains essentially a "word" or command of God. As such a command is needed, according to Genesis, to enable the lower elements to bring forth life, it is natural that the "word" should be given a place in this stage of the work. Once united with the Demiurge, it disappears as a separate factor, and the Demiurge, equipped with the power of the "word," acts as a Platonic creator should.'[82] This Hellenistic-Jewish Logos is in some sense the prototype of the Christian, and as both the *Poimandres* and Valentinianism originate in Egypt, some closer connexion may be suspected.[83] It may also be remarked that the Gnostic Demiurge, like that of the *Poimandres*, usually operates in accordance with the will of the supreme God.[84] This may indicate that in origin the Demiurge was merely a subordinate creator, as in the general tradition, and not a hostile power, but, on the other hand, it may be a vindication of the omnipotence of the supreme Being.

The Gnostic Demiurge plays a part analogous to that of Satan in Jewish and Christian theology, and this leads to a further point. Athenagoras treats Satan as an angel who exercised his freedom of will in rebelling against God, and who now appears as the ruler of this world.[85] This theory he supports by a chain of evidence from Greek sources concerning the demons, and despite the obscurity of his narrative we can detect something of the contemporary speculation on the subject. Some held that all was under the sway of Τύχη or Εἱμαρμένη, blind chance or inexorable fate, while others claimed that there was a purpose, a Providence, at the root of all things.[86] The demons have led men astray into the worship of vain gods and idols, and their chief, the prince of this world, sets himself up as God.[87] Given the Gnostic sense of the evil of this life, the association of fate with the planets and of the planets with the cosmic powers,[88] and some such demonology as that which lies behind Athenagoras, the Gnostic theory of the Demiurge was a natural result. For the existence of such a demonology the frequent references in the New Testament to the prince of this world,[89] the rulers of darkness,[90] the principalities and powers,[91] are ample evidence. The Gnostic theory need not therefore be traced back to remote antiquity; the elements which combined to form it are more immediately present in the environment of the earliest Gentile Christians, and, indeed, probably also in that of the early Church in Jerusalem. The Demiurge of Gnostic theory is simply the Satan of Jewish and Christian theology, the chief demon of current thought, transformed by the dominant Gnostic pessimism into the creator of the world, its present ruler;[92] the functions and titles of the Creator in the Old Testament are transferred to him, but traces of the older view persist in the appearance of demons below the cosmic powers. This suggestion is confirmed by the words of Porphyry concerning the demons:[93] 'After this they turn us to worship and sacrifices to the benefactors, as though they were angry. Now these and similar things they do because they wish to make us depart from the right knowledge of the gods and turn us to themselves. . . . For they wish to be gods, and the power pre-eminent among them is ambitious to appear to be the greatest god.'

There is nothing in Porphyry's description which is not directly appropriate to the cosmic powers of Gnosticism. The conception of the Demiurge is therefore due immediately to a development of the current philosophy, although, of course, elements in that philosophy may derive ultimately from much older sources. For instance, in Babylonian mythology the gods come down to enjoy the savour of sacrifice,[94] as here the demons delight λοιβῇ τε κνίσῃ τε.[95] Christianity as represented by the New Testament and by apologists like Athenagoras had adapted something of this philosophy for its own purposes, but the Gnostics go much further. A similar adaptation was doubtless made by the Jews earlier, but they had a contribution of their own to make, in their demonology,[96] while again the figure of the Demiurge in Gnosticism is only a distorted image of the Old Testament Yahweh. Once the identification was made the rest was a matter of adapting and reinterpreting the Scriptural narratives.

The concept of the Demiurge is particularly interesting for our purpose since it shows the interaction of Judaism and the current popular philosophy. Judaism seems to have drawn its demonology ultimately from Persia, Satan being modelled on Ahriman,[97] and here again we see the concurrence of Jewish and Hellenistic thought. The ideas adopted into Judaism came by various roads into popular philosophy also, partly at least, no doubt, through the medium of Judaism itself.[98] The Gnostic theory is largely an intensification of earlier ideas, and here Jewish and Graeco-Oriental elements are blended into a new and far more radical theory of the nature of human existence.

The separation of the Demiurge from the supreme God is not yet complete in the Hermetic $\kappa\acute{o}\rho\eta$ $\kappa\acute{o}\sigma\mu o\nu$,[99] while the identification is maintained throughout by the Catholic Church.[100] The appearance of a separate Demiurge in the Platonist Numenius is ascribed by Norden to the influence of Valentinianism,[101] and certain variations of opinion which appear to be indicated in our sources seem to show that the distinction grew up within Gnosticism itself, and that it was long before a clear and coherent theory was evolved. The cosmogony of Genesis, as interpreted by Jews of the Dispersion and later by Christians, had certain affinities with current philosophical speculation, based on the *Timaeus* but admitting elements from various other sources, some of which had also influenced Judaism. The occurrence of such ideas in the Hermetica, where Christian influence is unlikely,[102] suggests that the theory originated in the contact of Judaism with that philosophy, although its final development does not appear until the second century.

The Demiurge is frequently the chief of seven powers,[103] associated with the planets, although in some systems he seems to stand alone.[104] He is usually represented as setting in order the region of the Hebdomad, which is the realm beneath the heaven, and this function corresponds roughly to the account of Creation in Genesis; unfortunately our sources, apart from the *Poimandres*, do not afford sufficient details for a close comparison, although the reinterpretation of the Old Testament in such systems as those of Justin and the *Apocryphon Johannis* deserves attention. He is also the giver of the law, and speaks through the prophets, again corresponding to the God of the Old Testament.[105] The Jewish God, Creator and Giver of the law, has been interpreted by the Gnostics in an anti-Jewish fashion in the interests of their dualistic cosmogony. At certain points there is a closer agreement between the Hermetic theories and the Jewish than between the latter and the Gnostic, but this is sometimes due to the survival in the Hermetica of detailed cosmogonies for which we have no Gnostic counterparts.

The ignorance of the Demiurge concerning the supreme God is naturally inferred from the fact that the latter is unknown[106] until he chooses to reveal himself. But such ignorance about God is also a reproach, an evil among men.[107] Here again there are similarities in the Hermetic literature,[108] while Reitzenstein refers to certain Egyptian theories for explanation.[109] This, however, is only a further indication of the variety of the sources which contributed to the thought of the period in which Christianity arose. Dodd has no difficulty in finding Jewish parallels for the contrast of ignorance and knowledge, again indicating the affinity of the Hermetic writings to Hellenistic Judaism.[110] One peculiar feature, however, occurs in the theory of Basilides, where ἀγνωσία is the appointed lot for the Ogdoad and the Hebdomad, with the souls which belong to them, at the ἀποκατάστασις.[111] For them the desire for higher things is death. So too in Valentinianism it is the desire of Sophia to know the Father, or according to another account to create like him, which is the cause of her misfortunes.[112] The latter account finds a parallel in the *Poimandres*,[113] where in regard to the fall of the primal Man it is said that he desired to create, having beheld the creation effected by the Demiurge. Once again Dodd shows the affinity of the Jewish and Hermetic doctrines, although admittedly this particular point of Man's desire to create is not discussed.[114]

The idea of the Logos need not long detain us, since here we find parallels in orthodox Christianity; the Gnostic Aeon may be traced to Christian influence at least as easily as to Jewish. It need only be remarked that in the contemporary philosophy there appears a λόγος as intermediary between God and the world. The Jewish counterpart to this λόγος is first Wisdom and later, as in Philo, the Jewish Logos. The Prologue to the Fourth Gospel presents the first verse of Mark in terms of the Jewish Wisdom-Logos interpretation of Genesis,[115] and here both Judaism and Christianity are influenced by contemporary thought. Christianity, however, has an original contribution to make, in that the Logos doctrine is only an interpretation of the historical person of Jesus. 'What is original and new in the Johannine proclamation is precisely this, that the gracious mission of the Logos is presented not in the exaltation of individual souls but in a unique Person of history.'[115a] Nowhere outside of Christian circles do we find the idea that the Logos could become incarnate.

In this connexion it is worthy of note that the Fourth Gospel was a favourite book at least among the Valentinians.[116] In view of this, the revelation of God to the Aeons through Monogenes in Valentinianism is most readily to be understood as an application of John: θεὸν οὐδεὶς ἑώρακεν πώποτε· ὁ μονογενὴς θεός, ὁ ὢν εἰς τὸν κόλπον τοῦ πατρός, ἐκεῖνος ἐξηγήσατο,[117] although the Valentinians have transferred the scene of the revelation from this world to the Pleroma. The idea of creation through the divine word can be found in Genesis,[118] as well as in many other systems of thought.

The most natural explanation of the many parallels which we find in this connexion is that all derive from similar efforts to interpret various theories in philosophic terms. In each case there is no doubt some element already present which gives scope for such a reinterpretation, as in the Genesis narrative. The Logos then is the Jewish, based on the current philosophy; the Fourth Gospel derives it from the speculations of a circle like that of Philo, although apparently independent of him,[119] and applies the theory to the interpretation of the life and work of Jesus. In Gnosticism the appearance of Christ as the Logos, or as a separate Aeon beside the Logos, is an adaptation of the Christian view to Gnostic ideas.[120]

Of the other Aeons, apart from Sophia, little need be said. Those of the Valentinian system may as Tertullian[121] suggested be purely metaphorical, although reasons have been sought in earlier speculations for the occurrence of the particular figures 8, 10, 12, and 30. That the supreme God is comprehensible only to Mind is quite good Platonism; the fact that when Mind is hypostatized

there is no expression of its thought is explained by the statement
that such expression was prevented by a higher power: the Father
did not choose to reveal himself—a Gnostic refinement of the older
view.[122]

Only the Ophite Son of Man seems to call for closer study. This
designation might naturally be derived from the fact that its bearer
is son of Anthropos or the Primal Man, but it seems much more
probable that this being would have been given a name if there
had been nothing in previous thought to suggest the title. It would
appear therefore that the title is copied from the Jewish apocalyptic
figure, or perhaps more probably from Christian usage.[123] In the
latter case the relative simplicity of the Ophite system seems to
indicate an early date, but this particular feature may be a later
accommodation to Christianity. 'Son of Man' does not appear to
have had any great importance in Judaism, although possibly certain
circles were tending towards an equation of the apocalyptic figure
with the Messiah.[124] A link with Christianity is to be found in the
use of the term by Jesus,[125] but this only raises further problems,
since the connexion is not at all close. We must conclude either
that there was some earlier theory about the Son of Man which
has escaped our knowledge or that the formulators of the Ophite
system knew of Jesus' use of the term and of the place assigned to
him in Christian thought, but that like so many other Gnostics
they separated Christ the Redeemer from the second power in
their hierarchy. As Ophitism seems in many respects to be pre-
Christian we should then have a clear example of the assimilation
of Christian elements into an earlier and primarily alien scheme.

The figure of Sophia, however, calls for a much more detailed
treatment. In the *Poimandres*,[126] after beholding the archetypal
universe in the light which is Νοῦς, the seer asks: τὰ οὖν στοιχεῖα
τῆς φύσεως πόθεν ὑπέστη; To this the answer is: ἐκ βουλῆς θεοῦ,
ἥτις λαβοῦσα τὸν λόγον καὶ ἰδοῦσα τὸν καλὸν κόσμον ἐμιμήσατο,
κοσμοποιηθεῖσα διὰ τῶν ἑαυτῆς στοιχείων καὶ γεννημάτων
ψυχῶν. Reitzenstein[127] notes the rare occurrence of the word
βουλή in the singular in the Hermetic literature, as well as a difference in the use of the word. He finds the explanation in the Isis-
cult, where Isis is 'wie σοφία und βούλησις auch φύσις und γένεσις'.
In the text of his book he compares a passage from Plutarch: ἡ

γὰρ Ἶσίς ἐστι μὲν τὸ τῆς φύσεως θῆλυ καὶ δεκτικὸν ἀπάσης γενέσ-
εως. καθὸ τιθήνη καὶ πανδεχὴς ὑπὸ τοῦ Πλάτωνος .... κέκληται,
διὰ τὸ πάσας ὑπὸ τοῦ λόγου τρεπομένη μορφὰς δέχεσθαι καὶ ἰδέας
.... καὶ παρέχουσα γεννᾶν ἐκείνῳ κτλ.[127a] This leads to an
account of the two Ὧροι, the younger who is εἰκών τοῦ νοητοῦ
κόσμου αἰσθητὸς ὤν,[128] and the elder who is not the κόσμος but
εἰδωλόν τι καὶ κόσμου φάντασμα μέλλοντος. Here Isis is the
female principle who gives substance to the ideal form.

Reitzenstein further refers to Philo,[129] who says: τὸν γοῦν τόδε
τὸ πᾶν ἐργασάμενον δημιουργὸν ὁμοῦ καὶ πάτερα εἶναι τοῦ γεγο-
νότος εὐθὺς ἐν δίκῃ φήσομεν, μητέρα δὲ τὴν τοῦ πεποιηκότος
ἐπιστήμην. ᾗ συνὼν ὁ θεὸς οὐχ ὡς ἄνθρωπος ἔσπειρε γένεσιν,
ἡ δὲ παραδεξαμένη τὰ τοῦ θεοῦ σπέρματα τελεσφόροις ὠδῖσι
τὸν μόνον καὶ ἀγαπητὸν αἰσθητὸν υἱὸν ἀπεκύησε τόνδε τὸν κόσμον.
'This idea Philo cannot have derived from the Biblical glorification
of σοφία which immediately follows (Prov. 8. 22); rather must the
doctrine which was in general circulation be discovered in the
Jewish Scriptures, and justified from them. But it can have been
in general circulation only in Egypt.'[130] Reitzenstein also claims
that Philo is acquainted with the doctrine of the younger and the
elder Horus,[131] and declares that these ideas are neither Jewish nor
Graeco-Jewish, but Egyptian.[132]

Professor Dodd rejects Reitzenstein's view.[133] 'Reitzenstein (who
regards this passage as part of an interpolation into the original
Poimandres) finds here a doctrine of a female divine being who
receives the word, as σπέρμα, into herself, and brings forth the
world, and he connects it with widespread mythological ideas.
But the whole of this is simply read into the passage, which contains
not the remotest hint of a sexual process.' Dodd then goes on to
consider the Jewish affinities of the passage, and remarks that 'in
Jewish thought Σοφία came to be hypostatized and personified as
the divine agent in creation, the τεχνῖτις πάντων (Wisd. 7. 22).'[134]
Further, the influence of the Isis-theology upon Judaism, if such
there was, 'must have been exerted at a period long antecedent to
the Poimandres.'[135]

This, however, is not all that may be said. Reitzenstein quotes
also Irenaeus on the Valentinians: ταύτην δὲ τὴν μητέρα καὶ
Ὀγδοάδα καλοῦσι καὶ Σοφίαν καὶ Γῆν.[136] These he claims to be

well-known epithets of Isis, who is, therefore, in his view the Sophia of Valentinianism.[137] If it be added that this Sophia is also called Holy Spirit, which is the name of the female principle of Ophitism,[138] a clear chain of connexion becomes evident. The description of the Ophite Holy Spirit given by Irenaeus is closely similar to that of the *Poimandres*, and also to the words of Philo quoted above. On the other hand, all three accounts are much modified in comparison with the account of Plutarch, while again there is a variation in Ophitism and in the Valentinian theory. Briefly, the Valentinian Sophia-Achamoth is equivalent to the Ophite Sophia-Prunicus, the higher Sophia to the Ophite Holy Spirit.[139] It is the latter who is the receptive female principle, while it is the former who is the Mother and Ogdoad. The functions of Isis, if such they be, have been partitioned between two separate Aeons. This seems to indicate that neither the Ophites nor the Valentinians had a thorough and first-hand knowledge of the Isis-theology. They simply adapted what they knew and what had been handed down to them by tradition for their own purposes. And it is not difficult to discern the possibility of a Jewish contribution to the process.

Thus far the accuracy of Reitzenstein's claim that the titles of Sophia in Valentinianism are those of Isis has been taken for granted, as has his theory that this concept is dependent on the Isis-theology. Cumont,[140] however, has remarked, and Reitzenstein himself admits,[141] that there was no regular theology in the mystery cults, and Cumont refers explicitly to the cult of Isis.[142] In view of the influence exercised by the contemporary philosophy in other aspects of Gnosticism, it is probable that the same is true here.

In that case we have a development within Judaism of Sophia as a counterpart to Isis-Astarte, which in course of time provides the Jews with an intermediary corresponding to the λόγος of current thought.[143] In the pagan cults, which were likewise attempting to interpret their myths in philosophical terms, we find Isis as the intermediary between the supreme god Sarapis and the κόσμος, and similarly in other religions. The important point is that the tendency to regard the supreme god as completely transcendent led to the sense of the need for some mediating power. The Jewish philosophical interpretation, therefore, occasioned in the first place

Logos

O

by the need to offset the lure of the worship of Isis-Astarte[144] but later adapted to a more 'philosophical' use, eventually meets the pagan interpretation on the same ground, and the common material is carried over into Gnosticism. There is, of course, the possibility that Judaism exercised some influence on its pagan competitors, especially since in one case at least Wisdom replaces Isis in a hymn to Sarapis.[145] It is also possible that the influence of the Isis-cult may be entirely unnecessary. As Hatch remarks, 'on the one hand, there had long been among the Jews a belief in the power of the *word* of God: and the belief in His wisdom had shaped itself into a conception of that wisdom as a substantive force. On the other hand, the original conception of Greek Philosophy that Mind or Reason had marshalled into order the confused and warring elements of the primeval chaos, had passed into the conception of the *Logos* as a mode of the activity of God. These several elements, which had a natural affinity for each other, had already been combined by Philo . . . into a comprehensive system: and in the second century they were entering into new combinations both inside and outside the Christian communities.'[146] If, however, the Jewish theory was due simply to the contact of Judaism with the contemporary philosophy, it seems difficult to account for the appearance of Wisdom at all; it would have been easier for the Jews to develop the logos-theory at once, while again the contacts between Wisdom in Jewish writings and the Isis of pagan sources seem to indicate some connexion,[147] although certainly any such connexion took place long before the first century A.D.

The process of development may then be conjecturally outlined thus: to counteract the influence of the Isis-cult, the Jews developed the concept of Wisdom, as she appears in the Wisdom of Solomon and other Jewish-Hellenistic works, but other factors also enter in, among them the necessity of opposing the cult of Astarte, with whom Isis was united, while the sexual features of the original Isis-myth are considerably modified. A similar train of ideas is to be found in Philo, with whom the modified doctrine reappears in Egypt. Finally it appears in the *Poimandres* and in the Ophite and Valentinian systems. In the meantime both the Jewish theory and the Isis-myth had been accommodated to the dominant philosophy of the time, and it is in this form that the latter appears in Plutarch.

There is no reason to suspect a genealogical relation between the various links in the chain, except in a general sense or in regard to the dependence of Valentinianism upon Ophitism. Traces of Jewish influence upon the *Poimandres* have been demonstrated by Dodd, and Jewish influence upon Gnosticism seems almost certain, but such an influence cannot be definitely linked with the name of Philo. We have, in fact, evidence of Jewish adaptation of certain features associated with Isis, and of the use of these features again in later systems, probably under Jewish influence. The *Poimandres* is dated by both Dodd and Reitzenstein as belonging approximately to the beginning of the second century A.D., which means that it is slightly later than Philo and contemporary with, if not earlier than, the Gnostics. Plutarch represents a purely pagan tradition of about the same period, with no apparent Jewish influence, but all illustrate the tendency of the time towards a philosophical interpretation of religion.

The appearance of this particular feature in Ophitism, moreover, may perhaps serve to confirm the suggested location of the Ophites, or at least of some of them, in Egypt. On the other hand, the secondary character which it displays, and the evident Jewish influence, if the above conclusions be correct, may be held to discount that suggestion. Fuller evidence is necessary for a definite decision here.

We may conclude this section with a brief glance at the remaining figures: the cosmic powers, the angels, and the demons. These are best examined together, since there is some confusion among them.[148]

According to Philo, the angels of Moses are the demons of the Greek philosophers, conceived as souls peopling the air, some of whom descend into matter to become men;[149] elsewhere the angels are the philosophic λόγοι.[150] This is simply the theory of Posidonius,[151] who in his view of the soul departs from orthodox Stoicism. To him the air is full of souls, each of which is an igneous breath of an extremely subtle nature; at death, the soul leaves the body and returns to the air, where it rises until it reaches air of its own quality. The pure pass at once to the higher regions, while those laden with matter hover in the denser atmosphere near the earth, and in due course resume their punishment in new bodies.

In *de Gigantibus* 7ff. Philo reads this theory into Genesis 6, where the *bne elohim* (LXX ἄγγελοι)[152] descend to earth to mate with the daughters of men.[153] The Biblical narrative is treated as an account of the descent of souls into bodies, as also in the interpretation of Jacob's dream,[154] where the angels on the ladder are souls ascending and descending, some returning to the higher regions, others drawn down by the lure of mortal life, while others again, the perfectly pure, ascend or descend in fulfilment of their function as angels or 'messengers' of the Great King.[155] The Gnostics have the former passage of Genesis in mind but make different use of it. In Ophitism, the cosmic angels unite with Eve,[156] while in Valentinianism the angels who accompany the Saviour unite with Achamoth.[157] Here the Ophite exegesis is more accurate than that of Philo, probably because they have no need to distort the story, since they have already accounted for the human race and seek simply to explain the narrative in a way consistent with their system. Philo, on the other hand, is trying to discover Posidonius' theory in the Jewish Scriptures, regardless of the fact that he has already given a different account of the creation of man according to the first two chapters of Genesis. The Valentinian account is vaguely reminiscent of Philo, the offspring of the union being a spiritual seed which eventually becomes part of man, but this similarity is obscured by the wrappings of mythology which surround it.

The cosmic powers again are described in various systems as quarrelling among themselves over the leadership,[158] or as disputing over the pre-eminence which each claims for his own nation. This agrees with Jewish tradition concerning the angels who were appointed over the nations.[159] Finally, it has already been noted that four of the seven cosmic powers in Ophitism as presented by Irenaeus and in the Ophite diagram bear Old Testament names for God, the other three being due to magic.[160] Of the four Old Testament names one is Iao, which appears frequently in magical texts, and also occurs as a magic word in Valentinianism.[161]

The obvious conclusion once again is that the Gnostic theories have their origin in the convergence of Jewish and pagan views. The cosmic powers, angels, and demons of Gnosticism derive from a view of the world such as that which lies behind the New Testament. The distinction between Satan, the ruler of this world, on the one hand, and the planetary powers who govern man's destiny on the other, may be implicit in the language of Paul, although, as has been noted, this distinction is not always carefully observed. Certainly it could easily be read into Paul's words by later thinkers.[162] ·In Judaism, angelology and demonology took on an increased importance in the post-exilic period, largely under Persian influence.[163] The pagan world had its own views of a similar sort, and was dominated by superstition of one kind or another.[164] The Gnostics have simply separated the planetary powers, who hold man under their sway throughout his life, from the swarm of demons whose influence is more occasional, and from the angels, who may be either friendly or hostile. In some ways the Gnostic view is an attempt to bring order into chaos by systematizing the various theories that were current into one comprehensive scheme.

The Jews had a reputation as magicians, sorcerers, and exorcists, as may be seen from contemporary references, and the adoption of Iao by pagan magicians is not surprising in view of the efficacy of Jewish exorcism, which was naturally ascribed to the peculiar potency of the God of the Jews.[165] Jewish and pagan ideas are in this field blended in a bewildering syncretism which is the more striking in view of the comparative freedom of Judaism from syncretism in other respects; but just here we are dealing precisely with those classes in Judaism which were perhaps most prone to syncretism and apostasy, the lower and less educated who were addicted to magic and a prey to superstition.[166] Philo represents the position of the more educated, prepared to accept the contemporary philosophical theory where it could be accommodated to Judaism, yet assured that within Judaism he was free from the domination of the stars; but for such as him there were other temptations. Paul, too, admits the current scheme, but is confident that Christ has secured for the believer the victory over these adversaries. The Gnostics have taken over the contemporary view, with all its Jewish elements and all its magical accretions, and adapted it to their own scheme, although they have not succeeded in removing the confusion and obscurity in which it lay.

The Gnostic theories of the powers and emanations of God bulk large in our accounts of the various systems, but it was not here that the danger for Christianity lay. Plato had used myths to express philosophical ideas in a comprehensible way; Philo shows the tendency of the time towards mythological expression, whether by interpreting myths in terms of philosophy as was done in the mysteries or by the discovery of philosophical truths in the Jewish scriptures and the justification of these truths from the scriptures; Paul could accept much of the contemporary philosophy in his effort to present the Gospel to the Gentile world. The Gnostics simply carry the hypostatization of divine attributes and abstract ideas to a further degree. The fundamental error lies not here but, as in the case of the early heresies assailed by Paul, in a wrong attitude towards God and towards the world, in the emphasis on γνῶσις over against ἀγάπη, and above all in the depreciation of the historical Jesus and His death upon the Cross.

2. *The creation and nature of the world*

Something has already been said in this connexion in discussing the theory of the Demiurge, but there are other features which remain to be considered. The first and most obvious is a point of difference, namely, that in Judaism we have simply the universe comprising heaven and earth and sea, while in Gnosticism there seems to be a complete supra-mundane world, if not more than one. Prior to Valentinianism, however, the difference is more apparent than real. The Gnostic scheme presents the conventional Hellenistic theory, in which earth is the lowest stage of the ladder, or the inmost of several concentric spheres. Above or around the earth are a number of heavens, in some cases three, in others seven,[167] and above these again is the realm of the fixed stars. This scheme could obviously be adapted to Judaism, and we have clear evidence that the Jews did, in fact, make use of it.[168] The 'heaven' in which God dwells is then placed in the seventh sphere or, if God be considered as beyond the planetary system altogether, in the sphere of the fixed stars.[169] Jewish speculation of this sort could also take account of pagan theories concerning the ages of the world, but the Jewish reverence for the number seven, representing the Sabbath, sometimes led to difficulty.[170] Christian thought, although sometimes handicapped in other respects, was more easily able to adopt a view which placed the abode of God beyond the 'heavens,'[171] while the Gnostics go still further. The seventh sphere is the realm of the Demiurge, who is also the God of the Jews, identified as by Tacitus with Saturn; the eighth, under the firmament, is the abode of the Great Archon, the fallen Sophia, or Achamoth, while the firmament itself is the boundary between this phenomenal world and the true ideal world beyond.[172] Within this ideal world are the various divine beings, the attributes of God or emanations from him, the process of development culminating in the Valentinian πλήρωμα of Aeons.

This theory, then, is an adaptation of the cosmogony of Genesis by the assimilation of elements from current speculation, which was itself a Stoicizing adaptation of the cosmogony of the *Timaeus*.[173] The simple scheme is expanded by the insertion of the planetary heavens, and the abode of God is removed further from the world until it is finally beyond the universe properly so called, but the broad outlines of the picture as a whole are still those of Genesis. Differences really begin to appear with the Valentinian theory of the Pleroma, but this is largely an attempt to incorporate in the ideal world not only the attributes of God, as expressions of His nature, but also the archetypes of things on earth, including the 'ideas' of the virtues. The Valentinians have tried to effect a complete Platonic reduplication, finding the archetypes of the things on earth in the ideal world. In the other systems this elaboration has not yet taken place, or is only in process. The fall of Sophia from the higher world is an attempt to account for the existence of this world, since the Platonic view adopted by Philo,[174] which ascribes the origin of the world to the goodness of God, was impossible on Gnostic presuppositions. This fall of Sophia is an adaptation of the fall of man, which is presented both in Judaism and in the Hermetica as a fall into matter.[175]

There are three general theories of creation,[176] first, that the world was created directly by God or by lower powers created by Him or emanating from Him; secondly, that it was by a divine word, or some similar means;[177] and thirdly, that it was through the fall of a divine being. These are not always distinct, but there are traces of each in different Gnostic systems. Moreover, the first two are both possible for Judaism, while the third is reminiscent of the ancient myth of Tiamat, which seems to have had some influence on Jewish thought.[178] A divine word appears in the Hermetic cosmogony, while Philo by using the term λόγος is able to combine the Jewish theory as presented in Genesis with that of contemporary philosophy. As has already been observed, he speaks also of an archetypal universe, a κόσμος νοητός, existing in the mind of the Creator, and there is evidence that a similar theory was current among the rabbis.[179] On the other hand, the type of cosmogony which appeared where there was little or no influence from the *Timaeus* or from Genesis is shown by the papyri examined by Dieterich;[180] in his chief text creation is a sort of magical process, a series of gods coming into existence through successive laughs by the primal god. There are, however, Jewish features in this document, such as the use of Iao, while other points may have some connexion with Gnosticism.[181] The long series of gods, for instance, recalls the Gnostic emanations,[182] while the theory of creation by the falling of a 'dew' of light is in some ways similar to the Ophite theory of the fall of Sophia;[183] and again, the laughter and tears of the papyri recall the passions of Sophia in Valentinianism.[184] But it should be observed that the passions mentioned in the Valentinian theory are those of the contemporary Stoicism, and known to Philo,[185] who speaks of πάθος in one passage as ἀνείδεον οὐσίαν.[186] As there were four passions and also four elements, it was comparatively easy to identify them.

From the evidence so far adduced it seems clear that in this connexion we have three influences at work: on the more philosophical level Judaism is in close contact with the current systems of thought, and has adopted a considerable proportion of pagan speculation into the frame of its cosmogony. Some such philosophical Judaism has contributed considerably to Gnosticism, but at the same time other elements are due, on a much lower level, to magic. Here again, however, some forms of Jewish thought were in close contact with heathenism, and the Gnostics have, in fact, drawn in varying degree upon all three.[187]

In most cases, creation seems to take the form not of *creatio ex nihilo* but of the ordering of a pre-existing chaos or of matter which is in some form already present.[188] This could readily be derived from Genesis, where the earth is at first 'without form and void,' or in the Greek version 'invisible and unformed.' So in the

Poimandres there is a wet substance already in existence; the Hermetic λόγος is at first merged in this moist substance, but later ascends to unite with the Demiurge.[189] So too in Ophitism, Sophia falls into the deep (here apparently the elements), but struggles free from the waters to ascend again, forming the heavens from the body which she leaves behind.[190] Dodd, following Gunkel, is inclined to ascribe such passages as that in *Poimandres* (and similar sections in the Old Testament) to the early creation-mythology of Israel, and claims that the Hermetist is here well within the limits of Jewish tradition.[191] 'He might well have learned from his Platonic teachers that the primal formless stuff of the universe was "never still, but in discordant and disorderly motion" (*Tim.* 30a). But there are elements in his picture of the raging ocean of darkness which do not seem to come from Platonic sources, and are readily accounted for by familiarity not only with Gen. i but with Hellenistic-Jewish cosmology as a whole.'[192] The same may also be true of Ophitism, save that here the formless substance is equated with the elements.

In some schemes the ordering of chaos is accomplished by two or more powers operating successively, one of whom forms the Ogdoad, another the Hebdomad, and presumably the other six the cosmic spheres over which they preside.[193] The interest for the Gnostic, and especially for the Valentinians, is not so much in the creation of this earth as in the development of the supra-terrestrial regions, and consequently we have no detailed account of the creation of the world. This may also, however, be due to the failure of our authorities to report such an account. The earth is in any case a prison, and the important thing is the means of escape from this life.

Various trends of Greek philosophy contributed to the idea that matter as such is evil, but this theory is much more fully developed by the Gnostics, in accordance with their general view. It is not clear that matter is of itself evil in Philo,[194] but such ideas seem to be current in the period. They derive a certain philosophical justification from Plato, but the Gnostic development goes far beyond his view, combining dualism of various kinds into a comprehensive depreciation of this world and life on earth. The idea that the female gives substance only but not form, again, may go back to some remote mythology, but it could readily be given a Platonic interpretation as matter awaiting the impress of the idea.[195] Matter does appear as female in Philo,[196] while something may be due to the mere fact that ὕλη in Greek is feminine.

The seven heavens seem to be Persian or Chaldeo-Persian in origin, but it is perhaps significant that the location of Paradise above the third heaven agrees with Jewish thought, itself influenced by Persian ideas.[197] It was in the fourth heaven, according to the Jews, that Adam dwelt before the fall, and here too he is placed by the Valentinians.[198] There appears to be no reference to this theory in Philo, who is, however, normally opposed to astrological ideas, but the words in which Paul describes his vision imply that Paradise is there.[199] At the same time it should not be forgotten that Greek thought regarding the abode of the dead underwent a considerable development at least from Homer onwards,[200] as did the ideas of other peoples. Some of these developments, transforming the realm of departed souls from the nether regions of the earth to some part of the heavens, may have coincided with Jewish belief. We have already noted certain points of contact between Philo and Posidonius regarding the souls in the air.[201]

Finally, views differ as to the Creator: in Judaism it is God himself, with Wisdom, or in Philo the Logos, appearing on occasion as assessor or intermediary, or in the case of the Logos as pattern or as instrument; in Christianity there is a growing tendency to ascribe a prominent part in creation to Christ as the Logos.[202] Pagan theories either present God as creating, directly or through an intermediary, or else develop a sort of evolutionary view. In Gnosticism the tendency is either to assign creation to a subordinate power or powers hostile to man, or to adopt the evolutionary theory. The former is the more usual, although at times the two are confused.

To sum up, the dominant philosophy of the Hellenistic world had found a satisfactory cosmogony in the *Timaeus*, although other theories were also current. This was readily assimilated to the narrative of Genesis, as in Philo, and the resulting cosmogony, or something similar, has influenced the Hermetica; Christianity itself follows more closely on the Old Testament tradition, using the Platonizing adaptation at need and admitting a considerable number of elements from current thought, as did Judaism, in the interests of philosophical respectability, but the Gnostics once again carry the adaptation further, blending in various elements from other theories and in particular from magic. Their view of the world, apart from these accretions and the strong pessimistic tendency, is largely that of the contemporary world, the view which is in the background of the New Testament. It may be safely said, therefore, that here again the convergence of Judaism and the current philosophy played a major part in the rise of Gnosticism.

3. *Anthropology*

The essential feature here is that man really belongs not to this world but to a higher, heavenly world. This, of course, goes back at least to Plato, and was a commonplace in the Hellenistic Age. It appears in Philo and in the New Testament,[203] while even before Plato it appears in the Orphic myth of Zagreus. But this superficial similarity, and the common use of the idea that men are strangers and sojourners on this earth, aliens whose true abode is elsewhere, must not be allowed to blind us to the characteristic differences between the Biblical and the pagan views. In the former, man is regarded as created in the image and likeness of God, but by disobedience he has become alienated from Him; the barrier is constituted by sin. The latter attempts to account for the dual nature of man by some theory of a divine principle which has somehow entered into the material realm. The Biblical view, of course, may originally have been a similar attempt to explain the dualism of human nature, but the course of its development has greatly transformed it.[204] So Jesus conceives of his mission as being 'to seek and to save that which was lost,'[205] while the forgiveness of sins remains the characteristic of the Christian Gospel.[206] The mystery religions may have imposed on their initiates some obligation of moral amendment,[207] but they had no thought at all of forgiveness of sins.

The pagan view makes man a compound being, a soul imprisoned in the body. The latter, being material, is evil, but the soul, although hampered by the body, is always aspiring to escape. Such a view could be read into the Biblical narratives, as in some cases by Philo,[208] and there are obvious points of contact with Paul's distinction of σάρξ and πνεῦμα,[209] but nevertheless the difference remains. As Kennedy puts it, after reviewing Reitzenstein's claims that Pauline usage is dependent on the mystery-religions, 'Nothing adduced is strictly relevant to the profoundly ethical contrast which Paul draws between σάρξ, "flesh" (not σῶμα), and πνεῦμα "spirit." '[210] The background for Paul's thought here is adequately supplied by the Old Testament.

The Gnostics, however, both could and did assimilate the Biblical and pagan views. This means that the forgiveness of sins disappears, while the Incarnation in the full sense becomes quite impossible. The passion of Christ, so fundamental to Paul and to all orthodox Christian theology, is either ignored or explained away by some Docetic theory,[211] while salvation is secured through a mystic γνῶσις, imparted by the Redeemer. In this case, therefore, Gnosticism represents a submersion of Christianity in current paganism, with even less retention of Christian ideas than is found elsewhere. Both Christianity and Judaism before it had, however, adopted certain elements from contemporary thought for their own purposes, and these shed light on the growth of the Gnostic theory.

Gnosticism, like paganism, attempts to explain the dual nature of man by some theory of a divine principle which has somehow entered into the material world. The most extreme form appears in certain varieties of Valentinianism, where men are distinguished in three classes, the hylic, who have no part in the divine principle and are doomed to perish; the psychic, who have freedom of will either to ascend or to descend, but may not enter the Pleroma, and the pneumatic, who alone are predestined to full salvation.[212] More usually men are distinguished according to the preponderance of one element or another,[213] and it is possible to pass from one grade to another through receipt of the enlightening γνῶσις. Here Gnosticism reflects a confusion apparent very early in philosophy, all men being considered to possess the divine spark, while only some—who possess the divine spark!—are destined to salvation.[214]

The differences between the various theories of which we know are all differences of opinion as to how man came into his present state, and what is the means of escape. The Orphics spoke of the devouring of Zagreus by the Titans, the Stoics of a divine seed or spark, a portion of the immanent Logos, and these ideas could be blended with the Platonic idea that the body is the tomb of the soul and with the myth of the Primal Man to form a view in which an ideal Heavenly Man falls into matter, or is imprisoned in matter.[215] This again could be read into the narrative of the fall of Adam.[216] Another view held that some of the souls which inhabited the regions of the air nearest to the earth had descended into matter to become men, and this could be read into the story of the angels in Genesis 6.[217] The reasons assigned are often ingenious, and some theories recall ancient myths, but the latter fact need mean no more than that these myths were pressed into service by the thinkers of the period in order to express their own views. Thus Orphism, sometimes alleged as a source for Gnosticism, is important here only as mediated through other systems. It was no longer a vital force in this period.[218] Again, the myth of the Primal Man accounts only for the presence of the divine element in man. We are not here concerned with the alleged Heavenly Man Redemption Myth.[219]

Philo shows how these ideas could be read into Judaism. The Primal Man is, of course, Adam, but the fall is reinterpreted as a fall into matter.[220] Elsewhere the Logos is the ideal man, the ἄνθρωπος θεοῦ, the image of God.[221] The divine seed or spark may be found in the narrative where God breathes life into the man who has been formed,[222] while the souls which descend are the angels of Genesis 6. Man as man is ignorant of his true glory, at the mercy of his lower appetites, and must be quickened by the grace of God, his mind must rule the other parts of his soul, he must be roused out of his sleep and turn to strive up the path to his true abode.[223] Here he is but a stranger and a sojourner.[224]

Philo's general point of view is clear enough, but it is more difficult to follow the details of his thought, since he introduces so many views, not always consistently, to meet the needs of his text. Yet it is obvious that he is reading contemporary thought into the Old Testament. Some of his views appear also in the Hermetica, which are at least partly under Jewish influence,[225] and the Gnostics again plainly move in the same fields of thought. One striking feature is the interpretation of the 'coats of skin' in Genesis: in

Philo, in the Hermetica, and in Valentinianism the χιτῶνες are interpreted of the earthly body with its covering of skin.[226]

Within certain limits, the Gnostic theories differ widely, but all maintain the same central feature: man is a stranger, nay, a prisoner, in this life, whether he be as to the Ophites the creation of the Demiurge,[227] who knew not that he was conveying to his creature the divine seed, or as to Saturninus the image of a higher being, created in his likeness by the cosmic powers, whether the divine element be due ultimately to some pre-mundane fall as in Valentinianism,[228] or to the existence in the world of a portion of the divinity once implanted in it, which has not yet escaped, as to Basilides. All again accept the view that this life is dominated by the planets, or by powers which govern them, and all seek some means of ascending beyond the heavens to the higher world. Here mysticism and magic are perhaps more prominent than philosophy, but Posidonius had held that souls ascended on leaving the body until they reached air of their own quality. As in Philo, the Hermetic writings, and the New Testament itself,[229] the philosophical injunctions to sobriety and watchfulness were adapted to the needs of religion, although the Gnostic antinomianism sometimes led to other results.

In regard to the theory of Saturninus we may observe that in the Hermetica the powers are smitten with love for the Primal Man,[230] while in late Jewish and Jewish-Christian literature, above all in the Clementine writings, there is a tendency towards the glorification of the First Man.[231] Here Jewish thought seems to be moving away from the Old Testament towards a conflation of Adam with an alien Heavenly Man.[232] Again, the man moulded from the dust of the earth would naturally be assumed to lie like a statue, and the body is, indeed, so described by Philo;[233] the inbreathing of the divine spirit is, of course, easily derived from Genesis 2. 7. Thus it would seem that Saturninus has blended the latter account from Genesis with some conception of a heavenly ideal man, and that Jewish speculation may have prepared the way for his views. A further point concerns the interpretation of the 'dust of the earth': Philo, the Gnostic Justin, and the Valentinians all emphasize that this was not just any earth, but the best and finest.[234]

Man's subjection to fate does not appear in Philo, or at least not so prominently as in contemporary thought and in Gnosticism, but reference may be made to Paul, for whom, however, Christ has delivered the Christian from the power of the stars, just as to Judaism the Jew is free from fate.[235] The idea of men as female, destined as brides of the angels, also finds parallels in Philo, where Sophia is now female, mating with the patriarchs, but again male, implanting in them the seeds which they as female bring to birth.[236] Furthermore, the Gnostic distinction of men into different classes finds a certain preparation in Philo and in Paul, who both speak of νήπιοι and τέλειοι, of ψυχικοί and πνευματικοί,[237] while Philo distinguishes the perfect man from the man who is still progressing in several passages.[238] But this is largely metaphor, whereas in Gnosticism a real distinction is made.[239] Finally, there are traces in Judaism of the idea that the first man was bisexual,[240] but, on the other hand, the idea that two natures of men were created by God does not appear.[241]

In this section of our study the evidence for Jewish influence is not perhaps so strong, and more must be ascribed to current thought in the pagan environment, yet enough has been said to show that here again Jewish and pagan ideas converge. It is, however, rather a matter of Jewish assimilation of pagan ideas than of an independent development, and it must be admitted that here Gnosticism parts company with Judaism and Christianity.[242] Philo reads the ideas of the contemporary philosophy into the Old Testament, and that philosophy also colours the New Testament, but although Philo tends to waver Judaism and Christianity in general adhere to the Old Testament conception of man. Gnosticism, despite certain affinities with Jewish and Christian thought, in the main adopts the views of the pagan world.

4. *Salvation*

Man is in this world a stranger and a sojourner, 'a pilgrim in a land unknown.' In consequence, one constantly recurring theme of the Gnostics is the question of the way back to his true home, the way of salvation. Here Gnosticism is in contact with a wide range of ideas, but the existence of theories of salvation does not in itself point to any close relation between one type of thought and another. There are differences in regard to the evils from which salvation is sought, the means by which it is to be attained, and the content which is ascribed to it.[243]

The word σωτηρία does not always mean 'salvation' in our sense. This is its primary meaning in the Septuagint and in the New Testament, but it may also connote deliverance from peril, the preservation or safe keeping of property, security or safety, as in the case of the State, or bodily health and well-being.[244] The latter meanings are common in the papyri, and appear in at least two passages of the New Testament, but 'as a rule in the NT σωτηρία, following its OT application to the great deliverances of the Jewish nation as at the Red Sea, etc., came to denote Messianic and spiritual salvation, either as a present possession or as to be realized fully hereafter.'[245] Again, the Old Testament idea has undergone a long process of development: at first a deliverance from danger or peril, and especially from the hands of the enemy, it refers particularly to national and political deliverance, to peace, security, and plenty; with the growth of the Messianic idea there is a tendency towards a technical theological sense—the deliverance is to be brought in with the Messianic age; with a deepening sense of moral evil, it acquires a more ethical and spiritual meaning, as deliverance from sin as well as from the consequences of sin, while the destruction of the Jewish state led to an increased emphasis on man as an individual rather than as a member of the community; finally, there was a considerable development in regard to the idea of man's destiny after death.[246] The pages of both Old and New Testaments reflect the various ideas which were current. Christianity fell heir to the Old Testament tradition, as interpreted by the Pharisees, for whom the ethical and spiritual aspect predominates over the more materialistic. Rabbinic Judaism continued the process of development in its own way, along lines distinct from those followed by Christianity.[247]

In the pagan world our interest centres chiefly on philosophy and the mysteries, but we may note at once that Greek thought had undergone a similar process of development. The old Greek religion was concerned primarily with the well-being of the State, but the decline of the city-state brought an increased importance to the individual man, while Greek ideas as to the future life also went through many changes. The Homeric Hades, like the Jewish Sheol, is an abode of shades, the scene of a shadowy existence which is but a poor substitute for this life. Later theories on both sides not only gave fuller content to the realm of the blessed but also forecast a place of punishment for the wicked, and called upon men to live the good life on pain of eternal torment.[248]

Despite certain similarities, however, the Greek and Jewish views are quite distinct, although Greek influence may perhaps be found in some of the later Jewish writings of the Hellenistic period. One characteristic difference is that the Jew, regarding man as a whole, speaks of a resurrection, the Greek, following Plato, of the immortality of the soul. This latter doctrine was not, however, everywhere accepted, although there was a tendency, except in Epicureanism, to make room for survival in some form.

Some philosophers limited their view to this life, and taught that by reducing his interest in external goods a man might become independent of fate, that the unhappiness of mankind was due to desire for worldly goods, or to fear of the loss of such goods as were already possessed. Beyond death was nothing; the body might return to earth, the soul to the divine fire, or death might be simply the end of existence, an annihilation; in any case there was nothing beyond the grave. Men were concerned with this life alone, and true happiness was to be achieved by becoming independent of the world, accepting such blessings as might come, but free from care for anything but virtue. So the earlier Stoics admitted at most a survival until the next universal conflagration, after which the course of history would begin again,[249] and the Epicureans, anxious to eliminate the fear of death as a source of unhappiness, denied survival altogether. Posidonius, however, admitted some hope of survival for a few favoured mortals, who had been more than mortal from the first, and by blending with his Stoicism an Orphic-Platonic theory of reincarnations, left the way open for a future life.[250] This earthly life was the punishment undergone by the souls which were not sufficiently pure to ascend beyond the lower spheres, to enjoy in the higher regions the ineffable bliss of 'watching the stars go round.'[251]

The ordinary man clung to some idea of survival, and continued to look for some religion that would confirm his faith. The appeal

P

of the mysteries lay in the fact that by initiation he could be united
to the god, even deified, and pass beyond the heavens to the higher
realms.[252] The immortality reserved for the few was thrown open
to all, provided that they fulfilled certain conditions. Whether or
not there was in these cults any obligation to lead a better life, the
primary condition was initiation, but clearly there was a possibility
of the accommodation of these theories to a Stoicism like that of
Posidonius. Philosophy in general, therefore, reflects one side of
the ordinary conception of σωτηρία, that of well-being or security,
aiming as it does at the successful realization of a happy life in this
world. The mysteries, with such philosophies as that of Posidonius,
reflect the other, which regards salvation in the full sense as lying
beyond the grave and seeks to attain happiness in a future existence,
whether by initiation or by strenuous moral effort, whatever be
the fate of man in this life.[253] Conditions in the last century of the
Republic, amid the violent upheavals and reversals of fortune
which marked that period, favoured the development of the latter
view: this life could not be all—there must be some future existence
in which all wrongs would be redressed. Yet at the same time men
were ready to hail as saviour any leader who brought about,
even temporarily, the restoration of some measure of peace and
security.[254]

The pagan idea of salvation is primarily that of release from fate,
from the strains and stresses of this life, from the bondage of the
stars. The Jewish and Christian idea was rather of deliverance from
sin. Here the Gnostics followed the pagan view, but even to some
Christians redemption was not so much from sin as from the
demons,[255] and in any case both to Jew and Christian redemption
from fate was bound up with deliverance from sin; the powers
whom Christ had conquered had no longer any authority over the
Christian, while the worshipper of Yahweh was free from the sway
of lesser powers. At the same time, Judaism offered the prospect
of the practical realization of a happy and moral life,[256] and so
could appear as a philosophy, with a lofty ethic, its prestige enhanced
by the claim of Josephus[257] that the law fulfilled its purpose, being
known and obeyed by all. In Philo, the more nationalistic elements
of the Messianic hope are allegorized into symbols of moral progress: the Messiah becomes the philosopher-king, the Stoic sage,

and Moses wins the enlightened by his spiritual qualities.[258] This type of Judaism is thus similar to one form of contemporary philosophy, that which laid the chief emphasis on the present conduct of life; it is not, however, due to pagan influence, but is the outcome of the teaching of the prophets, the elements common to both worlds, such as the necessity of sincerity and purity of heart for true worship,[259] being emphasized at the expense of those which had a less universal appeal.

On the other hand, the apocalyptic form of Judaism, which awaited the coming of a Messiah who should restore Israel to her former glories and extend Jewish dominion throughout the world, has its parallels in visions of a golden age such as that of Virgil's Messianic Eclogue. This type of thought was alien to such men as Philo, but it was a common view in the time of Jesus and was held by some of his early followers. His rejection of such a destiny for himself led to their defection, and the Christian theory of the Messiah took a different form, which was 'to the Jews a stumbling-block, to the Greeks foolishness.'[260] The Gnostics, true to their primary views, agreed with the Greeks. The Jewish Messianic Age, however, despite its materialistic interpretation, is different from the pagan golden age: the vindication of the righteous is effected by a catastrophic divine intervention, and is normally regarded as future, however imminent. The keeping of the law is the condition not of happiness in this life but of future bliss, although a Jew might rejoice in the obeying of its precepts and an apologist pass lightly over the differences between the two views.

The essential feature in the Gnostic view of man is that he is really a divine being imprisoned in this material world and separated by the barrier of the seven heavens from his true abode. Salvation from fate, from the body, from the bondage of matter, from the changes and chances of this life, and all the ills to which the flesh is heir, is attained by $\gamma\nu\tilde{\omega}\sigma\iota\varsigma$, which may mean anything from knowledge imparted in a mystic initiation to a purely magical knowledge of names and spells. To Judaism, as to Christianity, the barrier is constituted by sin, and the true way of reconciliation is by penitence and faith. To the Jew, of course, obedience to the will of God is the first requirement, but there is scope for repentance and a return to obedience in the event of failure;[261] the Christian is more doubtful of man's self-sufficiency, and salvation here depends upon faith in God who has manifested His love in the death of His Son. In this respect Gnosticism is fundamentally different, yet there is a certain similarity. In particular, while in the normal Jewish view men are saved by their works, or by repentance, Philo at times makes salvation a matter of works and γνῶσις, the latter being a deeper understanding of the secrets revealed by Moses. In Christianity, again, the attempt to expound the meaning of the redemption wrought by Christ sometimes leads to language very like the Gnostic.[262] The tension between redemption by man's own effort and redemption by divine grace is less prominent in Judaism than it later became in Christian thought, but it appears very clearly in Philo.[263] Here man is alienated from God, and hence stands in need of purification; he must struggle upwards towards the vision, seeking to ascend to God. But man of himself is helpless, and therefore stands in need of redemption.[264] Again, man must seek God, but only a few find him, although the search in itself is sufficient for a share in the good.

In a sense, Philo represents the meeting of the ways. Philosophy calls for effort, while the mysteries offer a redeeming enlightenment. Judaism also calls for effort, but has too a sense of human need. In Christianity the need is more prominent, although moral effort finds its place. In Gnosticism the need is predominant, and effort finds little room, but the terms in which the theory is expressed are those of the pagan world. Both as regards the evils from which the release is sought and as regards the means of escape, Gnosticism is conditioned by some such philosophy as that of Posidonius, with elements from pagan religious thought. The fundamental difference between the Gnostic-pagan and the Jewish-Christian views lies in the fact that in the former the need for salvation is due to the subjection of a divine being to the sway of fate, while in the latter it is due to an alienation from God effected by man's own disobedience, and in the other fact that Gnosticism leans to magic in its view of the means by which salvation is to be gained. Philo has something of the Gnostic idea of the acquisition of ἀφθαρσία through γνῶσις,[265] and, as at other points, is closer to Gnosticism than either Christianity or philosophy, but this is due to his assimilation of pagan ideas. Judaism in general has little to contribute, and the main source here is some 'philosophical' adaptation of the ideas of pagan religion. With the view that the soul journeys through the heavens to its true abode, however, we are again in contact with Judaism, although the ultimate source is beyond Jewish belief.[266]

Finally, man in salvation is freed from the power of fate and restored to his divine abode, there to enjoy a blissful immortality in communion with God. This involves a deliverance of the spirit from the body, and is obtained as a right by those who can make good their claim. When we recall that in some systems salvation at its fullest is confined to the πνευματικοί, who are rather more than mere mortals like the rest of men, the contribution of Posidonius becomes clear. The inferior souls ascend to the sphere appropriate to them, the various garments of the soul are restored to their rightful owners, the powers which govern the seven heavens; the idea of the ἀποκατάστασις is Stoic, although the Gnostics give it a slightly different meaning, while a Jew might find it in the words of Genesis: 'dust thou art, and unto dust shalt thou return.'[267]

To the Jew, as to the Christian, much of the content given by the Gnostics to salvation is implied in his own scheme, but to the Christian, at any rate, the primary ideas are the forgiveness of sins, reconciliation with God, and eternal life, the first two of which are not known to the Gnostic. Instead of deliverance from the body, Paul speaks of a new and glorified body, suited to the new conditions of life.[268] Moreover, these blessings are obtained not of right but as the gift of God, not because man is essentially divine but because God is gracious and long-suffering and plenteous in mercy.

To sum up, we must distinguish between those theories which offered happiness in this life, with or without the vision of God, such as philosophy and Judaism in some of its forms, and those of a more eschatological trend, which promised a future bliss. The aim which each of the latter seeks to attain is in some form communion with God or the vision of God, but as they set out with different views of the nature of man and of the burden from which he must be freed so their doctrines differ as to the means of escape and the details of the expected salvation. It may be, indeed, that we should distinguish three types: a this-worldly, an apocalyptic, and a mystical; but in this case the distinctions might be difficult to draw. Where the Jew sought to conciliate his Gentile neighbour, or to accommodate Judaism to philosophy, where the Christian stressed release from fate rather than from sin, in short, where the differences were minimized and the similarities enhanced, Jew and Christian, pagan and Gnostic might walk together, but in truth their ways diverge. All have the same trials to face, the same difficulties to meet in this life, but their approach, their estimate of the relative importance of these difficulties, is different. Despite a certain similarity in the end they seek to attain, the bondage from which they seek release, the means of escape and the ultimate goal are again different. There are higher and lower levels in each, contacts more or less close with other views, but ultimately, despite considerable similarity in details and the adoption of many features from Judaism and from Christianity, it must be admitted that Gnosticism here stands apart from both.

No mention has yet been made of the idea of the Redeemer, but here again the same is true. There are similarities and differences, but in the end Gnosticism is fundamentally un-Christian and un-Jewish.

5. *The Redeemer*

In most Gnostic systems there appears the figure of a Redeemer, who is usually in some way associated with the Jesus of orthodox Christianity, if not identified with him, and who performs similar functions.[269] Sometimes the human Jesus is one of the forms in which the divine Redeemer manifests himself, the earthly vehicle of the transcendent Christ, or again, Jesus and Christ are different beings, although each has soteriological functions. Perhaps in no other instance have we so clear an illustration at once of the similarities and of the differences between Gnosticism and Christianity, as well as of the relation of each to the contemporary modes of thought. Certainly few Gnostic doctrines present so many intricate problems for solution.

The general Gnostic theory is comparatively clear, although the various systems differ as to details. Man is essentially a divine being, imprisoned in the body, and of himself he is powerless to escape. He therefore requires the assistance of a higher power, greater than those who hold him in subjection, a being who can rouse him from his stupor and impart to him the knowledge and the power which he needs. This has obvious affinities not only with Christianity but also with many other theories, and we are at once faced with the question of the relation of all these views to each other. The Zoroastrian concept of the Saoshyant, the many 'saviours' of the Hellenistic world, the Jewish Messiah, all could to some extent be invoked to explain both the Christian and the Gnostic views, while some would trace the whole to an alleged Hellenistic-Oriental redemption myth which centres in the Primal Man. Some of these parallels, however, are neither close nor exact, while in other cases it is at least doubtful whether the theory in question was in existence at the beginning of the Christian era and, if it was, whether it could have exercised the influence which is ascribed to it.[270] Again, theories which on a superficial survey seem to be closely akin sometimes prove on closer examination to be widely different.

There are several features in Gnosticism which seem to indicate an influence from Iranian theories, whatever the medium through which such influence came. Some scholars have, indeed, claimed that these theories influenced Christianity, but although there seems to have been some adaptation of Persian ideas by Christians at a later date,[271] this was not a primary factor in the earliest stage, as will appear. There is evidence, moreover, that Persian doctrines were interpreted later in a Christian sense.[272] With Gnosticism the situation is quite different: there is so much clear evidence of the adoption of alien elements that no possible influence may be overlooked.

The Iranian theory of salvation[273] is one of deliverance from evil, both moral and physical, in this life and of the securing of eternal happiness hereafter, but it has nothing to correspond to the Christian doctrine of atonement. Man has the choice of serving Ormuzd or Ahriman, and each works out his own salvation. The Saoshyant is one of the three last great prophets, and more especially the last, who presides at the resurrection of the dead and the regeneration of mankind, and prepares the ambrosia which gives immortality.[274] These three Saoshyants are begotten of the seed of Zoroaster, or are reincarnations of him, and all three are born of virgins.[275] The last is a victorious warrior-king who is to overthrow evil and establish the reign of justice. This theory has little in common with the Christian,[276] unless it be presented in a spiritualized form, but certain features do appear among the Gnostics, some of whom seem to have possessed documents containing a Hellenized version.[277] Again, most of it appears in Mithraism, together with other elements, and Mithraism, although too late in time to have influenced Christianity in the first instance, was in the later years of the Empire a formidable opponent, from whom the Church took over many things. In the present connexion, Bigg[278] has noted the resemblance of certain Mithraic ideas to theories derived by Clement from Theodotus.

The myth of the Urmensch-Redeemer has been adequately examined by others, and the view that such a myth, if it ever existed, exercised a formative influence on the early Church is now generally rejected.[279] Quite apart from the idea of a redemption myth centring on the Primal Man, however, there was definitely a theory of the fall of such a Primal Man, as we have seen.[280] This does not make the Urmensch a redeemer, but merely explains the existence of the divine element imprisoned in the world, and may take various forms. Sometimes the heavenly man descends and rises again, and at death there is an $\mathring{\alpha}\pi o\kappa\alpha\tau\acute{\alpha}\sigma\tau\alpha\sigma\iota s$; this is simply the common Hellenistic myth of the soul. Another view is that the heavenly man falls and is redeemed by another figure, as in many Gnostic theories; the way here is to some extent prepared by Paul's reference to the First and Second Adam,[281] but the idea may be much older, in which case Paul is using mythology for the purposes of his mission.[282] A third view is that of a heavenly man from whom the earthly race of men takes its origin, whether as made in his image or as possessing his spirit, and who descends to redeem them; something of this sort might seem to lie behind Philo's theory of the two men.[283] The two latter views are admittedly close in some respects to the alleged 'redemption myth,' but in neither case is it fundamental to the writer's thought. Paul is developing the antithesis between Adam, through whose disobedience men are in bondage to sin, and Christ, through whose obedience and death they are set free. Christ and Adam are each representative of humanity as a whole, but the same ideas are expressed elsewhere in totally different language. For Philo, as Kennedy remarks,[284] the hypothesis of an influence from the Urmensch theory is unnecessary, since an ideal man is postulated already in the Platonic view which he is following; moreover, it is not clear that this ideal man does descend as redeemer at all.[285] But whether or not such a myth existed in the time of Paul the theory of a divine Redeemer who descends to save mankind does appear in Gnosticism in a form similar to that suggested. This may be a Gnosticizing interpretation of Christianity or, perhaps less probably, due to the influence of some such alien myth.

In the Hellenistic world as a whole the prevalence of a yearning for salvation is very clear. This was one reason for the spread of the mystery-cults, but their gods were not the only 'saviours.' The word σωτήρ means a saviour or deliverer, a preserver from disease, ills or hurt. It is applied to Zeus in dedications of offerings after a safe voyage, but also to other gods or tutelary deities, to rulers such as the Ptolemies or the Roman Emperors, and even to public officials.[286] By constant use the title became so degraded as to be almost meaningless, although at its best it might embody a high ideal.[287]

Attempts have been made to prove the dependence of Christianity upon the mystery-cults, or upon the cult of the emperor, but neither of these is sufficient.[288] The former were for the most part originally fertility cults, based on a myth of the death and regeneration of the vegetation-god; the latter, although directed towards an historical person, depends where it is not pure flattery upon the hope that the ruler will be able to ensure the prosperity and security of his subjects.[289] Christianity is centred on an historical person and offers among other things freedom from fate, where that is sought, with regeneration into a new life, thus combining something of each; but it has a deeper insight into human need, and above all it is rooted in a living faith in Jesus for which no theory of dependence can account. In course of time, however, elements from the environment formed by these cults were baptized into the service of the Church; their ideas provided one of the many forms which were employed to express the Christian Gospel, but in the process these ideas were themselves transformed.[290]

The contemporary philosophy on the whole had no redeemer, although an individual teacher might be hailed as saviour by his pupils, as having delivered them from the fear of fate.[291] On the other hand, the aim of this philosophy was very largely the deliverance of the soul from its prison, and it was philosophy which provided the vocabulary for the religions of the time. Moreover, certain sayings of the great philosophers bear a striking resemblance to the demand of Jesus for personal allegiance to and trust in himself,[292] while at a somewhat later date Apollonius of Tyana is presented by his biographer as the Messiah of a reformed paganism.[293] This is regarded by Bigg[294] as 'the story of the Gospel corrected and improved' in accordance with pagan views, although Norden[295] would seem to place the dependence on the other side.

The obvious Jewish parallel is the doctrine of the Messiah, which to some extent underlies the Christian estimate of Jesus. Here again an alien origin has been postulated, but again such a view is unnecessary, although foreign influences entered into the development at a later stage.

The first point to be observed is that not all the 'Messianic' passages so called refer to a personal Messiah, some being visions of a Golden Age with no Messianic figure at all.[296] Again, many prophecies which have received a Christological interpretation were not originally so intended. The idea of the Golden Age is thought to be more original, that of the Messiah being sometimes combined with it later. The word Messiah means 'the anointed,' and as such is applied to priests and kings, in virtue of their consecration to office. According to Gressmann,[297] the term is used in pre-exilic times for the political ruler, but after the Exile first for the ruling high priest, which in his opinion indicates that the original significance was one of consecration as priest-king; later it is transferred to any priest. The Messiah may be the king of the ideal future, but in the Old Testament he is not yet the ruler of the eschatological kingdom. So Mowinckel would reserve the title Messiah for the eschatological figure of later Judaism, as distinct from the reigning earthly king.[298]

In the Old Testament the Saviour is almost without exception God Himself, and where the Messiah appears he is always subordinate to Yahweh. The fact that in the Septuagint the word σωτήρ is sometimes used of men does not affect the argument; these exceptions are 'deliverers' in the ordinary sense of the word, regarded as raised up for the purpose by Yahweh, who is ultimately the real Saviour. In other words, the anointed king might be a deliverer, but was not inevitably so regarded. His original function was political, not soteriological or eschatological. With the passing of time, however, there was a tendency for the two ideas to coalesce, for the Messiah, the idealized 'anointed of the Lord,' to become the eschatological Deliverer.[299] This later technical sense appears first in the Apocrypha.

The primary idea in the original Messianic belief is in a sense akin to that which appears later in the application of the title σωτήρ to the Roman emperors, namely that the king in question would inaugurate a new era of peace and prosperity. The title is applicable to any Jewish king, just as the hopes of the empire rose again at each new accession, even that of a Caligula or a Nero.[300] In one case, that of Cyrus, the title is conferred on a foreign ruler, but this is exceptional.[301] In the later developments the Messiah becomes more prominent, and there is a growing eschatological emphasis. The fall of the Jewish kingdom and the consequent frustration of the popular hopes led to the expectation of an idealized ruler who would restore the lost glories of Israel.

The teaching of the Old Testament may be summarized thus: (a) the Messiah occupies a comparatively subordinate position, and his coming is not an essential feature. The primary element in the expected deliverance is the activity of Yahweh himself. (b) There is constant reference to the Davidic dynasty, of which the Messiah is to be a scion. With the decline of the state this dynasty is idealized, and the restorer of its glories is naturally expected to be no ordinary man. (c) The Messianic belief is an element in popular religion, and hence is used with reserve. Finally, some have held that the Messiah is the divine *Heilbringer*, the Urmensch of the Heavenly Man redemption myth, but this is not proven. Others consider the Messianic expectation peculiar to Israel, explaining it as a fusion of national hopes of a Davidic king with eschatological hopes of a Golden Age.

In the period between the Testaments the Messiah is sometimes ignored, but elsewhere appears as an eschatological figure. References are now more frequent, but his coming is still not an essential element. In the first century A.D. this expectation was more universal among the Jews than ever before, but it is not taken very seriously by Philo and Josephus.[302] There is a tendency in Maccabean times to regard him as Levitic, but later speculation reverts to the Davidic view.[303] The theory remains mainly an element in popular belief, but there are tendencies which enhance the position which the Messiah holds. Foreign influence may have affected certain details, particularly in apocalyptic,[303a] but any extensive dependence is doubtful.

For the existence of the Messianic hope in the Dispersion we have on the one hand the evidence of the Sibylline Oracles and the Zadokite fragment,[304] together with the fact that such a hope was widely diffused in the first century, a fact confirmed by the persistence of the idea in Rabbinic Judaism, although here the political and apocalyptic aspects are abandoned. On the other hand there is the evidence of Philo and Josephus, who both almost completely ignore it. This may be due in part to a desire to conciliate the Gentile by suppressing the more nationalistic aspects of Judaism, or again, as Noel suggests,[305] the wealthier Jews may have been too comfortable in the Gentile world to risk endangering themselves and their property in a Jewish insurrection which they could see was doomed. In the latter case, the Messianic belief may have been prevalent among the lower classes, although rejected by the rich; as has been noted, it was essentially an element of popular religion. The silence of Philo, moreover, confirms the view that the contemporary pagan philosophy made little room for a redeemer except in the rather restricted sense of a revealer of Gnosis, in which the part could be adequately filled by Moses.[306]

As Moore puts it,[307] 'the Jews had no doctrine about the Messiah invested with the sanction of orthodoxy.' Consequently a breach with the synagogue was not at first inevitable for the early Christians, who could continue as pious Jews maintaining in addition to their Jewish faith a belief peculiar to themselves in the identity of the promised Messiah with the historic Jesus. The *testimonia* adduced for the Passion appear to have been first so used by Christians,[308] as the evidence at our disposal does not seem to warrant the conclusion that the Jews had a doctrine of a suffering Messiah.[309] On the other hand, the identification of the Messiah with the Son of Man seems due to certain developments of apocalyptic.[310]

Christianity takes up various strands of Jewish thought and combines them into one,[311] but the combination is not merely a matter of theory; it depends entirely upon the historical personality of Jesus. The Messianic confession is the presupposition of the Church's tradition, and, moreover, this confession 'cannot have originated except upon grounds already given in the life and mind of the Crucified himself.'[312] Several features of the Christian doctrine appear in Jewish writings, but the content which they now receive is different. Others again appear to be of foreign origin, but they have been subordinated and adapted to new purposes. The question is not whether alien elements are present, but what use has been made of them.[313]

Professor Manson accordingly finds no real debt to Jewish Messianism or pagan theories of a world-saviour, apart from the common use of the same titles.[314] In time, of course, foreign elements enter in, as forms for the expression of the Christian Gospel, but this influence is only secondary. Paul may be acquainted with some pagan theories, but the essential matter of his Gospel is independent of extraneous influence.[315] Again, there is 'no reliable proof that the Iranian "Urmensch" or First Man belief anywhere developed a real redemptive significance in association with the last things except in Jewish and Christian circles or under their influence.'[316]

The point of all this is that it seems to indicate that the Gnostic redeemer is not pre-Christian, but simply a more radical interpretation of the Christian Jesus in terms of current belief.[317] The Zoroastrian doctrine of the Saoshyant is the nearest in form, but this theory exercised but little influence on Judaism and even less on philosophy. It must have penetrated Western thought, therefore, by way of popular belief and magic, although the mysteries, and especially those of Mithras, may have played a part; on the other hand, it may be doubted whether Mithraism was as yet sufficiently prominent to exert such an influence. Jewish Messianism may have made some contribution, but only in a paganized form, since the general trend of Jewish thought is different in this respect from the Gnostic. Even if we accept the statement of Goodenough[318] that 'the distinctive contribution of Hellenistic Judaism was to identify the Gayomart—Heavenly Man—Adam of the East with the Greek Logos, and thereby with the κόσμος νοητός of Platonism' we have only a theory of man's existence and not of his redemption. Again, a theoretical abstraction of features common to the many saviours of the contemporary world to form a composite figure who was later identified with Jesus must be regarded as extremely doubtful.[319]

This is confirmed by the theories of the Gnostics themselves. If there were a pre-Christian theory we should expect a greater measure of uniformity than we actually find; and here, if van Unnik is correct, the *Gospel of Truth* may prove to be of fundamental importance, since although clearly Gnostic it centres upon the Jesus of the Christian faith. In philosophy and in the Hermetica γνῶσις is in itself sufficient;[320] it may be imparted by an earthly teacher, or by a god as in the mysteries, but there is no real idea of a descent to earth or of an incarnation.[321] Again, in some forms of Ophitism, the most likely of all to be pre-Christian, the redeemer is absent altogether. In the system of Simon Magus, Simon himself is the redeemer and appears in one form as Jesus, while in various other theories a supernatural Christ enters into the human Jesus;[322] in all these the Passion is eliminated by some Docetic view.

Basilides, according to Hippolytus, admitted no descent at all;[323] Christ is the son of the Great Archon and informs him of his true position; the light which thus fills the Ogdoad is imparted to Jesus the son of Mary, who is destined to be 'the first-fruits of the distinction of that which had been compounded.'[324] Finally, in the developed Valentinian theory we have apparently three Christs: the first with the Holy Spirit forms a syzygy produced by Monogenes after the fall of Sophia, and teaches the other Aeons concerning the incomprehensibility of the Father; the second is Jesus, formed by the union of the gifts of the whole Pleroma, while the third is a psychic Christ, the earthly vehicle of the divine redeemer.[325] Even the Valentinians themselves seem to have suffered from some confusion here, since at least one version makes Christ the offspring of Sophia, the first to be redeemed. This would most naturally refer to the psychic Christ, save that this redeemed being leaves Sophia to enter the Pleroma. Again, it is not clear whether the

Christ who confers form on Achamoth is the first or the second, or whether the Paraclete is the second or a different being entirely. From the context, however, it would appear that the former is the first Christ and the Paraclete Jesus, the second Christ and Saviour.[326]

The one essential feature common to all is that where a Redeemer appears an attempt is made at an interpretation of the Christian theory which would be acceptable to contemporary belief. Apart from Christianity there appears to be no real reason for the assumption of a descent into a human body, but if the Gnostics were starting from the Christian doctrine they had to find room for the incarnation. Whatever the contemporary views which influenced the development, the Gnostics are here primarily dependent on Christianity itself. Ostensibly Christian thinkers, they could not ignore the cardinal Christian doctrine. The absence of a redeemer thus points to the existence of pre-Christian forms of Gnosticism.[327]

In regard to the Redeemer, then, Gnosticism is both like and unlike Christianity, similar as a rule in the general outlines but differing in details. The divinity of Jesus is enhanced at the expense of his humanity; the Passion is unthinkable for a Greek, to whom the divine is impassible, as to the Jew, to whom crucifixion involves a curse, and is consequently eliminated.[328] The death and resurrection, so central for the orthodox Church, find little or no place. Again, the functions of the Redeemer differ. Salvation for the Gnostic is no longer from sin, but from fate, and consists not in a redemption and transformation of the whole man, but in the release of a divine nature imprisoned in the body of each. Finally, the means is not faith and love, a confident surrender of the self to the Redeemer, but a knowledge imparted by him.

A starting-point for each of these views might be found in Christianity, especially in its Pauline form, but the Gnostics have gone to the extreme of accommodation here. Jesus is presented as he ought to have been in the opinion of the age, anything to which exception might be taken being minimized if not suppressed. In this case Judaism has exerted an influence chiefly, perhaps entirely, through the medium of Christianity. Contemporary philosophy has provided the standard to which the theory must conform, the forms for its expression, but the primary factor is the Christian doctrine of Christ, although the final results produced by the Gnostics are very different from the classic Christian doctrine.

NOTES TO CHAPTER VII

[1] Some points of contact have already been noted, e.g. by Mansel. According to Casey (*Excerpta* 18), Theodotus' theory of the Name was derived from Philo, who identifies the Logos with the Name of God (see above, p. 170). The possible influence on Gnosticism of Jewish eschatology and of the doctrine of the Two Ages must also be taken into consideration (for these cf. Bousset-Gressmann 242ff. *et al.*).

In regard to the Logos, Wolfson (*Philo* 1. 230) notes that Philo uses the term as a substitute for Aristotle's term 'mind' ($\nu o \hat{v} s$). Wolfson (ibid. 374) distinguishes three stages in the existence of the Logos in Philo: (*a*) the Logos and the powers are all in God and all identical with God, the Logos being the mind of God and the powers the content of that mind; (*b*) the Logos is a created incorporeal mind and the powers and ideas the content of that mind; (*c*) the Logos is a mind immanent in the world, and the powers its content. Some of these points would appear to be significant, especially for the developed Valentinian theory.

[2] See above, pp. 103, 118, 151. For the inspiration of life into the lifeless corpse, see *Op. M.* 134; for the fall of a spiritual being into matter, *De Gig.* 6. See above, p. 104, and Knox *PCG* 80ff., 99, 127.

[3] The idea of this world as in subjection to evil powers has links with Jewish apocalyptic thought (see *SJT* 6. 136ff., Bousset-Gressmann 251ff.). Note also 1 John 5. 19 and similar passages.

[4] Cf. above, p. 45, and below, p. 200. The OT passage in question is Genesis 6. 1–4. For Jewish elaborations of the myth see Moore index (2. 457), Bousset-Gressmann 251f., 332f., 491f.

[5] The evidence seems to suggest a development similar to that conjectured for Wisdom (above, p. 37ff.). A female demon Ruha figures in Mandeism [see Bousset *Hauptprobleme* on the Mother (chapters i and ii), and Knox *PCG* index s.v. Ruha]; but this would seem to be the final stage in a long process of development.

[6] The fact that some of these features are ultimately of pagan origin does not alter this conclusion. The use of the OT indicates that Judaism was the medium by which these ideas passed into Gnostic thought.

[7] *Poimandres* 250.

[8] Cf. Cumont *Rel. Or.* xii: 'Bien des croyances de l'ancien Orient . . . sont parvenues en Europe par une double voie, d'abord par le judaisme plus ou moins orthodoxe des communautés de la Diaspora.'

[9] Cf. Goppelt 135: 'Das dem Synkretismus zuneigende Judentum war ein idealer Treffpunkt der entscheidenden Motive: in ihm konnten sich iranisch-babylonische und griechische Vorstellungen leicht im Zeichen

dieses Existenzverständnisses begegnen. Es kann darüber hinaus auch sachlich zur Gestaltung der gnostische Erlösungsbotschaft beigetragen haben.'

[10] Cf. above, p. 73ff., on the Dead Sea Scrolls. It is part of the merit of Nötscher's book there cited that he is careful to observe this distinction (cf. Rost's review in *TLZ* 1957, 267).

[11] Cf. above, p. 74, on the Dead Sea Scrolls.

[12] Jonas (1. 256ff.) discovers four main types: the Iranian (Mani), the Syro-Egyptian (Valentinus, etc.), the Alexandrian-Christian (Origen) and the Neo-Platonic. Of these the second 'fast alles umfasst, was die Häresiologen als Gnosis bekampften.' Cerfaux (*Recueil Cerfaux* 1. 278) distinguishes two movements, 'l'un plus philosophique avec Alexandrie comme épicentre et l'autre plus mythique et magique (épicentres en Babylonie et en Égypte). Goppelt (164ff.) surveys the different areas in turn (Palestine, Syria, Egypt,' Rome and the West, Asia Minor), and reviews the various sects within his general framework of the relations of Christianity and Judaism. Cerfaux notes 'la conception, désormais trop négligée, des premiers historiens du gnosticisme: Alexandrie fut la forteresse du mouvement de gnose' (1. 269).

[13] See *Beginnings* 5. 154ff.

[14] *ZNTW* 1904, 121ff.

[15] But according to Hippolytus (*Phil.* 7. 33, cf. 10. 21) he was skilled in the learning of the Egyptians. Sanders (*The Fourth Gospel in the Early Church*) argues that the Fourth Gospel was written in Alexandria, and recalls that the *Alogi* condemned it as the work of Cerinthus.

[16] Legge 2. 28ff., 45 note 1. Hippolytus (*Phil.* 5. 6ff., cf. 5. 2) is concerned to show the relation of the Naassenes to the Phrygian cults, and this relation may be accepted (cf. Goppelt 134). But it is not clear either that the Naassenes are to be identified with the Ophites, or that they are fully representative of Ophitism, although there are points of contact (Bousset *Hauptprobleme* index s.v. Gnostiker, Naassener, Ophiten). On the Naassenes and the Attis-cult see Bousset ibid. 183ff.

[17] Legge 2. 45 note 1. Cf. Bousset *Hauptprobleme* 80.

[18] The following points may be mentioned in favour of an Egyptian origin: (*a*) the affinity with Valentinianism; (*b*) the occurrence in Egyptian religion of triads of gods; (*c*) the place assigned to the Mother (corresponding to Isis); (*d*) the address to Hermes (or the Ἀγαθὸς Δαίμων) as being of serpent form in prayers of a Hermetic type (supra, p. 138 note 35); (*e*) the parallel between Isis and the Ophite Holy Spirit and Sophia (for which see below, p. 195ff.). Cerfaux (1. 264ff.) stresses the influence of the Isis-myth on Gnosticism. Some of these points, however, are equally valid for a Phrygian origin, while it is clear that the 'Ophite' systems were strongly syncretistic. Cf. Reitzenstein *Poim.* 82ff. (Hippolytus), 162ff. Bousset (*Hauptprobleme* 25ff.) argues for a Babylonian origin. The fact that the figure of the Mother does not appear in Saturninus or Basilides (Syria) or in the Naassene system (Phrygia?), while Simon (Syria) shows only slight

traces, may perhaps confirm the association with Egypt, although allowance must be made for the influence of astrology (Babylonia?). The formation of the heaven from the body of Sophia-Prunicus recalls the Babylonian myth of Tiamat (cf. Legge 2. 44 note 3). Certainly sects of an Ophite character existed in Egypt later, as the Nag Hammadi library shows (see *The Jung Codex* and literature referred to there).

[19] *Rel. Or.* 17ff.

[20] Cf. Bousset *Hauptprobleme* 319ff.

[21] Cf. Quispel *Gnosis als Weltreligion* 9: 'So hat dann angeblich beinahe der ganze Vorderorient zu den Ahnen des Gnostizismus gehört.' Cerfaux (1. 263ff.) stresses the influence of the Isis-myth, but although the Nag Hammadi library was found in Egypt Quispel observes 'Hier allerdings ziemt, wenigstens einstweilen, die grösste Zuruckhaltung' (ibid.).

[22] It may be noted here that Jonas (1. 335ff.) further divides the various sects according to the sex of the fallen 'principle' into 'male' and 'female' groups. Cf. Rudolph, *ZRGG* ix (1957) 14.

[23] For the Magi in relation to Hellenistic thought see Bidez-Cumont *Les Mages Hellénisés*.

[24] Cf. Goppelt 135: 'Ist es zufällig, dass die wichtigsten geschichtlich fassbaren Erscheinungen vorchristlicher Gnosis, der Gnostizismus des jüdischen Täufertums, die samaritanische Gnosis und die ältesten gnostischen Offenbarungsschriften auf einem entscheidend vom Judentum beeinflussten Boden erwachsen sind?' It should be noted that Goppelt follows Jonas' definition of Gnosticism, which is wider than that here adopted (cf. above, p. 65ff).

[25] So Simon and others tried to obtain the powers which the apostles displayed (Acts. 8. 18ff., 19. 13ff.). To them these powers appeared to be magic.

[26] Canon Knox considers that Philo represents the common Jewish-Hellenistic philosophy of a very large element of educated Judaism (see his Schweich Lectures 34ff., and cf. above, p. 34ff.), but in the present connexion a considerable restraint seems necessary in order to avoid undue exaggeration of his influence. Cerfaux (1. 277) notes that the opposition encountered at Alexandria by Clement and Origen presupposes that the religion of the *simpliciores* was there traditional. To Cerfaux, Bauer's theory that Christianity entered Egypt in Gnostic guise is 'perhaps not very probable' (ibid.; cf. above, p. 49 note 4).

[27] This statement, written in 1945, would now appear to require modification in the light of the Dead Sea Scrolls (cf. Braun in *Revue Biblique* 1955, 5ff., Albright in *The Background of the NT and its Eschatology* 153ff.), but as C. K. Barrett has aptly remarked, Palestine itself was part of the Hellenistic world (*The Gospel according to St. John*, London 1955, 32). According to Barrett (who does not take the Scrolls into account), 'the most illuminating background of the fourth gospel is that of Hellenistic Judaism' (ibid. 33).

[28] Cf. Knox *HE* 35: The similarities between Philo and the NT are intelligible since 'both go back to a common tradition of hellenistic Jewish interpretation of the OT to the Greek world. The differences represent the difference between the religion of the primitive Church and a peculiarly pedantic exposition of the Judaism of Alexandria.' Cf. also *Exp. Times* lxv. 47ff., *Novum Testamentum* i (1956) 225ff.

[29] Cf. Dodd *Interpretation* 10ff., and part II of *The Bible and the Greeks*; van Moorsel, *The Mysteries of Hermes Trismegistus* (Utrecht 1955); Festugière *La Révélation d'Hermès Trismégiste* (Paris 1944–54).

For the text of the Corpus, see the edition by A. D. Nock and A. J. Festugière (Paris 1945).

[30] Bousset (*Hauptprobleme* 12) thinks the equation of the Ophite Ialdabaoth with Yahweh is probably not original. The transformation of Ialdabaoth into the OT Yahweh Sabaoth is completed when we find in Epiphanius that some Gnostics held Barbelo (i.e. Sophia) to be the mother of Sabaoth (ibid. 14). If this be true, then anti-Semitism has adopted an older theory for its own requirements, but other factors may also have contributed. On Bousset's view that the Seven and the Mother are the old Babylonian deities, the question arises how they came to occupy the lower or intermediate positions which they have in Gnosticism (ibid. 27ff.). One form of syncretism arises from the incorporation of the gods of the conquered in the pantheon of the victors, naturally as inferior powers, and this may have operated here (cf. ibid. 38ff.). The OT creator is then identified with one of these creator powers. In his excursus (351ff.) Bousset finds the origin of Ialdabaoth in pagan speculations concerning Cronus-Saturn and the planetary hebdomad. Yahweh being commonly equated with Saturn (cf. above, p. 16), the further identification was easy. But cf. Quispel in *Eranos Jahrbuch* xxii (1953) 199, who derives the name from *Yalda' Bahoth*, 'Son of Chaos.' R. M. Grant (*Vig. Chr.* xi. 148f.) suggests a derivation from *Ia-el-zebaoth* (=Yahweh Elohe Zebaoth).

[31] For Marcion see Kirk 218ff., Bousset *Hauptprobleme* 109ff., Goppelt 268ff. The latest full study is that of Blackman, *Marcion and his influence* (London 1950). According to Bousset, Marcion transformed the opposition of the good and evil spirits, found in 'oriental-Persian dualism,' into an opposition between the Unknown God, the Father of Jesus, and the God of the OT. For the controversy between Bousset and Harnack over Marcion, see Kirk 503f. Further material in Turner, *The Pattern of Christian Truth*.

[32] *Der vorchristliche jüdische Gnosticismus.* This is an attempt to substantiate the thesis advanced in an earlier work, reviewed by Schürer in *TLZ* 1898.

[33] *TLZ* 1899, 167ff.

1. *The Idea of God*

[34] *Judaism* 1. 129; cf. ibid. 176, 357ff., 417ff. On Gnostic doctrines of God cf. Wolfson, *Philosophy of the Church Fathers* 1. 520ff., although some of his conclusions must be taken with reserve.

[35] In Gnosticism this care, where it appears, is confined to the γνωστικοί. The πάτηρ ἄγνωστος or πάτηρ τῶν ὅλων is not really a Father as to the Jew.

[36] Cf. Bousset *Hauptprobleme* 85.

[37] Cf. Causse 133ff., Guignebert 120ff., Moore 1. 367ff.

[38] Wendland (*HRK* 184) remarks that many ideas from the Graeco-Oriental world had penetrated into Jewish literature, and especially into apocalyptic. It should be observed, however, that some of these ideas had been so completely assimilated as to become almost Jewish and lose their alien character.

[39] Cf. Dodd *BG* 137.

[40] e.g. Wisdom, Soph. Sol. 9. 9, cf. 7. 22 etc.

[41] For this view in Jewish apocalyptic cf. Bousset-Gressmann 251, 331ff.

[42] Above, p. 32ff.

[43] In this connexion something may be due to the influence of Hellenistic magic which, impressed by the efficacy of Jewish exorcism, could not ignore the Jewish God of the ineffable name. Jewish influence on magic may have contributed in no small measure to the growth of what we know as Gnostic thought, since here again Jew and pagan came together, despite their differences. See Knox *PCG* 40ff., Reitzenstein *Poim.* 14 note 1.

[44] So Moore (1. 368) says that in the Jewish view God, though supra-mundane, is not extra-mundane. On the Fatherhood of God see Moore 2. 201ff., Guignebert 125ff.

[45] *Die Frömmigkeit Philos* 87. For Greek and Christian thought in this connexion see Hatch 171ff., and especially 238ff.

[46] *Agnostos Theos* 83ff. The contemporary dedications 'to the unknown gods' (above, p. 88 note 45) do not affect this conclusion, since it is there not a question of a theory of the nature of God as unknown, but of a consecration to a god (or gods) whose name is unknown to the worshipper when he sets up the inscription. Cf. Casey, *Excerpta ex Theodoto* 101 on Exc. 7. 1. See also Burkitt in *JTS* 15. 455ff. for criticism of Norden's theories.

[47] For LXX see Hatch and Redpath s.v. ἄγνωστος; for the NT, Moulton and Geden, s.v., where the sole reference is Acts 17. 23.

[48] Norden 84. For Christian examples cf. Athenagoras x and Geffcken's notes (*Apologeten* 180).

[49] ibid. 24ff.

[50] ibid. 27. Norden compares Is. 40. 26, Ps. 8. 2ff., 19. 2ff., but says there is no possibility that the passages in Soph. Sol. and Paul were derived thence. Similar passages occur in Philo and the Hermetica (Norden loc. cit.). On Philo *de Monarch.*, quoted here, see further ibid. 85f. Cf. Philo *LA* 3. 97ff. See also Knox *HE* 31ff. on the ideas derived from popular Greek philosophy by the synagogue; also Dupont 20f. on Rom. 1. 19ff.

[51] Rom. 1. 20 (see Norden 24ff.); cf. also Philo *de Mut. Nom.* 2 (Norden 86).

[52] Cf. Kirk 106 note 4, and his summary 110. Wolfson (*Philo* 2. 113ff.) claims that the idea is not found in Greek philosophy before Philo.

[53] Cf. Norden 83ff. (not truly Greek), 65ff. (Gnosticism and the Hermetica), 73ff. (the Catholic Church), 77ff. (the Platonists). Norden himself finds the idea rooted in a spiritualized Jewish Christianity of the earliest period (77).

[54] ibid. 97.

[55] ibid. 87ff. Norden regards γνῶσις θεοῦ as a central idea of Oriental religion (ibid. 95ff.). But see also Dupont, *Gnosis*.

[56] ibid. 87, cf. 97ff., Kirk 211 note 3. See also pp. 70, 107 above.

[57] Norden 63 and note 1, cf. 95ff.

[58] The significant features are: (i) an increased transcendence of God; (ii) a mystical approach to the idea of knowledge of God, resulting in the view that God is unknown except He reveal Himself. Here Christianity stands within the Hellenistic circle (Norden 98; cf. Matt. 11. 25, 27 and parallels). Cf. Norden 95 for NT references. Dupont, however, notes that the impossibility of seeing God is a theme familiar to the OT (113), and finds the background of Paul's thought in Jewish ideas.

[59] Norden 85. In *de Ebr.* 19 Philo by implication rejects the Gnostic view, but cf. *de Mut. Nom.* 7ff.

[60] ibid. 85f. Note p. 86: 'zwar der Ausdruck ἄγνωστος wird nicht gebraucht, vielmehr die üblichen ἀόρατος καὶ νοητός, aber da trotz des wiederholten Gebrauchs der letzteren Bezeichnung die Möglichkeit vernunftmässiger Erkenntnis Gottes negiert wird, so stehen wir hier doch bereits mit einem Schritt jenseits der hellenischen Spekulation.' The reference here is to *De Monarch.* i. 4ff. (*CW* v. 8ff.), where Philo argues that the existence of God may be known from His works, but that His nature is incomprehensible. None the less, the search must be attempted (*CW* v. 9, 36ff.). For effort on the part of man see above, p. 47, and Kirk 38ff. For Philo and Palestinian Judaism cf. Moore 1. 360ff.

[61] Cf. Norden 109. Bousset (*Hauptprobleme* 90) notes that the supreme Being now and then appears in Gnosticism as θεὸς ὕψιστος. Admitting the frequency of the designation in later Jewish literature, he nevertheless thinks it derived from religions where monotheism was less dominant. The idea itself in his view points to polytheism; but it could also meet Jewish monotheism half-way. See above, pp. 11ff., 33 and references there.

[62] Norden (70f., cf. 77) reckons it among the earliest elements of Gnosticism, and considers it taken over from earlier systems (68f.). He argues for an Oriental origin (113ff.). Something may be due to Posidonius (see ibid. 99 and the frequent mention of his work as a source for the thought of later writers; numerous references in the index, ibid. 403).

[62a] On the Gnostic Creator cf. Wolfson, *Philosophy of the Church Fathers* 1. 538ff.

[63] Timaeus 41Aff. Here the Creator says: 'Θεοὶ θεῶν, ὧν ἐγὼ δημι-

ουργὸς πατήρ τε ἔργων.' But in 40c earth is φύλακα καὶ δημιουργον νυκτός τε καὶ ἡμέρας.' The word δημιουργός has therefore not yet become a technical term in its later sense. Cf. Liddell-Scott-Jones s.v. See also Athenagoras vi and Geffcken's notes (Apologeten 174f.). For the idea of secondary creators see Dodd BG 136ff. In the Hippolytan account of Basilides both Ogdoad and Hebdomad are called δημιουργός (above, p. 125).

64 Drummond I. 75ff., Knox PCG 1f., 65f. See also Athenagoras xxii and Geffcken's notes (Apologeten 205ff.).

65 Drummond I. 96ff. Strictly speaking, God to the Stoics is not so much the Creator as the universe itself, but later Stoicism had adapted the cosmogony of the Timaeus (Knox PCG 65).

66 οὐ δημιουργὸς μόνος ἀλλὰ καὶ κτίστης, de Somn. I. 76 (cf. Geffcken 86 for parallels from the Apologists). See above, p. 41ff., and see also Moore I. 380ff.

67 See above, p. 40f.

68 See above, p. 37; also Knox PCG 159ff., PCJ 98 and notes.

69 Reitzenstein Poim. 22ff. For the identification of Hermes with the Δαίμων see ibid. 18, 126. Cf. also Dieterich Abraxas 62ff. For the 'Αγαθὸς Δαίμων as 'Αγαθοήλ in Jewish magic see Reitzenstein 18 note 8.

70 A stage towards the Gnostic view may be represented in the Poimandres, where the Demiurge is the God of heaven (Yahweh?) but not the supreme God (cf. Dodd BG 138). But here the Demiurge is not yet hostile, playing the part of the intermediary λόγος of other systems. From the fact that the distinction is not made in the κόρη κόσμου Norden argues that part of this treatise dates from a time before Christian Gnosticism had reached its height (Agnostos Theos 65ff.). But the problem is not so simple—there is no Demiurge in the Gospel of Truth, but Ialdabaoth plays the part in the Apocryphon of John (see above, pp. 156, 151).

71 e.g. Apology viii. This is a refutation of polytheism, but part of it could also be used against the Gnostic theory. As for Philo, so for the Apologists God is κτίστης καὶ δημιουργός (cf. above, note 66). Cf. Irenaeus, quoted above, p. 102, and see also Bidez-Cumont 1. 228ff.

72 Cf. Bidez-Cumont, loc. cit.: 'Les philosophes grecs conçoivent généralement le démiurge comme subordonné a l'Être Suprême, et même il devient pour le pessimisme gnostique une puissance malfaisante, l'auteur d'un monde mauvais.' The 'Greek philosophers' are, however, only those who admitted a creator as well as a supreme God.

73 De Is. et Os. 46 (369D). But others call the better 'god,' the other 'demon.' This occurs in a passage which presents a dualistic view similar to the Gnostic and some contemporary theories. Whether it is authentic Mazdeism or Mazdeism interpreted in terms of the contemporary philosophy is a question for specialists in Iranian theology. For an introduction to Zoroastrianism see Zaehner, The Teachings of the Magi (London 1956). In his larger work Zurvan: A Zoroastrian Dilemma (Oxford 1955) 143,

Zaehner admits a certain inter-action between Zoroastrian and Gnostic ideas, but is doubtful of extensive Iranian influence upon the West. Moreover the Zervanite doctrine is not pure Zoroastrianism but a Zoroastrian heresy, 'a classic example of religious syncretism.'

[74] In some texts, however, Ormuzd stands outside the opposition of good and evil, and the opponent of Ahriman is one of the subordinate beings, not Ormuzd himself. Cf. Causse 152, Bidez-Cumont loc. cit., Clemen *ET* 115. See also *ERE* 1. 237ff.

[75] Cf. Bidez-Cumont 1. 62ff., and the works of Zaehner cited above. For Persian religion in Greek writers see Knox *PCG* 204ff. Bousset (*Hauptprobleme* 116) claims that the Gnostic dualism is conditioned by Persian religion, but admits (118) that this dualism had been greatly transformed.

[76] Cf. below, p. 191.

[77] *Hauptprobleme* chap. I and Excursus, 351ff. (but cf. Quispel in *Eranos Jahrbuch* xxii (1953) 195ff.). A closer link may perhaps be found, however, in the *Poimandres* (above, note 70). Cf. also Legge 2. 46 note 3.

[78] Bousset loc. cit. Cf. above, p. 16.

[79] See above, p. 131.

[80] See Dodd *BG* 141ff., and for the λόγος ibid. 115ff. Reitzenstein (*Poim.* 66f.) considers this fusion Egyptian, but cf. Dodd 141 note 1. Cf. also Cyril ap. Reitzenstein *Poim.* 243 note 3. Bousset (182 note 3) considers the statement a later interpolation. Note, however, that the λόγος of *Poimandres* is not the same as the Philonic λόγος (Dodd *BG* 120).

[81] But as creator of the seven Administrators (the planetary gods) and therefore as god of fate he could readily be understood as hostile. Here again the *Poimandres* represents a step towards the Gnostic view. Dodd (*BG* 138ff.) considers that the Hermetist is here following a less orthodox Jewish theory, known to Philo but rejected by him.

[82] Dodd *BG* 142.

[83] Dodd has clearly demonstrated the dependence of the *Poimandres* on Genesis, or on Jewish speculations based on Genesis. We have no such detailed cosmogony for the Gnostics, but the general similarity seems to point to Jewish influence here also. Certainly both Justin and the *Apocryphon of John* reinterpret the OT for their own ends.

[84] See Dodd *BG* 142f., and for the Gnostics cf. above, p. 125. The same thought may be present in Valentinianism (cf. above, p. 131) and could be readily understood in other theories where it is not explicitly stated.

[85] *Apology* xxivff. Cf. Geffcken 214ff. This goes back, of course, to Jewish apocalyptic (cf. Bousset-Gressmann 251f.).

[86] Cf. references above, p. 28f.; Bevan *Hellenism and Christianity* 94, Dieterich *Abraxas* 93ff.

[87] Cf. Athenagoras loc. cit., and Porphyry, cited below. On Jewish and Christian demonology in relation to current thought see Geffcken 214ff.

[88] The distinction between demons and cosmic powers is not always

carefully observed. Thus in Valentinianism the devil is Cosmocrator (above, p. 132)—a relic of pre-Gnostic thought, before the Demiurge assumed the functions of Satan. Cf. Saturninus (above, p. 103). For the idea of evil spirits dwelling in the air, derived by Moffatt from Parsism, see Eph. 2.2, 6. 12 (Clemen *RGE* 111, referring to Moffatt in Hibbert *Journal* 1903–4, 353).

[89] ἄρχων τοῦ κόσμου τούτου: John 12. 31, 14. 30, 16. 11. Cf. ἄρχων τῶν δαιμονίων: Matt. 9. 34, 12. 24 and parallels (Mark 3. 22, Luke 11. 15); ἄρχων τῆς ἐξουσίας τοῦ ἀέρος: Eph. 2. 2. Cf. Bernard's note on John 12. 31 (*ICC* 2. 441). Cf. also Luke 4. 6, on which Creed refers to Bousset-Gressmann 514ff.

[90] κοσμοκράτορες τοῦ σκότους: Eph. 6. 12; cf. ἐξουσία τοῦ σκότους Col. 1. 13, Luke 22. 53?

[91] ἀρχαί Rom. 8. 38, Eph. 6. 12; ἀρχαὶ καὶ ἐξουσίαι 1 Cor. 15. 24, Eph. 1. 21, 3. 10, Col. 2. 10, 15; κυριότητες, ἀρχαί, ἐξουσίαι Col. 1. 16; ἄγγελοι καὶ ἐξουσίαι 1 Pet. 3. 22; δύναμις καὶ κυριότης Eph. 1. 21; δυνάμεις Matt. 24. 29, Mark 13. 25, Luke 21. 26 (parallel passages), Rom. 8. 38, 1 Cor. 15. 25.

Note that both ἐξουσία and δύναμις frequently appear in other senses also.

[92] Various factors contributed to the process, but the course of reasoning is fairly clear. Satan is the ruler of this world over against God. This present age is evil, and the body a prison; the real Hell is this life (Posidonius—see above, p. 62 n. 205). Man belongs to a higher realm, but is now under the sway of fate, which is governed by the planets. The evil powers being associated with the planets, so is Satan, and it is no long step to make him the creator. In any case Yahweh is in Gentile eyes a planetary deity (Saturn), and therefore hostile, while he is also creator in the OT. Influence from more ancient mythology is, of course, not excluded. For Satan and Saturn cf. Reitzenstein *Poim.* 74ff. Jewish angelology and reverence for the στοιχεῖα may also have played a part (cf. Reitzenstein ibid. 77, Geffcken 49ff., 82f. and index s.v. Elemente Gotter). Athenagoras (xxiv) makes Satan lord of matter and of the forms in it, a development of Platonism which may also have operated in the growth of the Gnostic theory. See also Knox *PCG* 150ff. on the Colossian heresy. Note further that Saturninus ap. Hippol. identifies the God of the OT with Satan (above, p. 113 n. 51), although Wendland rejects the MS reading in favour of that of Iren. etc.

[93] τρέπουσίν τε μετὰ τοῦτο ἐπὶ λιτανείας ἡμᾶς καὶ θυσίας τῶν ἀγαθοεργῶν ὡς ὠργισμένων. ταῦτα δὲ καὶ τὰ ὅμοια ποιοῦσιν μεταστῆσαι ἡμᾶς ἐθέλοντες ἀπὸ τῆς ὀρθῆς ἐννοίας τῶν θεῶν καὶ ἐφ' ἑαυτοὺς ἐπιστρέψαι .... βούλονται γὰρ εἶναι θεοὶ καὶ ἡ προεστῶσα αὐτῶν δύναμις δοκεῖν θεὸς εἶναι ὁ μέγιστος, de Abstin. 2. 40, 42, quoted by Geffcken 220.

[94] Gilgamesh Epic (see King, Schweich Lectures 1916, 84).

[95] These words are a quotation by Porphyry (loc. cit.) from Homer

(*Il.* 9. 500, cf. 4. 49, 24. 70), which suggests that there is no need to go to Babylon for the idea. It is already present in Greek mythology, as indeed in the views of sacrifice held by most early peoples. Cf. Bevan, *Stoics and Sceptics* 108 note 1, and Athenagoras xxvi: οἱ προστετηκότες τῷ ἀπὸ τῶν ἱερείων αἵματι καὶ ταῦτα περιλιχμώμενοι; xxvii: λίχνοι περὶ κνίσας καὶ τὸ τῶν ἱερείων αἷμα ὄντες.

[96] Jewish demonology had, however, undergone various influences in the course of the history of Israel. See *HDB* 1. 590ff., Oesterley *Jews and Judaism* 278ff., Clemen (*ET*) 111ff., Causse 148ff. But 'the antithesis of God and the angels over against daemons as necessarily evil was spread by Judaism and Christianity' (Nock *Conversion* 105). Cf. also Knox *PCJ* 111 note 12.

[97] Cf. Clemen *ET* 113ff., Cumont *Rel. Or.* 143, Causse 152.

[98] Cf. Cumont, quoted above, p. 228 note 8.

[99] Norden 65ff.

[100] ibid. 73ff. Norden sees here an influence of Gnosticism on the development of Christian thought. The unknown God gained entry into the Church, but doffed his heretical garb. 'Der Dualismus des ἄγνωστος und des δημιουργός wurde aufgehoben, d.h. die ursprüngliche Identität ... wurde nun wiederhergestellt.' It seems, however, more correct to say that the Church never abandoned the identity, although Gnostic influence contributed to an increasing transcendence in the idea of God. Cf. Hatch 251ff.

[101] ibid. 72, 109. Cf. Dodd *BG* 136f.

[102] Cf. Norden 5 (referring to Reitzenstein *Poim.* etc.), Dodd *BG* 204.

[103] Cf. Saturninus (above, p. 103), Ophitism (118), Valentinianism (131). The theory of Saturninus seems to have certain affinities with that of Exc. 10, where see Casey's notes (*Excerpta* 106ff.). In Basilides the Demiurge is the Hebdomad, but there seems to be no mention of the Seven (ap. Hippol., above, p. 125). On the Seven see also Bousset *Hauptprobleme* 9ff., and compare the *Poimandres* (Dodd *BG* 138ff.).

[104] So apparently Cerinthus (above, p. 102) and possibly Basilides ap. Hippol. (above, p. 125).

[105] In Saturninus prophecy is in part due to the creator angels, in part to Satan (above, p. 103), which may mark a stage in the development of the Demiurge theory. In Ophitism (above, p. 118) some value is accorded to the OT by the statement that Sophia through the prophets kept alive in man the memory of the primal light. But cf. Iren. 1. 28. 5 *ad fin.* Reference may also be made to the Epistle of Ptolemy to Flora (above, p. 143 note 118), where the OT is assigned to various authors, part to God, part to Moses, part to 'the elders of the people.'

[106] In Valentinianism the supreme God is unknown even to the higher Aeons, apart from Monogenes—the fullest development of this theory (above, p. 129).

[107] Corp. Herm. VII (Dodd *BG* 181ff.). Cf. Norden 64 note 2, 67f. for

ἀγνωσία = ἀσεβεία. There is a certain inconsistency in blaming men for their ignorance while the possibility of knowledge is denied. But, of course, the 'Gnostic' is able to reveal the secret.

[108] Dodd, loc. cit.

[109] *Poimandres* 117ff. Cf. also the ignorance of Ahriman (*ERE* 1. 237f.). Paul in 1 Cor. 2. 6ff. speaks of a hidden wisdom, which none of the princes of this world knew. A similar idea seems to lie behind the οἰκονομία of Ign. Eph. 18ff. (see Schlier, *Religionsgeschichtliche Untersuchungen zu den Ignatiusbriefen*, Beihefte zur ZNTW 8, Giessen 1929).

[110] loc. cit. See also Dupont's discussion of the Pauline passages relating to ignorance and knowledge (*Gnosis: la connaissance religieuse*, Louvain 1949).

[111] Above, p. 126 (Hippolytus). Cf. Philo *de Post. Caini* 15, where the realization of the incomprehensibility of τὸ ὄν is in itself a boon.

[112] Above, p. 129. Cf. Exc. 31. 3: ὁ δὲ βουληθεὶς αἰὼν τὸ ὑπὲρ τὴν γνῶσιν λαβεῖν ἐν ἀγνωσίᾳ καὶ ἀμορφίᾳ ἐγένετο.

[113] *Poimandres* 13 (Reitzenstein *Poim.* 331).

[114] *BG* 152ff. The desire to create seems to be introduced to account for Man's descent into the sphere of the Demiurge where, endowed with various gifts by the powers, he falls victim to the charms of Nature.

[115] Cf. Knox *HE* 55ff. For the relation of the Philonic and Christian doctrines see the works cited above (chapter II) on Philo, and the introduction to Bernard's commentary on John (*ICC*).

[115a] Windisch 114. Cf. also 115: 'So ziehen sich durch das ganze Evangelium Wendungen und Worte, die als Anlehnungen an Philo und charakteristische Abweichungen von seiner Position betrachtet werden können.' See also *Exp. Times* lxv. 47ff., *Novum Testamentum* i. 225ff., Mackintosh *The Person of Jesus Christ* (Edinburgh 1937) 116f. Wolfson (*Philosophy of the Church Fathers* vol. i) seems unduly to exaggerate the influence of Philo on early Christian thought. His use of the adjective 'Philonic' is accurate enough in the sense that the ideas referred to do occur in Philo, but carries with it a suggestion that other writers derived these ideas *from* Philo, which is quite another matter.

[116] Cf. Sanders *The Fourth Gospel in the Early Church* 47ff.

[117] John 1. 18. The MSS vary between θεός and υἱός, while some versions have neither. Irenaeus reads θεός (4. 34. 10), but υἱός (4. 34. 6, 3. 11. 9). Cf. Casey 100 on Exc. 6. 2, and see Bernard (*ICC*) ad loc. Cf. also Matt. 11. 25–30, on which see Norden 277ff. On John 1. 18 see also Knox *HE* 58 and note 3 there. For the revelation of God through Monogenes see Exc. 7; but in Iren. 1. 1. 2 Monogenes is prevented by Sige from effecting the revelation. See Casey 8, and notes on Exc. 6–7, 29.

[118] Cf. Dodd *BG* 115ff., Dieterich *Abraxas* 21ff., 71ff.

[119] Cf. references above (notes 115, 115a); the Dead Sea Scrolls must also be taken into account here (above, p. 52 note 41).

[120] The appearance of the λόγος in the *Poimandres* is not necessarily due

to a Christian source (Dodd *BG* 121 note 1). For Hermes as *Λόγος* and *Νοῦς* see Dieterich *Abraxas* 62ff.

[121] See above, p. 144 note 124. One reason for the number of Aeons in this system is the desire to find an archetype within the Pleroma for various phenomena of this life (e.g. there is an ideal or archetypal Man and an archetypal Church). Other Aeons represent attributes or aspects of the divine nature, or 'ideas' of virtue. Cf. Harvey cxxff.

[122] Cf. above, note 117.

[123] Cf. Mowinckel, *He that Cometh* 346ff., who refers to parallels and sources in the environment of Judaism (422ff.), and traces the concept to the oriental myth of the Primordial Man. But see also Quispel in *Eranos Jahrbuch* xxii (1953) 195ff.

[124] See Manson, *Jesus the Messiah*, esp. 171ff., and cf. Dodd *BG* 156f. Also Mowinckel 360ff.

[125] Cf. Bernard on John (*ICC*) cxxiiff.

[126] *Poim.* 8 (Reitzenstein *Poim.* 330). On the figure of Sophia cf. Dix in *JTS* xxvi. 1–12.

[127] *Poimandres* 39 note 1; cf. Dodd *BG* 128f.

[127a] *De Is. et Os.* 53–54.

[128] Cf. Plato *Tim.* 92C.

[129] *De Ebr.* 30 (176. 3 Wendland). For Sophia as *μήτηρ* cf. also *de Fug.* 109, L.A. 2. 49, *QDPSI* 54 (Goodenough, *By Light, Light*).

[130] *Poimandres* 41. But the sequel seems to show that Philo is simply presenting philosophy in a mythological form adapted to the text under consideration (see *de Ebr.* 33ff.).

[131] *QDSI* 31 (63. 6 Wendland).

[132] op. cit. 42.

[133] *BG* 127ff.

[134] *BG* 131. Cf. above, p. 37ff.

[135] ibid. note 1. For other presentations of this theory of Sophia and Isis, in addition to that of Reitzenstein, see Goodenough *By Light, Light* (Yale 1935) and Pascher *Konigsweg* (Paderborn 1931). Both received a comparatively favourable review in *TLZ* (1934, 177ff., 1936, 175ff.), but cf. reviews of Goodenough in *Gnomon* 13. 3. 156ff. (A. D. Nock) and *JTS* 28. 414ff. (G. C. Richards). See also above, p. 27 note 139, and Ringgren *Word and Wisdom* (Lund 1947).

[136] *Poimandres* 44 note 2; Iren. 1. 5. 3 (1. 1. 9 Harvey).

[137] Cf. above, p. 130ff.

[138] Cf. above, p. 117. Drummond (1. 215) remarks in regard to Soph. Sol. that Spirit and Wisdom are different names for the same reality. Thus Valentinianism returns to the earlier Jewish conception. The Gnostics seem also to have tried to combine the Christian triad of Father, Son, and Holy Spirit with certain pagan triads which had originally no connexion with it. Only the Spirit could be identified with the female principle, but Jewish ideas may have facilitated the process. For the Christian triad see Clemen

RGE 125ff. Cf. also Aphraates ap. Dix, *JTS* xxvi. 11, and compare the whole article.

[139] To the Barbelognostics (Iren. 1. 29. 4 = 1. 27. 2 Harvey) the fallen goddess is Spiritus Sanctus, Σοφία, Προύνικος (Bousset *Hauptprobleme* 13); but in *Apoc. Joh.* 36. 16–38. 14 Sophia is distinct from the Holy Spirit, 'whom men call Zoe, the Mother of all' (38. 10ff.; Till *BG* 116). The latter is identified by Till with the Epinoia of Light on the basis of 53. 4–10 [cf. perhaps 71. 7, where, however, the text of a Nag Hammadi MS differs (Till *BG* 182–3)]. The description of the Father of all as Holy Spirit (22. 20) is uncertain, since the end of the line is missing and has to be supplied (Till 84 note), but seems to be confirmed by 34. 17, 46. 19 and the reference to the sin against the Holy Spirit in 70. 19. Cf. John 4. 24, 2 Cor. 3. 17.

See Bousset *Hauptprobleme* 9ff. on the Seven and the Mother, together with 56ff. and his description of the Simonian Helen (but this is based on Epiphanius), and 325f. on the Jewish connexions. There seems to be a relation between Isis and the figures of the Ophite and Valentinian systems —of the four epithets claimed for Isis by Reitzenstein the Ophite Sophia has three (Mother, Ogdoad, Sophia), the Valentinian all four. But the Jewish Wisdom may have influenced the development.

[140] *Rel. Or.* 81 etc.

[141] *HMR* 27.

[142] loc. cit. Cumont notes the flexibility of the Egyptian religion, which was always in agreement with the dominant philosophy. Against the influence of the mysteries see Dieterich *Abraxas* 60, and for the popular philosophy ibid. 58ff.

[143] See above, p. 37ff.

[144] Cf., however, Ringgren, *Word and Wisdom* (cited above, p. 53 note 66).

[145] Knox *HE* 5 note 3: 'apparently because a colourless Wisdom is not, as Isis, whom we should naturally expect here, a dangerous rival to Sarapis.' Sophia appears also in certain magic prayers which show similarities to Gnosticism (Dieterich *Abraxas* 24ff.).

[146] Hatch 199f.

[147] Cf. Knox in *JTS* 38. 230ff. What is clear is that in the figure of Sophia we have another convergence of Jewish and Graeco-Oriental thought, associated with the current theory of mediation and influencing the Gnostics. For other views as to the origin of the figure see Clemen *ET* 323f.

[148] Cf. above, p. 190f; also Casey *Excerpta* 105f. on Exc. 10, and references there.

[149] *De Gig.* 6, *de Somn.* 1. 141. In *de Plant.* 14 the angels are the 'heroes' of Greek philosophy, i.e. semi-divine beings. Cf. also *de Conf. Ling.* 174. For 'heroes' see Cumont *After-life*, index s.v. Cf. also Athenagoras xxivf.

[150] *de Conf. Ling.* 28, *de Mig. Ab.* 173.

[151] Cf. Bevan *Stoics and Sceptics* 105, with *de Gig.* 7ff., *de Somn.* 1. 135ff. See generally Cumont *After-life* 28ff., etc., Bevan 98ff., Knox *PCG* 72ff. Cf. also Knox *HE* 59 note 1. Further references in Kirk 33 and notes.

[152] 'The LXX translators have been at pains to replace the plural *Elohim* or *bne Elohim* by ἄγγελοι, where these terms represent beings with a recognized status within the Jewish system,' and by other terms in other cases (Dodd *BG* 223 note 3; cf. ibid. 22f.). According to Hatch and Redpath υἱοὶ τοῦ θεοῦ appears in Gen. 6. 4 and in some versions of Gen. 6. 2. In Deut. 32. 43 the three authorities cited differ; here there is nothing to correspond in the Hebrew text. Elsewhere we find ἄγγελοι used. For Gen. 6 see also Philo *QDSI ad init.*, and Jude 6ff. with Mayor's notes (*Expositor's Greek Testament*, London 1910). It may be recalled that it was the use of this legend which for a time convinced Schoeps of the existence of a Jewish Gnosticism in the Dead Sea Scrolls (see above, p. 75). It should be noted that there are distinct similarities between the theory of Posidonius here and that of Basilides ap. Hippol (see above, p. 125ff.).

[153] For Jewish use of this passage see Moore index (2. 457). He remarks: 'It was only when they descended to dwell in this world that the evil impulse had dominion over them' (1. 483 note 6). So in the *Poimandres* it is after Man has entered into the sphere of the Demiurge that he falls victim to the charms of Nature (cf. Dodd *BG* 152ff.).

[154] *De Somn.* 1. 133ff.

[155] *De Somn.* 1. 140f. Cf. Plutarch *de gen. Soc.* 24, quoted by Bevan *Stoics and Sceptics* 112f., who compares *de Somn.* 1. 147.

[156] See above, p. 137 note 16; in *Apoc. Joh.* 62 it is Ialdabaoth himself who seduces Eve.

[157] See above, p. 131.

[158] e.g. Simon (Iren. 1. 16. 2), Ophitism (above, p. 118), Basilides (above, p. 124). See also Casey's notes on Exc. 69ff. (*Excerpta* 154ff.).

[159] In Deut. 32. 8 LXX the Most High 'set the bounds of the nations according to the number of the angels of God.' Cf. Moore 1. 403, 406, etc. In Philo *de Somn.* 2. 114 the stars are in rivalry. Similar ideas, however, appear elsewhere (Reitzenstein *Poim.* 111ff. and notes there). In Saturninus we have a revolt against the supreme God (Harvey 197, Latin). This may suggest that a myth like that of the fall of Lucifer (cf. Athenagoras, above, p. 190) or the Titans has been carried over into Gnosticism. Apart from Saturninus it remains a revolt against the God of the OT. Note that in Saturninus ap. Hippol. the God of the Jews is identified with Satan (above, p. 113 note 51, cf. p. 236 note 92).

[160] See above, p. 139, and for the *Apocryphon Johannis* p. 151. Moreover, the four OT names are among the seven 'special names' of God (Moore 2, 134 note 5). Three of them occur in Dieterich's papyrus (*Abraxas* 4 line 24. 5 line 1).

[161] See Iren. 1. 1. 7 (Harvey 33). For Iao in magic see Knox *PCG* 34 note 4, 41ff., 48, Nock *Conversion* 62f., 111, Dieterich *Abraxas* 21f. (in texts, ibid. 4 lines 24ff,. and p. 17), and especially Goodenough *Symbols* index s.v. For Hermes and Iao see Dieterich 71. The use of the word in line 97 of the reconstructed text (Dieterich 19) finds a parallel in Valentinian-

ism (above, p. 130) sufficiently close to suggest dependence on the part of the latter. But as Dieterich (83) dates his cosmogony provisionally in the second century A.D. the case may be the reverse, or both may depend on some older source.

[162] We should most naturally understand references to the rulers of this world or to the prince of the power of the air as meaning Satan and his angels (see references above, p. 236), but this world of darkness, or the air which surrounds it, extends only to the sphere of the moon, with which begin the planetary heavens whose rulers govern man's destiny (cf. Knox *PCG* 152, 187 *et al.*). In 1 Cor. 2. 8 the reference seems to be to the latter (Knox *PCG* 109 etc.), but in 2 Cor. 4. 4 similar words are used of Satan (ibid. 93). Thus if Paul made the distinction he did not consider it specially important. The Gnostics have transferred most of the attributes of Satan to the chief cosmic power, although they retain the sublunar devil.

[163] See Oesterley *Jews and Judaism* 266ff., 278ff. For Samael, one of the names given by the Ophites to the serpent (see Harvey 236 and note 4 there), cf. Clemen *RGE* 152 on Mid. Rabba to Deut. 31. 14. Cf. also Strack-Billerbeck I. 153: Ferner ist daran zu erinnern, dass alle Völker nach jüdischer Anschauung unter der Leitung von mehr oder weniger gottfeind-lichen Engelfürsten stehen, insonderheit die damalige römische Weltmacht unter der Leitung Sammaëls (= Satans) selbst.

[164] See Geffcken index s.vv. Engel, Dämonen; Bidez-Cumont index s.vv. anges, démons; Bigg *The Church's Task* 74ff.

[165] Cf. Knox *PCG* 41ff., *PCJ* 208 note 9.

[166] The names of the Ophite powers may therefore be significant, as may the frequent occurrence of Iao in magic. In some respects Gnosticism is very close indeed to magic. Cf. Knox *PCG* 211 note 3.

2. *The creation and nature of the world*

[167] Cf. Moore I. 368 note 2, Cumont *After-life* 106. According to Bidez-Cumont (I. 229f.) the original Persian scheme comprised three heavens, but was modified with the adoption of the 'Chaldean' scheme of the seven planetary spheres.

[168] Cf. Moore loc. cit., etc.

[169] Cf. Knox *PCG* 8, 44. In *QRDH* 99 those of a Chaldean mind put their trust in 'heaven,' but he who has migrated thence in 'Him who rides on the heaven and guides the chariot of the whole world, even God' (Loeb translation).

[170] Knox *PCG* 6ff.

[171] ibid. 8.

[172] In Ophitism the heaven formed by Sophia seems to be the firmament (i.e. Ogdoad = firmament), but in the Latin version Sophia for a time *remansit sub caelo quod fecit* (Iren. I. 28. 2, Harvey 229), i.e. the Ogdoad is really under the firmament. So in the theory of Basilides the firmament is above the 'heaven' of the Great Archon (supra, p. 125) and in Valentinianism

the boundary (Horus or Stauros) separates Achamoth, the Ogdoad, from the Pleroma. Cf. Knox *PCG* 155, and for Horus note 2 there.

[173] Cf. Knox *PCG* 65.

[174] For Plato cf. *Tim.* 29D; for Philo, Drummond 2. 54.

[175] Cf. Knox *PCG* 83f.

[176] On Christian and Gnostic theories of creation see Hatch 190ff.

[177] Cf. Dieterich *Abraxas* 21ff., Dodd *BG* 115ff., etc.

[178] This, however, is rather remote and not strictly parallel. More probably the doctrine of the fall of Sophia is an attempt to surmount the difficulty which the imperfection of the world presented to advocates of an evolutionary theory. See Hatch loc. cit., and for Tiamat Legge 2. 44 note 3.

[179] Moore 1. 266f. For Philo see above, p. 42, and for the archetypal universe in the *Poimandres* Dodd *BG* 110ff. Wolfson (*Philosophy of the Church Fathers* 1. 544) observes: 'The Sethians seem to be following Philo in taking the act of creation to consist of two creations, the creation of an intelligible ideal world and the creation of a visible corporeal world.'

[180] *Abraxas*; see also Reitzenstein *HMR* 216ff. Dieterich, however, finds influence from the Septuagint in the seven acts of creation (39ff.). Jewish influence is only to be expected in a cosmogony which appears in 'the Eighth Book of Moses,' but there are also other elements, while some of the other documents to which Dieterich refers are less affected by Judaism. The whole belongs to the realm of magic and popular superstition.

[181] op. cit. For Iao cf. above, note 161.

[182] The generation of seven gods in this cosmogony by successive laughs is, however, more closely akin to the generation of the cosmic powers. See Casey *Excerpta* 105f. on Exc. 10.

[183] Cf. above, p. 117f.

[184] Above, p. 130. Cf. Dieterich 24ff. See also Exc. 45 with Casey's notes, and Dieterich 86ff.

[185] *de Conf. Ling.* 90.

[186] *de Conf. Ling.* 85. Cf. Iren. 1. 1. 2f. [πάθος of Sophia, consisting in desire (ζήτησιν τοῦ πατρός Harvey 15), followed by pleasure (? γλυκύτης ibid.), grief and fear (Harvey 16)] and 1. 1. 7 [desire of Achamoth for Christos, grief and fear at failure to attain him (Harvey 33ff.). The Horus of the latter passage duplicates that of the former]. Note also σύστασιν καὶ οὐσίαν τῆς ὕλης and the quotation from Hippol. *Phil.* 6. 32 in Harvey (35 note 2). In *Apoc. Joh.* 55. 3ff. (Till *BG* 150) the material body is created from the four elements, i.e. from matter, and from darkness, desire and the ἀντικείμενον πνεῦμα. Irenaeus (1. 27. 2, Harvey 226) mentions ζῆλος, φθόνος, ἐρινύς (for which Zuntz (*JTS NS* vi (1955) 243f. conjectures ἔρις) and ἐπιθυμία as the four constituents of κακία, but these do not appear in the Coptic text of the Apocryphon. Schmidt suggested that these were the five rulers of the underworld. See *JTS NS* vii (1956) 248ff. It would seem that in both systems an attempt is being made to find room for the

'passions' of current philosophy. Note also *Apoc. Joh.* 65. 14ff., where wrath, envy, fear, desire, and satiety appear to belong to the 'temptations of wickedness' which the pure endeavour to avoid.

[187] Cf. Dieterich 136ff.

[188] But cf. Basilides ap. Hippol. 7. 22. 2ff. For chaos = $\ddot{v}\delta\omega\rho$ in Zeno see von Arnim *SVF* 1. 103 and references there.

[189] See Dodd *BG* 103ff. Note the occurrence of an upheaval of some sort in almost all the theories, from the Abraxas cosmogony to Valentinianism. This agrees with the Platonic view, but also with the Jewish (see below).

[190] Above, p. 117.

[191] op. cit. 106f.

[192] ibid.

[193] This is explicitly stated for some systems, but not for others. The theory of two $\delta\eta\mu\iota\upsilon\rho\gamma\upsilon\iota$ appears most plainly in Basilides ap. Hippol. *Phil.* 7. 23ff., where there are apparently no other powers concerned (cf. above, p. 125). A similar view appears, however, to be involved in Ophitism ap. Iren. 1. 28. 2f. (Harvey 228ff., cf. above, p. 118) and in Valentinianism ap. Iren. 1. 1. 7ff. (Harvey 31ff., cf. above, p. 131). Cf. also note 172. The Ogdoad and Hebdomad have been understood here to refer to the eighth and seventh spheres respectively, but it would also be possible to interpret the Hebdomad as the seven planetary powers headed by the Demiurge, and correspondingly the Ogdoad as the same group with the addition of the eighth power Sophia-Achamoth or the Great Archon. In this case the Hebdomad is also the whole region beneath the heaven of the fixed stars, the Ogdoad the whole realm outside the Pleroma. This, however, involves an inconsistency in Hippolytus' account of Basilides, where the Ogdoad is set in order by the Great Archon, and the Hebdomad is subsequently ordered by a second Demiurge.

[194] See above, p. 45.

[195] Cf. *de Fug.* 12, where the Logos is 'the seal by which each thing that exists has received its shape' (Loeb translation). Clement of Alexandria can speak of Christ as the $\chi\alpha\rho\alpha\kappa\tau\dot{\eta}\rho$ of the glory of God, 'stamping on the mind of the gnostic the perfect vision after his own image' (*Strom.* 7. 16. 6; cf. *Studia Patristica* 1. 434 and references in note 6 there).

[196] *De Ebr.* 61, alluding to Plato *Tim.* 51A etc. (see Loeb edition of Philo *ad loc.*).

[197] Cf. Clemen *RGE* 151-2, Bidez-Cumont 1. 230.

[198] Cf. Casey *Excerpta* 144. Other passages speak of the third heaven. See also Bidez-Cumont 1. 230 and notes there. 'The location of the original Paradise in the third heaven . . . is traceable to a rabbinical source' (Knox *PCJ* 114 note 14). Cf. also the Ophite account of the fall, Iren. 1. 28. 4, where Ialdabaoth is said *proiecisse Adam et Evam de paradiso*, and later they are said to have been *deiectos a coelo in hoc mundum*. See Harvey's notes, 233ff. In the *Apocryphon Johannis* 55f. (Till *BG* 150ff.), Paradise belongs to

the creation of Ialdabaoth and is intended to prevent Adam from returning to the world of light; but it fails of its purpose, and hence Adam and Eve are expelled (ibid. 61f., Till 162ff.). There appears to be no reference to the location of Paradise, but it may be noted that the word *plasma*, which Harvey (234) explains as referring to both Adam and Eve, is preserved in the Coptic of the Apocryphon as a description of Adam [48. 17, 55. 10; cf. also the *Sophia Jesu Christi* 119. 12ff. (Till BG 278)].

199 2 Cor. 12. 2ff.

200 Cf. Rohde *Psyche*, Cumont *After-life*.

201 See above, p. 199.

202 It may further be remarked that 'the interpretation of ἀρχή in Gen. I. I and John I. I as a metaphysical principle occurs frequently in early Christian literature' (Casey *Excerpta* 100 on Exc. 6. 2). Moreover, there was a Jewish interpretation of the *reshith* of Genesis (equated with the Torah) as an instrument in creation (Dodd *BG* 109; cf. also Dodd, *Interpretation* 86, Davies *PRJ* 150ff.). As Dodd remarks, Philo does not follow this in *Op. M.*, but in *de Conf. Ling.* 146 the Logos is ἀρχή, which may indicate acquaintance with similar theories.

3. *Anthropology*

203 Cf. *de Ag.* 65, *de Conf. Ling.* 77f., *de Cher.* 120f., *de Plant.* 17, and for the NT Heb. 11. 13, 13. 14, 1 Pet. 2. 11, Phil. 3. 20. Eph. 2. 19 looks at man from the other angle, as alienated from heaven, but restored to citizenship in Christ.

For Gnostic anthropology see Quispel in *Eranos Jahrbuch* xv (1947) 249ff. (Valentinus), xvi (1948) 89ff. (Basilides), xxii (1953) 195ff., Schlier in *Anthropologie Religieuse* (ed. Bleeker, Leiden 1955) 60ff. (Naassenes), Rudolph in *ZRGG* ix (1957) 1ff. Dodd (*Interpretation* 111 note) observes: 'the earliest documents for the "Ἀνθρωπος-myth, in any form relevant to our purpose, are demonstrably exposed to Jewish influence, and Jewish speculations on Adam would seem to have been at least as influential as ideas borrowed from Iranian sources. See W. D. Davies, *Paul and Rabbinic Judaism*, ch. 3.'

204 For Jewish views on the dual nature of man see Moore 1. 451f. It should be observed that in the Book of Enoch the legend of the Watchers is employed as an alternative theory to that of Adam and Eve (see Tennant, *Sources of the Doctrines of the Fall and Original Sin* 181ff.). This is a development of Gen. 6. 1–4, whatever the original meaning of this passage, and this, rather than the Paradise-story, 'was the earliest basis for popular Jewish speculation as to the origin of the general sinfulness of the world' (ibid. 236). See on the whole subject Tennant op. cit., Williams *Ideas o the Fall* (London 1929).

205 Luke 19. 10.

206 Cf. above, p. 76.

R

[207] See Angus *The Mystery Religions and Christianity*, esp. 244ff., and for the forgiveness of sins in Judaism Moore 2. 415 (index s.v.).

[208] Cf. *QDSI* 150, *de Ag.* 25, *de Mig. Ab.* 7ff., and see Chapter II above. Moore (1. 452) remarks that in *Op. M.* 135 Greek philosophy has contributed everything but the text.

[209] Cf. above, p. 77.

[210] *PMR* 154.

[211] In this respect the *Gospel of Truth* is a remarkable exception (see above, p. 163); but a Gnostic would probably explain the references to the Passion as applicable only to the human Jesus and not to the divine Christ.

[212] See above, p. 132. A triple classification (good, bad, and 'middling') appears also in Judaism, but this is obviously different. Cf. Moore 1. 485, 495. The Gnostic view may, however, derive from a similar root. Philo accepts the Platonic division of the soul (e.g. *LA* 1. 70 and Loeb edition *ad loc.*), of which the same may be said. It may be that the Gnostic theory is the outcome of their experience as missionaries of the Gnostic creed (cf. the explanations of the parables of Jesus in the Gospels, e.g. Mark 4. 11ff.): some men cannot, or will not, listen, and are therefore held to be predestined not to hear.

[213] In the Dead Sea *Manual of Discipline* iii. 13–iv. 26, it is said that God has appointed two spirits, a spirit of truth and a spirit of perversity, that man may walk with them until the day of his visitation; according to their adherence to one or other of these two spirits men are judged. So also in the *Apocryphon Johannis* 67 (Till *BG* 174f.) those into whom the divine spirit enters are delivered from evil, whereas those dominated by the ἀντίμιμον πνεῦμα are led astray. The Manual is, however, still far removed from Gnosticism in the strict sense (see *Vig. Chr.* xi (1957) 99ff.).

[214] Cf. above, p. 113 note 48. The failure of some to accept the message proclaimed might be ascribed to their 'sleep of intoxication,' but there seems to be a growing tendency to make the distinction one of essence. Exc. 17 avoids the difficulty of an immanent λόγος which still requires enlightenment. The divine influence is not part of man's οὐσία, and hence there is room for election. Cf. Casey *ad loc.* Some early Fathers distinguish between the εἰκών of Gen. 1.26 and the ὁμοίωσις, the former being the common possession of all mankind, the latter realized only in Christ (cf. *Studia Patristica* 1. 420ff.).

[215] Kennedy considers the Urmensch myth unnecessary for Philo, since the ideal man is already postulated in his Platonic theory (*PCR* 78f.). Cf. Manson *Jesus the Messiah* 182, and for the fall of Man in *Poimandres* Dodd *BG* 145ff. For the Urmensch see Bousset *Hauptprobleme* 160ff., who remarks that he does not play a dominant role in most Gnostic systems. Cf. also above, p. 45f., and Creed in *JTS* 26. 113ff.

[216] Knox *PCG* 81 note 8, *Pharisaism and Hellenism* 76.

[217] Cf. above, p. 199f.

[218] Bidez-Cumont I. 97.

[219] See Manson 174ff., Dodd *Interpretation* 111 note, Quispel in *The Jung Codex* 76ff.

[220] In *Op. M.* 151ff., *LA* ii, the Fall is allegorized into an account of 'how Mind was misled by Pleasure into an unhallowed union with Sense' (cf. Dodd *BG* 148).

[221] e.g. *de Conf. Ling.* 41, 62f. Cf. above, p. 42. But in *de Somn.* I. 74 the εἰκών seems to be the soul.

[222] *Op. M.* 134ff. The breath is πνεῦμα θεῖον (135), and there is precedent in Stoicism for the close association of πνεῦμα and the pure fire (Dodd *BG* 122f.). The Ἀγαθὸς Δαίμων is addressed as ὁ ἐμφυσήσας πνεῦμα ἀνθρώποις εἰς ζωήν in a papyrus quoted by Reitzenstein, *Poim.* 15 (for man as spirit imprisoned in the body cf. ibid. 84). Moreover, the earth from which man was formed was not just any earth, but the best and purest (*Op. M.* 137); cf. the Valentinian view, Iren. I. 1. 10 (Harvey 49 and note 1), Exc. 50, and that of Justin (above, p. 122).

[223] See above, p. 47, and for Philo's views on the relations of God and man in general Kennedy *PCR*. Cf. *Ev. Ver.* 22. 13ff.: He who thus possesses Gnosis . . . knows even as a person who, having been intoxicated, becomes sober. On the Philonic conception of 'sober intoxication' cf. Lewy, *Sobria Ebrietas* (Beihefte zur *ZNW* 9, 1929).

[224] Cf. above, p. 207.

[225] But, as Dodd shows, at several points the Hermetica are dependent not on Philo but on a Hellenistic Judaism of a similar type; so too there is no proof of acquaintance with Philo on the part of the NT writers, although similar ideas occur. The same may also hold for Gnosticism, all being adaptations of more or less the same material to meet similar needs.

[226] For Valentinianism cf. above, p. 132; for the Hermetic writings see Dodd *BG* 191ff., and for Philo the references in Dodd loc. cit. The phrase δερμάτινος ὄγκος occurs again of the body in *de Post. Caini* 137, *de Conf. Ling.* 55. See also Knox *PCG* 83, and references for Nadab and Abihu and for Er, ibid. 104, 137. Bigg (*Platonists* 204 note 4) refers to Orig. *c. Cels.* 4. 40. For patristic use of the passage see Tennant *Doctrines of the Fall* etc. 320 note 1, Williams *Ideas of the Fall* 229 note 1 and references there. Hippolytus (*Phil.* 1. 24, Wendland p. 28) ascribes the idea to the Brahmins. In the *Apocryphon of John* the body of Adam is made from the four elements (54–55).

[227] This is, of course, the Biblical account, suitably amended to comply with the premisses of Gnosticism. The *Apocryphon of John* seems to combine the Ophite theory with that of Saturninus—unless Irenaeus has omitted something [Iren. I. 28. 3 (Harvey 232) quotes Gen. 1. 26 *ad imaginem nostram*]. Certainly the use of Gen. 1. 26 and 2. 7 is clear enough.

[228] Compare the Hermetic view (Dodd *BG* 145ff.). Note that in Valentinianism man is created κατ᾽ εἰκόνα καὶ καθ᾽ ὁμοίωσιν by the Demiurge (above, p. 132). This view, like those of the Ophites and Saturninus, seems to be merely a Gnostic adaptation of Gen. 1. 26ff. For Philo and

Valentinianism here see above, note 222, and on the whole subject *Studia Patristica* I. 420ff.

[229] Cf. Dodd *BG* 179ff. Note the affinities of the Hermetica and Hellenistic Judaism, and the points of contact afforded by the OT. For the NT cf. I Cor. 15. 34, I Thess. 5. 6, 8, I Pet. 4. 7, 5. 8. See also Lewy *Sobria Ebrietas*, Bultmann *Theology* I. 174f.

[230] Cf. Dodd *BG* 156f., and compare *Apoc. Joh.* 48. 4–14 (Till *BG* 136f.).

[231] Dodd loc. cit., Manson *Jesus the Messiah* 177ff. Cf. Clemen *RGE* 74f.

[232] Manson 178; cf. also Mowinckel *He that Cometh*, esp. 420ff.

[233] *de Ag.* 25. Cf. Reitzenstein *Poim.* 84 for a similar idea in the Naassene preaching, which may represent a stage in the development of the theory. In Enoch 42. 1f. it is said that Wisdom found no place for herself on earth, and so returned to heaven (Clemen *RGE* 229); this may have contributed to the idea of the divine being who was too spiritual for this earth, but it is only a remote parallel, and perhaps not strictly relevant. In Tatian (*Or.* 7) the man made in the likeness of God became mortal by reason of the fall, when the 'more powerful Spirit' departed from him. In *Studia Patristica* I. 427 note 8 it is suggested that there may perhaps be some connexion between this δυνατώτερον πνεῦμα and the διάφερον πνεῦμα of the Valentinians (for which cf. Sagnard *La Gnose valentinienne* index s.v.).

[234] See above, p. 146 notes 159–60, and add to the references there Sagnard 391 *et al.*

[235] Cf. Knox *PCG* 111ff., and for the Jew as free from fate ibid. 100. On the heavenly journey of the soul see Kirk 16 note 1.

[236] *de Fug.* 51 etc. Cf. Exc. 21–22. In *de Cher.* 50 the soul is παρθένος after union with God, not γυνή, i.e. the course of events on the natural plane is reversed. See further Clemen *RGE* 121 and note 4. The idea which he quotes from Hippolytus of the soul becoming male through the operation of the spirit (from the Eleusinian mysteries) also finds an echo in Gnosticism. Cf. Exc. 79 and Casey's references to other sections. Cf. also *de Somn.* I. 200 and Bousset *Schulbetrieb* 113f., 114 note 1. The conception of the heavenly counterpart of the soul properly belongs to Zoroastrianism (Knox *PCG* 137). Cf. Bigg *Platonists* 239.

[237] e.g. de Mig. Ab. 46; I Cor. 2. 6, 3. 1, 13. 10, 11. For ψυχικός and πνευματικός cf. I Cor. 2. 14, 15. 44, 46, on which see Kennedy *PMR* 138ff. Cf. Jude 19.

[238] *LA* iii. 140; cf. ibid. 129ff., 147 and the various allegorizations of the patriarchs. Thus in *de Mut. Nom.* 60ff. the change of Abram's name to Abraham is represented as marking an advance from astrology to piety.

[239] Compare the difference between the positions of Clement of Alexandria and the Gnostics (see *Studia Patristica* I. 434 and references there).

[240] Moore I. 453, Davies *PRJ* 46, 48, 54.

[241] The view of Saturninus (see above, p. 103) was that two kinds of men, good and evil, had been created by the angels, for which there seem to be no Jewish parallels, evil in man being attributed rather to the evil

impulse [Moore 2. 413 (index)]. The idea of the two men in Philo, heavenly and earthly, is quite distinct. Cf., however, *LA* iii. 104. In the Dead Sea *Manual of Discipline* (iii. 13–iv. 26) there are two *spirits*, but men seem to have the choice, and the responsibility, of following one or the other.

[242] Cf., however, Quispel in *Eranos Jahrbuch* xxii (1953) 195ff.

4. Salvation

[243] Cf. generally Knox *PCG*, index s.v. Salvation.

[244] See Liddell-Scott-Jones x.v., and for 'salvation' in Hebrew thought Mowinckel 47, 69.

[245] Moulton and Milligan *Vocabulary* s.v.

[246] See *HDB* iv. 357ff., *ERE* xi. 109ff., Moore index s.v. Salvation. Moore claims (1. 321) that 'there is no indication that pious Jews were afflicted with an inordinate pre-occupation about their individual here- after.' Their salvation was bound up with that of Israel. Bultmann notes (*Theology* 1. 93) that the early Church simply took for granted salvation for the fellowship of God's people into which the individual is incorporated, and that this 'essentially differentiates it from the propaganda of other oriental religions of redemption.' Gnosticism on the other hand 'lacks the specific characteristics of Church-consciousness: a knowledge of its soli- darity with the history of the People of God and a binding tie to the document of salvation, the Old Testament' (ibid. 107). The speculations on the pre-existence of the Church to which Bultmann refers (ibid. 94) would seem to account for the appearance of Ecclesia as an Aeon in the Valentinian Pleroma.

[247] See the article Salvation (Jewish) in *ERE* loc. cit. It may be noted that much of the material which Goodenough claims as evidence for the persistence of a hellenized Judaism even after A.D. 70 is drawn from tombs and funerary ornament (see his *Jewish Symbols in the Greco-Roman period*). For Gnostic catacombs in Rome see Carcopino *De Pythagore aux Apôtres* (Paris 1956), on which see Toynbee's review in *Gnomon* 29 (1957) 261ff.

[248] See generally Rohde *Psyche*, Cumont *After-life*. Tarn (196ff.) notes the parallel development of individualism and universalism in Israel and in Greece.

[249] Cf. the Sacred Discourse of the Corpus Hermeticum (Dodd *BG* 230ff.).

[250] According to Rohde, however, he did not proclaim more than the qualified immortality of the older Stoics (*Psyche* 518 note 60).

[251] Bevan *Stoics and Sceptics* 111. For Posidonius see Knox *PCG* 73ff. The souls of the great and good come from the gods and return at death to the gods, but a similar destiny seems open to the pure. A further develop- ment exempted the wise man, like the Gnostic, from the need for religious observances (Cumont *After-life* 124).

[252] For salvation in the mysteries cf. Kennedy *PMR* 199ff.

²⁵³ For philosophy and the mysteries in this connexion see Cumont *After-life* 110ff., and for the Hermetica Dodd *BG* 170ff.

²⁵⁴ Cf. Knox *HE* 37ff.

²⁵⁵ Nock *Conversion* 222.

²⁵⁶ Cf. above, p. 15.

²⁵⁷ C. *Apien.* 2. 15, 16–19, 22. 30, 31–2, 38; cf. Philo *QDSI* 148.

²⁵⁸ Bréhier 3ff. Cf. Bousset-Gressmann 440ff. on Philo's detachment from everyday life: 'Das Lebensideal Philos ist das des griechischen von der Welt und ihrem Lärm zuruckgezogenen Weisen' (ibid. 443). Self-denial and αὐτάρκεια are the ideals of the philosopher.

²⁵⁹ Cf. Philo *de Plant.* 107ff., and for similar ideas from the Graeco-Roman world Clemen *RGE* 128ff., 272. On the Philonic passage cf. Moore 1. 504, concerning the prophetic teaching about sacrifice. Once again distinct resemblances are to be found in the sect of the Dead Sea Scrolls. Mowinckel (*He that Cometh* 267 and note 2 there) notes an unresolved tension in Jewish thought between 'those elements which were political, national, and this-worldly, and those transcendental and universal elements which belonged to the world beyond.'

²⁶⁰ 1 Cor. 1. 24.

²⁶¹ For repentance in Judaism see Moore 2. 440 (index s.v.). For Philo see Kennedy *PCR* 116–141 (repentance, faith, immortality).

²⁶² Cf. Torrance *The Doctrine of Grace in the Apostolic Fathers* (Edinburgh 1948). On the Gnostic side, compare the *Gospel of Truth* (see above, p. 155ff.).

²⁶³ See Windisch *Frömmigkeit*, and Kennedy *PCR*.

²⁶⁴ This redemption consists for Philo, as for the Hermetica and some Gnostics, in the impartation of γνῶσις, i.e. it is really revelation. In other types of Gnosticism redemption is a form of sympathetic magic, the Redeemer accomplishing what the soul ought ideally to do of itself, and thereby enabling it to fulfil its destiny (cf. Bevan *Hellenism and Christianity* 104f.).

²⁶⁵ See Windisch 4ff.

²⁶⁶ See Kirk 16 note 1.

²⁶⁷ Gen. 3. 19. Cf. Philo *de Post. Caini* 5, *de Mig. Ab.* 3 for similar ideas, and Dodd *BG* 230ff.

²⁶⁸ 1 Cor. 15. 35ff. For comparison of Paul's view with that of the mysteries see Kennedy *PMR* 180ff. *et al.*

5. The Redeemer

²⁶⁹ For Gnostic Christology cf. Wolfson, *Philosophy of the Church Fathers* 1. 552ff., and see also Houssiau *La christologie de saint Irénée* (Louvain 1955). Quispel (*Eranos Jahrbuch* xxii (1953) 234, *The Jung Codex* 78) claims that it was from Christianity that the concept of redemption and the figure of the Redeemer were taken over into Gnosticism.

²⁷⁰ On the 'Heavenly Man redemption myth' cf. references above, and see last note. Black in *SJT* 7. 177ff. observes that the pre-Christian 'Gnostic

Redeemer' proves on closer examination to be 'largely a scholar's recon-struction' from later sources. On the other side see Mowinckel 420ff.

[271] Cf. Bidez-Cumont 1. 50ff. See also Zaehner *Doctrines of the Magi*; *Zurvan: A Zoroastrian Dilemma*. In this connexion it is of interest that among the documents found at Nag Hammadi are an Apocalypse of Zostrianus and perhaps also an Apocalypse of Zoroaster (Puech in *Coptic Studies in Honor of W. E. Crum* 107f., 132ff. and in *The Jung Codex* 21; cf. Quispel *Gnosis* 6f. Doresse in *Coptic Studies* 255ff.). These are already mentioned by Porphyry in his life of Plotinus.

[272] Bidez-Cumont 1. 221.

[273] See *ERE* 11. 137bff., art. Salvation (Iranian). Cf. also Bidez-Cumont, index to vol. 1 s.v. Messie, Saoshyant, Sauveur. The date of some of these theories is, however, uncertain.

[274] Ignatius (Eph. 20) speaks of the bread of the Eucharist as $\phi\acute{\alpha}\rho\mu\alpha\kappa\sigma\nu$ $\mathring{\alpha}\theta\alpha\nu\alpha\sigma\acute{\iota}\alpha\varsigma$ (cf. references in Bultmann *Primitive Christianity* 227 n. 46). According to Pfeiffer (153) the mysteries of Isis were believed to be 'the remedy which gives immortality' (Diod. Sic. 1. 25). But Diodorus says only that Isis was supposed to have discovered $\tau\grave{o}$ $\phi\acute{\alpha}\rho\mu\alpha\kappa\sigma\nu$ $\mathring{\alpha}\theta\alpha\nu\alpha\sigma\acute{\iota}\alpha\varsigma$, which she used to resurrect Horus. Cf. also Howard *The Fourth Gospel in Recent Criticism and Interpretation* (4th ed., revised by C. K. Barrett, London 1955) 155f.

[275] For ideas of a virgin birth cf. Nock *Conversion* 232.

[276] The common elements are the virgin birth and the final victory of the Saviour, with the idea of the resurrection (mediated through Judaism). If this theory influenced Christianity at all it was itself transformed: the virgin birth is separated from its eschatological context and related to the earthly life of Jesus, while the final victory belongs to the Second Coming. Again, this is myth, while Jesus is an historical figure. At most, therefore, this theory has been pressed into service by later Christians who noticed the similarity. It does not account for the Christian doctrine. Cf. Bidez-Cumont 1. 53.

[277] See Bidez-Cumont 1. 153ff., and note 271 above.

[278] *Christian Platonists* 239. For Mithraism cf. ibid. 237ff.

[279] See Manson *Jesus the Messiah* 174ff., and references above, note 219.

[280] See above, p. 207ff.

[281] 1 Cor. 15. 45–49. On this passage see Manson 188f.

[282] This is only possible if some such myth as that of Gayomart and the Saoshyant was in existence at the time in circles where it could have been known to Paul. For the passages which have been held to indicate Paul's knowledge of such a myth see Knox *PCG* 220ff.

[283] *Op. M.* 134 etc. For the Logos as the Heavenly Man cf. *de Conf. Ling.* 146 (Manson 188). A closer approximation to the 'Heavenly Man Redeemer' is found in Saturninus, but it is not clear that the Saviour is there the heavenly being in whose image man was made, rather than

another figure entirely. In the latter case the theory belongs to the second type.

[284] *PCR* 78. On the other side see Clemen *ET* 153, who discusses both the passages here mentioned.

[285] Cf. the quotation from Windisch, above, p. 72.

[286] See Liddell-Scott-Jones s.v., Moulton and Milligan *Vocabulary* s.v., and Wendland in *ZNTW* 1904, 335ff.

[287] Cf. Wendland loc. cit., Knox *HE* 37ff.

[288] For the mysteries cf. Kennedy *PMR* and similar works; for the emperor-cult Wendland op. cit. 335. On the relation between Christianity and the Mysteries cf. Metzger in *HTR* 48 (1955) 1ff. and references there.

[289] Cf. Mowinckel 21ff. on the Israelite idea of kingship in relation to the ideas of other ancient cultures.

[290] Cf. Nock *Conversion* 234ff.

[291] Cf. the language used of Epicurus by Lucretius, *de Rerum Natura* i. 62–126, iii *ad init.*, and references in Liddell-Scott-Jones s.v. σωτήρ: 'of a philosopher or guide; especially of Epicurus.'

[292] Cf. Nock *Conversion* 181.

[293] Bigg *Platonists* 244ff.

[294] ibid. 246.

[295] *Agnostos Theos* 197 etc. According to this the Church clothed the simple teaching of Jesus in words whose form and content derive from the itinerant 'prophets' who went about claiming to be saviours. Of these Apollonius was one.

[296] See *ERE* 8. 570ff., with *HDB* 3. 352aff., 2. 458b (Incarnation), 4. 357bff. (Saviour), 5. 295bff. (Messiah), and Moore index s.v. Mowinckel would reserve the title Messiah for the eschatological figure of later Judaism, as distinct from the reigning earthly king (*He that Cometh* 3, 451f.), although there is a 'logical and historical connexion between the concept of the Messiah and the ancient Israelite idea of the king as "Yahweh's Anointed"' (ibid. 21). See also Klausner, *The Messianic Idea in Israel* (tr. W. F. Stinespring, London 1956).

[297] *Der Messias*.

[298] Cf. above, note 296.

[299] For the distinction between the earthly Davidic Messiah and the heavenly pre-existent Son of Man (two different expectations) see Duncan *Jesus Son of Man* 59ff., and cf. Mowinckel index s.v. Son of Man. Gressmann (230) claims that the eschatological element is inherent in the Messianic belief from the beginning. In his view the prophets took up the popular expectation of a coming ideal king, which was of a political character, and gave it a deeper moral and religious content. Note his summary, 268ff. But cf. also Mowinckel 14 etc.

[300] Cf. Gressmann 195, Mowinckel 96ff.

[301] Elmslie (*How Came our Faith*, Cambridge 1948, 340ff.) thinks the words *to Cyrus* in Is. 45. 1 no part of the original text.

[302] Cf. above, p. 9, and *HDB* 5. 300f.

[303] Cf. Mowinckel 286ff. On the 'two Messiahs' of the Dead Sea Scrolls see ibid. 289, Kuhn in *NTS* i (1955) 168ff., La Sor in *Vetus Testamentum vi* (1956) 425ff., Brownlee in *NTS* iii (1956) 21ff., 198ff.

[303a] Cf. *HDB* 5. 297b.

[304] For additional references on the Zadokite fragment see Kirk 61 note 2; see also Charles *Religious Development between the Testaments* (London 1942) 234ff. The Zadokite fragment must now, however, be linked with the Dead Sea Scrolls, on which see above, p. 73ff.

[305] *Life of Jesus* 33ff. Conversely hatred of the Herods and of Rome may have contributed to the popularity of the Messianic expectation among those who found the yoke of foreign domination irksome.

[306] This seems to afford additional evidence against Goodenough's theory of a Jewish mystery-cult. Moses is at most the hierophant of the cult suggested, although he might appear in the guise assumed by Poimandres in the Hermetica [note the identification Moses-Hermes-Thoth (Dieterich *Abraxas* 70). For Hermes and Poimandres see Dodd *BG* 99. Cf. also above, p. 28 note 147]. The Messiah might on the other hand have been transformed into a cult-hero to anticipate Mithras, but this is not the case. In Philo the Saviour is God alone, although He may make use of His powers as intermediaries.

[307] *Judaism* 1. 90, cf. 121, 162.

[308] ibid. 185f.

[309] ibid. 551; cf. *HDB* 3. 354b. Gressmann (309) identifies the Servant in Isaiah with the Messiah, but even if this be accepted it does not affect the conclusion, since the Servant Songs do not seem to have exercised any real influence on later speculation. Manson (168ff.) notes that the Targum on Is. 52. 13–53. 12 while identifying the Servant with the Messiah diverts from him the element of suffering and so completely transforms the whole passage, while Gressmann himself admits that Judaism in the time of Jesus was dominated by a completely different conception of the Messiah (336). Cf. Mowinckel 213ff., 325ff., 410ff. 'The thought of the suffering Servant of the Lord had, broadly speaking, no influence on Messianic conceptions in the OT and Judaism' (ibid. 256). For the Targum see also Mowinckel 330ff.

[310] ibid. 186, cf. 2. 335ff. On the interconnexion of these with the Servant see Manson, esp. 171ff. But the idea of glory through humiliation 'had not entered into the Messianic calculations of Judaism' (ibid. 116).

[311] Cf. *ERE* loc. cit., *HDB* 3. 356f.

[312] Manson *Jesus the Messiah* 2.

[313] Thus the Son of Man concept may have been derived by Judaism from Persia, but if so it has been subordinated to Jewish ideas (cf. Manson 183, Clemen *RGE* 69ff.).

[314] ibid. 12; cf. also Clemen *RGE* 62ff. For the title κύριος see the articles collected in *Recueil Cerfaux* 1. 1–188.

[315] ibid. 190.

[316] ibid. 100.

[317] There are two possibilities: (a) that there was a complete Soter myth, later transferred en bloc to the historic figure of Jesus (cf. Reitzenstein *HMR* 60 for an example, and generally *ERE* 6. 237); (b) that elements from various myths were employed in presenting the historic Jesus. The latter seems more probable, but there is no room for dogmatism. In either case the essential factor is the historic Jesus, who had somehow to be fitted in. Cf. also note 319.

[318] *By Light, Light* 361.

[319] Cf. *ERE* 6. 237. The existence or non-existence of a composite pre-Christian redemption myth is not a matter for dogmatism, and certainly various features were abstracted from the saviour gods of the mysteries and applied to Jesus. Again, when the Gnostics tried to interpret Jesus for their time such ideas were the natural medium. The primary impulse, however, comes not from these myths, nor from any popular conception of a redeemer based upon them, but from the Christian Gospel. It is a paganization of the Christian Jesus, not the imperfect harmonization of a Christian Jesus and a pagan Soter. But for the historic Jesus the Gnostic Redeemer might have been unnecessary, and certainly would have been even more different from the Christian figure. On the other hand, influences which have had only a secondary effect upon Christianity are often much more prominent in Gnosticism.

[320] Cf. further Bevan *Hellenism and Christianity* 95ff. He observes that the Redeemer has two functions: (a) to bring γνῶσις, in which case he is parallel to those of the mysteries and the Hermetica; (b) to do what the soul ought of itself to do, and thus 'to bring power to the fallen Divine element in man by a process of sympathetic magic.'

[321] The idea of an incarnation was repellent to the contemporary world (Nock *Conversion* 236). On the other hand there are several parallels for the Passion (ibid. 234f.).

[322] So in Ophitism and Valentinianism, but there is no sign of this in the *Gospel of Truth*. In Cerinthus the natural Jesus is inspired with the Spirit of God at his baptism, while in Saturninus and Basilides (ap. Iren.) the Saviour Christ appears as a man. The primary idea seems to be that Jesus somehow escaped the Passion, the descent of the supernatural Christ into the human Jesus being a later development.

[323] See above, p. 125.

[324] i.e. the first-fruits of them that are saved (cf. 1 Cor. 15. 20ff.). Paul's κεκοιμημένοι might have been interpreted in terms of the Poimandres (27: ὦ λαοί, ἄνδρες γηγενεῖς, οἱ μέθῃ καὶ ὕπνῳ ἑαυτοὺς ἐκδεδωκότες) as meaning those who have still to be roused to knowledge, i.e. to salvation.

[325] Compare Ophitism, where Christ is associated with the Holy Spirit, but descends into the human Jesus. Here Christ is the offspring of the Holy Spirit, who in Valentinianism is identified to some extent at least

with Sophia. This may have given rise to the confusion noted below, but the fault may be that of our sources. Note further that the Ophite Son of Man has no soteriological function.

326 Cf. Sagnard *La Gnose valentinienne* 647f. (index s.v. μορφή etc.).

327 Such earlier forms may not, however, be 'Gnostic' in the strict sense, but only 'pre-Gnostic' or 'gnosticizing.' Cf. p. 73ff. above on the Dead Sea Scrolls. The view that the ideas of the sect of the Dead Sea Scrolls account for the origins of Christianity would now appear to be ruled out, although points of contact are apparent and the Scrolls certainly do illuminate the background of the primitive Church. See most recently Daniélou *Les Manuscrits de la Mer Morte et les Origines du Christianisme* (Paris 1957), Rowley *The Dead Sea Scrolls and the NT* (London 1957).

328 The fact that the *Gospel of Truth* is in this respect so much nearer to 'orthodox' Christianity would seem to confirm van Unnik's theory that it was written by Valentinus shortly before or shortly after his break with the Church.

CHAPTER VIII

DIASPORA, SYNCRETISM, AND GNOSTICISM

THERE remains only the summing up of the results which have been reached, and the formulation of the conclusions which may be drawn concerning the contribution made by Diaspora Judaism towards the development of Gnosticism. The two parts of our study are clearly complementary: but for the Diaspora the Gentile Mission could not have had the success which it enjoyed, if, indeed, such a mission had been possible at all; there would thus have been no Gentile Christianity, or at best only a very feeble plant which would soon have withered, and there would have been no Christian Gnosticism. The Church would not have suffered the troubles which accompanied its growth, but would have remained an obscure sect adhering to a peculiar variety of Jewish Messianism. In regard to Gnosticism itself, certain Jewish theories, often of a syncretistic nature, contain the germ of later Gnostic ideas, or help to explain their development. On the other hand, Gnosticism leads us out of the Jewish-Christian environment into the wider field of the pagan world, and provides a standard by which to measure the debt of Judaism and of Christianity to the contemporary paganism. All three have been modified by their contact with the surrounding world, but where in the Dispersion and in Christianity the process of assimilation has been largely kept under control, and the borrowed elements subordinated to the essential message of each, in Gnosticism the control has gone. The Gnostics may have been Christians in intention; their theories are fundamentally pagan. Their lack of control over the process of assimilation at once brings them closer to the pagan world and at the same time sets the more orthodox theories in a very different light. Judaism, especially in the Dispersion, and Christianity are both in a sense syncretistic religions, but in comparison with the Gnostic their syncretism was extremely mild.

It is not possible fully to understand the growth and development of Christianity without reference to the contemporary world, and there can be nothing but gain in the restoration of the documents of the early Church to their contemporary setting; but as has been emphasized above, attention must be paid to details of chronology and to the meaning which words and phrases possessed for their author at the time when he wrote. After the fall of Jerusalem in A.D. 70 Jewish Christianity recedes into the background, while Judaism itself for the most part entered on a different course of development. It was left to the Church to take up the heritage of the Dispersion and to achieve a synthesis of Jewish and Graeco-Oriental thought. On either side there is a long history of development, with, in the later stages, a considerable influence from each upon the other. Some stages in this history are obscure, but the final outcome is comparatively clear.

In the Hellenistic world at large we have first of all the breaking down of the old national barriers and the foundation of larger empires by Alexander and his successors, culminating in the establishment of the Roman Empire by Augustus. The rivalries of the Diadochi to some extent formed new barriers, and it is only with the triumph of Rome that the blending of Greek and Oriental reaches its height, yet within each of the great kingdoms there was a mixed population of various races, each with its own beliefs. Even in Greece itself there were slaves and merchants from all parts of the Eastern Mediterranean, who formed small societies for the observance of their ancestral worship. Communication between one region and another became increasingly easier, and here again the peak was reached with the supremacy of Rome. In the realm of thought, the old Greek religion had been largely discredited by the criticisms of the philosophers. Some sought a substitute in philosophy, others in the increasingly popular mystery cults. The speculative tendencies of the age favoured some sort of monotheism, while the various cults appropriated to themselves ideas from each other and from philosophy. On the lower levels magic and superstition were rife.

The mysteries were not the only medium by which Oriental ideas entered into Greek thought, since several prominent figures in the philosophy of the Hellenistic period, particularly among the Stoics, were of Semitic origin, although some of them may have been born of Greek parents in a foreign land. But whatever the source of the different ideas, whatever the medium through which they penetrated into Greek thought, the characteristic feature of the period is a religious and philosophical syncretism which seeks to blend diverse elements into a consistent whole. It was essential for any religion which sought to win adherents that it should be in conformity with the views of the current philosophy, and some cults showed themselves uncommonly pliable. On the other hand, philosophy itself took on a semi-religious character. The dominant note in contemporary thought is that man is a divine being imprisoned in a mortal body and subjected to the whim of fate. Under the influence of astrology, fate itself is associated with the planets, and salvation means escape to the realm beyond the seven planetary heavens. As methods of securing this escape some proposed initiation, others a mystic knowledge open only to the few, others magic spells, others again ascetic practices and austerity of life. The philosophy of ancient Greece, of Plato and Pythagoras, is combined with that of Zeno, with the theories of contemporary science, with ideas more or less primitive from religions of all kinds, according to each man's taste, but through it all there sounds a note of uncertainty, of dissatisfaction. The men of the age were uneasy, anxious, yearning for a real assurance of peace and security.

In the Dispersion, and to a smaller degree in Palestine itself, the Jews came into contact with this type of thought, and their reaction was quite unique. Despite various concessions, the characteristic attitude was largely one of resistance. The mysteries found their theology in the current philosophy, and adapted their myths accordingly; Judaism appeared with its sacred Book translated into Greek, and claimed that the philosophy was there already. There is evidence that the Septuagint made a considerable impression upon those Greeks into whose hands it came, but the very process of translation had transformed the Old Testament, while the methods of interpretation then in use facilitated the discovery of philosophy in the Scriptures. But the majority of Jews refused to make any sort of concession to contemporary religion. There was syncretism in their use of Greek ideas to further the interests of Judaism, but there was none of that other kind of syncretism which consisted in the merging of the gods of two different faiths.[1]

Within the general process of accommodation to the contemporary environment there were several degrees of approximation. The majority seem to have been orthodox, although prepared to adopt Hellenistic thought for Jewish purposes. Others like Philo were perhaps inclined to go further, but still remained primarily Jewish. In some cases the Jews of Palestine were able to exercise more freedom in this respect than their compatriots of the Dispersion, but in the main both are fundamentally loyal to the faith of their fathers. In addition to these two main groups there were others more or less accommodating: some who rejected all contact with the Gentile, others who went much further even than Philo. The greatest laxity appears to have been in Phrygia, but there is occasional evidence of apostasy elsewhere, while it is clear that the Jews had a reputation in the world of magic. Apostasy and syncretism, however, except in the general sense of syncretism noted above, affected at most only individuals or small groups, and the majority of Jews remained loyal. On the other hand, there is no question of a closed doctrinal system accepted by all. There was considerable freedom of thought even in orthodox circles.

Judaism both could and did profit by its contact with the Hellenistic world. New problems were, posed, new answers suggested, and the general result was a widening and enriching of Jewish thought. At the same time Judaism had something of its own to offer to the Gentile, and so Jewish ideas passed into pagan use. Many Gentiles, moreover, were attracted to Jewish worship, whether as full proselytes or as adherents, and when the Christian mission began many of these passed into the Church.

The earliest Christians were Jews, and it was to the Jewish synagogue that Paul turned when he set out on his journeys. The success of his efforts soon made the Gentile element the more predominant in the Church, but this success was largely due to the preparation which had preceded it. A sense of need had long been felt in the pagan world, and various attempts had been made to satisfy it. The Dispersion had adapted some of the current ideas for its own use, and Christianity followed the same path. Paul and John and the other New Testament writers all use the Greek language which was then the universal tongue. Often they are primarily dependent on the Jewish Scriptures, but in their Greek form, while again they derive many of their metaphors and ideas from the surrounding world. The different writers use different idioms, but the message is the same; many of the idioms are drawn from the environment, but their use is unique. The Gospel is not merely another mystery-myth, nor is Jesus merely another mystery-saviour, although the language of the mysteries or philosophy or the terminology of the emperor-cult may be employed in the proclamation of the message. It is not the words that matter, nor the ideas, but the use to which they are put; the ideas of the contemporary world are transformed when they are applied to the service of Christ.[2]

In the long history of their development both Jew and Greek had come in contact with many systems of thought. The Jew in particular had been at a very early stage in contact with all the cultures which contributed to the later syncretism. Egypt lay to the south, Babylonia to the north, and each held sway over Palestine in the earliest days of Israel. In the period of the Hebrew kingdom there were friendly relations with Phoenicia, while after the Captivity the country passed successively under the yoke of various powers, Babylon and Persia, Alexander and the Diadochi, with the old rivalry of Egypt and Assyria springing to life again in the conflict of Ptolemy and Seleucid. Finally, after a brief period of independence the Jews became subjects of Rome. From each of their earlier overlords they absorbed something which became a part of their own religion, and this was to some extent of advantage when they found themselves confronted in the Hellenistic world with a syncretism of elements from all these sources, elements of which some had possibly passed through a Jewish medium into the Graeco-Roman world. This is important for the understanding of Gnosticism, since the Gnostics take up so many such elements. On the other hand, there are remarkable similarities in the primitive beliefs of widely different peoples, and the mere proof of similarity does not always point to an influence of one upon another. The source of Gnosticism has been found in various systems of antiquity, but ultimately we have no sure ground beyond the syncretistic environment of the Diaspora. A particular theory may go back to Egypt, but another is due to Persian influence; it is in the blending of such ideas in the Hellenistic world that we find the true source of Gnosticism.

In words already quoted, Gnosticism is an atmosphere, not a system; it is the general atmosphere of the period and affects to some extent all the religions and philosophies of the time. The Gnosticism which appears in the history of the Church is only one form which it took, but while it was normal for the pagan world it was fundamentally alien to Judaism and to Christianity. In its widest sense the term covers most contemporary pagan thought, the Hermetica, philosophy, the mysteries; it has influenced Philo, Paul, and John, and continues to flourish for centuries. But we must distinguish this from the narrower sense. Paul and John, like Philo, accept much of the contemporary philosophy, but emphatically reject many Gnostic views based on that philosophy. The difference is that between acceptance of the current *Weltanschauung* and acceptance of all its implications, especially when the latter conflict with the fundamental ideas of Judaism or of Christianity. If the similarities are undoubted, the differences are no less clear, and justify the drawing of this distinction.

When the Church came into contact with paganism there were various possibilities: some rejected any sort of compromise, while others went too far; others again took a middle path. It is to the third group that Paul and those like him belong. They profited from their association with non-Christians to find new methods of winning others, new ways of presenting the message which they sought to convey; but they adhered steadfastly to the central truths of their faith. The Gnostics are either Christians of the second group or pagans who wished to appropriate something of Christianity without fully accepting or understanding it.

In the wider sense it is evident that there was a Jewish Gnosticism. Philo could in a sense be called a Gnostic, much as Paul or Clement of Alexandria, but in the narrower sense adopted in this study he is not a Gnostic, although there are indications that Christian Gnosticism was foreshadowed, if not actually anticipated, by a Jewish. Such a pre-Christian Jewish Gnosticism would be not so much a system as a tendency of accommodation to the environment, as was Christian Gnosticism later. Within it we should find a number of systems like those of the various later sects, and it

s

might be possible to trace a chain of development from the earlier to the later groups. But however that may be, Philo himself stands at a point intermediate between Judaism of the more strict type and Gnosticism. Dodd, for example, remarks that he is 'a teacher standing on the Jewish side of the dividing line, who is glad to use all the resources of pagan religious philosophy to elucidate the mysteries of his own Scriptures,' while 'the author of *Poimandres* is a colleague on the other side of the line who welcomes the wisdom of the Hebrews as giving an august sanction to the doctrines of his own philosophy.'[3]

Even apart from Philo there are features which may be due to Jewish influence—certain aspects of the Gnostic doctrine of God, for example, and more especially the portrayal of the Demiurge, which owes something to the Old Testament Creator and something to demonology; or again, the figure of Sophia and some aspects of the lower powers, which have a certain affinity with Jewish theories. There are further traces of such an influence in the accounts of the creation of the world, and more again in those of the creation of man. The use of Old Testament names and even of quotations seems to confirm this view, although Reitzenstein remarks,[4] with reference to the use of Jewish names and formulae in magic, 'They show not acquaintance with the Jewish or Christian religion, but lack of knowledge.' The names are there, but they have been wrested from their context and employed purely as magic spells; there is often no sign that their true meaning, or that of the Jewish faith from which they were derived, was clearly understood. In the case of Gnosticism the situation is somewhat different, since some systems are quite certainly reinterpretations of the narratives of Genesis, but once again it may be questioned whether their authors had any real comprehension of the true significance of the Jewish faith.

Practically all the Jewish elements can be traced to other sources, as is done, for example, by Reitzenstein, but this does not alter the fact that they appear in Judaism, while the form in which they influence Gnosticism seems to be very often that which they had in Judaism. Again, many of these elements were probably incorporated into Jewish thought at a very early stage, and most of them had been completely assimilated. It is of particular interest to observe the number of cases in which Gnostic theories seem to be due either directly to a convergence of Jewish ideas with those of the contemporary philosophy, or to a development based on such a convergence. This is significant, since there was a tendency for Jews to suppress or minimize those points which were alien to the pagan world, and to emphasize the points of similarity.

Clear evidence for Jewish influence upon Gnosticism in any particular case is seldom available, but there is more to show that Judaism was a contributory factor. By taking those views in which Judaism and paganism more or less concurred, the Gnostics could make some pretence of satisfying both; nor did they entirely escape the error of mistaking superficial similarity for a real identity. It is also possible that the Septuagint itself exercised some influence, as a religious book of peculiar potency, in circles which had little or no real contact with Judaism. Different elements appear in different systems, as is only natural. We are dealing not with the development of a single system of doctrine but with a number of theories all of which show certain similar tendencies. The inconsistencies within individual systems may be due either to indiscriminate mutual borrowing by the Gnostics themselves, seeking to satisfy all demands without excessive regard for coherence, or to confusion on the part of our authorities, who may have transferred to one sect views which are akin to those which it advanced but which are really at variance with its general theory, and properly belong to some other group. As the *Apocryphon of John* now shows, Irenaeus has attempted to summarize and to some extent collate various theories, which would be accessible to and understood by his readers, but are now for the most part lost.

In short, Gnosticism in the broader sense is a general tendency of the period which saw the birth of Christianity, and makes its presence felt in various ways in all the thought of the time. In a narrower sense the name is applied to certain types of speculation which appeared in the first two centuries of the Christian era, and whose chief characteristic was the assimilation of Christianity more or less completely to the ideas of the contemporary world. These Christian Gnostics thus apply to the Christian Gospel the ideas of the wider Gnosticism around them, but in the process the essential message of Christianity is lost. The origin of the movement has

been found in many different systems of religion, but whatever the
ultimate source of individual elements, the movement as a whole
derives from a syncretism which blends them all, a syncretism
current in the first centuries of the life of the Church. To this
syncretism Judaism had made its contribution, partly by mediating
elements from other sources, partly by advancing views of its own,
but on the whole Judaism itself was not greatly affected.

Influences from this world of thought appear in the New Testament, where as yet they are only secondary, although on occasion
the need arises for the refutation of some theory which gives them
the chief place. In the New Testament 'the regulative motive is
that supplied by the originating impulse of Christianity itself.'[5] In
the Hermetic documents, parts of which may go back to the first
century, we have an example of the contemporary pagan form of
thought, while in Gnosticism we have a fusion of the two. 'If we
could imagine a recension of the *Poimandres* in which the figure of
Christ was introduced as an after-thought, either as identified with
one of the divine powers—Logos, Demiurge or Anthropos—or as
the medium or the original recipient of the revelation, then we
should have a work strictly analogous to such early Gnostic teaching
as that of Justin, or the Naassene, or even in part of Basilides. The
more definitely Christian Gnostics of whom Valentinus is the type
believed that acceptance of the central Christian doctrines supplied
that which was lacking to complete the great synthesis to which
religious thought was tending. They constructed vast systems on
the basis of earlier speculations, in which the redemption wrought
by Christ was made to provide the final clue to the mystery of
things. But the central mind of the Church rightly judged that in
these systems the distinctive truths of Christianity were swamped
in alien speculations, and called a halt to the process of synthesis.'[6]
It need only be added that these 'distinctive truths' included the
incarnation in its full sense and the death and resurrection of
Christ.[7]

On the other hand, Gnosticism was not without its good points.
It provided to some extent an intermediate stage between paganism
and Christianity, and many no doubt who had first been drawn by
some form of Gnostic doctrine later entered the Church to be
faithful Christians. Again, Gnosticism was an experiment in the

performance of a task which had to be done—the accommodation of Christianity and Hellenistic culture. Its very errors were a warning to others, while it also forced the orthodox to consider seriously what was to be accepted, what rejected, in the philosophy of the contemporary world. When all is said, however, despite its Jewish and Christian elements, despite its contribution to Christian thought as an experiment in accommodation, despite the good intentions of some at least of its exponents, Gnosticism is not Christian, but a phase of heathenism.

NOTES TO CHAPTER VIII

[1] This creates a certain difficulty, since the one word 'syncretism' has to do duty for two separate things. Norden (109) prefers to use 'theocrasia' for the blending of gods in paganism, but this has the disadvantage of being too like the completely different word 'theocracy,' while again there does not seem to be any adjectival form available apart from 'theocratic,' which is even more open to this objection. We must therefore confine ourselves to remarking that 'syncretism,' used of Judaism or of Christianity, may mean something very different from the same word applied to the mystery religions.

[2] So Mowinckel (*He that Cometh* 57, 75) observes 'Israel did not take over either Canaanite religion, or the sacral kingship which was connected with it, unaltered.'

[3] *BG* 246f.

[4] *Poimandres* 14 note 1: 'Sie zeigen nicht die Bekanntschaft mit der jüdischen oder christlichen Religion, sondern die Kenntnislosigkeit.'

[5] Dodd *BG* 247f.

[6] ibid. 248.

[7] Admittedly certain Gnostic documents, such as those in the Berlin Codex, purport to give the teaching delivered by Christ to his disciples after the Resurrection, but this does not affect the fact that the characteristic Gnostic tendency was to minimize or eliminate the death and resurrection of Jesus, and to stress as the means of salvation the gift of γνῶσις.

BIBLIOGRAPHY

This list includes only the works chiefly consulted, and does not contain those to which only occasional reference has been made.

ANGUS: *The Environment of Early Christianity* (London and New York 1914, 1920).
  The Mystery Religions and Christianity (London 1925, 1928).

BETHUNE-BAKER: *Introduction to the Early History of Christian Doctrine* (7th ed., London 1942).

BEVAN: *Hellenism and Christianity* (London 1921; second impression 1930).
  Stoics and Sceptics (Oxford 1913).
  The Hellenistic Age (with W. W. Tarn and J. B. Bury: Cambridge 1923).

BIDEZ AND CUMONT: *Les Mages Hellénisés* (Paris 1938).

BIGG: *The Christian Platonists of Alexandria* (Oxford 1886).
  The Church's Task in the Roman Empire (Oxford 1905).

BOUSSET: *Hauptprobleme der Gnosis* (Göttingen 1907).
  Jüdisch-christlicher Schulbetrieb in Alexandria und Rom (Göttingen 1915)
  Die Religion des Judentums (3rd ed., revised by H. Gressmann, Tübinge. 1926).

BRÉHIER: *Les Idées philosophiques et religieuses de Philon d'Alexandrie* (Paris 1908; 2nd ed., Paris 1925).

BULTMANN: *Primitive Christianity in its Contemporary Setting* (ET, London 1956).
  Theology of the New Testament (ET, 2 vols., London 1952, 1955).

BURKITT: *Church and Gnosis* (Cambridge 1932).

BURROWS: *The Dead Sea Scrolls* (New York 1955; London 1956).

CASEY: *The Excerpta ex Theodoto of Clement of Alexandria* (Studies and Documents I, London 1934).

CAUSSE: *Les Dispersés d'Israel* (Paris 1929).

CERFAUX: *Recueil Cerfaux* (Gembloux 1954).

CHARLES: *The Apocrypha and Pseudepigrapha of the Old Testament* (Oxford 1913).

CLEMEN: *Religionsgeschichtliche Erklärung des Neuen Testaments* (Giessen 1909; 2nd ed. 1924; ET, Edinburgh 1912).

CONYBEARE: *Philo on the Contemplative Life* (Oxford 1895).

CROSS (ed.): *The Jung Codex* (London 1955).

CUMONT: *After-life in Roman Paganism* (New Haven 1922).
Astrology and Religion among the Greeks and Romans (London and New York 1912).
L'Égypte des Astrologues (Brussels 1937).
Les Religions orientales dans le paganisme romain (4th ed., Paris 1929; ET, Chicago 1911).

DAVIES: *Paul and Rabbinic Judaism* (London 1948).

DIETERICH: *Abraxas* (Leipzig 1891).

DODD: *The Bible and the Greeks* (London 1935).
The Interpretation of the Fourth Gospel (Cambridge 1953).
The Background of the New Testament and its Eschatology: Essays in Honour of C. H. Dodd (Cambridge 1956).

DRUMMOND: *Philo Judaeus* (London 1888).

DUPONT: *Gnosis: La connaissance religieuse dans les Épitres de saint Paul* (Louvain and Paris 1949).

FOERSTER: *Von Valentin zu Heracleon* (Beiheft zur ZNTW, Giessen 1928).

FRIEDLÄNDER: *Der vorchristliche jüdische Gnosticismus* (Göttingen 1898).

GEFFCKEN: *Zwei griechische Apologeten* (Leipzig and Berlin 1907).

GOODENOUGH: *The Politics of Philo Judaeus* (New Haven 1938).
By Light, Light (Yale 1935).
Jewish Symbols in the Greco-Roman Period (New York 1953-).

GOPPELT: *Christentum und Judentum im ersten und zweiten Jahrhundert* (Gütersloh 1954).

HATCH: *The Influence of Greek Ideas on the Christian Church* (London and Edinburgh 1892, 1904).

HOOKE: *The Labyrinth* (London 1935).

HOONACKER: *Une Communauté Judéo-Araméenne à Elephantine* (Schweich Lectures 1914: London 1915).

JACKSON AND LAKE: *The Beginnings of Christianity* (London 1920).

JOHNSTON: *The Doctrine of the Church in the New Testament* (Cambridge 1943).

JONAS: *Gnosis und Spätantiker Geist* (Göttingen: vol. i, 1934, 1954; vol. ii, pt. 1; 1954).

JUSTER: *Les Juifs dans l'Empire romain* (Paris 1914).

KAUTZSCH: *Apokryphen und Pseudepigraphen des AT* (Tübingen 1900).

KENNEDY: *Philo's Contribution to Religion* (London 1919).
St. Paul and the Mystery Religions (London 1913).

KIRK: *The Vision of God* (London 1932).

KNOX: *St. Paul and the Church of Jerusalem* (Cambridge 1925).
  St. Paul and the Church of the Gentiles (Cambridge 1939).
  Pharisaism and Hellenism (in *Judaism and Christianity*, vol. ii).
  Some Hellenistic Elements in Primitive Christianity (Schweich Lectures 1942: London 1944).

LEGGE: *Fore-runners and Rivals of Christianity* (Cambridge 1915).

LEWY: *Sobria Ebrietas* (*Beiheft zur ZNTW*, Giessen 1929).

LOEWE (ed.): *Judaism and Christianity* (vol. ii, London 1937).

MACGREGOR AND PURDY: *Jew and Greek, Tutors unto Christ* (London 1936).

MANSON: *Jesus the Messiah* (London 1943).

MEYER: *Ursprung und Anfänge des Christentums* (Stuttgart and Berlin 1923).

MOORE: *Judaism* (Harvard, 1927, 1930).

MOWINCKEL: *He that Cometh* (Oxford 1956).

MURRAY: *Five Stages of Greek Religion* (London 1935).

NOCK: *Conversion* (Oxford 1933).
  The Pagan Background of Early Gentile Christianity (in Rawlinson, *Essays on the Trinity and the Incarnation*, London 1928).

NORDEN: *Agnostos Theos* (Leipzig 1913; reprinted 1923).

OESTERLEY: *Jews and Judaism in the Greek Period* (London 1941).
  (ed.): *Judaism and Christianity* (vol. i, London 1937).

OESTERLEY AND ROBINSON: *History of Israel* (Oxford 1932).

PEET: *The Literatures of Egypt, Palestine, and Mesopotamia* (Schweich Lectures 1929; London 1931).

PFEIFFER: *History of New Testament Times* (New York 1949).

PUECH: *Le Manichéisme: Son Fondateur, Sa Doctrine* (Paris 1949).
  Les nouveaux Écrits Gnostiques découverts en Haute-Égypte, in *Coptic Studies in Honor of W. E. Crum* (Boston 1950).

QUISPEL: *Gnosis als Weltreligion* (Zürich 1951).
  'La conception de l'homme dans la gnose Valentinienne,' *Eranos Jahrbuch* XV (1947) 249ff.
  'L'homme gnostique: doctrine de Basilide,' ibid. XVI (1948) 89ff.
  'Der gnostische Anthropos und die jüdische Tradition,' ibid. XXII (1953) 195ff.

REINACH: *Textes d'auteurs grecs et romains relatifs au Judaisme* (Paris 1895).

REITZENSTEIN: *Die Hellenistischen Mysterienreligionen* (3rd ed., Leipzig 1927).
  Poimandres (Leipzig 1904).

RINGGREN: *Word and Wisdom* (Lund 1947).

ROHDE: *Psyche* (*ET*, London 1925).

Sagnard: *La Gnose valentinienne et le témoignage de saint Irénée* (Paris 1947).

Sanders: *The Fourth Gospel in the Early Church* (Cambridge 1943).

Schoeps: *Urgemeinde, Judenchristentum, Gnosis* (Tübingen 1956).

Schürer: *The Jewish People in the Time of Christ* (*ET*, Edinburgh 1885–6, 1890; 4th German ed., Leipzig 1909).

Stewart: *A Man in Christ* (London 1935).

Sukenik: *Ancient Synagogues in Palestine and Greece* (Schweich Lectures 1930; London 1934).

Tarn: *Hellenistic Civilisation* (2nd ed., London 1930).

Thomas: *Le mouvement baptiste en Palestine et Syrie* (Gembloux 1935).

Turner: *The Pattern of Christian Truth* (London 1954).

Völker: *Fortschritt und Vollendung bei Philo von Alexandrien* (*TU* 49. 1, Leipzig 1938).
   Der wahre Gnostiker nach Clemens Alexandrinus (*TU* 57, Berlin 1952).

Wendland: *Die Hellenistisch-Romisch Kultur* (3rd ed., Tübingen 1912).

Windisch: *Die Frömmigkeit Philos* (Leipzig 1909).

Wolfson: *Philo* (2 vols., Cambridge, Mass., 1948).
   The Philosophy of the Church Fathers (vol. i, Cambridge, Mass., 1956).

Texts: (a) Greek

Josephus: trans. Thackeray, Loeb Classical Library, London (1926–30).

Philo: ed. Cohn and Wendland (Berlin 1896–1915); trans. Colson and Whitaker, Loeb Classical Library (London 1929–).

Eusebius: *Praeparatio Evangelica*, ed. Gifford (Oxford 1903).

Hippolytus: *Philosophoumena*, ed. Wendland (Leipzig 1916).

Irenaeus: *Adversus Haereses*, ed. Harvey (Cambridge 1857).

Origen: *Contra Celsum*, ed. Koetschau (Leipzig 1899); trans. Chadwick (Cambridge 1953).

Clement of Alexandria: *Excerpta ex Theodoto*, ed. Casey (London 1934); ed. Sagnard (Paris 1948).

Ptolemy: *Epistle to Flora*, ed. Quispel (Paris 1949).

Corpus Hermeticum: ed. Nock and Festugière (Paris 1945).

Dittenberger: *Orientis Graecae Inscriptiones Selectae* (Leipzig 1903).

Preizendanz: *Papyri Magicae Graecae* (Leipzig 1928, 1931).

(b) Coptic

Evangelium Veritatis: ed. Malinine, Puech and Quispel (Zürich 1956).

Cod. Berol. 8502: ed. Till (*TU* 60, Berlin 1955).

REFERENCE BOOKS, ENCYCLOPAEDIAS, PERIODICALS

CAH   *Cambridge Ancient History* (Cambridge 1923–).

Cumont: art. Hypsistos in Suppt. *Rev. Inst. Pub. Belg.*, 1897.
art. Sabazius in *CR Acad. Inscrr.* 1906, 63ff.

ERE   Hastings: *Encyclopaedia of Religion and Ethics* (Edinburgh 1908–)

Exp. T. *The Expository Times.*

Gnomon

HDB   Hastings: *Dictionary of the Bible* (Edinburgh 1898–).

HTR   *Harvard Theological Review:*
    29. 1. 39ff. 'The Guild of Zeus Hypsistos' (Roberts, Skeat, and Nock).
    31. 3. 191ff. 'Jewish Liturgical Exorcism' (Knox).

JBL   *Journal of Biblical Literature.*

JEH   *Journal of Ecclesiastical History.*

JNES *Journal of Near Eastern Studies.*

JQR   *Jewish Quarterly Review.*

JRS   *Journal of Roman Studies.*

JTS   *Journal of Theological Studies.*
    Moulton and Milligan: *Vocabulary of the Greek New Testament* (London 1914–1929).

PW   Pauly-Wissowa-Kroll: *Real-Encyclopädie der classischen Altertumswissenschaft* (Stuttgart 1894–).

RB   *Revue Biblique.*

SAB   *Sitzungsberichte der k.p. Akademie der Wissenschaften zu Berlin* 1897, 200ff. (Schürer).

TLZ   *Theologisches Literaturzeitung.*

TWB Kittel: *Theologisches Wörterbuch zum NT* (Stuttgart 1933–).

Vig. Chr. *Vigiliae Christianae.*

ZNTW *Zeitschrift f. die NT Wissenschaft.*
    1904, 335ff. (Wendland).
    121ff. Simon Magus (Waitz).

ZRGG *Zeitschrift f. Religions- und Geistesgeschichte.*

ZTK *Zeitschrift f. Theologie und Kirche.*

INDEX

Abraxas, 124, 141, 244
Achamoth, 130–2, 173, 197, 200, 203
Adam, 57, 78, 104, 118, 131, 151–2, 164, 169–70, 172, 206, 209–10
Christ and Adam, 170, 220
Alexander of Abonoteichus, 25, 95, 101
Alexander, Tiberius, 19, 24, 50
Alexandria—
    Christianity, 30, 117, 133–6, 230
    Gnosticism, 126–7, 176–7, 229
    Judaism, 10, 21, 27, 30–63, 79, 179–80
Allegory, allegorical method, ix, 9, 17, 35, 46, 51, 73, 110, 123, 134
Angels, angelology, 10, 33, 41, 46, 94, 100, 102–3, 118, 121–4, 130–1, 152, 199, 200–1
Anthropos (Aeon), 117, 119 (Ophite), 128–9 (Valentinian)
Apocalyptic, 19, 54, 61, 75, 183–4, 195, 215, 225, 228
Apocatastasis, 142, 193, 217
Apocryphon Johannis, 87, 109, 110, 138, 139, 140, 149–55, 162–3, 169, 193, 234, 240, 243, 244, 246, 247, 248, 263
Apologetic, Jewish, 25, 26; cf. Propaganda
Apostasy, 4–5, 14, 35–6, 181–2, 259
Apotheosis, 47, 70, 214
Archon, the Great, 125 (Basilides), 126, 141, 203, 244
Aristobulus, 28, 35, 38–9, 51
Asia Minor—
    Jews in, 3, 11–14
    Gnostics, 111, 177–8
    Cf. also Phrygia
Astrology, 4, 10, 13, 16–17, 31, 33, 46, 78, 79, 105, 258
Athenagoras, 188, 190, 191

Babylonia, 3–4, 7, 10, 189, 229, 231; cf. Astrology
Barbelognostics, 109, 149, 240
Baruch, 122
Basilides, 99, 123–8, 140, 176, 178, 193, 210, 226, 229, 241, 244, 254, 264
Body, 58, 114, 124, 152; cf. also Coat of Skin, Soul
Bythos, 117, 119 (Ophite), 128–9 (Valentinian)

Cabbala, 91
Cerinthus, 99, 100, 101, 102, 114, 177, 254
Christ, Christology, 93, 104–5, 218–28; 102 (Cerinthus), 103 (Saturninus), 117–18 (Ophites), 122 (Justin), 124, 126 (Basilides), 129–30, 132 (Valentinians), 150, 152 (*Apoc. Joh.*), 163 (*Gospel of Truth*), 190 (Valentinians)
'psychic' Christ, 132
See also Redeemer
Citizenship, Jewish, 24–5, 49
Clement of Alexandria, 28, 49, 54, 67, 128, 134–6, 220, 244, 248
ps. Clementines, 210
Coat of Skin, 132, 165, 209–10
Cosmocrator, 132 (cf. 33, 236)
Creator, Creation, 37–45, 61, 102, 103, 105, 123–5, 131–2, 184, 187–93, 202–7; see also Demiurge

Dead Sea Scrolls, 5, 19, 52, 54, 73–5, 81, 94–5, 97–8, 166, 246, 249, 250, 253, 255
Demiurge, 56, 125, 130–2, 156, 166–7, 184–5, 187–93, 202–3, 205, 210, 262
Demons, 23, 103, 120, 132, 190–92, 199–201, 214
Dew of light, 117–18, 204
Dionysus, 11–12, 45
Docetism, 103, 110, 113, 134, 137, 163, 169, 208, 226
Dositheus, 91
Dualism, 45, 58–9, 74, 114, 188

Ebionites, 50, 94, 102
Eden, 122 (Justin)
Egypt, 28, 30–1, 110, 177–8, 196, 260
    Jews in, 2–3, 24, 31
Elephantine, 2, 18
Elohim, 122 (Justin), 139 (Ophites), 152 (*Apoc. Joh*)
Elyon, 13, 32
Ennoia, 100, 104, 109–10, 128 (Valentinians), 136 (Ophites), 150 (*Apoc. Joh.*)
Enoch, 23, 245, 248
Essenes, 50, 73; cf. Dead Sea Scrolls
Eugnostos, Epistle of, 87
Eve, union of angels with, 137, 140, 152, 173, 200; cf. Achamoth, 131

271